SOUND RECORDING
PRACTICE

SOUND RECORDING PRACTICE

A Handbook compiled by the
Association of Professional Recording Studios

Edited by
JOHN BORWICK

London
OXFORD UNIVERSITY PRESS
New York   Toronto
1976

Oxford University Press, Ely House, London W.1

GLASGOW NEW YORK TORONTO MELBOURNE WELLINGTON
CAPE TOWN IBADAN NAIROBI DAR ES SALAAM LUSAKA ADDIS ABABA
DELHI BOMBAY CALCUTTA MADRAS KARACHI DACCA
KUALA LUMPUR SINGAPORE HONG KONG TOKYO

ISBN 0 19 311915 3

© Oxford University Press 1976

Filmset and printed in Great Britain
by BAS Printers Limited, Wallop, Hampshire

Foreword

As a contribution to recording knowledge and standards, the Association of Professional Recording Studios is proud to present this handbook. It collects in a single volume a distillation of the experience and knowledge of a score of sound-recording experts. Whilst the authors have all been chosen from those engaged in this exciting field in the British Isles, their work is universally recognized by the success of British recordings as well as by the use of British equipment in studios throughout the world.

Studio personnel, both senior and junior, have a duty to keep abreast of developments in the technical and artistic spheres of their profession and ever since the APRS was formed in 1947, one of its prime aims has been the encouragement of the highest technical and operational standards.

The pace of technical advance was never greater than it is today and yet, ironically, harassed studio managers, engineers, and producers have less time than ever to sift through the numerous magazines and manufacturers' brochures in search of all this complex and vital data. I believe, therefore, that this comprehensive manual will provide a most useful digest of the present state of the recording art—a bird's-eye view of the work and ideas of people engaged at all stages in the chain of sound recording.

The needs of the aspiring entrant to the profession have not been overlooked. Reading this book will, by itself, provide an invaluable grounding in the special terminology of recording and something of the flavour of the atmosphere which pervades this exciting and ever-changing medium. There are numerous references to existing literature and international standards, and a substantial glossary of terms.

I would like to thank everyone concerned with the production of this handbook and I commend it heartily to all those with an interest in sound recording at the professional level.

Jacques Levy
Chairman
Association of Professional Recording Studios

Editor's Preface

In planning this Handbook, the Association of Professional Recording Studios saw no need to duplicate the more formal and theoretical material already available in numerous textbooks and learned journals. Rather it was the intention to present in one comprehensive volume a digest of the experience, techniques, and philosophy of leading practitioners currently working in sound recording and broadcasting. Thus the APRS was committed to a policy of persuading a score of busy men to turn their backs on their beloved control consoles, multitrack recorders, synthesizers, and music scores long enough to put down on paper such details of their *modus operandi* as would be most helpful to others in the industry and to that vast army of aspirants who are continually knocking on studio doors trying to get in.

By turning to experts in the various branches of sound recording, the Association ensured a degree of up-to-dateness and personal involvement that would have been lacking in a textbook writer, however competent. At the same time, this has inevitably led to a variety of styles in presentation from chapter to chapter. One thing that shines through all the contributions is the enthusiasm that working in recording or broadcasting always seems to generate. It is no exaggeration to say that sound engineers and producers really love their work. This makes them amateurs, in the original sense of the word (Latin *amare*=love), but their professionalism is also clear for all to see.

While saluting the authors, I cannot omit a word of thanks to the APRS Executive Committee, and in particular the Sub-Committee comprising Richard Petrie and Michael Beville, for the helpful way in which they guided and sustained my ministrations on the manuscripts and illustrations. The draughtsman John Webb also deserves high praise for his painstaking artistry as does my wife Sheila for her considerable secretarial contribution.

John Borwick
Haslemere
Surrey

Contents

Chapter Six   **Extra Facilities**   By Michael Beville (Audio and Design Ltd.)

Chapter Seven   Monitoring Systems   By Stephen Court (Court Acoustics)

Chapter Eight   Magnetic Tape   By Angus McKenzie (Angus McKenzie Facilities Ltd.)

TECHNICAL INTRODUCTION

CHAPTER ONE

The Programme Chain

John Borwick

Sound recording is an artistically rewarding occupation. At the same time, it makes use of many quite complex technical principles and the equipment in particular seems to become more technologically elaborate year by year.

It makes sense therefore, while referring the reader to specialized texts for a deeper treatment of acoustics and electronics, to begin with a few of the more vital definitions and explanations. As a preliminary, we shall outline the programme chain from studio to listener.

The making of a gramophone record

The sequence of stages in the production of a gramophone record is outlined in Fig. 1.1. Many variations on this basic scheme may occur but this division into stages is typical and provides a convenient framework for a preliminary survey of the terminology. It is helpful to look for ways in which the quality of the recording might be degraded at each stage and the types of skill required to keep the quality as high as possible.

Stage 1: Planning. While mercenary considerations may be forgotten during the excitement of the music making and recording sessions, it is of first importance that records do ultimately make money. The planning stage must therefore include a study of the existing recorded repertoire before any given work is scheduled for recording. However popular the work is felt to be, its marketability must be coldly assessed in terms of the record buying climate, the suitability of the artists available and even the image of the particular record label. Only then can the questions of dates, recording venue, contracts, and detailed costing be considered.

Stage 2: Direct recording to tape. The acoustic energy radiated by the sound sources (instruments and voices), modified by the acoustic characteristics of the hall or studio, is converted into electrical energy by the microphone(s). The electrical signal is amplified, mixed, and corrected as necessary at the control console and passed to the tape recorder. Here the electrical energy is converted to magnetic energy for storage and subsequent reproduction. The

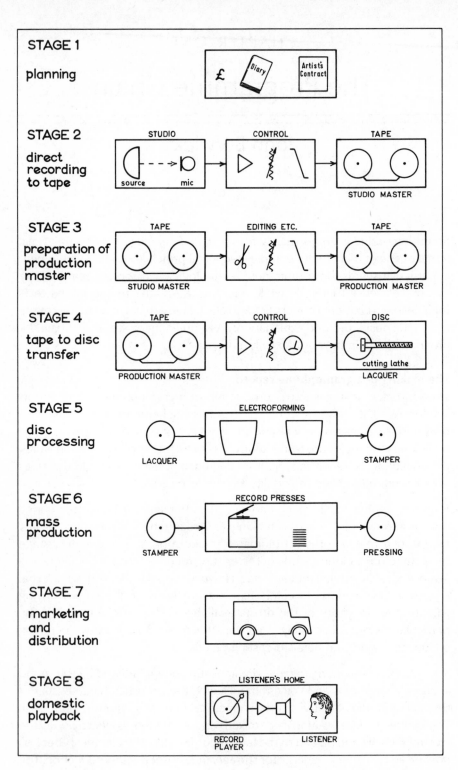

STAGE 1
planning

STAGE 2
direct recording to tape

STUDIO — CONTROL — TAPE
source — mic
STUDIO MASTER

STAGE 3
preparation of production master

TAPE — EDITING ETC. — TAPE
STUDIO MASTER — PRODUCTION MASTER

STAGE 4
tape to disc transfer

TAPE — CONTROL — DISC
PRODUCTION MASTER — cutting lathe — LACQUER

STAGE 5
disc processing

LACQUER — ELECTROFORMING — STAMPER

STAGE 6
mass production

STAMPER — RECORD PRESSES — PRESSING

STAGE 7
marketing and distribution

STAGE 8
domestic playback

LISTENER'S HOME
RECORD PLAYER — LISTENER

Fig. 1.1
The stages in the production of a gramophone record

usual procedure is to record all takes and re-takes (followed by any multi-track overdubs, etc.) so that this Studio Master contains all the programme material, leaving the final choice of best takes until later.

Best layout of the instruments calls for detailed knowledge of their directional characteristics so that the sometimes conflicting needs of the microphones and the performers can be met. The hall or studio will presumably have been chosen because it has sympathetic acoustics. Even so, the amount of reverberation and its tonal quality (all reflecting and absorbing surfaces have an effect on the balance of frequencies) will need close study. Considerations of extraneous noise may also inhibit the freedom of choice in positioning of microphones.

The choice and disposition of microphones, and the subsequent mixing, frequency correction, etc., involve techniques which vary from engineer to engineer. Some guidelines are given elsewhere in this book. Control of the dynamic range, proper alignment of the tape machines and even careful handling of the tapes are all matters which need scrupulous attention if the Studio Master is to attain optimum quality.

Stage 3: Preparation of the production master. A perfect take is most unusual. Generally the best passages from several takes will be selected and spliced together to form the Production Master. Also, particularly in pop recording, the Studio Master will have been built up from several synchronized takes on multi-track tapes (8, 16, or 24 tracks) and will require to be mixed down ('reduced') to a two-track stereo version (or perhaps a four-track quadraphonic one) for production purposes.

While most of the value judgements at this stage remain artistic ones, they depend for their realization on expert knowledge of the particular equipment and technical facilities available. The mere act of copying from the Studio Master to a Production Master (in the general case where the original studio tape, suitably edited, cannot go forward to production) creates a second generation recording in which the signal-to-noise ratio will have been degraded. Noise reduction systems, notably Dolby A, have done much to obviate this potential source of increased noise.

It is important for the engineer making the Production Master to strive for optimum sound quality, and minimum noise, at this stage since the recording is now at its peak and all subsequent processes must be expected to downgrade the quality to some degree. He must also take careful account of the problems inherent in disc cutting (Stage 4). These include a strict adherence to standard peak levels on the tape, with high amplitudes at extreme bass frequencies avoided where possible. In stereo recordings, it is important to restrict out-of-phase components as far as possible since this results in vertical motion of the cutting stylus. Proper regard to this question of phase really begins at the studio and is a strong argument against multi-microphone and split microphone techniques. The exceptionally clean quality of sound sometimes obtained on one-microphone tracks in pop recordings (or coincident pair stereo recordings) is often remarked upon and can be attributed to the avoidance of spurious phase effects.

Stage 4: Tape-to-disc transfer. For record making, the finally edited and reduced Production Master tape is played and the electrical signals used to drive the cutter head stylus on a disc-cutting lathe. The Direct Disc ('lacquer' or 'acetate') requires great care in terms of depth and level of cut. Limiting and compression may be necessary, despite attention to this factor at the studio, and such techniques as vari-groove will be used to ensure the best compromise between peak recorded level and maximum duration per side.

In the programme chain for manufacturing tape cassettes and cartridges, there is an equivalent transfer stage to derive the high-speed Production Master tape from the standard 38 cm/s (15 ips) one.

Stage 5: Disc processing. The 'lacquer' disc is first sprayed with silver, to make it electrically conducting, and then put through a series of electroforming processes to produce successive metal parts as follows:
  (a) the Master (a negative)
  (b) the Mother (a positive)
  (c) the Stampers (negatives)

Stage 6: Mass production. The metal stampers for the two sides of a record are placed in the two plattens of an automatic press which, on closing, will mould a 'biscuit' of vinyl material into the final 'pressing'. The thermoplastic cycle of preheating, pressing, cooling, and releasing takes about 30 seconds. The discs are then trimmed and put into their sleeves.

Cleanliness is obviously important throughout a pressing plant and a vigilant programme of quality control checks to discover stamper wear or blemishes before a large number of wasted pressings is produced.

Tape duplication is a longer process and more costly. Banks of slave recording machines are fed with the signals from the replayed Production Master. High speed duplicating is employed at up to 32 times normal running speed (609·6 cm/s for the master). Such time consuming operations are then needed as identification of the programme start, the attaching of leader tapes, inserting in the cassette body, sealing, labelling, and boxing.

Stage 7: Marketing and distribution. Assuming that all the planning details were carried out as described under Stage 1, the record company can now follow this up by proper attention to packaging the product—sleeve design, libretto booklet printing, sleeve-note writing—marketing, distribution, and promotion. Suitable advertising will be necessary, and advance copies of the records made available to reviewers and broadcasting organizations, so as to acquaint as many as possible of the potential purchasers with the recording's special virtues.

Stage 8: Domestic playback. In the purchaser's home, the record player or hi-fi system re-converts the recorded waveforms into acoustic energy via the loudspeakers. The sound waves will again be modified by the acoustic properties of the living-room and there will be other restrictions because of the generally lower listening level, higher level of background noise, and other domestic circumstances and distractions.

These factors should ideally be borne in mind at all stages of recording. For example, a slightly drier acoustic than the norm for a particular type of music may be aimed at, to allow for the small amount of reverberation added by the listening room. The full dynamic range of which the studio equipment may be capable will often be compressed deliberately in acknowledgement of the narrower range acceptable in many domestic situations or reproducible on much domestic equipment. The effect of a reduced listening level will often be assessed by the studio engineer when making a final decision on the balance of bass and treble frequencies, and he may even switch over to a domestic-sized speaker to gauge the deleterious effect on his recording in, say, the relative balance of soloist and accompaniment (backing).

No operating skills can be assumed on the part of the home user. Equipment and records must therefore be designed to be as foolproof as possible and, where special instructions are needed as to choice of stylus type or record care, the record companies have a duty to educate users through dealer literature, sleeve notes, leaflets, etc. Even so, the quality of reproduction will vary from poor (with a simple mono record player) to such excellence (with a properly set up hi-fi system) that the full impact of modern recording techniques can be enjoyed in the home setting.

Units

With an eye to standardization and the international scene, it has been decided to employ metric units throughout this book. For the benefit of British and American readers, however, the Imperial equivalents are often given in parentheses—particularly for such common items as disc diameters and tape speeds.

The form of metric units employed is that of the 'Système International d'Unités' (which is abbreviated to SI in all languages). The main features of the system are outlined in Appendix A.

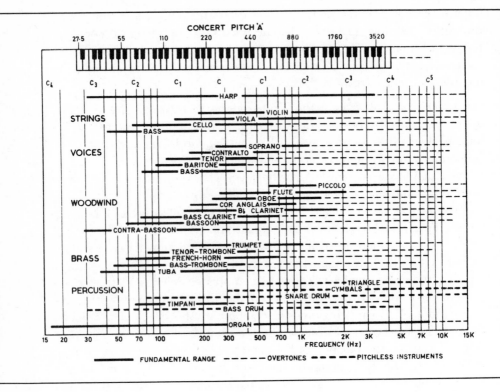

Fig. 1.2
The frequency range of musical instruments and voices

Apart from all the basic units of length, mass, etc., there are two units which occur very frequently in audio. These are the Hertz and the decibel. (The latter is not strictly a unit but rather the *name* for a dimensionless ratio.)

The Hertz (Hz) is what used to be called 'one cycle per second' and is simply used in stating the frequency (rate of vibration) of a sound emitting source, or the air particles in the path of a sound wave, for example. Frequency is closely related to our estimate of musical pitch and Fig. 1.2 illustrates the frequency range of various instruments and singing voices. The true range of notes (the fundamentals) is shown by the full horizontal lines and the broken lines show the extent of the overtones or harmonics. The piano keyboard at the top of Fig. 1.2 has been marked to show that the successive octaves above and below concert pitch A (440 Hz) have frequencies obtained by multiplying or dividing by a factor of 2. It is because the ear estimates pitch intervals in terms of the *ratio* of the frequencies, rather than the frequency difference, that a logarithmic scale is always preferred to a linear one when plotting frequency on graphs.

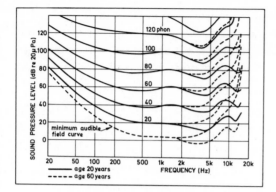

Fig. 1.3
Equal loudness contours for pure
tones (Robinson and Dadson)

The human ear responds to sounds in the range approximately 20–20,000 Hz, but is less sensitive to high and low frequency sounds than mid-frequency ones. This is illustrated in the equal loudness curves plotted by Robinson and Dadson by averaging the results obtained on a large number of listeners (Fig. 1.3). These curves are tending to replace the classical ones published by Fletcher and Munson in 1933, though the phrase 'the Fletcher-Munson effect' is still used to describe the fact that the ear's relative sensitivity to high, low, and middle frequencies changes with the listening level.

Just as the ear estimates pitch intervals by reference to the ratio of the two frequencies, it assesses the extent of a loudness increment in terms of the ratio of the sound intensity levels. We have seen that the frequencies of audible sounds range from about 20 to 20,000 Hz, a ratio of 1,000:1. By comparison, the range of audible intensities (represented by the difference between the two thresholds in Fig. 1.3) is from about 10^{-12} to 1 watt per square metre, a phenomenal ratio of 1,000,000,000,000:1. This enormous range again suggests the use of a logarithmic scale, which in any case accords well with the ear's method of estimation.

If we work from a standard intensity at the Threshold of Hearing, I_0, we can specify all other intensities, I, in terms of *intensity level*, L, by the expression

$$L = 10 \log \frac{I}{I_0} \tag{1}$$

the results being in *decibels*, abbreviated dB.

Table 1.1 illustrates this use of the decibel further by interpolating some approximate musical dynamic markings between the threshold limits. It will be seen that music occupies a range of some 60 dB on this scale; naturally a wider dynamic range may occur in large-scale orchestral works or in amplified pop music.

In many situations the *sound pressure level* is more applicable (and easier to measure). The threshold sound pressure, P_o, is 20 micro-Newtons per square metre (or P_a/m^2) and, since intensity is proportional to the square of sound pressure, the expression for sound pressure level L_p for any given sound pressure becomes

$$L_p = 20 \log \frac{P}{P_o} \text{ dB} \tag{2}$$

By direct analogy in electrical circuits, the expressions for stating electrical power and voltage levels corresponding to (1) and (2) become

$$\text{Power level} = 10 \log \frac{W}{W_o} \text{ dB} \tag{3}$$

$$\text{and Voltage level} = 20 \log \frac{V}{V_o} \text{ dB} \tag{4}$$

The reference (zero) power level, W_o, is generally taken as 1 milliwatt, and then *m* is added as a suffix to give *dBm*. Strictly speaking, the expression for voltage levels holds only if the two voltages in question are measured across identical impedances. In Post Office and studio applications, the open wire impedance of 600 ohms is taken as standard and so the reference voltage corresponding to 1 mW in 600 ohms becomes 775 mV (0·775 volt), calculated from the formula $W = V^2/R$.

Unfortunately, the expression dBm has come into common use for voltage levels as well as power levels (with reference to 1mW) and the dB has become commonly used as a measure of voltage ratio without specifying the imped-

Table 1.1: *the scale of sound intensities*

Dynamic level	Intensity	Ratio	Level (dB)	Typical noise levels
Threshold of pain	1	10^{12}	120	Pneumatic drill
fff	10^{-2}	10^{10}	100	Underground train
f	10^{-4}	10^{8}	80	Noisy office
p	10^{-6}	10^{6}	60	Large shop
ppp	10^{-8}	10^{4}	40	Suburban home
Threshold of hearing	10^{-12}	1	0	Soundproof room

ances across which the voltages are measured. In BBC practice, for example, the form dB(v) is sometimes used to distinguish the cases where the imped-ances are not necessarily equal.

Quality criteria

A critical ear is a prerequisite for everyone working in sound recording. Value judgements have to be made on the 'live' and reproduced sounds at every stage. This process of quality monitoring has to be seen as quite different from, and more highly skilled than, mere listening for musical enjoyment.

Recording engineers and producers must develop the ability to con-centrate their aural attention on each individual feature of the reproduced sound—to the exclusion of others. The musical performance and inter-pretation must be assessed separately and then, for quality assessment, the listener must switch his attention to the various technical aspects of the sound, one by one. Sometimes the switching will be done slowly and deliber-ately—as when checking a new microphone balance: with experience, it can become a continuous, rapid process carried out almost subconsciously during monitoring.

The main technical criteria of sound quality which require continued assessment will now be considered separately.

1. Frequency response. As was shown in Fig. 1.3, audible sounds range in frequency from about 20 Hz to 20,000 Hz (20 kHz). So far as possible, the recording and reproducing chain should be able to respond equally over the full range. In other words, the graph of output signal level for a constant applied input level should ideally be a straight line. In practice, fluctuations in level of about 1 decibel would probably go undetected by even the keenest ears. Changes outside these tolerance limits (20–20,000 Hz ± 1 dB) do become important, however, and affect the tonal balance of bass, treble, and middle frequencies (presence).

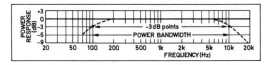

Fig. 1.4
Power/frequency response of an amplifier

In the general case of an amplifier, for example, the response will fall away at each end of the 'pass band', as shown in Fig. 1.4. The power bandwidth is then defined as the frequency range between the points where the power has fallen to half (− 3 dB).

2. Dynamic range. It was suggested in Table 1.1 that musical sounds range in intensity over about 60 dB. In practice, a range of 70 or 80 dB can occur in a full-scale symphony orchestra (not to mention a modern pop group) and the levels arriving at a recording console may exceed this, since microphones may be placed at widely different distances from the instruments.

It therefore becomes necessary to steer the signal levels between the twin rocks of over-modulation on the one hand (resulting in tape saturation or amplifier clipping) and under-modulation on the other (resulting in merging of the quietest musical passages with the level of inherent background noise). The dynamic ranges of various media (often expressed as the signal-to-noise ratio) are listed in Table 1.2. It will be seen that a degree of compression will often become obligatory and that studio engineers must therefore develop skills in controlling programme volume and doing so with as little detriment to the music as possible.

Table 1.2: typical dynamic ranges (dB)

Symphony orchestra	75
Grand piano	70
Studio amplifier	85
Professional tape machine	65
LP gramophone record	50
Domestic cassette recorder	40
AM radio transmission	30
Musak tape	20

3. Distortion. We can define distortion as any unwanted change in waveform between two points in the chain of recording and reproduction. It is possible to distinguish between different types of distortion as follows:

(a) *attenuation distortion:* is variation in gain or loss at different frequencies. Most common is a loss of high frequencies, for example in tape recording or in landlines. It is often wrongly referred to as 'frequency distortion' and is not generally serious since it can be corrected by means of equalization (see Fig. 1.5), the process of passing the signal through frequency correction circuits giving a mirror image response of the known distortion curve.

(b) *phase distortion:* generally accompanies attenuation distortion and correcting the latter will usually reduce the former. It arises when the trans-

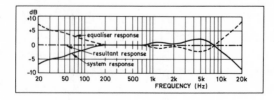

Fig. 1.5
Showing how a flat frequency response can be obtained from a system by passing the signal through an equalizer having a 'mirror image' response curve

mission time through a part of the chain is different at different frequencies, for example in interstage coupling in an amplifier. It would appear that the ear cannot detect simple waveform shifts due to phase distortion but tests indicate that the effect on transients, for example, is important. For stereo and quadraphony, of course, it is necessary to preserve phase relationships between channels over as wide a portion of the frequency spectrum as possible.

(c) *non-linear distortion:* produces harshness of sound, due to more energy being thrown into the upper harmonics, and is caused by non-linearity of the transfer characteristic at any point in the chain. In Fig. 1.6, for example, the transfer characteristic AB may be considered linear over a small portion only. An input waveform W of small amplitude will therefore produce

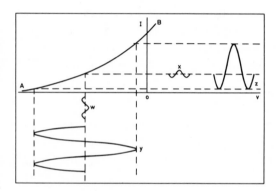

Fig. 1.6
Showing how distortion of the signal waveform is caused by non-linearity of the transfer characteristic AB

an undistorted output waveform X. However, if the input amplitude is allowed to rise as at Y, the curved nature of the line AB will severely clip the signal peaks as shown at Z. It will be appreciated that non-linear distortion is generally associated with high signal levels or poor centring of the system (biassing) on the linear portion of the curve.

Non-linear distortion is perhaps the most serious form of signal degradation. It cannot be corrected by equalization and it is noticed by all critical listeners—though, oddly enough, the human hearing mechanism is itself non-linear and generates distortion on sounds with intensity levels above about 50dB. Non-linear distortion can be sub-divided into three basic types, all of which tend to occur together.

(i) *harmonic distortion* is the production of spurious harmonics (multiples) of the input frequencies. It is relatively innocuous at small percentages, since there will be masking by noise, etc. and most musical sounds already contain substantial components at harmonic frequencies. The average person will begin to detect harmonic distortion at amounts equal to about 0·3%–1·0%, therefore figures below 0·3% are desirable.

(ii) *intermodulation distortion* is the production of spurious combination frequencies between any two input frequencies. Dissonant sum and difference tones will result and measured values of below about 1·2% should be aimed at.

(iii) *amplitude distortion* is a change in system gain at different input signal amplitudes. It is used deliberately, for example, in limiters and compressors. In serious cases of amplifier overloading, or overdriving of a loudspeaker, it results in clipping of the waveform and very obvious distortion or even breaking up of the signal.

(d) *scale distortion:* is not a measurable form of signal degradation like the types considered above. It is the term used to describe the physical impossibility of a relatively small sound source (loudspeaker) in a small space (living-room) being able to reproduce with 100% realism the spatial effect of a large orchestra in a concert hall. To some extent, the various surround sound techniques, such as quadraphony and dummy head (*kunstkopf*) stereo, are endeavouring to recreate the impression of being present at the actual performance.

4. *Noise.* Any unwanted sound which is reproduced or generated by the system, as an accompaniment to the desired signal, can be described as noise. It is worthwhile to distinguish between ambient noise and system noise.

(a) *ambient noise:* in a well designed studio or concert hall will already be at a low level (see Table 1.3) and can often be reduced further by close microphone techniques. There is then a risk, of course, of picking up the noises of pages being turned, mechanical action in such instruments as the harp and harpsichord, or even breathing.

Table 1.3: typical ambient noise levels

Location	dB
Recording studio	20–25
Broadcasting studio	20–30
Concert hall	25–35
Quiet home	33–39
Average home	39–47

The higher ambient noise levels in the listener's home has the advantage of masking the recorded noise to some extent and of course contributes to the need for a measure of compression, as discussed in Section 2 above. The way in which ambient noise can affect our listening habits is evident if one compares the apparent loudness of music, and the nuisance value of inherent noises, on daytime and late evening listening.

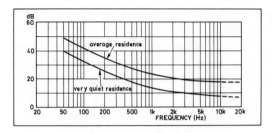

Fig. 1.7
Noise spectrum in average and very quiet homes

As Fig. 1.7 illustrates, the noise spectrum in a room tends to have a falling response at high frequencies, as does the spectrum for conventional music. (Electronic music may disobey this rule—as it does many others.)

(b) *system noise*: tends to have a flat frequency response and so becomes more obtrusive at high frequencies. (One thinks of amplifier and tape noise as hiss.) In fact, thermal noise in amplifiers, etc. is proportional to bandwidth and temperature. It is the first stage noise which is most important—because it is boosted by the later stages. Note, however, that any EQ (equalization) applied later will modify the noise spectrum. The signal-to-noise ratio of an amplifier is the ratio, expressed in dB, of the rated output to the residual noise. Typical S/N ratios are:

Capacitor microphone	60dB
Studio amplifier	85dB
Professional tape machine	65dB

Note, when a 'weighted' noise figure is quoted, this has been measured through a network which takes account of the ear's frequency response at low levels. It is thus a better indication of the true nuisance value of the noise and will be a bigger ratio (less noise) than the unweighted figure.

Noise at very low frequencies will be due to mains hum (at 50 Hz or 60 Hz plus harmonics) or motor rumble (in the 25–200 Hz region), etc. This will obviously be more in evidence when loudspeakers with extended bass response are employed and may set up standing waves in the listening room to give up to 15 dB variation in sound level at different positions in the room. Crosstalk between adjacent tape tracks and amplifier channels may be regarded as a special case of noise (see Section 6 below).

5. *Wow and flutter*. The ear is a relatively poor judge of absolute pitch but can detect very tiny *changes* in the pitch (frequency) of notes when a refer-

ence is present. In live sound, this means that gradual drifting in pitch, perhaps with an unaccompanied choir, may go unnoticed, whereas mis-tuned individual instruments or voices will sound dissonant. In reproduced sound, there is a similar inability to judge the precise running speed of a record player or tape machine, whereas any cyclic fluctuations in speed are readily recognized by the pitch wobbles produced.

Such short-term speed fluctuations are collectively referred to as wow and flutter: wow is slow speed changes at 20 Hz or less, often attributable to an off-centre gramophone record or buckled tape spool; flutter is a higher rate speed fluctuation perhaps due to a damaged capstan or pressure roller. In practice, some amplitude modulation will usually accompany the fre-quency modulation and an odd feature is that wow and flutter are generally more evident when listening to loudspeakers than headphones because of the change in standing wave effects on reflected sounds.

In general, pitch hearing acuity is poorest at low frequencies, the minimum perceptible pitch change being about 3% at the bass end and only 0·3% at middle and high frequencies. The presence of wow is most obvious on the sustained notes of piano or organ, while flutter is most easily detected on woodwind. Professional tape recorders have a total wow and flutter content of about 0·08% but there is an unfortunate variation in the way the figure is measured and quoted—peak or rms, weighted or unweighted—so that care is needed in comparing the specifications of different machines. Most wow and flutter meters will also measure long-term speed changes, or drift.

6. *Crosstalk.* In multichannel systems there is an additional criterion, the need for the separate channels to be reproduced without interchannel inter-ference or crosstalk. In two-channel stereophony, for example, any crosstalk will degrade (narrow) the stereo image and in four-channel quadraphony the positioning of voices and instruments will be blurred or shifted. The crosstalk level in 'unwanted' channels should be no higher than − 20 dB relative to the wanted channel, at least in the mid-frequency range. The directional effects are also dependent on the phase relationships of the original signals being pre-served on their transmission through the recording and reproducing chain. This makes special demands on such factors as amplifier design, tape head azimuth, and the landline or radio links in broadcasting.

THE STUDIO

CHAPTER TWO

The Acoustics

Alex Burd

When mention is made of acoustics, the average studio engineer probably thinks immediately of 'panels of little holes'; no apology is offered for taking a wider brief than this in the following description of studio acoustics. The application of absorbing treatment to modify the character of sound within an enclosure is the final stage in acoustic design; it may be the only stage to be carried out when modifying existing premises for studio use but, for the provision of fully satisfactory conditions, all the steps which are described in this chapter are of importance.

The studio is intended for the production of sound and for its conversion into electrical signals by means of microphones or other transducers. Sound is a pressure variation arising from vibration of strings or surfaces, or from modulation of an airflow; it is transmitted through the air—or to a lesser extent through structures—and is subject to attenuation, masking, reflection, diffraction, interference, or absorption. It is the control of each of these processes that produces an environment which is sympathetic to the performers and also provides the engineer with the flexibility required for his operations. These two aims may sometimes conflict and a compromise solution has to be found.

The two main factors involved in the studio environment are background noise and the acoustic quality of the studio. It is necessary to start by defining the level of background noise that will be permitted and then developing a structure and selecting equipment compatible with this decision. The acoustic quality is set by the size and shape of the studio, by the selection of acoustic absorptive materials and their disposition and by the furnishings and operation of the studio. These factors will now be considered in turn.

Background noise
The background noise which can be permitted in a studio depends on the type of programme material to be produced and on the microphone techniques. Obviously one can accept a higher noise level for a pop group

being recorded with close microphones than for a harpsichord or a drama production; further, improvements in recording techniques permit a wider dynamic range to be accommodated with a consequent requirement for a lower background level in the studio. The background noise can be varied only to a limited extent after the construction of the studio, so its design value must be based on the most critical use expected.

For design purposes, acceptable noise levels will be defined by a spectrum relating the sound pressure level in a given bandwidth (octave or one-third octave typically) to the centre frequency of the band.

As already mentioned in Chapter One, sound pressure level (SPL) is the ratio of the actual sound pressure to a standard reference pressure (20 $\mu N/m^2$) which corresponds approximately to the minimum pressure audible to the ear; these pressures are normally the root-mean-square values averaged over a sufficiently long period. The limits set by 'just audible' and 'painful' sounds encompass an enormous range of pressures which is expressed most conveniently in a logarithmic form. The SPL of a pressure p is normally expressed in decibels, where SPL$= 20 \log p/p_0$ dB (p_0 is the reference pressure).

For convenience, single-figure noise levels are often quoted, the A weighted sound pressure level being the most common (in dB(A)). In this case the broad band electrical signal resulting from the sound pressure is weighted by a filter having a frequency response corresponding roughly to that of an aural equal loudness curve (40 phon). Sound levels are usually measured by a

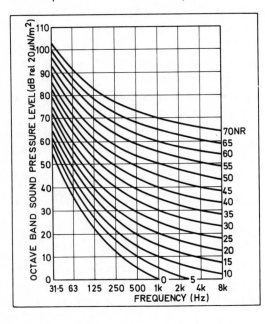

Fig. 2.1
Noise rating (NR) curves

sound level meter which consists of a microphone, amplifier, attenuators, filter or weighting network, rms detector and a meter having certain defined ballistic characteristics. In order to determine a meaningful value, it will be necessary to consider both the time and spatial variation of the sound level and to specify the relevant form of measurement. Where more than one noise exists, the total sound level will be the factor to be specified; incoherent signals add on an energy basis and thus two signals each require to be 3 dB lower in value, to achieve a given total sound level, while three signals must each be 5 dB lower.

Figure 2.1 shows a family of Noise Rating criterion curves prepared by the International Organization for Standardization. The acceptable background noise levels in studios will lie in the range NR 0 to NR 20 depending on the use of the studio and the operating intentions. Figure 2.2 compares the specifications for British and German broadcasting studios. The lower noise levels in German studios undoubtedly permit a greater range of dramatic voice effects, but the cost implications on all aspects of the building and plant are serious.

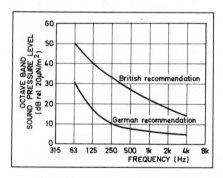

Fig. 2.2
Comparison of recommended studio noise levels in British and German practice

A good general-purpose studio will probably have a noise level not exceeding an NR 15 criterion curve (corresponding to say 20 dB(A)). To achieve such a standard, efficient anti-vibration mounts will be required for all ventilation plant and other rotating machinery; silencers will be necessary in all ventilation ductwork; air velocities at studio grilles will have to be low; chokes in fluorescent lighting fittings must be remotely mounted, and many other similar precautions taken.

Background noise in studios also results from sources outside the premises (aircraft, road traffic, building operations, etc.); it may be generated as vibration, conducted through the structure and radiated as noise (underground trains, footsteps, etc.); or it may arise from sources inside the building (lifts, other studios and control rooms, etc.). Site noise surveys will identify external sources; information from manufacturers or tests will determine internal noise levels; while the sound levels expected from other studios must be predicted from the expected operations.

This body of information, taken together with the acceptable levels required in the studio, provides the basis on which the structure of the studio building is designed.

Sound insulation

The sound reducing capabilities of a structure arise as a combination of its mass and its resonant properties; the 'sound reduction index' (SRI) is a measure of this ability. All partitions possess a range of frequencies within which they exhibit a mass controlled behaviour, where the SRI is proportional to the product of the mass per unit area and the frequency; thus for a given material the theoretical value of the SRI will increase with frequency by 6 dB/octave; while at a given frequency the SRI will increase by 6 dB for each doubling of the surface mass, i.e. a doubling of the wall thickness or a change to a denser material

This 'mass law' region is restricted in extent and modified in practice by the existence of a multiplicity of resonance conditions. The lowest frequency of resonance is that controlled by the mass and stiffness of the partition, the entire partition moving in phase; higher modes of vibration appear at higher frequencies and give rise to further minima, the depths of which are controlled by the internal damping and by the clamping conditions around the edges. Below the fundamental resonance, the behaviour of the partition will be stiffness controlled and its SRI will increase with reducing frequency; attempts to design partitions using this property have not proved sufficiently successful to warrant their use in practice. The higher modes of vibration in a randomly incident sound field combine in practical partitions to reduce the mass law increase to 5 dB per doubling of frequency or doubling of mass.

Figure 2.3 shows the SRI, averaged over the frequency range 100–3,150 Hz, for a variety of practical simple partitions plotted as a function of the mass of the partition. The straight line is a representation of the mass law.

A very significant resonance condition is that in which bending waves are excited in a partition by sound wavefronts passing over the surface. The velocity of the bending waves for a particular size and material of partition is proportional to the square root of the frequency; at a certain limiting frequency, the velocity of the bending waves equals the velocity of sound in air and wavefronts at grazing incidence will excite the resonance; above this frequency, there will always be an angle of incidence at which the wavefronts travel over the surface at the same velocity as the bending waves. This effect is known as the coincidence effect and results in a serious loss of insulation in lightly damped materials over a band of frequencies above the critical frequencies. Figure 2.4 shows the coincidence effect very clearly for a studio/cubicle window in which both glasses were of the same thickness.

The range of frequencies over which measurements of SRI are made, and over which a mean value is calculated from the individual one-third octave results, is 100–3,150 Hz. While this range covers the frequencies of interest in

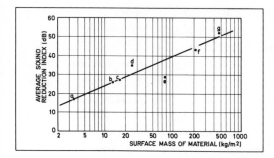

Fig. 2.3
Average Sound Reduction Index of various materials as a function of their surface mass.
Materials:
(a) 6 mm plywood
(b) 18 mm chipboard
(c) 6 mm glass
(d) 11 mm plywood with lead bonded (absence of resonances improves SRI)
(e) 50 mm woodwool with 2 × 12 mm plaster (serious resonances degrade SRI)
(f) 112 mm brick with 12 mm plaster
(g) 225 mm brick with 2 × 12 mm plaster

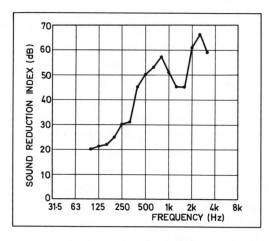

Fig. 2.4
Coincidence effect for two panes of glass 8 mm thick with a 100 mm cavity

domestic situations, it is inadequate for much studio use where the response of loudspeakers and microphones is maintained to much lower (and higher) frequencies. Manufacturers of proprietary partitions aim to optimize their performance within the above frequency range; resonances are shifted just outside the range and can give rise to howlround at low frequencies or audible break-through at high frequencies.

The use of a single-figure mean value has disadvantages that must be borne in mind. Such a single value can hide the existence of a serious dip in the SRI characteristic, which may be audible through the resultant energy leakage. An alternative form of single-figure value which eliminates this problem, but which is not so well known, compares the measured values with a grading curve. This curve is raised or lowered until a specified deviation between the two curves is not exceeded.

Simple mass law constructions are usable up to mean sound reduction indices of 50–55 dB; above this value, the mass becomes excessive and leads to a cumulative thickening of all walls and foundations. Multiple leaf constructions can give a gain over single panels, although in most practical situations the coupling between the individual leaves will restrict the frequency range within which the increase occurs. Where the spacing between the leaves is a fraction of a wavelength, they will behave as a single mass law partition. With rising frequency, a progressive gain over the calculated sound reduction index is found which depends on the spacing, and on the acoustic absorption within the cavity. At high frequencies, the SRI may be found to increase at 10 dB/octave indicating that the two leaves are acting independently.

The presence of more than one panel introduces additional resonances, at each of which a reduction in the insulation will result. The most important of these resonances occurs when the two panels move in anti-phase and the stiffness of the enclosed air is added to the mechanical stiffness of the panels themselves. Higher resonances due to cross modes of vibration within the air space can be well damped by the addition of absorption within the air space.

In practical terms we are interested in the reduction of sound level that is produced between the source of unwanted sound and the studio. This is a function not only of the energy that is transmitted through the wall (i.e. a function of the SRI) but also of the acoustic conditions within the receiving room. For a given acoustic power, a higher sound pressure level will result in a live room than in a dead room; most studios will contain sufficient absorption to give an effective gain over that calculated from the SRI.

This handbook is not the place to enter into details of sound insulation, but a few representative examples may serve to show the wide range of values required and to indicate the types of construction that are used.

In a typical studio centre, the roof may be required to exclude aircraft noise and an average sound level difference of 70 dB may be specified. A structure to achieve such a value could be an inner roof of 150 mm reinforced concrete, supporting a second lighter skin of woodwool slabs with suitable waterproofing and weather protection, on resilient pads.

Walls to exclude traffic noise will have to achieve at least 60 dB average sound level difference; one possible construction is a cavity wall having two leaves of 225 mm brickwork and a cavity of 50 mm minimum.

Walls between a studio and its own cubicle have to provide 45–50 dB average sound level difference; it is usually possible to achieve this value with a multiple leaf dry construction partition, but a single skin 225 mm brickwork, plastered to ensure that no air holes exist, is a simpler form of construction.

Control room windows to achieve compatible results must be of heavy glass and an air-space of minimum depth 200 mm with absorptive reveals is necessary. It is essential that the two glasses are of different thicknesses—say 8 mm and 12 mm—to ensure different critical frequencies for the coincidence effect.

Where ventilation ducts or other services pass through a sound insulating partition, it is of course necessary to ensure that the sound level difference by that path does not degrade the overall insulation. The use of attenuators, commonly called 'cross-talk silencers', is the answer in the case of ventilation ductwork, while other cable ducts are packed with sandbags or bags filled with mineral wool.

In cases where serious vibration problems exist or exceptionally high sound insulation values are required, it may be necessary to mount the studio resiliently. Such a case may arise in areas adjacent to studios designed to house 'pop' groups, where no control can be exercised over the sound levels generated by the playing. In such cases, sound levels of 120 dB(A) are common and levels 10 dB(A) higher than this are not unknown. The use of rubber pads or steel springs, together with additional precautions to damp out resonances in the structure, can permit the construction of a 'box within a box' design in which the transmission of vibration is substantially reduced.

Acoustic quality

Having constructed the shell of a studio that is not subject to interference by noise from either external or internal sources, it is now necessary to ensure that it sounds 'right' to those who use it—both artists and engineers. The sound that is heard live in a studio, or at a microphone output before processing, is a combination of the direct sound from the source together with a multiplicity of reflections from the surfaces of the studio and from the furnishings and fittings.

When a short sharp sound is produced in the studio, it is possible instrumentally to display the pattern of reflections that results; this display is known as the impulse response. In the early part of such a display, shown in Fig. 2.5, the first signal which has travelled direct from source to microphone can be seen, followed by several discrete reflections which are spaced apart by time intervals of several milliseconds. After a time which will be a function of the size of the studio, the reflections are seen to arrive so close together that it is impossible to separate them. These later signals arise from multiple reflections within the studio and, since energy will be lost from the sound wave each time it is reflected by a surface, the sound field will gradually die away. This region, known as the reverberation, was the first part of the characteristic of sound in an enclosure to be systematically explored and it probably remains the most important single feature of the sound field.

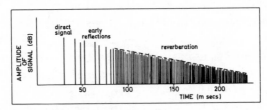

Fig. 2.5
Impulse response of an auditorium

Within the impulse response there exist regular series of reflections arising from the major surfaces of the room. These correspond in the frequency domain to the frequencies at which the path contains a whole number of half wavelengths of the sound, and they are known as the natural modes or eigentones of the room. Figure 2.6 shows the three lowest modes that can exist between a pair of plane parallel surfaces; these series, arising from the three pairs of surfaces in a rectangular room, comprise what are known as the axial modes of the room. The other series are the tangential modes, in which two pairs of surfaces contribute, and the oblique modes, which involve all three pairs of surfaces. The axial modes have been shown to be the most significant by virtue of the energy they carry and the duration of their decay.

An undue concentration of modes in one frequency region will often be heard as an accentuation of sounds around that region. By analogy with optical terminology, in which light of a particular colour arises from an electromagnetic vibration of a particular frequency, such an emphasis is called a colouration. If two (or more) dimensions of a room are the same, or a simple multiple of each other, then two of the axial mode series will be the same or will have many common terms. The acoustic designer's aim of a uniform distribution of sound is thereby made more difficult to achieve.

In small rooms, the lowest frequencies in the axial modal series lie in the speech frequency region and are spaced well apart in frequency. The twelve lowest axial modes calculated for an echo room are shown in Table 2.1: the dimensions of this room were deliberately adjusted to distribute the modes.

One important example of an axial mode is the regular series of reflections set up between a pair of plane parallel reflecting surfaces: this is known as a flutter echo. This type of response is particularly apparent in an otherwise dead room and can result from comparatively small areas such as control

Table 2.1: modal frequencies of a room

Dimensions		Length	(x)	5·03 m				
		Breadth	(y)	3·96 m				
		Height	(z)	3·05 m				

n_x	n_y	n_z	Frequency (Hz)	n_x	n_y	n_z	Frequency (Hz)
1	0	0	34·02	2	0	1	88·25
0	1	0	43·20	1	2	0	92·89
1	1	0	54·99	2	1	1	98·25
0	0	1	56·15	3	0	0	102·00
1	0	1	65·65	0	2	1	103·08
2	0	0	68·08	1	2	1	108·54
0	1	1	70·85	2	2	0	110·03
1	1	1	78·59	0	0	2	112·30
2	1	0	80·63	1	0	2	117·34
0	2	0	86·44	0	1	2	120·32

room windows or doors. The cure for a flutter echo may be the addition of more absorption, or the angling of one of the surfaces.

The decay of the sound field in a room was studied by Sabine in the early part of this century. He noted that the reverberation time was a function of the volume of the room and of the total amount of absorption that it contained. He derived the relationship

$$T = \frac{\text{const} \times V}{\bar{\alpha}S}$$ where T is the reverberation time
V is the volume of the room
S is the surface area of the room
$\bar{\alpha}$ is the average absorption coefficient.

When the dimensions of the room are in feet, the constant of proportionality is 0·049; for metric measurements the constant is 0·161.

The reverberation time is defined as the time taken for the sound to die away to one-millionth of its original energy although, of course, measurements are seldom possible over such a wide range (60 dB). The average absorption coefficient is obtained by adding together all the individual items of absorption and dividing by the total area

$$\bar{\alpha} = \frac{1}{S} \left\{ \alpha_1 S_1 + \alpha_2 S_2 + \ldots \ldots \right\}$$

The above formula assumes a continuous absorption of sound whereas, with the exception of air absorption, the removal of energy is a discontinuous process occurring each time a wavefront is reflected from a surface.

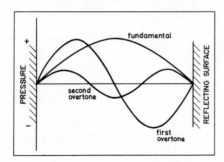

Fig. 2.6
Modes of vibration (eigentones) between two parallel reflecting surfaces

Modifications to the formula have been made by several people, the most successful being that by Eyring in 1930; the formula becomes

$$RT = \frac{0 \cdot 161\ V}{-S\ \log_e (1 - \alpha) + 4mV}$$

The 4mV factor accounts for air absorption which is significant at high frequencies and in rooms of large volume.

The optimum value for the reverberation time of an enclosure is a function of the volume and of the use for which it is intended. For a given type of studio it is normally found that the optimum value increases with volume. Thus for classical music values from 1·0 to 2·0 secs are typical, while for small studios suitable for speech values between 0·3 and 0·4 secs are adequate. The recommendations given by the BBC are shown in Fig. 2.7.

Studios for multi-microphone recording comprise a special and rapidly growing class in which the aim is to give the studio engineer the maximum freedom to adjust the relative balance between different groups of instruments. The lack of internal balance in a band in which, for example, a relatively small number of strings are matched with a strong brass section may now be corrected by the increasing electronic sophistication of the control desk. However, the implication on studio design is that the sound from one group of instruments must be satisfactorily separated from that of a neighbouring instrument. This is particularly true in stereophonic recordings, where the positioning of an instrument in the sound stage

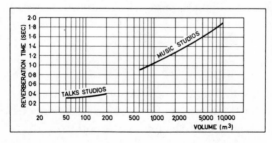

Fig. 2.7
Recommended reverberation times for broadcasting studios (courtesy BBC)

will almost certainly differ from its geographical positioning in the studio. Spurious pickup of one instrument on the microphone of a nearby instrument will lead to incorrect positioning of its image or, more commonly, an unacceptable broadening of the image as the adjacent microphone is faded up. The solution to this problem lies partly in an acoustic design which gives the greatest possible fall of sound level with distance and partly in the correct choice and positioning of studio furnishings.

Acoustic conditions which approximate to those found in the absence of reflections lead to a fall of sound level of 6 dB for each doubling of the distance. While it is possible to instal acoustic treatment which will absorb substantially all the sound incident upon it, this is an extremely expensive form of treatment and leads to an acoustically oppressive atmosphere. It is sufficient, and usually all that is possible in practice, to design for an average absorption coefficient of 0·4; the practical limitations of the surface area available, together with the probable economic limit on the materials that can be installed, make it difficult to exceed this figure.

While it is not sufficient to specify a reverberation time, the necessary treatment on the surfaces will ensure that a low reverberation time results. Typically studios of less than 1,000 m³ volume will have reverberation times less than 0·5 secs.

Although such dead conditions assist the technical requirements for the production of sharply defined images on the sound stage, they do not provide a comparable stimulus to the performer. Musicians in general need to be able to hear themselves in order to produce a good tonal quality, and they need to be able to hear each other in order to achieve an ensemble. Local reflecting surfaces are normally appreciated by the strings, and in most other cases there will be adequate spill-over from one area to another to assist in achieving ensemble. However, on occasions it may be necessary to dispense with natural acoustics and rely on headphone or loudspeaker foldback to enable players to hear each other. When such measures are accepted then an even greater flexibility results: for instance different studios can be used for strings and brass, or recordings need not be made simultaneously, etc.

Acoustic absorbers

It is necessary to adjust the absorbing characteristics of all studios in order to achieve correct acoustic conditions. To this end, materials which absorb sound in particular frequency ranges have to be selected in the correct amounts and installed in the optimum positions. Acoustic absorbers operate by dissipating the energy stored in the oscillatory pressure waves as heat either in internal losses in vibrating materials or as viscous losses in air movements in porous materials.

1. *Panel absorbers:* When a panel or membrane of a mechanically lossy material is excited into vibration by sound waves, energy will be dissipated. If such a panel comprises the exposed face of a closed box, a low frequency resonator is formed; the resonance frequency is controlled by the mass of the panel and the stiffness both of the material itself and the enclosed volume of air. Thus variation of the weight of the material or of the depth of the air-space will adjust the frequency at which maximum absorption occurs. In some cases it will be necessary to introduce additional damping into the box in the form of porous material; this must be mounted directly behind the membrane, since this is the position at which the particle velocity is at its greatest.

An extremely efficient form of membrane absorber developed in the BBC Research Department uses bituminous roofing felt as the membrane; this material has a low inherent stiffness and a considerable variation of resonance frequency results from alteration to the depth of the air-space. Results for this type of absorber are shown in Fig. 2.8. Most other thin panel materials will act in the same fashion but usually without achieving comparable bandwidths of absorption or allowing adjustment over a comparable frequency range.

2. *Helmholtz resonators:* An alternative absorber for use at low frequencies is formed when an enclosed volume of air is coupled to a studio through a 'neck'. This form of resonator is well known to all who have blown over the neck of a bottle. The resonance results from the movement of the mass of air contained in the neck controlled by the stiffness of the enclosed volume of air; the frequency is governed by the volume and by the size of the neck and tuning can be accomplished by changing one or the other. It will always be necessary to add a resistive material in the neck, to ensure absorption of energy over a useful bandwidth. Such absorbers have been used on occasions to damp out particular low-frequency modes in small rooms.

3. *Porous absorbers:* The greatest range of absorbing materials lie within this general classification; mineral wools and hanging curtains, woodwool slabs and unplastered blockwork walls all dissipate energy by viscous loss in their pores. Provided the material is sufficiently dense, efficient absorption will result at high frequencies. As the thickness of the material is increased, the absorption will extend to lower frequencies; to some extent the same effect results from increasing the density of the material but this may lead to increased surface reflection at higher frequencies.

The first maximum in the absorption occurs at a frequency for which the thickness of the material is one-eighth of a wavelength; doubling the thickness will lower this frequency by one octave. Progressive doubling of the thickness of absorbing material becomes expensive and it is useful to note that there is not a great loss of efficiency if a thin layer of porous material is backed by an air space to give the same total depth. Results typical of the behaviour of such porous absorbers are shown in Fig. 2.9.

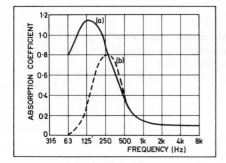

Fig. 2.8
Absorption coefficients of membrane absorbers: (a) 300 mm, and (b) 25 mm deep air-space

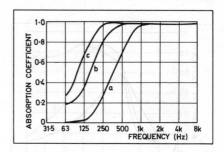

Fig. 2.9
Absorption coefficients of porous absorbers: (a) 25 mm layer, (b) 50 mm layer, and (c) 25 mm absorber plus 175 mm air

The absorbing characteristics of this type of absorber can be modified by the use of a perforated facing material. Perforation providing a distributed open area of 25% or greater will not significantly modify the absorber characteristic within the normal audio-frequency range. Reduction of the open area will cause a progressive cut-off of high frequency absorption. When low percentage perforations are reached (say 5% or less) the behaviour is more like that of a surface containing a large number of Helmholtz resonators in which the perforation acts as the neck and the appropriate part of the space behind each perforation acts as the enclosed volume. Resonance absorption characteristics in the range 70 Hz to 1,000 Hz can be produced by selecting the appropriate perforation and depth of air space; typical results for absorbers which have been produced as a range of manufactured modular absorbers are shown in Fig. 2.10.

Acoustic treatment of a studio

Knowing the volume and proposed use of the studio, a preliminary calculation is carried out to determine the total amount of absorption required at each frequency to achieve the optimum reverberation time. If the shell of the studio exists, a measurement of the reverberation time will reveal the inherent absorption of the structure; if the design is being undertaken in advance of the construction, then the structural absorption will have to be calculated on the basis of values obtained previously. The difference between the absorption required and that arising from the structure represents the amount that must exist in the completed studio from all other causes—furnishings, persons, air absorption (if the studio is large) and added absorbers. It is most common in studio design to seek the same reverberation time at all frequencies, although some authorities prefer a rise at low frequencies to give added warmth.

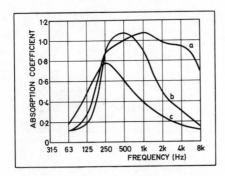

Fig. 2.10
Absorption coefficients of perforated faced absorbers: (a) 25%, (b) 5%, and (c) 0·5% perforated face

The selection of materials to achieve the design reverberation time is done by an iterative procedure, making due allowance for those items which are necessary for the occupation of the studio (carpet, chairs, etc.) and for these that may be desirable from other points of view (suspended ceiling, curtains, etc.).

The absorbing behaviour of materials is dependent on the sound field in which they are placed. The maximum absorption is normally found in a diffuse field, that is one in which the sound is incident uniformly from all directions. Since this condition is the one that can best be reproduced, it is specified for all standard laboratory measurements of materials.

A certain degree of diffusion is also necessary in studio conditions; this is normally obtained by eliminating major flat reflecting surfaces and substituting structural irregularities or areas having differing absorbing characteristics. The former method was most common in early recording studios but, when it was appreciated that patches of absorber could produce a similar effect, this led to a cleaner studio line having all surfaces flushed out to a common face.

Distribution of the absorption thus leads to the development of a diffuse sound field, to improved efficiency of absorption and to better agreement between reverberation times calculated on the basis of laboratory figures and those measured in the completed studio. The positioning of the absorptive treatment must bear in mind the requirements for diffuse conditions together with the prevention of flutter echoes and the elimination of strong reflections which may interfere with the direct signal or cause unwanted crosstalk at adjacent microphones.

Variable acoustics

Over the years there has been much interest in the concept of variable acoustics, the reverberation time of a studio being altered to suit the requirements of the production currently occupying it. In general, attempts to realize such a system have been poorly received; large areas of acoustic absorption have had to be moved physically and, because the effort involved is seldom available, some compromise condition is accepted for all productions and remains unaltered.

A recent development by the Institut für Rundfunktechnik has renewed interest in the possibility. It is fully automatic in operation and can be controlled, in the same way as an artificial reverberation unit, from a knob on the control desk. In this invention the required area of wall surface is partitioned to a depth comparable with that of the modular absorbers described earlier. When absorption is required, a resistive membrane is drawn over this surface by an electric motor to act as a wideband absorber. A suitable decorative perforated facing is used to conceal the entire operation from view. After calibration, the control can be scaled directly in seconds of reverberation time as for an artificial reverberation device.

Studio screens

Notwithstanding the provision of adequate acoustic absorption to achieve the design reverberation time, there remains in many studios a need for additional absorbers or reflectors in specific places. This may be necessary for the control of particular defects (flutter echoes, strong reflections from windows, etc.), to provide a local acoustic which differs from that of the remainder of the studio (live areas in otherwise dead studios, open-air conditions in drama studios), or more commonly to supplement the natural attenuation between adjacent instruments.

Traditionally such screens have been of a light construction, with one side reflective and the reverse absorptive. Since the overall depth is normally less than 25 mm, the possibility of achieving either high absorption or high reflectivity over a wide frequency range is limited. The reflective surface will probably be of painted hardboard or plywood; the absorptive surface will be of 12 mm porous absorber covered with a protective and decorative finish.

Provided precautions are taken to fit the screens closely together and to cover any gap that may exist at the foot, some 10–15 dB attenuation can be achieved between adjacent areas. The design of this type of screen will commonly incorporate a transparent area through which musicians can see the conductor; this area can be covered by a hinged panel of absorptive material if viewing is not required.

An alternative approach which sacrifices the light weight and ease of movement to obtain more efficient absorption has recently been described. In this screen the total depth is more nearly 100 mm and greatly improved absorption results. The control of the sound from percussion or other instruments enclosed by such screens is greatly improved and it is possible to work with a microphone close to the surface of the screen. Such a position can give greatly improved separation from instruments on the opposite side of the screen.

CHAPTER THREE

The Microphone Circuits

John Borwick

The need for extreme care in handling, suspending, and making cable connections to microphones cannot be too strongly stressed. Of all the equipment in a recording studio, it is the microphones which take the lion's share of being moved around and placed at risk amongst performers and audiences. Knowing this, the designers of microphones put robustness high on their list of design criteria—and one can think of early moving-coil microphones which were strong enough to use for hammering in tent-pegs. Robustness is a relative term, however, and the need for care arises from two main factors, the fragility of the moving parts and the extreme smallness of the electrical signal to be conveyed along cables prior to amplification up to 'line' level.

Moving-coil (dynamic) microphones are the most robust and, since the built-in permanent magnet already makes the unit fairly heavy, the designer will usually feel justified in making the case heavy too. Ribbon microphones also rely on the electromagnetic principle and weigh a fair bit. Yet it would be a mistake to regard ribbon microphones as other than extremely fragile. The ribbon itself is only a fraction of 1 μm thick and corrugated lightly across its width to enable it to be critically tensioned between the end clamps. Any slight movement of the microphone will set the ribbon in vibration at its resonant frequency (about 40 Hz) and produce bumping noises. This makes the ribbon microphone unsuitable for use on a television boom, in the open air, close to bass drums, etc., and even for some sopranos.

Capacitor (electrostatic) microphones can be very expensive and perhaps this has the psychological advantage of persuading all users that they need careful handling. The presence of built-in electronics—the head amplifier—also contributes to the reputation for fragility though faults here are not common. Most vulnerable is the thin diaphragm (about 6 μm thick) which clearly cannot withstand excessive shocks: even if physical breaks do not occur, there is a risk of sparking of the DC polarizing voltage.

Exposure to conditions of high humidity can make capacitor microphones noisy and engineers will often switch on such microphones an hour or more before a session to ensure 'drying out'.

Microphone sensitivity

The electrical output level from a microphone for a given sound pressure level should clearly be as high as possible, to provide a high ratio of signal to noise. The word 'noise' is here used to mean inherent electrical noise, interference, mechanical handling, cable rubbing, and indeed all the unwanted accompaniments to the desired signal before it reaches the control console amplifier. In practice, the microphones used in professional recording vary quite widely in sensitivity.

Microphone sensitivity is quoted in several ways and so some calculations may be necessary before comparing different manufacturers' specifications. A common method is to specify the output voltage (in millivolts) for a sound pressure level equivalent to conversational speech at about 20 cm distance. This is 74 dB SPL (or 0·1 Pascal) and output voltage values for some well known microphones are given in Table 3.1.

Instead of quoting the sensitivity in mV, some microphone manufacturers prefer to give a level in dB relative to 1 volt (so that 1 mV = −60 dB, for example). Yet another method attempts to avoid the difficulty that voltage levels will vary with the nominal impedance of different microphones by specifying the power level. The usual reference power is 1 mW and the sensitivity is then given in dBm for a Threshold of Hearing SPL of 0 dB (0·2 μPa). These different ratings are also listed in Table 3.1.

The main point to note is that microphone signals are of very small magnitude and so, for a reasonable signal-to-noise ratio, it is vital to limit extraneous noise to the order of a few microvolts.

On very loud signals, however, as in close microphone balances on a drum kit or guitar amplifier, there may be a real danger of overloading the microphone amplifier in the control console. Switched attenuators are therefore built into some microphones, or in-line attenuators can be purchased to give 10 dB or more reduction in signal level prior to the microphone circuit to the desk.

Microphone cables

Microphone cables for professional use have standardized over the years. In almost all cases a twin-conductor cable with metallic screen will be chosen. Several qualities are available, with either a metal braid or foil sheeting for the screen. The outer coating can be of rubber or plastic, the difference then being of operational convenience rather than strength, some cables tending to kink annoyingly and become difficult to wind in. For long runs of up to 100 metres, the cable will be wound on a drum and, if more than two or three drums are in use, a form of cradle will be a sound investment to make winding easier.

Table 3.1: sensitivity ratings of some typical microphones

Model	Type	Open circuit voltage (mV) (for 74 dB SPL)	dBv	Output power (dB rel. 0dB SPL)
AKG D202	2-way moving coil cardioid	0·16	−76	−150
AKG C451	capacitor series	0·95	−61	−135
AKG C414E	capacitor, variable	0·6	−65	−139
Beyer M201NC	moving coil hyper-cardioid	0·14	−77	−151
Beyer M88N	moving coil hyper-cardioid	0·25	−72	−146
Beyer M160N	double ribbon hyper-cardioid	0·1	−80	−154
Calrec CM1051C	capacitor cardioid	0·3	−70	−144
Neumann KM84	capacitor cardioid	1·0	−60	−134
Neumann KM88	capacitor, variable	0·8	−62	−136
Neumann U87	capacitor, variable	0·8	−62	−136
Neumann SM69	stereo capacitor	1·8	−55	−129
Schoeps CMT56U	capacitor, variable	1·0	−60	−134
Sennheiser MD441U	moving coil hyper-cardioid	0·2	−74	−148
Shure SM56	moving coil cardioid	0·16	−76	−150
STC 4038	ribbon figure-of-8	0·6	−85	−159

For shorter cables (8 metres is a convenient length) it is good practice to fold the cable end to end until it measures about 1 metre and then tie it in a loose knot for transportation or storage on a row of coat-hooks etc. This is better than rolling the cable in a small circle, which can so easily become tangled.

Balanced lines

The use of twin-conductor cables is referred to as balanced line working, to distinguish it from the single-core screened cable which uses the screen as the return wire of the circuit and is called unbalanced (see Fig. 3.1a).

While the screen in either case will give some protection against induced signals from stray magnetic fields, the balanced line is much better from this point of view, as will be seen from Fig. 3.1b. Any induced current caused by an external field which gets through the screen will flow in the same direction in both conductor wires, and will be of the same magnitude. The amplifier end of the cable is terminated in a transformer, either centre-tapped or

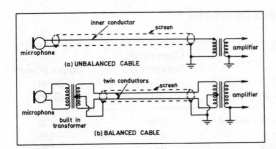

Fig. 3.1

Comparison of (a) unbalanced and (b) balanced cable working for microphone circuits

'floating', and the noise currents will flow in opposite directions through the primary winding and effectively cancel. Such care to eliminate unwanted signals is very important in microphone circuits, of course.

Another advantage of the balanced line is that it is automatically matched to the microphone in terms of impedance and permits very long runs, of as much as 300 metres, with no serious loss in signal strength or frequency response.

In recent years, though a few 30-ohm microphones still exist, a standard value of 200 ohms has evolved. This is simple to arrange for moving-coil and ribbon microphones, which have inherent impedances of around 30 and 1 ohms respectively, by building in a matching transformer. With capacitor (sometimes called electrostatic) microphones, the position is equally straightforward since a built-in head amplifier is the rule. This can be designed to match the extremely high impedance of the condenser diaphragm assembly (capsule) and yet provide a suitably low source impedance. Precise matching of impedances is not usually critical and the majority of professional microphones will operate satisfactorily into any impedance which is higher than its own source impedance. Thus a 200 ohm microphone can be loaded with 600/1,800 ohms. The position is somewhat confused by the fact that manufacturers will sometimes label microphones and amplifiers with the impedance to which they are meant to be connected, rather than their own impedance value.

Plugs and sockets

When a studio is being wired up from scratch, it pays to be generous in the number of microphone circuits and wall sockets provided. Eight microphone points would be a minimum in even a small studio, and 40 would not be too many for a larger, general-purpose studio. It might be thought that multitrack working, in which only small groups of musicians are recorded at any one time and overdubbed to build up the complete sound mix, would make fewer microphone points necessary. But fashions change and each studio must be ready to tackle a wide variety of recording assignments.

The microphone sockets should be arranged in groups of 4, 8, or 12 at positions around the walls which will make it easy to cover the working area with reasonably short-lengthed cables. Parallel groups of sockets might be installed on opposite walls, with one box suitably labelled Mic 1A, Mic 2A, etc., to keep floor cable lengths down to a minimum. An interesting example of parallel sockets is met in some small talks studios, where the alternative socket is wired with quite substantial bass cut and will be chosen by the engineer if room resonances are being a nuisance or he is using such a close microphone technique that the bass rise (due to the 'proximity effect') is making voices sound boomy.

Microphone sockets used generally to be mounted almost at floor level, in the skirting board, but a height of about 1 metre (3 feet) is more convenient, particularly if the labelling has to be read or locking latches have to be freed each time a plug is inserted or removed.

While several types of plug and socket have been used over the years, including Tuchel and DIN, the Cannon XLR series has emerged as a favourite with many users. In the code numbers for these connectors, the first number indicates the quantity of pins and the last group of numbers identifies the type (see Table 3.2), the odd numbers indicating a socket (female) connector and the even numbers a plug (male) connector. Thus XLR-3-12C is a 3-pin cable plug and XLR-3-13 is a 3-pin round panel socket. The panel and cable socket connectors contain a latching device to retain the plug, but this can be removed if not required.

Table 3.2: XLR connector types

	Socket (female)	Plug (male)
In-line cable connector	11C	12C
Round panel mount connector	13	14
Rectangular panel mount connector	31	32
Right-angle cable connector	15	16

An extension microphone cable would normally have XLR-3-11C (female) at one end and XLR-3-12C (male) at the other. A useful rule of thumb is that the pins point in the direction of signal travel. The built-in connectors on microphones are therefore of the plug (male) variety, whereas the connectors on walls and mixing console inputs are socket (female). A similar reasoning helps to identify the input and output connectors on tape machines, reverberation plates, etc. which use this XLR series.

To allow for the unexpected, it is useful to have a supply of 'sex change' adaptors with the same type of connectors at each end (both male or both

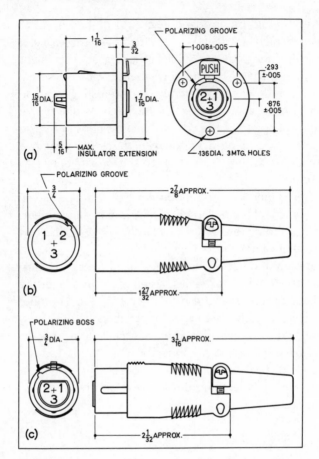

Fig. 3.2
Pin numbering and basic construction of (a) XLR-3-13 socket,
(b) XLR-3-12C plug, and (c) XLR-3-11C cable socket (dimensions
are shown in inches)

female). These can be made up on short lengths of cable (suitably colour
coded for easy recognition) or are available ready fitted in a metal casing
about 100 mm long. As an extension of this idea, XLR type in-line attenuators
can be purchased with a male connector at each end, and a balanced resistor network built-in to give such fixed attenuation values as 10, 15, 20, or
30dB (for a source and load impedance of 200 ohms).

Phasing

The most common pin wiring convention for microphones (a US standard,
though unfortunately not a universal one) is shown in Fig. 3.2. This makes
pins 2 and 3 the 'live' and 'return' wires respectively, with pin 1 screen

(ground). In fact, the metal sides of the socket hole No. 1 are longer than those of the other two to ensure that the screened connection on inserting the plug is made before the signal on pins 2 and 3. It is important to stick to one convention within any studio complex. Of course any wrong wiring of the screen will result in an obvious buzz or hum, but simple cross-wiring of pins 2 and 3 will reverse the polarity (phasing) of the signal and might not be immediately detected unless the engineer is using this cable for one microphone in a stereo pair. Therefore, if the cable used has red and white insulation on the twin conductors, for example, the studio might decide on red for 'live' (pin 2) and white for 'return' (pin 3).

Power for capacitor microphones

Capacitor microphones, unlike dynamic and ribbon types, require a feed of DC voltage both to power the head amplifier and apply a polarizing voltage to the diaphragm assembly. The most usual voltage is 48 V but other values down to 9 V are met.

Suitable mains units exist for each microphone type, rectifying the AC mains and producing a reasonably ripple-free DC current for one or more microphones (each drawing typically about 1 mA). There are even some microphones, such as the Neumann U87, which incorporate a compartment for insertion of small batteries, giving 200 hours running.

Increasingly common, however, and built into many modern consoles as a matter of course (and, for example, included in the Nagra IVS portable recorder) is a general purpose DC supply unit capable of running any number of capacitor microphones by the feed system known as 'phantom powering'.

In the most usual arrangement (Fig. 3.3) the positive DC side is applied through identical series resistors or a transformer centre tap to both the signal wires of a balanced line and the negative side to the screen. This obviously decouples the DC voltage, and any superimposed noise, from the signal and makes it safe to use the microphone circuits with dynamic or electrostatic microphones interchangeably.

Where phantom powering is not already provided, it is usually a simple matter to construct a suitable mains supply unit as in Fig. 3.4a or improvize a feed arrangement by taking a DC tap from a convenient rail in the console

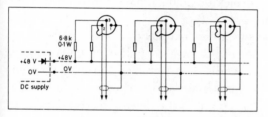

Fig. 3.3
Phantom powering of microphone circuits via identical series resistors to both signal wires of the balanced lines

capable of supplying the few mA required. The major microphone manu-facturers can supply details of the correct procedure. In Fig. 3.4b, for example, an arrangement using a Zener diode for stabilization is shown capable of producing the required 50 V phantom power voltage from any DC positive rail of between 100 and 400 V having a spare capacity of about 6 mA.

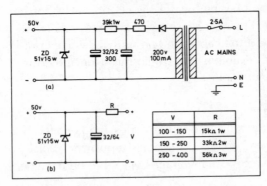

Fig. 3.4
Showing how a 50 V DC phantom power supply can be derived (a) from a simple mains unit, or (b) by tapping from a DC rail in the associated equipment

Some capacitor microphones, notably Sennheiser, employ a transducing element of much lower capacitance than usual and this forms part of a radio frequency circuit. The high-Q crystal controlled RF oscillator is said to give very low noise values. The high output level of the microphone and the built-in RF filter further assist in producing a very high signal-to-noise ratio.

Powering of such microphones is again via the signal leads but in a system referred to as A-B powering. This differs from phantom powering in that the cable shield is not part of the circuit. Although there is no danger to dynamic microphones plugged into an A-B powered line, the latter type of power supply unit normally has a switch to disconnect the DC when dynamic microphones are in use.

The patch bay

A cross-patching facility is a standard requirement, to allow the engineer to interchange his microphone-to-channel fader connections, either for operational convenience or to bypass a suspect faulty channel, etc. This is not normally provided at microphone level, because of the greater nuisance value of dirty contacts. Instead, the pick-up points will be at the microphone pre-amplifier output, channel pre-fade output, etc.

Some studios use larger Tuchel or Cannon plugs and sockets for the patch bay, but a more common system in Britain is to follow Post Office and BBC practice, using double-ended cords with standard 316 type tip-ring-sleeve plugs on each end. Of the various arrangements possible, a double row of sockets as shown in Fig. 3.5 is perhaps the most common. Type 500

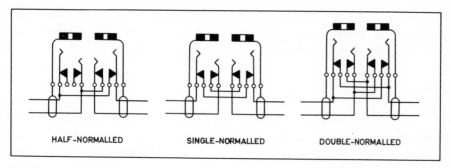

Fig. 3.5
Examples of jack field arrangements using normalled (straight through) connections on pairs of jack sockets

doublebreak jacks are used in the lower row of the popular 'half-normalled' arrangement for example to give a 'listen' and 'send' facility. Inserting a jackplug in the upper socket simply picks up the programme source A signal (for listening or feeding purposes) without breaking the 'normalled' connection to the lower socket (destination A). Inserting a jackplug in the lower socket automatically breaks the feed of programme source A to destination A and sends any signal on that jackplug to destination A instead.

Electret microphones

A relatively recent development in capacitor microphones is the electret. This is produced by techniques of applying a very strong DC electrostatic field to the plastic foil for the diaphragm during manufacture in such a way that a virtually permanent state of charge is set up. This eliminates the need for a DC polarizing supply to the microphone and, particularly when an

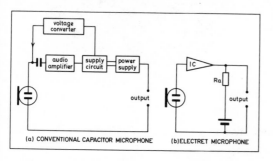

Fig. 3.6
Comparing the built-in circuitry for (a) a conventional capacitor microphone, and (b) an electret microphone

integrated circuit (IC) head amplifier is employed needing only a tiny 1·5 V or 6 V battery, both simplifies the cable arrangements and reduces the microphone size considerably. The simplification in the circuitry is shown in Fig. 3.6.

So far, electret microphones have mainly appeared in the lower priced bracket, but versions with fully professional standards of performance can be expected to develop.

Microphone accessories

The reliability and versatility of microphones can be extended by proper attention to the accessories, other than cables, with which they are used. A studio will soon acquire the booms and floor-stands that best meet all day-to-day requirements but there are numerous smaller items which should be kept at the ready.

These include stand adaptors and brackets—with and without some form of elastic suspension designed to attenuate structure-borne vibrations when used with a particular mass and design of microphone. Goose-neck and other types of extension mount are also helpful, as are stereo bars and

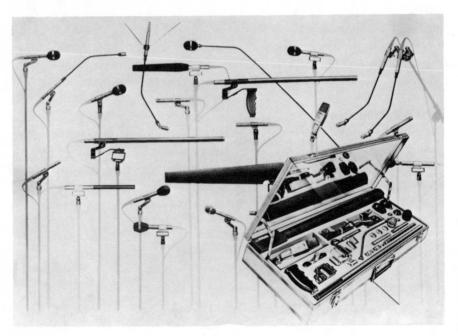

Fig. 3.7
Range of accessories available for a typical modern series of capacitor microphones (courtesy AKG)

attachments to simplify slinging from ropes or nylon cord. When slinging in outside locations particularly, it will be important to bear safety in mind as well as the ability to position the microphone precisely in three dimensions. A three-cord suspension will usually be best with provision for one cord and a safe microphone attachment which will make it impossible for the micro-phone to fall on the musicians or audience, in the event of a failure in the plug-socket connector, for example.

Windshields are made in various grades, only the larger ones comprising a thin acoustic screen in a double cage of open-work mesh being really effective for outdoor work, giving about 20–30 dB improvement. The simpler polyurethane foam types will often prove effective for reducing popping and blasting with vocalists, however, and at least have the advan-tage of keeping the singer's mouth at a few centimetres distance. Combined with some bass cut, they can reduce wind noise by 12–20 dB. A composite photograph of the accessories and carrying case available for one well-known microphone series is shown in Fig. 3.7.

CHAPTER FOUR

The Communication Circuits

Ted Fletcher

Studio managers are generally aware that the physical comfort of a singer or instrumentalist is important in achieving an acceptable performance, and it is therefore all the more remarkable that studio communication systems (foldback, talkback, cue and light indicators) often receive so little attention. A classical pianist can suffer a serious trauma when concentrating on, say, the quieter passages of a Debussy prelude if he is suddenly assaulted by a screaming, howling talkback system; by contrast, the foldback at a rock session must not only be capable of penetrating a sound level of 110 dB or more but also be extremely flexible.

In order to understand the problems, we must first define our terms and establish requirements.

Talkback is the general term meaning speech transfer between acoustically isolated areas.

Foldback originally meant the system whereby a performer was able to hear himself, the signal going from studio to control room and then folding back to the studio again. It is now more generally used in a looser sense as any information or cueing to a performer.

Cue is any audio or visual information concerning the timing or synchronization of a performance.

Talk to tape, also known generally as *ident* or *slate* (in film studios and elsewhere) is cue information spoken on a recording, normally by the engineer or producer; for example the script reference or music title, and number of the take.

Talkback and foldback in the small studio

Even in a small recording studio, with limited space for performers and perhaps no aspiration to technically ambitious work, the studio communication systems are still of utmost importance. It is essential to have communication both ways between studio and control room, and equally important to possess some form of foldback. Whether a combined foldback/talkback system is used, or each function is handled by a separate system, will be determined not only by economics but also by the type of work normally undertaken.

The simplest case would be that of a small music studio having a mixer equipped with a microphone, a key switch with 'talk to tape' and 'talk to foldback' positions, a pre-fade foldback gain control on each channel and, perhaps, a master foldback gain control. Such a system is shown diagrammatically in Fig. 4.1; in this example the foldback output from the mixer feeds direct to headphones.

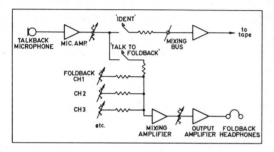

Fig. 4.1
Schematic diagram of talkback and foldback facilities in a small music studio

An arrangement of this kind provides identification on to the tape, communication between control room and studio, and foldback; but its limitations would quickly become apparent if it were employed in a studio accommodating a larger number of performers. The level of output from the mixer foldback amplifier would almost certainly be inadequate, and the single foldback system allows only a single mix from the mixer pre-fade.

Even in a small studio, however, there is much to be said for having separate foldback and talkback systems, with independent control of the programme foldback and information conveyed between control room and studio. If such an arrangement is adopted it is usual for the talkback to be fed to a loudspeaker and, while the foldback can also be on loudspeaker, it is more often on headphones in practice. The main advantage of having two independent systems, rather than a single combined one, is that foldback levels can remain preset while adjustments are made to the talkback.

Talkback and foldback in the large studio
In a studio catering for all forms of music recording, the systems become very much more complex, the basic requirements being that:

1. Sections of musicians must be able to hear their own individual mix of foldback at a level suited to their own requirements.

2. A conductor or director must be able to hear a complete mixed signal and be able to talk back to the control room.

3. Foldback should be available on both headphones and loudspeakers.

4. The control room should be able to talk to individual foldbacks or all foldbacks, as well as to the conductor.

To meet these requirements, mixer manufacturers tend to use multiple-foldback systems. A practical arrangement will be described in which the mixer basically incorporates six foldback circuits. Two circuits are driven from the input channels, pre- or post-fader, giving direct foldback of the performer to himself and to other performers. Two circuits are derived from a separate sync mixer from the multitrack tape machine, giving 'playback' of a pre-recorded track for synchronization purposes. The remaining two circuits originate in the main monitoring section of the mixer and provide the conductor with a total mix.

The talkback microphone has access to all foldback circuits, either separately or in any combination. The foldback circuits are normalled through to appear as multiple jack socket outlets on the studio floor, but may be cross-plugged to give various mixes and combinations on each circuit. For each circuit the feed to the studio floor is via a 25 watt amplifier arranged for 8 ohm drive. Thus loudspeakers or medium-impedance headphones may be used direct across the line with no significant level adjustment.

The two control room microphones (one each for engineer and producer) are omnidirectional to give their users freedom of movement. They also have a slight bass roll-off to take account of the reduction in acoustic insulation at low frequencies between control room and studio often found even in the best designed studios.

A separate private communication circuit between producer and conductor is provided by conventional telephone handsets, each terminal being equipped with a flashing light for calling. The light operating voltage is derived either from a telephone ringing generator or from some other local supply.

During the 'talk to foldback' function it is not advisable to silence the foldback signal on the circuit completely, nor is it advisable to insert the talkback over the foldback with no level variation. In practice the optimum reduction in foldback level seems to be 10 dB, which allows sufficient level for the performer not to lose track of the foldback, but retains intelligibility from the control room. A practical example of how this may be achieved without the use of relays is shown in Fig. 4.2.

It is essential that each of the foldback circuits appears on the main mixer select panel (and thence through to the conductor) so that the producer or engineer may set up the foldback balance and demonstrate it to the conductor if required. In this way the conductor can know what the producer is hearing in the control room.

In addition to the circuits already mentioned, the studio is provided with

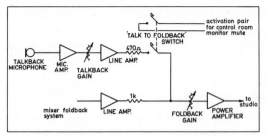

Fig. 4.2
One possible arrangement for 'talk-back over foldback' without the use of relays. (The line amplifiers are zero output impedance types similar to that in Fig. 4.3)

main playback speakers driven from the main monitor panel and interlocked so that they may become live only when listening from tape and when neither console nor tape machine is in the record mode.

The operation of a system of this magnitude can impose a considerable strain on the engineer. In order to reduce this, some manufacturers equip their talkback circuits with automatic gain control in the form of a very high-ratio limiter, thus ensuring that talkback signals appearing in the studio are always intelligible and at a fixed known level; the engineer is then relieved of the need for constant readjustment of talkback gain. The circuit diagram of a commercial AGC talkback system is shown in Fig. 4.3.

Additionally, to improve the intelligibility of the talkback signal from the control room to the studio, and to prevent acoustic feedback, it is normal for the talkback actuation switch to operate a separate circuit either to

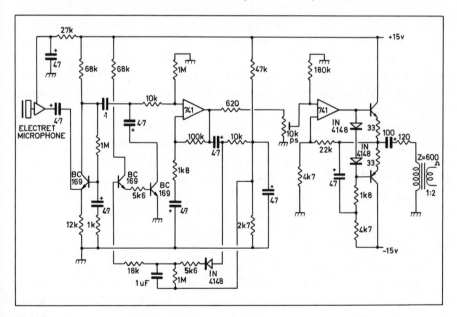

Fig. 4.3
Circuit of one form of AGC talkback amplifier (courtesy Stancoil Ltd.)

mute or dim the main monitor loudspeakers in the control room. A dimming system is preferable in use while a muting system is easier to instal; one or the other is of course essential when talkback microphones are equipped with AGC.

Talkback and foldback in broadcasting studios

A full discussion of all the facilities to be found in a broadcasting studio is beyond the scope of this book but, because many of these facilities are also found in studios which specialize in dialogue recording, some mention of them will not be out of place.

Whereas in such a studio the signal circuits are very much simpler than in a music studio (indeed, in many instances the operator has merely an input adjuster and a fader to control) the talkback and cue facilities, on the other hand, are required to be extremely comprehensive. It is not intended here to go fully into the various necessary system interlocks, but a brief examination of a typical small broadcasting studio can give some understanding of the sort of problem encountered.

It is necessary for an operator in a broadcasting studio to be able to:

1. Monitor the station output. This gives him an immediate check that the signal is leaving the studio.

2. Monitor off air, to ensure that the signal is getting to the transmitter.

3. Monitor the outputs of all associated studios.

4. Communicate with all other technical areas, i.e. other studios and rooms containing programme source equipment.

5. In addition, have available many of the facilities of a normal recording studio. For example he will require a 'talk to tape' facility for the preparation of pre-recorded programmes, but this facility must in turn be automatically disabled by going 'on air'.

Consider a 'self-drive' studio (i.e. a studio manned by a disc-jockey or presenter with no technical assistance) having an attached news booth and interview area. The first requirement is that the presenter shall be in constant easy contact with all other technical areas, particularly those which may supply contributions to his programme. This is accomplished by a comprehensive talkback system but with the difference that, whereas in a normal recording studio the 'reverse talkback' or 'receive' signals are passed through the programme microphone circuits, in a broadcasting studio they pass through a separate system which allows incoming calls to appear on a talkback speaker, the presenter's headphones, or the main monitor speakers, depending on the system design. To avoid interference and distraction, this 'reverse talkback' signal is muted when the presenter switches on his own programme microphone.

Additionally, the presenter has facilities to talk to a newsreader in the booth or to the foldback system in the interview area. The news booth may have a complete talkback terminal, making it a technical area proper.

Foldback systems in broadcasting differ from those in recording studios in one important respect. In a recording studio the performer hears a mix set up by the engineer to his specific requirements; in broadcasting, the foldback is a post-fade mix and corresponds closely to the main station output. During a news/magazine type programme the foldback often consists of a feed from the station's off-air receiver, enabling the participants to take their cues from the complete transmission loop; in other circumstances it may be necessary for participants to receive a 'clean feed', i.e., the programme without some particular source such as a simultaneous foreign language announcement or the speaker's own voice, which he may find distracting.

Lines, levels, and impedances

Practical systems in broadcasting closely follow time-honoured tradition based on the 600 ohm balanced line. For this there are very sound and sensible reasons, not the least of which is that all the problems have been solved and the system has such a long history that its every characteristic is documented somewhere; in short, it is a thoroughly known system, and it works. Simpler systems using unbalanced low-impedance lines for talkback are often employed in recording studios, but the crosstalk effects they produce are unacceptable in broadcasting.

However, with the advent of local commercial radio in Great Britain there has been increasing experimentation in broadcasting systems, including the application of many techniques used in recording studios. With care and thought this can lead only to improvement and better understanding by both sections of the industry. Source impedances of one ohm or less, which could be obtained only with great difficulty using valve circuits, are now easily achieved by transistors and a number of systems have been designed round the philosophy of very low impedance balanced sources feeding bridging loads, using dBm as a voltage measurement only: dBm$=0.775$ V. Such systems have many applications, particularly to foldback circuits, where pairs of 400 or 600 ohms headphones may be paralleled across one main foldback drive line.

At the same time it must be emphasized that such systems are not applicable to long lines where the characteristic impedance of the line itself is the important factor. In this case, there is no easy alternative to 600 ohm balanced working.

Light signalling and cueing

This chapter has been mainly concerned with audio communication between studio and control room, but no less important to the smooth running of a session are the light signalling and cueing systems. In this respect practice varies from one organization to another but one system in common use is described below.

A blue light, repeated inside and outside the operational areas, indicates that work is in progress, but for rehearsal purpose only. Entry and movement are therefore permitted but only in a way that will not cause interruption.

A red light, similarly repeated, indicates recording or transmission and must be strictly treated as an absolute barrier to all entry and unwanted noise, as well as a record indication to performers and a reminder to technical operators.

Studios specializing in dialogue recording frequently use a green cue light in addition to the two above. This is positioned on the studio floor or attached to a microphone stand and used for spot cueing of individual performers by the producer.

In a small studio a simple relay-activated light may be manually operated from the mixer deck, but in larger studios the system more usually comprises a blue light showing rehearsal plus a red light variously interlocked with recording systems on the mixer. In a recording studio the mains-borne click of a red light being turned on is of minor importance; but cue lights, often operated by back-of-fader contacts, must be capable of being switched on and off during performance without causing interference. If the light is mains-powered, the activating relay must be housed either in the lamp casing itself or in some other place that will remove the switching transient from the physical area of the mixer. Alternatively, cue lights can be run from separate DC power supplies or linked via opto-electronics to achieve complete freedom from interference.

THE EQUIPMENT

CHAPTER FIVE

Mixing Consoles

Richard Swettenham

In order to cover all the features likely to be met with in consoles for recording use, this chapter will describe the possible units and systems of a large desk for multi-track recording and subsequent mixdown, considered from the operational rather than the engineering point of view.

Microphone Inputs

The factors to be considered here are:

  Input impedance seen by the microphone
  Noise
  Frequency response
  Overload margin.

Nearly all studio microphones have nominal impedances of 30 to 60 ohms or 150 to 300 ohms and for practical purposes these may be regarded as nominally 50 or 200 ohms. Almost all capacitor microphones are supplied as 200 ohm, but some may have their internal transformers connected as 50 ohm. This gives half the output voltage, and thus may avoid overloading the input of equipment basically intended for dynamic microphones.

A dynamic microphone is not, of course, a pure resistive source and, at high frequencies, its impedance may be somewhat higher than the stated value. So exact matching of the amplifier input impedance to that of the microphone, while it would give 'maximum power transfer', might well degrade the frequency response. Microphone manufacturers normally state that the input impedance should be at least five times the quoted microphone impedance, and take their published response curves in this way. It is also important that the impedance does not drop seriously at low frequencies, due to lack of inductance in the input transformer. This is often a reason for apparent bass loss.

In some equipment it is still the practice to switch the microphone transformer primary winding in series or parallel for 50 or 200 ohm microphones. This of course gives a voltage step-up of 6 dB, and thus an improvement in signal-to-noise ratio. However, with most input amplifier designs, the noise improves when fed from a lower impedance source, so in the present state of the art it is questionable whether this switching is justified; almost all microphone types are available in the 200 ohm range, and the few which are not may simply be regarded as rather less sensitive types. It must also be clear whether any feedback gain change in the first amplifier reduces the input impedance below the minimum value.

Noise

In comparing manufacturers' specifications, it is essential to compare the stated test conditions and regard with caution any figures which do not state them clearly. Noise is normally specified at maximum gain, and is stated either as 'equivalent input noise' or 'noise figure'.

Equivalent input noise is the noise measured at the amplifier output in dBu (dB relative to 0·775 volt) plus the amplifier and transformer voltage gain in dB, when the input is terminated with a resistor of the normal microphone value (usually 200 ohms). Note that a 600 ohm source, sometimes specified, will produce an apparently worse figure, and a 30 ohm source (sometimes not mentioned) an apparently better figure.

> Example: Noise measured − 57 dBu, gain 70 dB,
> Equivalent Input Noise = − 127 dB.

The Noise Figure is the amount by which the Equivalent Input Noise is higher than the thermal noise of a 200 ohm (or other specified) resistor. Here the source value is part of the calculation, so the above ambiguity is avoided.

It is also necessary to state the bandwidth of measurement, or the weighting network used, and the voltage measuring instrument. A nominal 'rms' microvoltmeter will give a lower reading on noise than a peak instrument such as a PPM.

The above figures give a measure of the goodness of a microphone amplifier at highest gain. As the gain is reduced, the amplifier noise output will reduce at first in proportion to the gain, but then tend to level off towards a certain minimum noise at low gains (Fig. 5.1). Frequency response is mainly dependent on the quality of the input transformer and the impedances between which it works.

Overload margin

The overload margin at average input levels and medium gains will depend simply on the maximum voltage swing available at the amplifier output, as in the case of all amplifiers in the desk. But when the gain is low and input level high (as with close miking of instruments with capacitor microphones) the determining factor becomes the harmonic distortion due to saturation of the input transformer, particularly at low frequencies. To avoid this, a resistive pad may be switched into circuit in front of the transformer. In order to maintain the impedances of 1,000 ohms minimum towards the microphone and 200 ohms as a source for the transformer, this pad will have at least 14 dB loss, and 20 dB is usual.

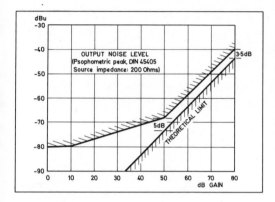

Fig. 5.1
Noise level limits for microphone amplifiers. (Source: Nordic Broadcasting Authorities' recommendations, 1972.) Note that the 'theoretical limit' shown works out to an equivalent input noise of only −124 dB, whereas lower figures are often quoted. This is because of the measuring method specified, which is not the one usually encountered

It would appear from the foregoing that the source of all short-comings in microphone amplification is the transformer, which suggests it should be eliminated. Unfortunately, transformerless differential input amplifiers have not so far reached the noise figure achievable with transformers. The transformer also provides isolation of the phantom supply voltage, normally provided for capacitor microphones, from the amplifier input.

Phantom power supply
Phantom operated microphones fall into two groups (as mentioned in Chapter Three); those which utilize 48 V directly for polarization and head amplifier powering, and those which generate their operating voltages by an oscillator-rectifier arrangement from the phantom supply. The latter types are intended to work from available voltages from 9 V upwards, with phantom splitting resistors chosen according to voltage. Since a control desk is liable to have to work with microphones of both types, the built-in desk supply will be 48 V and the resistor value chosen for the microphone type which draws the greatest current. The 'true 48 V' types draw very little current, so there is minimal voltage drop.

Gain settings
The key to the correct setting of microphone amplifier gain, with respect to both noise and overload margin against unexpected input peaks, is to keep the channel fader at the intended setting (e.g. 10 dB from maximum) when

the channel is contributing a signal to the mix that produces a peak level indication. This assumes of course that the group master faders are also at normal.

A useful approach to the correct situation is to set all faders to reference on a rehearsal and attempt to produce a plausible balance on the microphone gain controls. It should be realized that any downward movement of the fader from this position (other than to reduce the amount of that channel heard in the mix) is eating into the available headroom. *If restoring any fader to the reference mark causes the level meter to go over peak, then microphone gain must be reduced.*

An additional safeguard now becoming popular is the fitting of LED (light emitting diode) overload warning lights to each input channel. As will be seen later, these are best located after the equalizer.

Filters and phase reversal

As part of the input amplifier channel, a phase reversal switch and bandpass filters are often provided. It is questionable whether phase reversal on each input is worthwhile; except for the unlikely case of a wrongly wired microphone cable, its use is limited to dealing with cancellation effects due to microphone placement in the studio; if the console contains one or two patchable inverting amplifiers or transformers, this should take care of all such cases.

Filters have considerable use; the normal response specification of 20 Hz–20 kHz is usable only under ideal conditions; it is frequently desirable to curtail the LF response sharply below a certain frequency to cut off studio rumble, vibration of microphone stands and hum from guitar amplifiers. Typically, switched positions of 40, 80, and 120 Hz cut-off will be provided, with slopes of 12 or 18 dB per octave.

High-frequency filtering is less necessary in live recording. In reproduction from recordings or over lines, where hiss is noticeable, it may be useful to have a cut-off above the highest frequency of useful programme content. In live recording it may be helpful to cut off high-frequency overspill, e.g. from cymbals picked up on a microphone covering a bass instrument whose harmonics do not come far up the frequency range. Care must be taken that the characteristic 'edge' of a steep cut filter does not in fact make hiss more noticeable, and often a gradual high frequency roll-off is preferable.

Equalizers

The simplest equalizers found in studio equipment provide high and low frequency shelving curves similar to the treble and bass controls of domestic equipment. The next step is to provide a mid-frequency lift at various switchable frequencies from about 1 to 6 kHz. This is often called a 'presence' control as its effect is to make the signal affected stand out in the balance, as if closer to the microphone. But, if applied in an exaggerated way, it will give a hard metallic effect which destroys realism. Naturally the inverse of such a curve, a mid-frequency dip, is called in European terminology 'absence' and has a corresponding effect. Its use is to reduce those parts of the range of an instrument which 'stick out' too prominently in a mix, or to counteract in remixing the excessive use of 'presence' in the original recording.

It will be obvious that a normal shelving bass lift, which levels off and continues at a raised level down to the bottom end of the frequency range, will exaggerate any hum or rumble present in the input, which will in turn call for a low cut-off filter. For this reason there is a strong case for bass boost to be in the form of a broad resonant curve so that, if the 200–300 Hz region say is lifted to 'warm up' a male voice or a cello, the response will have returned to flat by about 60 Hz, and can then be allowed to continue flat down to say 30 Hz, allowing bass and bass drum to come through unattenuated.

From a similar point of view, a high-frequency boost should for most purposes level off by 10 kHz at the highest, and avoid exaggeration of hiss, mechanical noises from close-miked instruments and the like.

It has been standard practice in studio equipment for the controls of equalizers to have precisely calibrated switched steps of both lift or cut and of operating frequency. This enables precise settings to be written down and returned to, and makes it easy for a number of channels to be set to exactly the same response. However, there are many engineers who would prefer finer graduations than the steps of both frequency and amount usually provided. This has led to a fairly strong movement back towards continuous potentiometers and, most recently, to the introduction of so-called parametric equalizers. In these units the frequency spectrum is divided into several regions. The frequency of peak or trough is continuously tunable through each region by a potentiometer. The amplitude of the peak is also continuously variable and, lastly, the sharpness of the peak may be varied in steps or even continuously. The frequency regions may be arranged to overlap, any one region having a ratio of highest to lowest frequency of say 20 to 1, though an even higher ratio is possible. In some models the highest and lowest regions may be switched from a peak to a shelf form. In this way a very great degree of flexibility is available, at the expense of requiring a considerable number of panel controls. With such equalizers it is possible to produce some very strange and exaggerated effects, and it is important to bear in mind exactly what one is trying to achieve and proceed very logically in setting up the controls.

Studios also employ 'graphic' equalizers, so called because the user 'draws' a response curve with a number of vertical slide controls, each raising or lowering a fixed band of frequencies, typically in octaves or half octaves. These give a result similar to the parametric type but, unless there are many closely spaced sections, one cannot exactly simulate what is possible with a parametric type. Due to the number of variable controls, such an equalizer tends to consume a great deal more panel space than other types, so will usually be found as a 'patch-in' device, and not provided on every channel.

Equalizer overload

An equalizer, whether its circuit configuration is active or passive, will be designed to have the same maximum output level as the other amplifiers in the desk. So, with its controls at flat, it will not overload sooner than the microphone amplifier. However it should be realized that any considerable amount of boost applied to a frequency region where full level is present in the microphone amplifier, will result in a higher level at the equalizer output, using up more of the available headroom. Of course it will normally 'sound louder' and thus cause the channel fader to be pulled down. If the previously mentioned criterion of 'keep the fader up and the input gain down' is remembered, this should avoid any problem.

Conversely, if the equalizer applies a considerable cut to a high input level region, more signal may be present at the microphone amplifier output than is apparent. Probably the ideal solution is a LED overload indicator showing when *either* the microphone amplifier output or the equalizer output exceeds a certain level.

Insert points

After the equalizer (and occasionally before it as well) will commonly be found a break-in point at which a compressor or other processing element may be inserted. Sometimes the signal path will simply be led out via a pair of normalled jacks, but preferably there will be a switch in the channel, allowing the effect of the inserted device to be compared with the straight-through signal, or the device to be switched in and out on musical cues. It also avoids the signal passing through redundant wiring or transformers when nothing is inserted. Wherever possible, levels through a desk are arranged so that all insert points are at the same nominal level.

The channel fader

In recent years the large rotary stud faders once standard in professional equipment have given place to the straight line slide type which, with the exception of the quadrant lever, is now almost universal. Also, with the abandonment of constant impedance attenuator networks, the stud construction with precision resistors has been replaced by continuous tracks based on conductive plastic or carbon compounds. It has been accepted that precision of attenuation values is less important than smooth and noiseless control. Naturally, matching for minimum variation of loss between faders used for stereo and quadraphony has been a problem, but these tolerances have now been brought to an acceptable level.

Considerations in the choice of faders are mainly the smoothness of mechanical 'feel' and freedom from electrical noise, best judged by listening to the control of a steady tone or, better still, the application of a DC voltage to the fader. Other points are the susceptibility of the fader to damage by dust and liquids spilt on the console, and crosstalk through the fader when closed. To optimize this, a switch will be found in many faders which short circuits the slider to earth at the minimum setting. Another switch is usually available as an option for external wiring, to illuminate indicator lights or start remote tape machines or turntables. A further facility called 'overpress' may be provided by which, having closed the fader, a further pressure of the knob against a spring operates another switch which can connect the channel signal to a pre-fade listen circuit, or possibly switch the channel input to a different source.

Faders are available in Europe with built-in line amplifiers, usually of 10 dB gain, which make up the attenuation normally held in the fader, and provide a low impedance output to feed following equipment or serve as a desk output. However, this offers no technical or operational advantage over separate amplifiers.

PFL, AFL and Solo

The pre-fade listen (PFL) circuit provides a means to check (a) with a fader closed, that the correct signal is present at the correct level, and (b) the technical quality of the signal at a standard listening level, without disturbing the recording balance. Signals from one or more channels are switched to a mixing bus. The mixed signal may either appear on a small speaker in the console, or operation of the button on any channel will energize a relay which brings up the PFL signal on one monitor speaker while muting the others.

The after fader listen (AFL) circuit is exactly the same, but it takes its signal from the output of the fader. It is therefore heard at a level proportional to its level in the programme balance. Either PFL or AFL will enable the operator to judge how much 'overspill' signal from other instruments is entering any studio microphone. In American terminology AFL is often called 'Solo'. There is another possible facility, however, which we will call 'real Solo'.

As stated, AFL brings up the signal on one of the monitor speakers. If echo is being added to the signal, it will not be heard in the AFL mode, but may be added by pressing the AFL button of the echo return system at the same time. However, it is often desirable to hear one or more inputs at the same level and stereo position as they occupy in the mix, and with their proper echo. This is achieved with the real solo circuit. Each channel has a signal cut-off relay connected through the solo switch contact to a bus wire which is parallel along all channels. Normally this wire has no voltage on it but operating the switch on any channel lifts the relay of that channel off the bus, and applies operating voltage to the bus. Thus the cut relays of *all other* channels are operated, and all signals are muted except the ones selected. While AFL may be operated while recording, Solo will of course destroy the actual balance, so will be locked out of operation during a take.

Auxiliary sends from channel
A signal may be taken off before the channel fader via switches and level controls to feed one or more foldback (artist headphones) mixes. This is normally pre-fade, so that level changes made during balancing do not affect the headphones feed.

Echo send is taken through another set of switches and level controls, usually from a point after the fader, though a pre-post fader switch is often provided. In a console intended for general-purpose broadcasting or record-ing use, often no distinction will be made between echo and foldback, and each auxiliary feed will have a pre-fade, off, or post-fade switch.

Independent outputs
It is often required, particularly for broadcasting and live-event recording, to feed individual input channels to a multi-track recorder while at the same time producing a stereo or mono balance. In the simplest form, the signal after the channel fader and its following amplifier will simply be brought out to a jack. However there may be a conflict between the fader settings for the proper musical balance, and the requirement to record full modulation on all tracks of the multitrack. It may therefore be desirable to take the inde-pendent output from before the fader, through a level trim control and separate amplifier. There is the alternative of recording the stereo from the multi-track monitor system, which will be mentioned later.

Stereo and quadraphonic panning
In the early days of stereo, a relationship was established between the proportion of signal level fed to two loudspeakers and the apparent position of the sound source (Fig. 5.2). If the levels to left and right are controlled according to these curves, the sum of power outputs from the two speakers

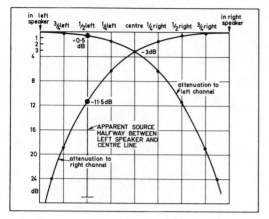

Fig. 5.2
Pan-pot law: the attenuation will give
constant loudness for a single source
panned across a pair of loudspeakers

will remain constant so that, when a source is panned from one speaker to the other, the loudness will not vary.

To produce the exact curves, a double stud potentiometer is necessary consisting of close tolerance resistors on a switch with as many positions as practicable. A fairly satisfactory approximation may be made with linear continuous pots, using one or other of the circuits shown in Fig. 5.3. Values are chosen so that the output level with the control central is 3 dB down on the level at one end of its travel. To maintain the law of the curves, the output of the pan-pot must be loaded as lightly as possible, so it may well be necessary to follow it by a pair of amplifiers, or at least emitter followers.

It should be noted that, while the 3 dB loss in the centre produces constant acoustic level from loudspeakers, if the two − 3 dB signals to left and right from the same source are added electrically to obtain a mono signal, the voltage sum will be doubled, and the mono will therefore be 3 dB higher with the pan-pot central than with the pot to one side. (The same will happen if the stereo recording is combined to mono in a playback system.) A 6 dB loss at the mid-point would remove this effect, but produce an apparent central level dip on a stereo pan. Where mono results are still considered important, as in broadcasting, a compromise value of 4·5 dB at the mid-point is therefore adopted.

For quadraphony, a peripheral positioning may be obtained by switching the two outputs of a stereo pan-pot to tracks 1–2 (normal front) 2–3 (along

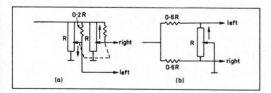

Fig. 5.3
Two forms of pan-pot (arrows clock-wise)

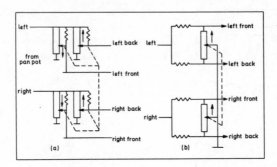

Fig. 5.4
Two forms of quadraphonic front-back pan-pot (to be fed from a normal stereo pan-pot)

right side) 3–4 (across back) and 4–1 (along left side). However, if the source is to be positioned in the 'solid area' between speakers (i.e. fed to more than two speakers at once) a front-back panning element must be introduced. This control is in effect handling two inputs (left and right) and proportioning each between front and back. Thus, if it is of the form of Fig. 5.4a it must have four elements and, if Fig. 5.4b, two elements. It will probably be most convenient to arrange that this front-back control is only switched into circuit when actually required.

The 'joystick' quadraphonic panner is simply the left-right and front-back elements combined into one mechanical construction, so that movement of the lever in the physical direction desired produces movement of the controls in two planes to position the image.

Again the actual potentiometers are either step switches or continuous track elements, the step type giving the most accurate positioning but, due to the physical size limitation, the number of steps cannot be great and on some programme material the step changes may be audible. The control lever moves through less than 90° in each plane, so that a continuous pot track directly operated has a small arc, which limits accuracy of resolution. Introduction of gearing, to use standard potentiometers, tends to worsen the feel of the lever. Mechanisms using rod-operated straight line potentiometers have now appeared which offer advantages in feel and construction, but accuracy is questionable.

The joystick should perhaps best be regarded as a special-effect device, patched in where actual two-dimensional movement of a source during an item is required. Except for rapid movement, all positioning may equally well be done with two rotary or slide controls.

Channel routing to groups

For multitrack recording, the ability to send any input channel to any group is essential. Basically this is a simple matter of switching but, in its physical layout, considerations such as minimization of crosstalk and operator preferences of presentation and indication have called for a good deal of ingenuity from designers, and represent a serious cost element in large consoles.

Routing systems can be divided into:

Rotary switch systems

Push-button systems

Pin matrix systems

Relay or transistor systems.

The simplest rotary switch arrangement selects the channel output to one of the available groups. If it is desired to record stereo pairs of signals on adjacent tracks, the switching in of the pan-pot can also connect a second switch bank to the next higher numbered group, i.e. selection of '1'+'Pan-pot In' gives panning between groups 1 and 2, and so on.

If it is desired to be able to record a channel on two tracks (possibly mixed on one, and by itself on the other) two separate switches will be provided. These may be fed either direct or through the pan-pot. One switch feeds to odd numbered groups, the other to evens. The only limitation is that the two groups selected cannot both be odd or both even. This meets almost all requirements. Indication of routing is by simple panel marking, or by dials illuminated from behind. The category of rotary switches also includes thumbwheel or lever operated types.

It is sometimes felt desirable to be able to route an input simultaneously to any or all groups. The traditional way of doing this is by push-buttons, often with illuminated caps. This is a straightforward and self evident system. The pan-pot, if inserted, will operate between two sets of buttons, again usually odd and even groups. The push-button system originated in four and eight group desks but, when applied to 16 and 24 groups, consumes a great deal of panel space.

A very reliable and low cost system is a pin or plug matrix located at one end of the desk. Only two signal lines from each channel enter the matrix, and one bus line out to each group mixing amplifier. Pins or plugs must be physically inserted to make each connection. However, there is normally no indication at the channel module of the routing selected. The author produced a system in which a double pin plug was used, the second pin connecting a DC supply to one of a bank of lamps illuminating figures in a small display panel over each channel.

Finally there are DC logic operated systems in which a button representing the channel and another representing the destination are operated to latch in a reed relay, or solid state audio switch, at the same time giving some kind of visual indication at the channel. Such systems, though elegant, are very costly in terms of the number of switching elements required.

Free grouping

A number of medium sized consoles, mainly for broadcasting use, have been designed on the principle of 'free grouping' which means that any channel may be used as a group or output. A certain number of channels is routed to a mixing bus which is then picked up as an input by another channel. The output of this channel may then be further regrouped with other such subgroups using another mixing bus, and the last channel will pick up this bus and will constitute the main output. Switching of channel inputs and outputs is so arranged that a channel cannot pick up its own output (Fig. 5.5).

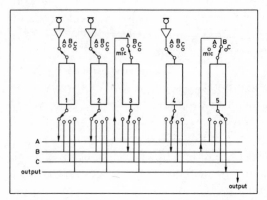

Fig. 5.5
Free grouping mixer principle. 1 and 2 are routed to subgroup A, which is controlled by 3. Output of 3 goes to B, as does independent input 4. C is not in use at present. Group B is controlled overall by 5, which is designated as the source of the main output

Mixing networks

The simplest mixing network may be used where a fixed number of sources is routed to a mix, or where the switching can be so arranged that each source not connected is substituted by a short circuit or dummy source resistance. A series resistor R from each source goes to the input of a line amplifier. Assuming say 20 possible sources, the input voltage will be divided in the ratio

$R : \dfrac{R}{19}$ or 1/20, or 26 dB loss, and the amplifier will be set for 26 dB gain.

However, if it is not practical for each unconnected source to be simulated, the loss of the simple mixing circuit will vary with the number of sources connected, from no loss at all with one source to the 26 dB stated for 20 sources. Obviously this is not acceptable, but the variation can be considerably reduced by fitting one shunt resistor across the amplifier input. For example, if the mixing resistors are 10 kohms and the shunt resistance is 500 ohms, the variation of loss between one and 20 sources is reduced to 6 dB. The variation will be further reduced by reducing the value of the shunt resistor, but this will call for increased gain in the following amplifier and thus a worsening of noise. A step-up transformer may be introduced before the amplifier to improve the noise situation.

The major alternative to the above arrangements is active or virtual earth mixing, which uses an inverting amplifier with feedback returned to its input through a resistor of the same value as the mixing resistors. The input of the amplifier is then a current summing point which has almost zero impedance. The voltage gain from any source to the mixing amplifier output is normally zero, though some gain can be produced if desired. The advantage of this system is that the level from one source to the mix does not vary significantly, however many sources are connected, up to the designed maximum. Also the noise produced by such a circuit, instead of being fixed by the gain required for the maximum number of sources, varies with sources connected and is minimum with only one source. Subject to careful practical design, this system is probably the most flexible and easy to apply in large consoles.

Groups

After the group mixing amplifier, an insert point will usually be provided, to accept a compressor or other device, before the group fader. After the fader, a feed to echo send may sometimes be provided.

As an aid to multitrack mixdown, a regrouping arrangement is useful. In the simplest form, it will consist of a single switch which returns the output of all odd numbered groups on to Group 1, and even numbered groups on to Group 2, which are then used as main stereo outputs. For quadraphony, groups may be returned in fours on to Groups 1–4. Channels not required to be sub-grouped may still be switched directly to Groups 1–4. A more flexible arrangement will be a selector switch routing the output of each group back to the mixing inputs of any other group.

Main outputs

It is conventional practice that the line outputs are capable of delivering a fairly high maximum level into a load, usually of 600 ohms. On comparing specifications, levels of $+18$ to $+26$ dBm (dB relative to 1 milliwatt in 600 ohms) are given. In actual studio operation this level of available output is of minimal importance. Headroom in the input amplifiers is important, as explained earlier. But after control by channel and group faders, and monitored by an output level meter, the level leaving the desk is unlikely often to exceed the nominal peak by any large amount. Indeed it must not, as excess levels reaching the tape will inevitably produce serious distortion. It is argued that on transient peaks the momentary level reached will not be indicated by a VU meter, which is quite true, and that the nature of tape overload is subjectively less unpleasant than the clipping of an amplifier. But, whatever the arguments about the practicability or desirability of 'getting more level on the tape' as a counter to noise or even to make use of tape overload as an effect, it is worth remembering that all studio recorders have an input gain adjustment which enables the tape to be fully loaded with an input of 0 dBu or often less. The fact that a VU meter with its standard series resistor reads 0 VU for +4 dBu is also unimportant, as the provision of small buffer amplifiers in front of VU meters is now very common practice.

The significant sources of noise in a mixing console are the microphone and mixing amplifiers, and the output level is not a factor in the signal-to-noise ratio of present-day equipment. Therefore studio engineers may do well to consider the operation of all equipment at 0 dBu for peak recording level.

Echo send outputs
The echo send signals from channels or groups will be combined on a mixing bus and amplifier, and passed by an overall level control to a line output to feed external echo devices. The sending circuit may also contain simple equalization, an insert point for compressor, etc. and a second switched insert for tape or digital time delay. Where this is used, a regeneration or 'spin' control will be provided giving repeat echoes round the delay device.

Echo return
From the chamber or reverberation device, the signal may be returned into an input channel or an echo return system, which is in effect a simplified line level input channel with equalization, fader and routing to groups and foldback (but of course no echo send).

Foldback outputs
In the simplest form, the foldback group will be the same as a direct echo send. It may also contain insert and equalization, and a relay for talkback into headphones. In a large desk, a second mixing matrix may be provided by which different combinations of say two mixes of signals from input channels, two from tape sync tracks, plus echo returns and external signals may be selected to four or more studio outputs. Provision may also be made to feed the foldback systems with the whole monitor mix as heard in the control room.

Multitrack monitoring
During the recording of a multitrack tape, it must be possible to monitor the input or recorded signal on all tracks, and present this as a reasonable representation of the final stereo or quadraphonic balance on the monitor speakers. Therefore for each track, after the line-tape switch, there will be the following controls:

(a) Foldback send pots (one or more per track). In early multitrack desks it was necessary to return each recorded track on to a desk input channel in order to send it to foldback. When there are plenty of input channels available, this is no disadvantage, and some engineers prefer it, but in smaller desks it occupies channels that may be needed for live recording of subsequent tracks.

It is necessary of course to provide the foldback feed from tracks with switching linked to the mode of the recorder, so as to prevent signal from the machine's playback head being fed to headphones when the machine goes from Sync to Record, or when the operator has selected to listen to playback in the control room.

(b) Level control. The general listening level will be set by the main monitor volume control. The individual track controls are then trimmed for a reasonable balance, so they will usually have a range of say +10 and −15 dB relative to a reference mark.

(c) Track Solo and Cut switches. These operate in the same way as described under Channel Solo and Cut. In this case the operation of Solo does not affect the recording, so it may be operated at any time.

(d) Monitor Echo Send. A level control and switch enables echo to be sent from a track round one of the echo systems and returned into the monitor system only. The switching for routing the return will be in the echo return module, if any. In a desk in which echo is normally returned to input channels, additional switching must be provided to bring echo back into the monitor system.

(e) Sync switch. When the main line/tape switch is on Line, the sync switch enables the operator to decide whether he will hear direct input to the track, or the already recorded signal from the machine's record head. (In the tape position of the main line/tape switch, playback will always be heard.) The detailed arrangement will vary between consoles, and will also depend on the make of multitrack recorder used. Relays may be provided to switch the monitoring of individual tracks back from sync to direct when the machine is put into record on that track.

(f) Stereo or quadraphonic monitor panning. These controls position each track signal on the monitor speakers during multitrack operations.

Record from monitor
Provision will usually be made to feed a stereo or quadraphonic recorder from the mixed monitor signals, before the main monitor volume control, so that a reference recording may be made simultaneously with the multitrack.

Main monitor controls

The signals from the track monitor system will pass to the main monitor section, which typically contains:

(a) Selection of monitor mode—multitrack, quad, stereo, and mono.

(b) Provision for checking quad as stereo, stereo as mono, and stereo phase.

(c) Main monitor volume control.

(d) Studio playback source selection and volume control.

(e) Switching to check echo send, foldback and external signals on main monitor speakers.

Provision is often made to transfer the main monitor signal on to small loudspeakers built into the desk, to simulate domestic radio and television listening conditions. When not in use for this purpose, such speakers are available for intercom with other control rooms, or pre-fade listening without cancelling the main speaker balance.

Metering

In a console with up to eight group outputs, it is normal to provide a level meter for each group. For 16 and 24-track working, there is a choice whether to have the full number of meters, or a switching arrangement. It is questionable whether an operator can really pay simultaneous attention to more than eight meters at the most, and there also arises the question of the optimum physical arrangement of these meters.

Logically, the easiest arrangement to scan is a square or rectangle. In an eight-track console, one therefore adopts a 4×2 layout. For 16 tracks, the commonest layout is 8×2 but, if the general module layout and overall height will permit it, a 4×4 pattern is preferable: 16 meters in a row is the worst of the choices, and is resorted to only when a low profile desk is essential for other reasons.

The above applies to conventional rectangular meter instruments; if edgewise instruments mounted vertically are adopted, the number which can be viewed horizontally is greatly increased, the positions of the pointers then being perceived as a 'graph' of levels in the group of outputs. In a console in which there is a module for each output group, an edgewise meter may be located above each such module. Except for the recording of live performances, it is most unlikely that all tracks of the recorder will be used at one pass of the tape. One therefore has the space and cost choice of 8 or 12 meters with switching; usually, for 16 track, meter 1 will read tracks 1 or 9, meter 2 will read tracks 2 or 10, and so on.

For mixdown, the two physically central meters of the group may be switched to read the stereo signal.

Types of meter

The level meters used in recording consoles are basically of two types, VU (Volume Unit) meters and PPM (Peak Programme meters).

The VU meter is an AC rectifier voltmeter, whose meter has a specified ballistic (i.e. rise time and overshoot) behaviour when it is connected to the signal source through a specified value resistor. Its performance is laid down by an American Standards Association specification, and it is important to realize that only meters conforming to this specification, and fed through the correct source resistance, give readings that can be meaningfully compared on programme material. Not every meter having the usual VU scale does conform, particularly in semi-professional equipment, though all such meters will normally give consistent readings for 0 VU on continuous sine-wave tone.

The normal sensitivity of a VU meter with its resistor (3·6 kilohms) is +4 dBu (1·73 volts) for a reading of 0 VU, and it is from this that the standard line level of +8 dBu for peak recording level derives. This may appear inconsistent but it is a property of the VU meter, due to its fairly slow rise time, that it will give a lower reading on average programme material than on steady tone. Hence the difference of 4 dB. American test tapes for recorders carry a tone at what is called 'Operating Level', that is the level which produces a reading of 0 VU. European test tapes carry a tone called 'reference level' or full recording level, which will be found to be approximately 4 dB higher. As a VU meter reads +3 relative to 0 VU at full scale deflection, the European level will drive it off the scale, thus it is usual, where such test tapes may be used, to provide a de-sensitizing switch for the VU meters. Opinions vary as to the amount of 'lead' that should be allowed between tone and programme, from the 4 dB mentioned to 6, 10, and even more. If a VU meter with resistor is connected across a 600 ohm source, it is possible to measure a small increase in distortion due to its presence. For this reason, and to enable the meter sensitivity to be adjusted about the standard value, it is common practice to give each VU meter a small buffer amplifier. This amplifier also permits a switched increase of sensitivity to read the frequency response section of a European test tape, which is recorded 20 dB below peak level.

We referred above to 'average programme material'. In relation to the readings produced on a VU meter, there is really no such thing and the permissible VU readings for different kinds of sound are something which must be learned by experience. The more sustained the sound, e.g. organ or slow chords, the closer the reading will be to a steady tone situation while, for sharp percussive sounds, the meter will underread considerably. In particular it should be mentioned that speech falls into the latter category, and should always be recorded well below 0 VU to avoid overloading.

The peak programme meter has a drive amplifier which detects and applies to the instrument the peak value of the audio voltage. It holds this value by charging up a capacitor which then discharges through a high resistance. Thus the peak value of a short transient will be held long enough for the instrument to rise to the correct scale reading, and then fall back slowly, so that the eye can register the value reached without being confused by very fast pointer movement.

It is possible to design a PPM with extremely fast rise time but, as certain transients are so short that if their full amplitude was taken into account they would produce a tendency to under-record the average level, allowance is made for the fact that distortion lasting a few milliseconds is not objectionable, and the electrical charging time of the capacitor is deliberately slowed. In the BBC programme meter circuit this charge time is 2·5 milliseconds. PPMs are normally semi-logarithmic, i.e. the scale is more or less linear in dB (whereas the VU meter is basically a voltmeter). The European peak meter circuits differ from the BBC standard in the rise and fall times and the number of dB on the scale length.

In Europe for many years the standard precision programme meter has been the so called light spot meter. This is a moving coil instrument on the principle of the mirror galvanometer in which the pointer is an image optically projected on the scale. These instruments were originally horizontal but, with the coming of multitrack consoles, are now made with vertical scales and stacked together with minimum width. This gives an excellent presentation but, due to the small quantity made and the precision required, any large number of such instruments is extremely expensive. Therefore other approaches have been made to obtain a display with the same virtues.

In the USA there have appeared a number of displays using rows of filament lamps behind a coloured screen. None of these has found wide acceptance, because of the rapid flickering of the top one or two lamps with level variation. Similar indicators using light emitting diodes (LED) are a very much more acceptable approach, but those which attempt to simulate the movement of a VU meter pointer suffer from the same flickering problem.

An indicator of the peak type with even four or six LEDs can give a very useful level indication for individual tracks, coupled with a few more precise meters switchable to signals of key importance. There are now available extremely precise LED programme meters with up to 70 discrete steps, and with a 'hold' facility allowing the highest value reached during a whole programme item to be indicated. Up to eight tracks, these instruments are perhaps the most elegant devices currently available. Where a large number of tracks is to be monitored, probably the most successful solution to the space and easy visibility problem is a cathode ray tube display.

Talkback

Talkback systems vary greatly in complexity according to the studio situation (see also Chapter Four). In a large console one is likely to find provision for:

   Talk to studio on loudspeaker
   Talk to each headphone circuit separately or all together
   Talk to conductor's stand or another control room
   Speak identification on to tape (Slate).

Provision will also be made in a large studio for a conductor to speak on a desk microphone to the control room, or to address an orchestra through the studio loudspeaker.

Console layout and ergonomics

Having reviewed all the possible features which may be included in a large console, and the very large number of manual controls which may thus be required, it will be evident that, to produce a workable unit, the layout and physical location of controls requires a great deal of intelligent thought. It is of little use to provide the maximum possible flexibility of adjustment if this will lead to a situation in which the operator is unable to reach controls which he has to operate simultaneously, or if the number and layout of these controls causes operator confusion and mistakes when working under stress. Thus the art of panel layout may almost be described as the intelligent

Fig. 5.6
A typical straight console layout (courtesy Helios Electronics Ltd.)

choice of what to leave out, and the organization of what remains in the most comprehensible form.

Present day control desks are of three main shapes—straight, L-shaped and wrap-round. The straight form is most suitable when the operational controls to be handled by a single operator fall within a span of about 1·6 metres (5 feet). Beyond this width may be controls used for setting up at the beginning of a session, patch fields, producer's space, and table-top space for auxiliary portable equipment. An operational control area much wider than this is impractical unless it is intended that two or more operators shall be used. This may often be the case in film and television work, but is hardly a practical proposition for normal music recording.[1]

A number of designs of L-shaped console has appeared in recent years. The tendency here is for the main channel inputs to be in front of the operator, modules concerned with track monitoring, echo and foldback being placed in the side section. Sometimes the track monitoring section will be expanded into what is effectively a second full mixer, complete with equalization, which constitutes the mix-down from multitrack to the final quadraphonic or stereo recording. Such a duplication of facilities, however, is extremely costly. The corner section between the two legs of the L-shape is extremely useful as a location for main monitoring controls, auxiliaries such as compressors, and possibly a small patching area.

The wrap-round layout, with various choices of angles (Fig. 5.7), offers what is in many cases an optimum solution. The requirements for convenient operation are precisely the same as for playing a large organ or flying an aircraft. The controls constantly being adjusted must fall under the operator's hands; those requiring occasional adjustment must be within arm's reach, but those set up and left for a whole session or series of items must not encroach on the valuable central space. Visual indications requiring constant operator attention must fall within the field of view without head movement. But nothing in this field must draw undue attention to itself by excessive brightness. Lamps indicating steady switching states should be very subdued, while brighter lamps at the extremes of vision are useful for signalling conditions requiring action. In Fig. 5.8 the areas 1 contain the most-used manual controls, overflowing if necessary on to 1A, provided the span is not too wide; and 2 the most important visual indications. The whole central panel can be spanned by the engineer without body movement, and the outer wings can be reached by leaning rather than moving

[1]Mention should perhaps be made of a console produced some years ago by the Decca Record Company for operatic recordings in which the producer sat in the centre with two mixing engineers beside him, one of whom took responsibility for the orchestral balance, and the other for the voices.

Fig. 5.7
A typical wrap-round console layout (courtesy Helios Electronics Ltd. and Strawberry Recording Studios, Manchester)

the chair. The corner quadrant panels 3 contain controls associated with monitoring, patching, feeds to foldback, etc. Panels 4 contain secondary visual indications such as echo meters and warning lamps. Areas 5 are for initial set-up controls. Depending on the number of channels, and hence width of the central section, talkback and remote controls are housed either centrally or in the small triangles at fader level. Normally there is room for two operators side by side should this be necessary. There is also

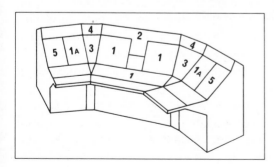

Fig. 5.8
Illustrating one possible scheme using a wrap-round console layout

the advantage that there are now two of the angular sections described above in which to fit monitoring and auxiliary facilities, in space which would not exist in a straight console. It is also argued by some acoustic consultants that a desk shape which is physically symmetrical with respect to the central line of the control room and loudspeakers makes a perceptible contribution to optimum stereo listening.

Automated mixdown

At the time of writing, the first generation of commercially available automated mixdown equipment is being evaluated in studios. The initial fears that such equipment would interfere with the skill and creativity of mixing engineers have now been dispelled. The optimum degree of automation in large desks is currently being determined, and operating techniques are being established. The prospect of automation has given a strong impetus to the design of voltage-controlled amplifiers which, though they have been in use for some years in music synthesizers, have only recently been brought to standards of noise and distortion acceptable for use in the main signal path for live microphone recordings. The first advantage of the introduction of VCAs into consoles is the possibility of ganging the level control of a number of channels (going to entirely different tracks) under one fader, thus easing the problem of reach and simultaneous operation without resorting to memory-type automation. However, the advantage of being able, by means of the memory facility of automated systems, to establish a complicated balance bit by bit without losing anything one has already done, and the further possibility of making modifications to individual channels while the overall balance remains as previously determined, are beginning to be accepted as really worthwhile advantages.

The first systems introduced have been based on the recording of data on the first of two tracks reserved on the music tape for the purpose. The tape is then replayed and the balance reviewed. On the next pass of the tape, the operator may revise the settings of some or all controls, and the revised data track is re-recorded on the second reserved track. The information being transferred unchanged from the first track is normally regenerated electrically, so that on subsequent repeated retransfers there are no cumulative changes of data track levels. The data will always be read from the record head in the 'sync' mode, otherwise on recording it would be moved along the tape in relation to the audio.

The above assumes the use of the normal record head of a multitrack machine, which has until now been accepted by system designers as an unavoidable requirement from the point of view of simplicity. It has been argued that the user would prefer the sacrifice of two audio tracks to the complications of separate bolt-on heads or sychronization of a separate recording medium for data. This policy places limitations on the data recording in that it has to be encoded in a form which will pass with complete integrity through the record and playback audio amplifiers, possibly containing transformers, and through an audio record head using normal HF biasing. Therefore the data bandwidth is somewhat limited, and the signal recorded looks very much like an audio tone interrupted or amplitude modulated.

The proprietary encoding systems will not be discussed in detail here. It is questionable, however, whether these 'simple' systems are the ideal solution, though there is a strong possibility that, on the argument of 'compatibility between studios', one of them will become the industry standard at least in the present generation of studio equipment. Whether compatibility of memory data between studios outside one organization is of any real significance is also debatable, unlike the case of noise reduction or quadraphonic matrixing where it is unavoidable. A good case may be advanced for normal instrumentation-type recording via standard data heads fitted to the recorder in a specified relationship to the audio record head. The associated read/write electronics may then be a 'black box' entirely unconnected with those of the recorder. When the data tracks are in use (assuming they occupy the position of audio tracks) the corresponding audio tracks are simply not placed in the record mode; but, if automation is not required, these tracks are free for normal use without any reconnection.

Existing systems are based on the repetitive scanning of all the faders and switches to be controlled, i.e. multiplexing at a regular rate. This means that the recorded data contains a great deal of redundancy, in that most of the voltages scanned will represent 'no change from last state', and this again is a waste of valuable bandwidth. However, the alternative of recording only changes, with addresses relating them to the controls concerned, calls for a much more complicated encoding system. Such an approach would also permit the storage of data on a separate medium, e.g. cassette or magnetic disc, which would not necessarily have to run in direct time synchronism with the music tape.

There remains in all systems the problem of relating, in the playback mode, the physical positions of faders and other controls to what is happening under the control of the recorded data. Early systems have provided the faders with meters indicating where they are 'supposed to be'. Modifications to the settings were then made by matching the fader with the meter reading and switching into 'data write'. In order to return to the original data track, the levels had again to be matched and the control switched back to 'read'. The inconvenience of this was overcome by introduction of the 'update' facility, by which the manual fader is set to a reference mark, e.g. 15 dB from the top, and an update switch operated. Any movement of the fader up or down from the reference is then added (plus or minus) to the existing programmed level.

Other schemes have proposed the physical movement of the fader lever, or a marker moving beside it, by a small servo-motor controlled by the memory signal. If it is the fader which is moved, the need for a voltage-controlled amplifier is avoided. Means must be provided by which the operator, on taking hold of the control to intervene manually, disengages the mechanical drive.

It would be possible to apply the same approach to equalizer controls, for example, though it does not appear economically feasible. It is very questionable whether automation of equalizer settings is in any case worthwhile by any method. Equalizers have been designed which are capable of voltage control but, with the operator's hands freed from fader operation, it seems reasonable that changes of equalization during an item, if any, can very well be done manually.

There is a case for a system which logs all control settings on a console in case work has to be interrupted and resumed later, but again the cost effectiveness of the hardware involved is doubtful, against the time-honoured practice of writing everything down after a session.

Finally, schemes have been proposed which would depart from the existing form of a sound control console and replace it by some kind of keyboard and display system, in which fader and equalizer settings are typed in and displayed, at the same time acting upon the audio signals in the control part of the system. This would entail an entirely new approach to sound control, and a new skill for operators to learn. It appears to have the weakness that all changes have to be thought of in quantitative terms and fed serially into the system, while in a present-day console an operator will 'feel' for the sound he wishes to hear and perhaps move several controls simultaneously.

As in all the other features discussed above, cost-effectiveness in terms of studio time and artistic result will be the determining factor in how far the sophistication of automated systems is carried.

CHAPTER SIX

Extra Facilities

Michael Beville

In the early days of multi-microphone recording, mixer desks, though massive in construction, were severely restricted in the functions they could perform by the large amount of space needed for valve circuitry. Facilities considered as basic today were more often add-on features mounted in the rack bay. Nowadays, units formerly found in the rack are increasingly being integrated into the desk itself. The capacity for transistor circuitry below the board can far exceed the space required for controls above it, and today's problems are primarily those of finger-space and ergonomics. However, the auxiliary equipment bay is still far from obsolete and desk designers will continue to provide insert points no matter how comprehensive the desk facilities.

Equipment usually classified as auxiliary includes such items as limiters, compressors, expanders, comprehensive equalizers (for example the graphic and parametric types), effects units (for phasing, ring modulation and time delay), noise reduction circuits, and reverberation systems. In practice, such devices are often the product of specialized manufacturers; the studio user selects those systems which suit his requirements, while the desk manufacturer limits his contribution to the provision of suitable interfacing arrangements.

Dynamic range

Before discussing such systems in detail, it would perhaps be useful to review the characteristics of the ear with special reference to its dynamic range. From the set of equal loudness curves already shown in Chapter 1 (Fig. 1.3) it was seen that the ear's response is far from flat and that it changes with varying sound pressure level.

In communication terms, dynamic range is the ratio between the quietest and loudest parts of an audio signal in a given context and period. The dynamic range of a recording or reproducing system will be the difference between the noise level at one end and the system overload point at the other. In the human auditory system, the dynamic range is not as great as may at first appear, since the ear incorporates what is in effect an automatic gain control device. Under extreme high level conditions, perception is attenuated and takes some time to recover sufficiently to be able to respond once more to low level sounds. Continuous subjection to high level sound causes fatigue, and engineers have noted that their judgement seems to be impaired after several hours of such exposure.

In considering dynamic range, account must be taken of the ambient sound level both in the recording and the reproduction environment. Ambient noise can to some extent be likened to the noise level in electronic systems. However, while ambient noise tends to be random and omni-directional in nature (the listener being able to direct his attention through it), the noise generated by electronic systems covers the whole audio band-width, is of high mean level and concentrated so as to radiate from the source of the audio signal itself. Therefore, whilst the listener will tolerate an audio signal dropping to the ambient noise level at times, he will object when the signal is partially masked by electronic noise.

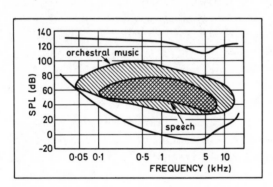

Fig. 6.1
The spectral energy distribution of speech and music

Figure 6.1 shows the spectral energy distribution of speech and music, indicating the typical dynamic range of each. The sound level of a full orchestra from a seat in the audience is probably of the order of 95–100 dB and higher under some circumstances. The skill of the engineer lies in tailoring the signal to fit the medium; but not only the medium, for consideration must also be given to the conditions under which the signal will normally be heard. Figure 6.2 shows typical dynamic ranges for various musical instru-ments and recording media.

Even when the signal has been accommodated to the limitations of the medium, there are environmental situations under which wide dynamic material would be spoilt because of low level signals being swamped by the ambient noise; alternatively, if the low levels were reproduced to be audible above the noise, then the high level content might cause discomfort to the listener.

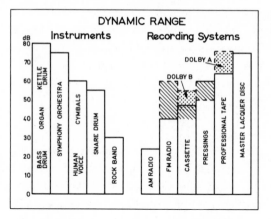

Fig. 6.2
Some typical dynamic ranges

Wide dynamic signals demand greater attention and listening conditions with low background noise. The listener tends to choose the right time and place for the full enjoyment of such signals. By contrast, the success of popular music probably owes much to its so-called 'easy' listening. In the home, the housewife will require that not too much of the signal gets lost in the ambient noise; in a restaurant, peak ambient noise will sometimes exceed the level of the background music and reliance is made on the listener's ability to discriminate in favour of the sound he wishes to hear. The dynamic range of the programme must therefore be very restricted, and may be as little as 10 dB.

Reduction in dynamic range can be effected manually, by changing the system gain, or automatically, by using a compressor. Manual control is effected by anticipating loud and quiet sections of the programme and changing the system gain slowly so as to maintain sharp contrasts. In Fig. 6.3 it will be seen that the operator (following a marked score) is gradually

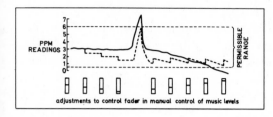

Fig. 6.3
An example of manual control of levels

attenuating the signal as a short peak is approached. When the peak occurs, he has attenuated the level by 6 dB; he then increases the gain by 10 dB to lift the following diminuendo.

While manual control is probably ideal for classical material, there is obviously much opportunity for error and, where rapid changes of level occur, it is impossible to effect any satisfactory compression of the dynamics within that section. Purists argue that automatic compression tends to flatten out the sound, but the degree of flattening depends on the compression slope used. Automatic compression and level control are widely used throughout all sections of the recording industry; in pop music, where impact and loudness are essential ingredients of the art form, they are indispensible.

Automatic gain control

In the early valve circuits, the most common gain controlling element was the variable-mu pentode valve, arranged as a push-pull pair to cancel distortion; its major problem was the so-called thump effect which would produce a DC shift at the output under dynamic conditions. It was necessary to trim the anti-thump balance control periodically for minimum effect. At their best, some valve units were excellent and are still highly valued.

The first transistor circuits to appear had a light dependent resistor as the control element (LDR) but their slow acting time tended to produce spectral energy distortion at high frequencies, since they allowed much of this region through before attenuating the signal, so emphasizing sibilants. The balanced diode bridge was also used in a transistorized circuit in the mid-1960s and produced an effective limiter, with an attack time of $20\,\mu s$. Shortly after this, FETs (Field Effect Transistors) were used as variable resistors with some success but, due to harmonic distortion and the low signal conditions under which they could be used, overall performance was not equal to the best valve systems.

This scene changed dramatically when it was realized that feedback applied to the gate of the FET device would reduce harmonic distortion by some 20 dB, thus enabling higher signal levels to be used whilst still achieving a most acceptable distortion level. Today most compressors and limiters on the market use the FET control principle.

A more recent innovation is the voltage controlled amplifier, which offers similar performance but has the advantage of improved control linearity thus simplifying the linking of units for stereo operation. Pulse Width Modulation, another system in use, samples the input signal at a fixed rate (e.g. chopped at 100 kHz) whilst the side-chain determines the sample duration and consequently the output level after the signal has passed through a low-pass filter acting as an integrator.

Limiters, compressors, and expanders

Limiters, compressors, and expanders are dynamic devices in which gain reduction is automatically controlled by programme level. Limiters and compressors increase attenuation progressively as the level rises above a pre-determined point; the expander increases it progressively as the level falls.

The limiter-compressor is an amplifier that maintains a fixed gain relationship between input and output at all signal levels below a chosen threshold. Beyond this point, for every dB increase at the input, the output rises by an amount determined by the ratio or slope selected. Figure 6.4 shows a device having two slopes of 2:1 and 20:1. It will be seen that the relationship between input and output is constant up to 0 dBm, beyond which level the 2:1 slope effectively reduces the output by 1 dB for every increase of 2 dB at the input. If the 20:1 ratio is selected, the output continues in a linear relationship until the level of +10 dBm is reached, when gain reduction commences. On this slope, the input must rise 20 dB over the threshold point for the output to increase by 1 dB. Such a tight slope is usually described as a limit-ratio, the difference between output and input at any time being described as the amount of compression or gain reduction; this is usually indicated on a meter scaled in dB.

At the point A in Fig. 6.4, where the two slopes intersect (+20 dBm input) the gain reduction on both is the same. The 2:1 slope at this point of intersection could be described as 20:10 and the limit slope as 10:0·5. Thus we have approximately 10 dB compression/gain reduction obtained in two different ways. On the softer slope it is effected gradually over the top 20 dB of the input signal; on the limit slope it occurs suddenly over the top 10 dB. The effect is obviously going to be a tighter and more constricted sound when the higher ratio of 20:1 is used. The softer slope preserves more of the original dynamic range, because an increase in level at the input, still results in a significant increase at the output.

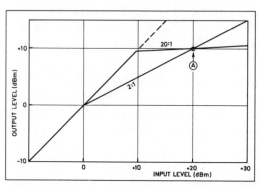

Fig. 6.4
Typical limiter-compressor slopes

Limiting

The function of a limiter is to limit the signal level at some specified point. Transients (peaks of short duration) are the signals most likely to exceed the predetermined peak recording level. Control of these will not directly affect the dynamic range of the signal because, when they do occur, gain reduction will be momentary and of a relatively low order of magnitude. The dynamic range of the recording or transmission system will be increased, however, because the engineer can safely reduce his system headroom and operate at a higher recording level without fear of overload. For most types of programme, a fast release time will be desired so that transients are punched down without apparently affecting the programme content. A tight compression ratio (greater than 10:1) would be used.

Compression

Compression is used to describe a process of gain reduction that is more or less continuous; thus the original dynamics are compressed, with a resultant increase in overall loudness. The compression ratio selected may be anything from the softest slope (say 2:1) to the tightest (say 20:1) dependent on the effect required.

Fixed gain versus variable gain

Two basic operational systems are used for limiters and compressors; variable gain and unity gain. Unity gain systems originate from a principle used in broadcasting, associated primarily with the action of limiting. A device is inserted in the line to provide overload protection and the threshold adjusted to the required level; when gain reduction occurs, the output is attenuated by exactly the amount of gain reduction. When the principle is applied to compression, as opposed to limiting, it becomes apparent that it does not provide an ideal solution, since 10 dB compression will result in attenuation of the line output by 10 dB and it will therefore be necessary to provide some form of gain in the following stage. Most practical unity gain systems provide built-in gain make-up so as to compensate for gain reduction (as compression), ensuring that the output level from the system is maintained at normal operating level.

Variable gain systems seem to have originated in North America, where they have been in common use; they became popular with British recording studios during the 1960s. Typical systems have an input and output attenuator, with fixed internal limiting and compression thresholds; these are pre-set for optimum signal/noise performance. The input of the system is adjusted to provide the amount of compression or gain reduction required, whilst the output attenuator is set to give the required peak level into the following system. It is normally possible to make a comparison between the direct signal and the compressed signal at the same peak level; thus the engineer can make a valid comparison and note the effect he is creating with reference to the input signal.

Depending on the exact arrangement, variable gain systems usually have a performance advantage over unity gain systems in that they can operate over a wide range of input and output levels without worsening their optimum signal/noise performance even at full gain. Figure 6.5 shows a typical example of a gain control amplifier system using an FET device as the attenuating element at the input. In order to keep the signal level low on the FET (to minimize harmonic distortion) an input attenuator is necessary with a fairly high gain (following) amplifier.

The limit threshold is usually set internally, but can be effectively varied by the output attenuator or a ganged input/output arrangement maintaining unity gain. Noise referred to the limit threshold (normal operating point) will be less than − 80 dB for a distortion of around ·05% at 1 kHz. The system has the advantage that make-up gain is built-in, so that there need be no loss due to compression. In systems employing following make-up gain, the noise will worsen with increased gain, whilst in the above arrangement the noise will never be worse than the figure stated.

The side-chain is an amplifier which rectifies the audio signal and provides a DC control voltage to the attenuating element. By arranging the side-chain in a feedback mode, non-linearities in the control device are corrected to provide accurate slopes. Figure 6.5 shows the use of several side-chains to give different gain control characteristics, thereby using the same variloss amplifier as limiter, compressor and expander. Note, the expander side-chain

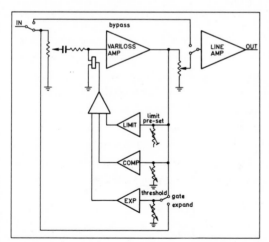

Fig. 6.5
Typical gain control amplifier system with a variloss amplifier and side-chains

is fed forward from the input and provides a 2 : 1 attenuating ratio; when fed from the output of the variloss amplifier it provides a gate slope of 20:1 ratio.

When using a limiter to handle transient peaks of short duration, a fast attack time is essential if the leaks are to be stopped. The attack time is the

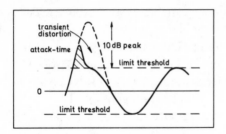

Fig. 6.6
Showing how transient distortion can arise from too fast an attack time in a limiter

period taken by the device to attenuate an input level that exceeds the threshold point, bringing it to its required level as determined by the slope selected. To control a 10 kHz tone within its first half-cycle would require the attack to be completed within 50 μs or less. Figure 6.6 shows what will happen to a waveform when it is attenutated by 10 dB within a short time period; it will be distorted, and this is an example of transient distortion. Fortunately, it is of such short duration that the distortion is normally inaudible. However, the tighter the slope the faster the rate of gain change and the worse the transient distortion will be.

A good case can be made for using slower attack times of around 1 ms when recording on to tape. Assuming good electronics, the fastest transients are lost by saturation of the tape and become inaudible, whilst longer duration peaks are controlled. This will have the subtle effect of easing to some degree any tightness in the limiting.

Attack characteristics

The limiter-compressor, being a dynamic device, is one of those instruments that can be fully evaluated for smoothness of operation and freedom from side-effects only by trial in operational conditions. The initial attack characteristics are all important and Fig. 6.7 illustrates some of the desirable and undesirable features. Figure 6.7(a) shows a fast attack time in which the signal is smoothly reduced to its predetermined static level; (b) shows a slower attack time with, once more, the gain reduced smoothly over a relatively short period of time; (c) and (d) illustrate over-limiting; here, although the initial attack is very fast, gain is reduced below its proper static level for a short

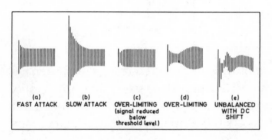

Fig. 6.7
The effect of different attack characteristics

period. This may result in a strangulated effect which is quite unpleasant. Figure 6.7(e) shows the thump effect that used to occur in valve limiters as a result of improper balance.

As the attack time is increased, more of the peak is allowed to pass before being attenuated; the effect dynamically (when the release time is fast and there is continuous gain change) is similar to a softer ratio. Observed on a PPM, the static level will be exceeded and the slope effectively altered. On some units, designed primarily as limiters with only one tight slope, a slower attack time is sometimes marked as 'compress'. With speech programmes, however, the use of slow attack times tends to emphasize sibilants, since it is just these peaks which are allowed to pass unattenuated.

Recovery time

The recovery or release function is possibly the most important variable for pop sound, since it controls loudness. Loudness is determined by the maintenance of high mean levels; the effect of compression is to increase the proportion of high level signal content. It is the release time which determines the moment-to-moment gain change within the system; the faster the unit releases, the more low-level signal is brought to a higher level (or, in the case of a tight ratio, to peak level). In the extreme case, with high gain reduction, fast attack and release, together with a tight ratio, levels approaching 100% continuous modulation can be obtained. On a PPM the dynamic range could be around 1 dB or less.

Figure 6.8 shows the recovery effect diagramatically: (a) illustrates the input signal being periodically pulsed to a level 15 dB higher than the continuous tone; (b) represents the control voltage in the side-chain of the limiter, the falling curve in the intervals being the recovery time as the RC network discharges. During this period, the gain is increasing (after 15 dB attenuation) and lifting the low level tone towards peak level. Figure 6.8(c) shows the output as the release time is increased until, in the third section, the interval is almost completely filled with the lower signal level now brought up to peak level.

As already observed, fast gain change causes transient distortion. With

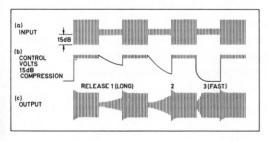

Fig. 6.8
The effect of different recovery times

very fast release times, the 'attack' effect becomes visible on low frequency waveforms, becoming progressively worse the lower the frequency and the faster the recovery time. The low frequency waveforms are being flattened and this is most noticeable under conditions of high gain reduction, coupled with a tight slope and a fast attack time. In practice it is surprising what the ear will tolerate, and therefore the engineer can get away with a good deal in pop applications, where extreme conditions of this kind can be useful.

When simply limiting peaks, the release time should initially be set fast, to perhaps around 25 ms. Gain change under these conditions is normally of a small order and of short duration; the ill effects on low frequencies, and the programme content in general, are inaudible. However, as gain reduction is increased towards the point where it becomes continuous, the effect on the programme will become apparent in the form of distortion and pumping, due to fast gain change on a tight slope. At this point, the process becomes compression rather than limiting, and a longer release time should be selected.

With an additional network, this can be done automatically so that fast gain change is allowed to occur only over a limited range, say 6 dB; when this range is exceeded, a longer release time is introduced and the user has what is sometimes called a 'gain platform', in the form of a fast release operating above a slow recovery time which is related to mean rather than peak level. This is a useful arrangement as it reduces modulation effects; considerable overall compression can be effected without being too apparent, and the system is ideal both for background music and for reducing dynamics in other media of very limited dynamic range (e.g. AM radio transmissions and optical film tracks).

Modulation effects

One of the problems experienced in compressing a mixed programme is that gain reduction tends to be controlled by one dominant instrument or sound, and this in turn modulates the remainder of the programme content. This effect can be mitigated in the release network in a number of ways: by using a soft compressor slope such that gain reduction is spread across a wide level of input; by using an RMS detecting network in the side-chain of the conventional limiter, or by using an equalizer in the side-chain to attenuate the dominant instrument. However, it should be noted that such modifications in the side-chain will alter the limiter response. The threshold will vary dynamically with softer slopes or an RMS network and with frequency if equalization is introduced. In general it is preferable to compress individual instruments or groups of similar instruments before the mix; the ear then has no reference level (other than noise and ambience) by which to recognize gain change.

Compression noise

With a straight compressor it is best to operate on the direct signal before going on to tape. It will be appreciated that, when the compressor recovers, the gain in the system increases and any low level programme content is brought to a higher level relative to the unprocessed signal. Thus any source noise is increased, and tape hiss in particular can become exaggerated. Microphone channels have a lower inherent noise level and can generally tolerate deterioration in this way but, if individual microphones are compressed, there will be an increase in inter-microphone crosstalk during pauses, together with an increased level of studio ambience.

Expander/Gates

In order to take the fullest advantage of multitrack techniques, there is a natural desire on the part of engineers to record tracks straight at the recording session and keep all options open. Compression and equalization at this stage can worsen the overall signal-to-noise ratio and diminish the advantage gained by noise reduction systems. This is where a device which attenuates all signals below a certain level can be most useful.

The expander/gate threshold sets the point at which attenuation commences; the rate at which the device attenuates is determined statically by its slope, and dynamically by the release or 'close' time. Obviously such a device must open quickly, to avoid loss of initial transients when high level programme again presents itself.

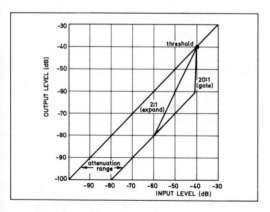

Fig. 6.9
Typical expander-gate slopes

As with the compressor, the expander will operate along a prescribed ratio/slope, commonly about 1:2 (for every 1 dB change at the input, a change of 2 dB at the output). Figure 6.9 shows such a slope, and how the amount of low level attenuation can be controlled by the range setting. It will be realised that, with this sort of slope, the relationship between noise and wanted signal can be improved by a factor of only 2, beyond which point the expander is held open by noise. In circumstances where noise and wanted signal are separated by only a few dB, a gate action is preferable. This is the complement of the limiter at low level; the slope will be some 1:20 (for a change of 1 dB at the input, the output can be attenuated by up to 20 dB dependent on the range setting).

In studio use, both systems come into their own in multitrack work, attenuating increased noise due to compression, or reducing inter-microphone pickup and undesirable ambience on channels as soon as they cease to contribute useful signal to the mixdown process. Thresholds will be adjusted just below the wanted signal, and attenuation effected quickly before noise becomes apparent. Good separation between microphones must still be maintained in the studio, since the expander is attenuating only the low level content, and there is always the additional danger that an extraneous signal may rise above the threshold and open the channel inadvertently.

Gates have not enjoyed a good reputation in the past, either because of slow opening characteristics (so that initial transients were lost) or because they were prone to 'hunting', in which slight signal variations around the threshold point could cause the gate to open and close repeatedly, with objectionable modulation effects. In modern designs there is no apparent transient loss and, by arranging the threshold to have a hysteresis effect such that the closed threshold is lower than the open threshold, hunting is largely obviated.

When treating older recordings with poor signal-to-noise ratios, a gate is useless and even an expander, with its softer slope, can provide only a limited improvement due to modulation effects and the change of noise level which itself becomes apparent. In such a case the expander range would be restricted to a few dB, the threshold being set to expand only a portion of the lower part of the signal and with slow attack and release times to reduce modulation effects. In general, this type of treatment is best performed with selective low level attenuation, as will be discussed later.

Combination units

From an operational viewpoint it is often preferable to compress on a soft slope, say 2:1, since the reduction in dynamic range is more subtle. However, for example in the case of a vocalist, there can still be sudden increases in output which must be contained either by selecting a tighter slope or, more ideally, by having a limiter circuit operating over the compressor. Such a combination has come to be known as a complimiter and it will usually be possible to control the individual compressor and limiter thresholds so that any amount of gain reduction can be effected in the compressor before the onset of limiting.

As already noted, one of the major problems with compression is that it worsens the source signal-to-noise ratio. For every dB compressed, source noise is effectively brought up by 1 dB. From a practical point of view, it is best to compress at the point in the system which has the best signal-to-noise ratio. Where there is no noise-reduction system in use, it is essential to compress low pitched instruments before tape because there will be no signal content to mask high frequency tape noise components.

Several compressors are available which combine compression with expansion in order to mitigate the effects of increased noise. Provided the expander range exceeds the total amount of compression, an overall improvement can be made; even so, this relies on good initial signal-to-noise ratio and a wide-band signal content to mask any noise.

Dynamic equalization

Conventional limiters attenuate the whole programme signal, gain reduction being triggered by signals at any frequency which exceed the threshold level. The modulation effect of dominant instruments has already been noted, but this can be particularly objectionable with high level, low frequency signals such as organ, bass drum, timpani and double-bass. It is often impossible to limit this type of programme since the modulation effect is quite obvious even with only a few dB gain reduction; middle and high frequency components are noticeably attenuated, along with a dramatic change in the ambient characteristics of the studio or concert hall.

Problems usually occur when transferring a recording from one medium to another (e.g. tape to disc, cassette or optical film track). With disc cutting, difficulties are often found in the low frequency or sibilant areas which can give rise to cutting and tracking problems. In the case of cassettes or optical tracks, sibilants and other high frequency content are notoriously troublesome and can often ruin a good copy. By this transfer stage, the final programme balance has been the result of many hours' hard work by artists and engineers; and the balance arrived at is what they hope the public will hear. The transfer engineer's job is to see that it gets on to the final medium with minimum change or loss. All too often the only choice is to lower the overall modulation level (which is generally unacceptable) or introduce some fixed attenuation in the troublesome frequency bands, which degrades the signal throughout the programme as a whole.

The problem of sibilants has been with the film industry in particular for many years, and circuits evolved in an attempt to solve this go under the general description of 'de-essers'. The usual approach has been to make the

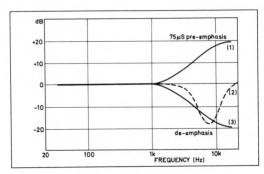

Fig. 6.10
FM broadcasting pre-emphasis and typical 'de-esser' threshold curves

side-chain of a limiter frequency conscious, so that the threshold is more sensitive at high frequencies than at low ones. Figure 6.10 illustrates typical 'de-esser' thresholds (curves 2 and 3). A limiter with threshold (3) would be ideal before a transmitter with a typical pre-emphasis to curve (1). However, note that limiting still affects the whole bandwidth. Another approach to the solution of high frequency problems has been the programme controlled filter, used for some time in disc cutting and, with the advent of relatively simple bandsplitting techniques, new possibilities are to hand.

Selective limiting and expansion

Units are available which enable the engineer to select any part of the audio bandwidth for separate processing, prior to it being added back to the main signal path. Thus sections can be attenuated momentarily without any effect on the rest of the programme. Bandsplitting can be achieved with high and low pass filters, or with notch filters. Figure 6.11 illustrates a system using a parametric notch filter to derive the notch content for processing.

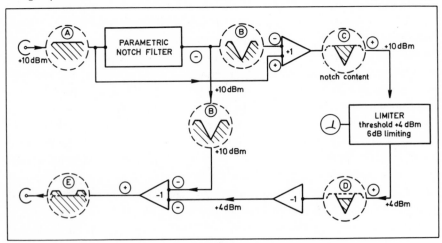

Fig. 6.11
Schematic diagram of a system giving selective limiting or dynamic equalization

A flat response input A, is added to inverse phase notch signal B in order to derive the notch content only at C. C is then routed for processing (limiting or expansion, etc); then, as D, is added in-phase to B, the result being E. When C and D are equal—i.e. no gain change—E will be identical to the input A. Any difference in C or D will result in the progressive appearance of a notch at the output E. In the example shown, input signal level is +10 dBm over the audio range; the limit threshold is established at +4 dBm so that C is held and cannot rise above this level (in this case giving 6 dB attenuation— gain reduction). Output E shows a notch of 6 dB in the selected region; but note that, at an input level of +4 dBm and below, E will again be identical to the input A. Selection is made by sweeping the notch over the frequency band and adjusting the 'Q' so as to encompass the troublesome region. To facilitate easy identification, the notch content alone can be monitored.

In the case of sibilants, the area can be accurately selected and separately limited without affecting extreme HF or programme frequencies below it. Low frequencies can be handled in the same way, and the limit threshold adjusted so that momentary attenuation occurs as soon as the safe level is exceeded.

It is important to realize that, under unity gain conditions, when the selected section is added back, the response at the output is flat and identical to the input. Momentary equalization is present only *above* certain levels in the selected area using limiter action. Below the limit threshold, the system response is once more flat, the programme being only momentarily altered or tailored to the new medium.

Using an expander on the selected portion, the equalization takes place at low signal levels *below* the expander threshold. This can be extremely useful for attenuating low frequency rumble or hum. The expander threshold is adjusted so that, just as the rumble ceases to be masked by the signal, the LF attenuation takes place. In the same way HF noise can be selectively attenuated at low level, when transferring older tapes to disc, for example.

Noise reduction systems

Engineers have long been aware of the need to improve the noise performance of the magnetic tape medium. This has indeed been tackled by the tape manufacturers, who have continually sought improvements in base and oxide materials to provide better performance tapes. However, the advent of multitrack recording techniques has tended to highlight the noise problem since the noise from tracks is additive on mixdown.

The problems of noise have been approached in various ways over the years. On individual recording/transmission systems, for example, complementary static equalization is used to optimize the system performance.

Tape, disc, and FM transmissions all use a degree of high frequency pre-emphasis at the input (see Fig. 6.10, curve (1)), while the reproducer/receiver uses a complementary de-emphasis curve (curve (3)). Thus the noise contributed by the recording or transmission system is attenuated at high frequencies by an amount that is determined by the chosen de-emphasis curve, while the overall balance of frequencies in the reproduced signal is the same as the original.

Such an arrangement takes advantage of the fact that the spectral distribution of energy throughout the audio band tends to fall off at high frequencies (see Fig. 6.1). When these standards were arrived at, this was more true than it is today since, in the intervening years, the improvements made in microphone bandwidth and compression techniques, coupled with the use of electronic sound generating devices in contemporary music, have tended to increase considerably the mean high frequency energy content. Thus such pre-emphasis systems are more prone to high frequency overload than they were, and no further reduction in noise can be gained by an extension of this principle (particularly in the tape medium, which becomes increasingly sensitive to saturation as frequency rises). Static equalization, whilst making a worthwhile contribution, fails to load the recording system fully under changing conditions of programme level and energy distribution. Thus some form of dynamic process is necessary.

Before considering noise reduction systems in detail, it is important to differentiate between two types of noise attenuating requirements. First, it may be required to reduce low level unwanted and spurious sounds which are already present in an audio signal; this would be handled by a single-ended processor, in the form of an expander or gate, operating either across the full bandwidth or selectively on a particular part of the audio spectrum. Hopefully this device would be operating below the level of the wanted signal, or only mildly affecting it. Then, although the dynamic range would not actually be increased, the signal would be cleaned up and become more acceptable on wide dynamic systems.

In the second situation, the signal is required to pass unaffected through a recording/transmission system whose dynamic range is not sufficient to accommodate that of the input signal. In this case the dynamic range of the intermediate system must be effectively increased, ideally to exceed that of the incoming signal. A complementary system should of course be used so that no changes occur in the reproduced signal relative to the input.

The search for a professionally acceptable noise reduction system has been long, the way being strewn with the skeletons of proffered solutions. The most promising line of experiment has always been the compander, in which compression is applied during the record process, to increase the mean level and the loading of the recording system, whilst a complementary expansion process takes place on replay. There are many problems associated with this approach, including poor tracking between the compressor and expander slope, both statically and under dynamic conditions, transient overshoot in the compressor leading to components outside the control of the system, modulation products due to gain change and the difficulties of synchronizing complementary dynamic operation. However, even if all these are overcome, a high level, low frequency signal such as a solo bass drum will fail to mask high frequency tape noise. Even more objectionable is the fact that the noise is then modulated so that, as the instrument plays, it is surrounded by a varying halo of noise. So, after thirty years of failure to establish a wide-band noise reduction system, the recording industry greeted Dr. Ray Dolby's novel system in 1966 with mixed feelings.

The Dolby 'A' system

Dolby's approach was ingenious. Instead of processing the high-level signal, as in ordinary companders, he decided to compress the low programme levels which contain the noise. He also tackled modulation effects and the problem of unmasked noise by bandsplitting the audio signal and processing it in four independent frequency bands. Thus, in the presence of a solo low-frequency instrument, the top two or even three frequency sections can be providing full or partial noise reduction within their respective spectra.

The major problem to be overcome in any such system is the method used to encode and decode the signal. An ideal system should obviously incorporate within itself the means by which a processed signal can be decoded to restore the original. In the Dolby system (Fig. 6.12) this not

Fig. 6.12
Compact form of Dolby A noise reduction system housing 16 processors in a single cabinet

inconsiderable problem is solved with remarkable simplicity. Figure 6.13 shows the signal path through the Dolby system. It will be seen that there is a direct signal path to which is added the differential component which

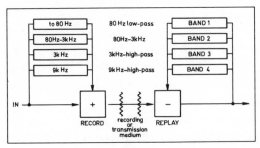

Fig. 6.13
Signal path in the Dolby A noise reduction system

encodes the signal and can subsequently be used to provide decoding by means of subtraction. This differential component (Fig. 6.14a) is obtained by the operation of a limiter on each frequency band; the amount of gain established in each compressor under quiescent or low level signal conditions will dictate the maximum noise attenuation possible in each section of the system. The design provides for noise reduction over the range 30 Hz– 5 kHz of 10 dB, rising to 15 dB at 15 kHz.

The effect of adding the differential component is shown in Fig. 6.14b. The pre-determined gain is present up to an input level of − 40 dB and then gradually returns to unity by an input level of approximately − 10 dB; above this level the direct signal is in no way affected. On replay, the effect of subtracting the differential component is to provide an exact inverse of the record process characteristic (Fig. 6.14c); a really elegant solution.

Transient overshoot in the compressors is prevented from becoming part of the differential component by the action of diode clippers operating above the limiter slope. This enables fairly slow acting time constants to be selected in the attack and recovery of the compressor. The diode clipping action is completely masked by the high level signal in the direct path and in any case the distortion components are low level, of short duration and cancel on replay.

The system is level sensitive and requires the establishment of a pre-determined level by means of a test signal (called Dolby Tone) which ensures that all tapes are recorded to an internationally established level to provide for accurate decoding between systems and studios.

From the professional user's standpoint, one of the major values of the Dolby system, besides its obvious use on master recording, is the possibility of making several subsequent generation copies in the encoded state.

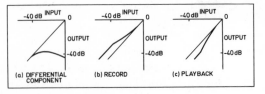

Fig. 6.14
The input/output transfer characteristics and differential component in the Dolby A system

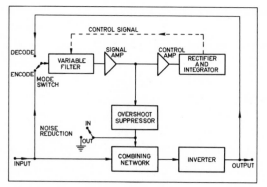

Fig. 6.15
Block diagram of the Dolby B system:
the circuitry can be switched to
encode or decode the signal

When finally decoded, the copies will, to all intents and purposes, be identical
to the decoded original master. For these reasons, the system has found
wide acceptance and established itself as an international standard.

Dolby 'B' system

The Dolby B system is licensed to consumer product manufacturers who
have used it widely to improve the performance of cassette machines in
particular, as well as some domestic open-reel machines. Its operation is
similar in principle to the Dolby A system except that it is much simplified
(Fig. 6.15). As Fig. 6.16 shows, the encoded signal covers a frequency band
from about 500 Hz upwards but this varies depending on the variable filter
in the secondary path. The maximum noise attenuation is restricted to 10 dB
(as opposed to a maximum of 15 dB at 15 kHz on the professional version).

DBX noise reduction system

Another important noise reduction system was developed by David Blackner
of DBX in the early 1970s. This system employs a wide range 2:1 compressor-
expander configuration using a voltage controlled amplifier. Since the system
provides a 2:1 relationship over its entire operational range, there are no
problems in accurately matching recording and replay levels. Noise reduction
in excess of 30 dB is achieved.

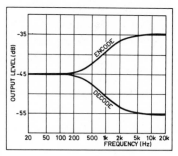

Fig. 6.16
Output response of Dolby B encoder
and decoder circuits under low-level
input signal conditions. Since the
operations are complementary, a flat
frequency response is maintained

With a linear compander system operating over a wide range, there are several problems, as we have already seen. The recording system noise will vary with the signal level and, while the ear can reject a constant hiss level, fluctuating background noise would be quite unacceptable. Blackner's solution to this is to provide considerable high frequency pre-emphasis, avoiding high frequency self-erasure and overload problems by applying the pre-emphasis before the level sensing circuit so that, under record conditions, it too is subject to the 2:1 compression slope.

Another major problem is the dynamic response of the system and the achievement of complementary operation under transient conditions. Peak and average sensing systems are rejected in favour of a true RMS detecting circuit, since it is only the RMS value that will remain constant, representing the energy sum of all frequency components present regardless of their phase relationships. Figure 6.17 shows a block diagram of the system.

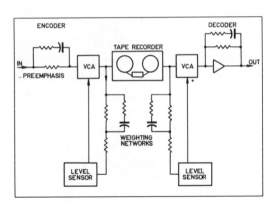

Fig. 6.17
Block diagram of the DBX noise reduction system

EQUALIZERS

There was a time, not so long ago, when established practice forbade the use of equalizers in mixing consoles. The argument (a perfectly tenable one at the time) was that the engineer's task was to produce a natural sound and, since microphones with a flat frequency response were available (notably the BBC's highly successful PGS Ribbon), equalization was not only unnecessary but actually detrimental to the objective being pursued. This school of thought succumbed to the pressure of two events: firstly, the almost simultaneous arrival of the pop group and the transistor; secondly, the rise of independent studios whose engineers, because of their independence and closer contact with the performers, were in a better position to experiment.

The term equalizer derives from the fixed gain and response shaping networks designed to compensate for losses occuring in transmission lines between one part of a communication system and another. Examples of fixed equalization standards have already been noted, which were selected to provide optimum system performance. Programme equalizers as used in mixing desks, or found in the auxiliary equipment bay, are used partly to provide correction for poor acoustic conditions or operator error, but in the main for artistic enhancement of instrument sound and texture. A versatile equalizer will enable the engineer to manipulate sounds so that they become quite different in character. In combination with compressors, equalizers assist in the production of impact and loudness effects by manipulating the energy spread throughout the frequency spectrum.

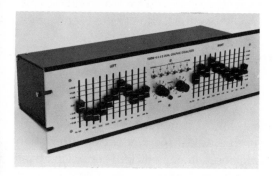

Fig. 6.18
A typical stereo graphic equalizer with eleven controls covering the frequency spectrum in each channel (courtesy Klark-Teknik Ltd.)

Graphic equalizers

The types of equalizer available are covered in Chapter Five. The most common equalizer found as a separate rack unit is the graphic type, with a range of slider amplitude controls which give a visual indication of the response curve being used (see Fig. 6.18). The versatility of the unit will depend upon the number of frequency points and this may range from as few as five to as many as 28 (providing control of each third-octave over the audio bandwidth). An example is illustrated in Fig. 6.19. The 'Q' or bandwidth of the peaking or dipping action can never be sharper than that of an

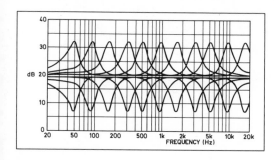

Fig. 6.19
Range of controls in a typical graphic equalizer

individual control section, but the effect can of course be broadened by use of the adjacent controls. The graphic equalizer is probably most useful for overall frequency balance adjustment.

Of late it has become the practice to 'voice' or equalize monitor loud-speakers in the control room so as to reproduce a smooth frequency response at the balance engineer's position (see Chapter Seven). Optimum results largely depend on the room being acoustically well designed in the first place. Whilst a third-octave equalizer is normally used, there is a growing opinion that a broader one-octave filter is better and likely to introduce less colouration. Such techniques are clearly very praiseworthy since, for the first time, they begin to provide a reference standard for monitoring against which balance engineers can work with greater certainty between studios.

Parametric and sweep equalizers

The other type of unit being increasingly used is the parametric or sweep equalizer (parametric meaning all parameters variable) in which a number of controls provide continuously variable frequency selection over a range of the audio spectrum. This enables an exact frequency to be located for boosting or cutting; amplitude controls adjust the amount of attenuation or boost on each section and, in addition, some bandwidth control (perhaps continuously variable) is usually provided. From the operational point of view this allows the engineer greater flexibility and is proving very popular in 'pop' recording applications. Figure 6.20 shows one parametric response section.

The control range of a versatile equalizer should be at least ± 12 dB and even greater (± 20 dB) for maximum flexibility on individual instruments either to clean up the sound or create 'new' effects. Although this degree of fine control was considered unnecessary by some engineers at first, their preconceived objections were quickly dispelled when they experienced for themselves the possibilities of wide range parametric equalizers.

Like compressors, limiters and noise reduction systems, equalizers are best evaluated in the studio under operational conditions, both from the

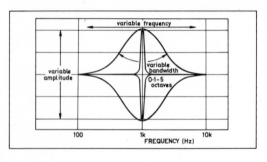

Fig. 6.20
Showing the range of control in one section of a parametric equalizer

point of view of simplicity of operation as well as effectiveness. Any system providing selective lift or cut will produce phase changes but this is not normally a problem when operating on separate channels, using close microphones and multitrack techniques prior to the final reduction. Of greater importance will be colouration due to poor design of the equalizer circuits along with possible degradation of transient performance.

REVERBERATION FACILITIES

Most pop recording applications rely considerably on the use of artificial reverberation. The availability of effective reverberation systems along with multitrack techniques has enabled small studios to produce 'big band' sounds apparently involving many more artists than the capacity of the studio would seem to allow. Contemporary studio design usually aims at a dead acoustic, to provide maximum separation between instruments by reducing reverberant sound to a minimum; the philosophy is that you can always add it later, but you can never get rid of it once it's there. All reverberation systems employ some form of delay line. This can be acoustic, as in the case of an echo chamber, electro-mechanical, as in the case of the spring, plate and tape delay systems, or completely electrical in the form of a digital delay line.

Reverberation is differentiated from a single echo by the fact that it comprises a number of repetitive peaks within a time interval; thus it consists of multiple echoes arranged in a diffused and reducing pattern such that none is identifiable in itself. Clearly the mathematical analysis for a given reverberant characteristic would be extremely complex. Figure 6.21 shows a suggested response curve plotted against time for both speech and music.

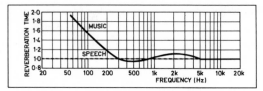

Fig. 6.21
Reverberation time/frequency curves for speech and music relative to the value at 800 Hz (after Beranek)

The echo chamber. Undoubtedly the most natural artificial reverberation is achieved by use of an echo chamber; i.e. a room specifically set aside and treated to provide an effective acoustic delay line. The walls are of hard, reflecting surfaces such as tiles, in order to give maximum reflections of the audio signal. Normally two microphones are arranged to provide stereo pickup from a single loudspeaker; they are placed so as to avoid direct signal pickup and obstacles may be introduced to break up the signal path further. An L-shaped room is favoured since this tends to avoid standing wave resonances as well as a direct signal path.

Fig. 6.22
Plate reverberation unit with front cover removed. (Note this is the EMT 140Q model designed for quadraphonic use with a single driver and four pick-up transducers)

The reverberation plate. A widely accepted form of artificial reverberation is provided by the reverberation plate (Fig. 6.22) patented and manufactured by E.M.T. The best known model consists of a large thin steel plate some 2·5 × 1·5 metres suspended in a framework. A moving coil transducer drives the plate while two asymmetrically placed ceramic units pick up the delayed signal after multiple reflections from the boundaries of the plate. The pickups are followed by equalized amplifiers to optimize the frequency balance of the reverberant sound. The reverberation time is modified by a mechanical damping system in close proximity to the plate. Being a somewhat cumbersome device, it is normally remotely sited from the control room and is usually found in cellars and little used corridors, care being taken to avoid sound transmission from the environment to the plate. A smaller transportable model is also manufactured.

The reverberation spring. Another reverberation system relies on vibrating springs as used in the Hammond organs. The Grampian model, for example, is a portable, battery driven unit which provides a convincing effect, especially on vocals. It employs a pair of mechanical spring delay lines with electromagnetic transducers providing drive and pickup. The delay times of the two springs are slightly different but of the order of 30 ms, the long reverberation being obtained by feeding the output back to the input and in this way creating a sustained effect of up to 2 seconds at 300 Hz, reducing to 1·5 seconds at the cut-off point of 6 kHz. A more recently introduced device is the AKG BX20 reverberation unit which is a torsionally driven spring

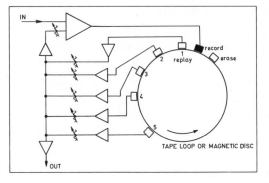

Fig. 6.23
Schematic diagram of a magnetic reverberation device using multiple replay heads

system and provides a delay time of 2 to 4·5 seconds. The unit is dual channel and can be controlled remotely.

Tape reverberation systems. A number of specialized tape systems have been evolved using magnetic disc or tape loops. In these a series of spaced replay heads provide varying amounts of delay which are then fed back to the input to provide reverberation. Figure 6.23 shows a multi-head tape reverberation system. In general these have not been designed to full studio standards, and the tape loop system has been marred by the tape-join every time it passes the heads. New moulded loops are now available, however, and this may encourage their consideration for professional use. Flutter-echo, using standard studio machines, is achieved by feeding the output of the replay head back into the record circuitry, but this is of somewhat limited use in providing reverberation, since there is only one fixed time interval between the successive echoes.

Standard tape machines are commonly used, however, to delay the studio signal before sending it to a reverberation system. This improves the reverberant effect since it is more natural (there always being a delay before first reflections in a hall) and it allows a lower level of reverberant signal to be used thereby reducing the give-away characteristics of the reverberation system. Some systems incorporate a limiter, to provide overload protection and avoid unpleasant ringing, and excellent effects can also be obtained by compressing the signal so that the reverberation is sustained; interesting crescendo effects can also be obtained in this way.

Delay lines. An increasing number of digital delay lines is now available and the cost, though still high, has been reduced over the years. The costly parts are the analogue/digital and the complementary digital/analogue converters. Once in digital form, however, the signal can be delayed for any length of time without degradation, dependent on the size of the digital store. Most systems are of modular construction, so that delay modules can be added and tapped anywhere along the digital route by an output digital/analogue unit. Delays from zero up to about 0·5 second are available on most systems, with very small increments between. Such devices offer better performance than tape delay, though at considerably greater expense. The digital system is ideal for introducing delays in sound reinforcement systems, for example, where it has been used to delay the signal's arrival at each loudspeaker by the same time that it takes for the direct voice to reach that point in the auditorium.

Tape phasing

The popularity of phasing as an effect seems to go in cycles of a few years. It can be produced by recording a common input on two machines simultaneously, then re-recording the mixed output from the replay heads on a third machine. The distance between the record and replay heads of one of the machines is varied slightly, e.g. with a pencil, or the machine speed is varied so that phase differences create the desired cancellation effects. The drawback, besides the number of machines used, is that it cannot usually be done in real time.

Several phasing devices have become available which provide phase delay at several points in the audio spectrum, and these can usually be shifted by an oscillator or by a control signal derived from the programme itself. Middle and high frequency sounds seem to phase best and give the most dramatic effects. The devices operate in real time, with the further advantage that programme controlled units can produce a given effect predictably on subsequent re-takes.

CHAPTER SEVEN

Monitoring Systems

Stephen Court

The monitoring system is a most important tool in the recording chain, and its quality is probably the greatest single contributor to the final product. It is analogous to the light by which an artist sees his painting, even more so in these days when recording is as much an artistically creative process as a purely 'photographic' one. Even though it may be argued that a deficiency in the original recording caused by inaccurate monitoring can be corrected in subsequent processes, aberrations in the monitoring system will inevitably reflect on the overall quality of the final recording.

What may have been considered an adequate system a few years ago has, in many cases, proved to be insufficient for modern 'state of the art' recordings. The considerable increase in the dynamic range of associated equipment, caused by sophisticated noise reduction systems and other design techniques, now provides the engineer with signal levels so low that they would have been considered impossible to cut on a disc ten years ago. At the other extreme there are explosive wavefronts from loud electronic instruments and close microphones which may have to be monitored at their full acoustic level. The tendency towards improved linearity of response at the expense of efficiency in loudspeakers intended for home use, now means in general that the design considerations for studio monitoring speakers are not the same as for the domestic market.

Another factor relating to the importance of consistency in monitoring is the increasing practice of transferring tapes in 'mid-process' from one studio to another. The sometimes awesome experience of hearing how a tape sounds radically different when it is played in different studios, even though they may be using identical equipment, shows that there must be deficiencies in many systems. It also suggests that one should not simply select a speaker which appears to do the job, but pay due attention to the combination of speaker and room to ensure system linearity.

Design philosophy
Since the monitor loudspeaker has to reproduce signals at their natural

acoustic level, the need has been for a system efficient enough to reproduce minute changes in level and subtle defects, yet able to handle enough power to provide sound pressure levels in excess of 100 dB with minimum distortion. Since the engineer spends many hours in front of the speakers, distortion, although not easily perceived, can cause considerable listening fatigue, and such a speaker is unsuitable for studio use. The theoretical ideal of a single transducer is unsatisfactory, since a cone large enough to move air at low frequencies would have too much mass to follow high frequency information. The use of several low mass transducers, although eliminating crossovers, creates other problems, especially phase distortion and polar non-linearity. For these and other reasons, the type of loudspeaker which has virtually monopolized the monitor market is the two-way system. This consists of a high efficiency bass unit in a large enclosure—usually ported to improve LF efficiency—crossing over at around 500–800 Hz into a horn-loaded compression driver—again to maintain system efficiency over the remainder of the spectrum.

The low mass diaphragm provides wide range HF response, and the horn increases efficiency and effects dispersion. Extra lateral dispersion is often provided by honeycomb elements or acoustic lenses. Accurately controlled dispersion is of prime importance, since the polar radiation should be sufficiently wide in the lateral plane to give the engineer an even response irrespective of his position at the desk, yet not so wide as to provide spurious reflections from the control room surfaces.

The two-way system has some limitations in that a single horn covering the entire HF spectrum becomes increasingly directional at high frequencies. This might lead to overcorrection at very high frequencies if the engineer is off axis and, a property of the horn itself, throat distortion which increases with level and frequency. For high level monitoring, therefore, a three-way system is preferred with the compression unit covering the fundamentals, which can have a larger diaphragm and throat, and a third unit to cover the harmonics above say 6,000 Hz. This also enables the system to cater for natural focusing at HF by providing a wide dispersion HF unit. Such systems usually provide better linearity in the midrange, to which the ear is most sensitive.

One step further from the three-way system is the four-way monitor, where the lower frequencies are sub-divided also. It may be impractical to use a single bass driver to handle extreme excursions from percussion and bass instruments, and at the same time the more delicate upper frequency transients from strings and voices, for example. Using a large cone area bass system covering the spectrum up to 300 Hz or so, then crossing over (electronically) to a smaller bass unit to cover the remainder of the spectrum up to the midrange driver, provides a more solid bass response and improved resolution in the upper bass end, by reducing IM (intermodulation) and FM (frequency modulation) or 'Doppler' distortion.

While it appears that we may be approaching the opposite extreme from the single transducer—one speaker per octave—the high levels and low distortion required in modern recording techniques have created a demand for more sophisticated systems than were required even ten years ago. A full-range electrostatic speaker might appear to offer the ultimate solution, but design technology suggests that electrostatic diaphragms capable of handling today's monitoring levels are still a long way off.

In loudspeakers where more than one transducer is used, passive cross-over networks predominate and, while careful design can greatly improve system linearity, such networks do tend to introduce losses and create distortion. Even a 3 dB insertion loss, wasting 50% of the power available, represents a considerable cost by today's standards. The use of electronic crossovers feeding separate power amplifiers eliminates this, as well as increasing system efficiency and reducing distortion. Another advantage, which will be discussed in detail later, is the ability of electronic crossovers to provide some control over the final system balance. Although using these between midrange and high frequencies is not totally necessary, their use between the bass and high frequencies can produce a considerable improvement.

Speaker evaluation and installation
The evaluation of loudspeakers suitable for studio monitoring is a highly complex task, since the process is so very subjective. There are numerous factors involved, often apparently contradicting each other but in all cases requiring extensive listening tests with the speakers in the actual positions in which they will be used. The main difficulty is that, when an engineer listens to a loudspeaker, he will not only be hearing the sound radiated from it, but a combination of that and the room acoustics. It is not unusual to move one's head a few inches from the operating position and hear a totally different response characteristic. Careful room design and desk positioning are clearly of prime importance so far as the speakers are concerned.

One would imagine that, when comparing loudspeakers on an A–B basis, the room contribution would be constant. But, since the loudspeaker radiation characteristics involve a change in the shape and intensity of the wavefronts, different room modes are likely to be excited.

Another problem is that the engineer will be inclined to prefer the loud-speaker which sounds 'best', i.e. flatters his recordings the most. While it is true that he does have to live with the sound, the function of a monitor is to tell him exactly what is going on to the tape and not to impress anybody in particular. It is difficult to be adamant about this, especially when speaker A shows up a fault in the balance, whilst speaker B happens to 'sound better' although it is a less accurate monitor.

It can be argued that to tell an engineer exactly what sound he is putting on tape is impractical, especially since recording is so much an artistic activity. Or, to put it another way, if his product is consistently good, it does not matter if he monitors on re-entrant loudhailers. The important thing is that it may sound good in that particular studio but, when it goes to another studio for reduction, or for cutting, the faults in the balance due to inaccurate monitoring are bound to show themselves. Apart from creating technical difficulties for the cutting engineers, it is not a particularly good advertisement for the studio concerned.

To sum up, while extensive listening tests are important, they should be carried out along with a series of properly conducted measurements if only to ensure that the ear is not being fooled.

The apparently obvious procedure is to listen to previously recorded tapes with which the engineer is familiar. Apart from the problems previously mentioned, however, he will also be listening to tapes which he balanced according to his own tastes. By so doing, he will have inadvertently corrected for any aberrations in the existing monitors. Any major differences in the performance of the speakers under test will therefore produce a change of balance and give a false picture of their true qualities. It is important, therefore, not only to listen to the playback of known tapes, but also to compare the speakers on live material and after having recorded a session via them.

A further factor, as already mentioned, arises from the interaction of speaker and room and the different results that even minute changes in speaker placement can produce. It is slightly ironic that a manufacturer may go to great lengths to reduce distortion or improve the impulse response in his speaker system, and yet it will be mainly judged on factors that can originate from peculiarities in the listening room. The point here is that a flat frequency response, according to the manufacturer's specification, is useful but academic so far as music is concerned for, in the final analysis, it is the most inconsistent factor and the easiest one to change. The solution, therefore, is to select a loudspeaker which gives the best performance in terms of clarity and definition and, providing it can handle the sound pressure levels required, have the complete system equalized if necessary for a flat response at the listening position.

The best test for this is to play individual tracks from a multitrack master which have undergone little or no correction, are at their natural acoustic levels, and provide a musically useful source unbiased by the aesthetics of the final production. Finally, playback of all the tracks will ensure that the speakers can retain their definition with a complete instrument line-up. Having done this—even if the speakers appear to be perfect—it is then necessary to measure the response at the listening position to ensure overall linearity. (Equalizing the system is dealt with later.)

One factor which governs the sound from a speaker system is the way in which it was designed to be mounted. When listening to loudspeakers, since the HF radiation pattern is typically narrow, anyone listening more or less on the axis will hear a large percentage of the total HF power radiated. At mid-frequencies the dispersion is usually wider, so that the listener receives a slightly smaller percentage but, since there is a lot more information in this part of the spectrum, the difference is minimal. At low frequencies, however, since bass radiation is naturally non-directional, he will hear only a small percentage of the total radiation. This applies especially if the speaker is mounted well out into the control room (Fig. 7.1). If the speaker is flush

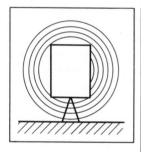

Fig. 7.1
Free standing loudspeaker
(4π)

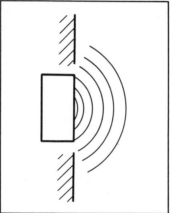

Fig. 7.2
Flush or wall mounted loudspeaker
(2π)

Fig. 7.3
Corner or ceiling/wall
mounted loudspeaker (π)

mounted (Figs. 7.2 and 7.3)—a procedure which one always tries to recommend—the control room walls become an extension to the speaker baffle, offering a theoretical 3 dB or greater increase in bass. This position also prevents back radiation from being reflected after a time delay and causing severe colouration of the low frequency response by addition and cancellation with the direct radiated signal. Flush mounting the speakers, giving an angular radiation characteristic between π and 2π, i.e. into a quarter or half sphere (Figs. 7.3 and 7.2), will give a noticeable improvement in the 'tightness' of the bass, as well as providing an increase in level. The actual amount will vary, since the room itself can give gain or losses at these frequencies due to standing wave effects.

In practice, it is a good idea to leave a space of approximately 25–50 mm around the speaker cabinet, the space being filled with rockwool or something similar. This provides some degree of mechanical decoupling between the speaker and the control room surfaces, while satisfying the requirements for flush mounting. Though this method of mounting is generally recommended, it is important to check whether the particular manufacturer intended his product to be used in this way, and even to find out how he tests his speakers. Since anechoic chambers are not very reliable at low frequencies, some manufacturers carry out their measurements in the open air—on the laboratory roof for example—i.e. under 2π conditions. Free mounting such a loudspeaker may leave the system bass light. By the same token, a speaker designed for flattest response under anechoic (4π) conditions will possibly sound boomy and lack resolution at low frequencies if flush mounted.

Very often the question of whether the speaker was intended for free standing or flush mounting will quickly become apparent on listening tests, and in any case most manufacturers recommend a certain type of mounting for their products. In all cases, eliminating radiation from behind the speakers is strongly recommended.

System equalization

The usual method for overall system measurement (Fig. 7.4) consists of applying pink noise (at the desk output), the speaker output being measured from a calibration microphone at the listening position(s). With a swept

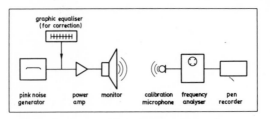

Fig. 7.4
Block diagram of a common method used to measure the acoustic performance of a monitoring speaker/room combination

frequency analyser, pen recordings are made to show the overall system response (see Fig. 7.5). Usually frequency runs at three positions are taken, and the results averaged to give a more accurate picture of the control room/speaker response.

A more efficient method is the pulse recording system which provides a coherent signal source, rather than random noise, synchronized with the measuring apparatus to give a fully integrated measurement. This is quicker,

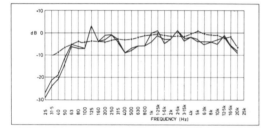

Fig. 7.5
A typical monitoring system response plot (at two microphone positions) from speakers whose laboratory responses were 40–18,000 Hz ±3 dB. The broken line shows the system response after changing the speaker positions and making structural modifications to the room

less costly, and more accurate. If it is required to move the speakers around in search of the best response, a real time analyser can be used, which gives a continuous response curve for the system: changes in the response can be observed graphically while changes are being made (Fig. 7.6).

All this equipment is very expensive so, if one is using a test rig hired for the purpose, it is worth taking extra time to make a tape recording of bands of pink noise. Since the system has been adjusted for flat response, it is then easy to draw a calibration curve for playing this tape over the system

Fig. 7.6
Using a real time analyser (Bruel and Kjaer) during calibration of the monitoring system in a modern studio control room

using a standard studio microphone (see Fig. 7.7), the calibration curve eliminating response variations in the studio equipment. The usefulness of this is that, should the speakers need to be changed or moved at any time, the system can be recalibrated without costly measuring apparatus. While more attention is being paid these days to speaker/room design from a structural point of view, our only concern here is to establish a method of assessing the linearity of a given monitoring system.

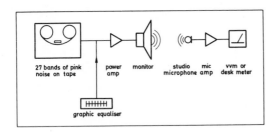

Fig. 7.7
Simple technique using the calibration curve derived from previous tests and a prepared tape of bands of pink noise

Having measured the system, any aberrations can then be corrected by inserting graphic equalizers in the output channels. Alternatively, if only small deviations are found, single cut or boost narrow-band filters can be inserted at these points only, at a considerable saving in cost. However, graphic equalizers are also useful for providing a means of varying the system response, should this be required at any time, perhaps following equipment alterations.

It occasionally happens that a system equalized for a flat response (or to IEC specification) produces a rather dry and boring sound, and requires modification if only to conform to the response in another control room which may not be very flat but does produce consistently good recordings. As mentioned previously, it is difficult to be dogmatic on this subject: customers go to a studio because they prefer the sound they get on a particular type of music. However, one would hope that this sound is derived from the studio itself and the skill of the engineers, rather than any specially coloured sound in the control room itself.

As a final point on the subjective question, most studios use a pair of domestic speakers in the control room which they can switch in to ensure commercial compatibility. It is also a useful idea to set up a pair of speakers in a separate room so that clients can listen to tapes and records with a system that provides a constant source of reference to the studio products. Using good quality, but domestic style, speakers may provide a better check on commercial suitability than the studio speakers which were designed to provide clinical monitoring at the desk position only.

This need to standardize on control room characteristics has long been recognized on the Continent, where some attempt is made to ensure that a tape recorded in one studio will sound the same when played back in another. Electro-acoustic equalization has been widely accepted in the United States also. It has to be remembered that equalization will not make a bad system sound good, but only improve an inherently good system. The considerable phase shift introduced by equalization can be practically imperceptible, providing it is the same on both speakers, but where more than 5 dB correction is found to be necessary, the reduction in headroom and therefore dynamic range should be considered. Should more than 5 dB correction be necessary, then it is a case for mechanical or structural modification by an acoustics expert. This is especially so when the response is satisfactory at the control position, yet standing waves and other factors give a different sound elsewhere in the room.

In conclusion, the fact that one has to consider such elaborate system modification techniques suggests that loudspeaker manufacturers and control room designers are unable to provide ideal results. However, since design and evaluation methods and individual tastes do vary considerably, it is not unreasonable to expect minor variations in the final system performance. While measurement is always recommended, severe corrections should be the exception rather than the rule. There is no basic reason why an 'off the shelf' system should not provide accurate monitoring without any need for drastic correction.

Monitoring electronics

The advantages of electronic crossovers for two-way and three-way speakers have already been mentioned, with the added possibility of providing a small degree of control over the overall system response. Whether electronic crossovers or passive networks are used, the power amplifiers associated with them have changed considerably over the past ten years. Before semiconductor power amplifiers came on the market, valve amplifiers had reached a peak of sophistication, and although small signal electronics have greatly improved with transistor design, semiconductor power amplifiers often leave a lot to be desired. Thus their choice is of paramount importance. Ten years ago it may have been safe to say that the speaker was the weakest link in the chain, but that does not necessarily apply today.

Much attention is now being paid to the impulse response of loudspeakers: but their improved transient response, combined with high sensitivity, makes them sensitive to faults in the driving amplifiers, especially at high monitoring levels. Not only have monitoring levels increased over the last few years but, with very close microphone techniques and wide dynamic range electronics, the actual peak-to-mean ratio of the sound heard on the monitors has changed radically. It is mainly for this reason that manufacturers' specifications are inadequate to predict the performance of monitor speakers being driven at consistently high levels. The most common fault encountered is the amplifier's inability to handle high power transients, and to recover fast enough in the event of signal overloading. Even when sinewave tests show that a unit meets the manufacturer's specification, the highly reactive load provided by efficient loudspeakers, especially below resonance, combined with the explosive wavefronts present in the sounds being monitored, considerably reduce the effective power handling of many amplifiers. Uneven clipping, dynamic offsets and poor overload recovery appear to be the most commonly encountered faults. Even minute static DC offsets are sufficient to bias the cone of a sensitive speaker, reducing its low frequency performance and resolution.

Such faults are often aggravated by poor damping, not only as a function of amplifier source impedance but also due to the long connecting leads between the power amplifiers and the monitor speakers, especially when the wire is of insufficient thickness. A common mistake is to assume that the damping factor is obtained simply by dividing the speaker impedance by the amplifier source impedance. In fact, damping depends on the resistance of the speaker leads and the speaker's own DC resistance, which can change due to heating when continuously monitoring at high levels. This might appear to be overcritical of amplifiers, especially since their consistency is generally better than that found in many loudspeaker systems, but faults in this field are by no means rare, and should be taken into account when installing a new monitor system.

As a summary, the following points are outlined for consideration:

1. On initial evaluation, ensure that the speakers are in the *exact* positions in which they will be used, and play dry recordings at first, since equalization via other loudspeakers might otherwise give a false tonal balance.

2. Pay attention to the clarity and definition of the various instruments rather than the overall balance, since subtle deviations in response can be corrected but poor resolution cannot.

3. Unless the manufacturer specifies free standing (where an air space should be provided under the speaker), flush mounting is recommended so that the control room walls become an extension of the speaker baffle. A space of 25–50 mm should be left around the speakers, the space being filled with rockwool or something similar.

4. Check amplifier/speaker compatibility. Observe the bass cone motion when switching on the power amplifiers. If the cone fails to return to its original position, there may be a DC offset at the power amplifier. Excessive cone motion on a bass drum suggests poor damping either from the amplifier

or because cables are too thin or too long. Placing the power amplifiers near the speakers is the best way to avoid this.

5. Even though the sound may appear good, have the system measured, and plot the overall system response.

The aim of this chapter has been not only to provide information on a subject that has probably been the centre of more attention than any other, but also to emphasize the importance of consistency in loudspeaker monitoring systems. It is only with consistency, not just from studio to studio, but throughout the world, that record companies can guarantee uniformity in studio sound irrespective of location.

CHAPTER EIGHT

Magnetic Tape

Angus McKenzie

Although the first recording tape was made before the beginning of the 1939–45 war, tape recording was not used commercially to any significant degree until some years after. The very first recording tape was made by BASF in Germany and consisted of rather crude iron oxide particles, coated on to a paper backing. The first machines employed DC bias and ran at a tape speed of 1 metre per second; to give a useable playing time, spools initially contained over 1,000 metres of tape. The earliest British tape was made by EMI at Hayes specifically for their BTR1 recorders running at 76 cm/sec (although some models were supplied to the Post Office running at a speed of 30 cm/sec). It is now apparent that the results obtained prior to 1950 were frequently better than was realized at the time. Although the tape itself was a considerable limitation, the replay heads and amplifiers were also very poor and many re-issues of early recordings now appearing on LP reveal quite good quality. By the early 1950s, EMI had developed their famous BTR2 recorder, which sold in remarkably high quantities throughout the world. The BBC bought several hundred machines and EMI were thus encouraged to develop their H77 tape for professional use. This EMI tape continued to be manufactured to virtually the same formulation for about ten years and gave a 6 dB improvement in signal-to-noise ratio over the early H50/H60 types. Many foreign tapes then became popular with studios, who were continually looking for better performance, and the most popular tapes in the early 1960s were Agfa type FR4 (acetate backed), BASF type LGS52 or its matt backed equivalent type LGR, and Scotch 111V. BASF then introduced a very high output tape type LR56 (matt backed) and Agfa their type PER555 and PER525 matt backed. These continental tapes clearly influenced the recording industry to a significant degree and competition became quite severe: EMI then developed many new tape types, including 811, 812, and more recently 815 (shiny backed) and 816 (matt backed).

Matt backed tapes were not produced in commercial quantities in the United States until fairly recently and, at the time of writing, the only significant American types are Ampex 406 and Scotch 206, with their higher output counterparts Ampex Grandmaster and Scotch 250. In Germany, however, BASF produced their SPR50LH tape whilst Agfa announced their PEM468.

Tape types

Recording tape can be classified in many different ways. Overall thickness is normally referred to as standard play, long play, double play, and triple play. Naturally the thinner the tape the greater the length that can be accommodated on any given spool. Tapes are also available with different types of backing material, namely matt backed, semi-matt backed and shiny backed. Originally most tape backing was acetate type and, whilst this tape tended to break rather than stretch, it was fairly popular amongst engineers since a stretch would make a recording unusable whereas a break could be edited together. PVC was also used but it stretched rather badly, and eventually polyester type backing was introduced and is now used by almost all tape manufacturers for all types of recording tape. Polyester is very tough and therefore cannot be easily stretched: therefore relatively few such problems arise provided recordings are made on standard play or the better types of LP tape.

The type of oxide employed is also of considerable importance since different oxides have totally different performances with respect to maximum operating level parameters at middle and high frequencies, oxide shedding, signal-to-print ratio, basic background noise, erasability, and sensitivity. Unfortunately it is not yet possible to design a tape that has the best possible performance in all respects, but most tapes made today are good and certainly appreciably better than even the best tapes of ten years ago.

Most tapes are available in various standard widths, 6·3, 12·7, 25·4, and 50·8 mm ($\frac{1}{4}$, $\frac{1}{2}$, 1, and 2 in.) though there is a tendency for some manufacturers to leave out one or two of these. This chapter deals only with audio tape but many other types of tape configuration are available for specialized applications in video, instrumentation, and computing.

Maximum operating level

When tapes are evaluated at 38 cm/sec, maximum operating level (MOL) at middle frequencies is almost always tested at 1 kHz in Europe. MOL is normally defined as being the magnetization in nanoWebers per metre (nWb/m) that corresponds to 3% third harmonic distortion of a 1 kHz fundamental tone. Modern tapes vary in this from a minimum of about 600 nWb/m to a maximum of about 1,400 nWb/m—an amazing difference. As will be seen in Fig. 8.1, the MOL at 1 kHz varies with bias current. A lower value of bias severely restricts the MOL, but at high frequencies the MOL is slightly improved. As the bias level is increased, the 1 kHz MOL improves up to a maximum plateau, whilst the HF MOL decreases. The bias setting is thus important and a compromise has to be reached between the relative MOLs. Bias current also affects other parameters which will be described later.

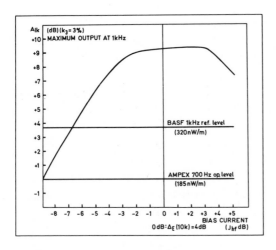

Fig. 8.1
Showing how the MOL of a typical modern tape (EMI 816) varies with bias current

The MOL performance of a tape also determines the relative distortion levels of the tape at lower levels and an examination of the characteristics of many modern tapes (see for example *Studio Sound*, February 1975) shows differences of third harmonic distortion at 1 kHz which are very dramatic. The lowest distortion tapes give only 0·1% distortion of middle frequencies at 320 nWb/m, whereas average tapes may be four times worse. Although most engineers are inclined to drive a tape at rather high peak levels, in order to obtain optimum signal-to-noise performance, others prefer to record at a lower peak level in order to achieve noticeably lower distortion, and use a noise reduction system such as Dolby or DBX. Noise should not normally become a problem and thus it seems that many engineers are needlessly driving their tapes too hard. Furthermore, if Fig. 8.2 is examined, the typical performance of an average tape will be noted at different high levels and it will be seen that high frequencies become squashed severely at very high levels. The actual squash at high frequencies is not the main problem, however, but the intermodulation distortion produced at high levels of combinations of high frequencies is, for this results in a very dirty reproduced sound on transients.

An important factor in the choice of a tape for a particular studio is the recording characteristic used. The 35μs IEC curve (DIN) at 38 cm/sec requires 3 dB more treble to be recorded for a flat overall response, and thus a tape

having a good MOL at high frequencies is essential. The NAB 50 μs characteristic, however, requires 3 dB less HF boost than IEC at 38 cm/sec and thus,
provided a tape has an acceptable MOL at high frequencies, a good MOL at
middle frequencies is highly significant. Remember that, for a given recording
level, the NAB 38 cm/sec curve gives 3 dB more high frequency noise on
playback than the IEC curve.

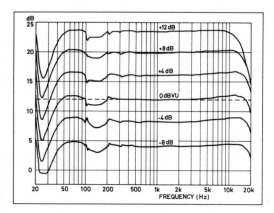

Fig. 8.2
Showing how the high frequencies
become suppressed (squashed) at
very high recording levels

Sensitivity

Tape sensitivity at middle and high frequencies again varies with bias. The
maximum high frequency sensitivity of a tape is always at a slightly lower bias
setting than that which gives maximum sensitivity at middle frequencies, but
an examination of the bias curves shows that the reduction in sensitivity, as
bias is lowered, is more rapid at middle frequencies than when the bias level
is increased above maximum sensitivity. Optimum bias must thus lie somewhere between the plateau of maximum 1 kHz sensitivity and slightly above
this point. The basic sensitivity of one tape at middle and high frequencies
can be very different from that of another, not only between brands but
between different batches of the same tape.

A machine that has been carefully set up for one tape may well give a significantly inferior performance on another and, to avoid variations in performance, it is advisable to standardize on one type for normal recording
in any studio complex. Sensitivity variations between one reel and another
of a particular type can be as wide as 2 dB, although a particular batch of
tape will not usually vary more than 0·5 dB. When ordering a large quantity of
tape, try and persuade the manufacturer to supply reels coming from the
same batch, rather than mixtures of batches taken from stores at random.
All professional tapes should have their batch numbers stamped on the
boxes, allowing easy checking.

Print-through

Many otherwise good recordings have been ruined by a sudden transient peak being heard at one or more revolutions of the tape spool before or after the transient. Such 'print-through', as it is called, is caused primarily by the percentage of spread in the size of oxide particles used, the wider the variation of particle size, the greater the tendency to print. Some oxides also show more tendencies to print than others, and so very wide variations in performance can be noted between different brands of tape. In general, tapes of European origin seem to be rather better than American tapes in this respect and, in particular, matt backed tapes have a significantly lower print than shiny backed types since the former usually have a thicker backing.

Measurements have shown differences in signal-to-print ratio of nearly 20 dB between different types of tape: engineers should note that tapes with bad print-through may cause recordings to become virtually useless commercially after a period of a few weeks, let alone years. Print-through can be significantly worsened by storage in too high an ambient temperature, or in environments in which the temperature varies over fairly wide limits. Archive tapes should be spooled through regularly to decrease the long term effects of print and, since any master should always be spooled through at least once before playback to reduce print further, it is conventional for studios to store masters 'end out'. This forces an engineer to spool the tape through before playback and thus reduces print.

Severe cases of print-through on an archive recording can sometimes be improved by passing the tape over a record head having a small DC current passing through it. Alternatively an extremely low bias current can be used to achieve an improvement. The amount of current required should be determined by pre-recording a high frequency on a tape and increasing bias from zero, without erase being present of course, until the output level decreases by 1 dB at 15 kHz.

Modulation noise

Modulation noise refers to any form of noise introduced in recording at frequencies other than the signal frequencies or harmonics. It increases in amplitude as the modulation level increases, and can be caused by problems in the manufacture of the tape itself or deficiencies in the tape transport mechanism. Different types of oxide give different modulation noise performance and, as with print-through, large variations in oxide particle size can tend to cause inferior performance. Short term variations in oxide coating thickness or in the homogeneity of the binder can also cause problems. Modulation noise has even been known to be exaggerated by printers' ink on a matt backing coming off on to the oxide side of tape one revolution away. Matt backed tapes have often tended to be worse in modulation noise characteristics, but recent advances in semi-matt backed types have shown considerable improvement.

Modulation noise normally occurs around the frequency being recorded and Fig. 8.3 shows a typical modulation noise curve around 1 kHz. Each vertical division represents 10 dB, while frequency is displayed horizontally from 750 to 1,250 Hz. Fortunately the main intensities of modulation noise are closest to the centre frequency, which audibly masks the noise. Subjectively, therefore, the effect of modulation noise is directly connected with the rate of fall off of noise away from the tone causing it. Figure 8.4 shows noise shoulders on either side of the recorded tone (975 to 1,025 Hz). The analysis on Figs. 8.3 and 4 has been made with only 1 Hz bandwidth for only with this remarkable resolution is it possible to see the noise shoulders. The shoulders are clearly symmetrical about the centre frequency, and thus correspond to

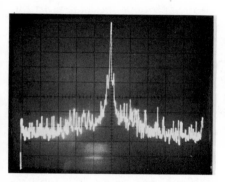

Fig. 8.3
Oscillogram of modulation noise around a 1 kHz tone. Each vertical division represents 10 dB and the frequency range shown is 750–1,250 Hz

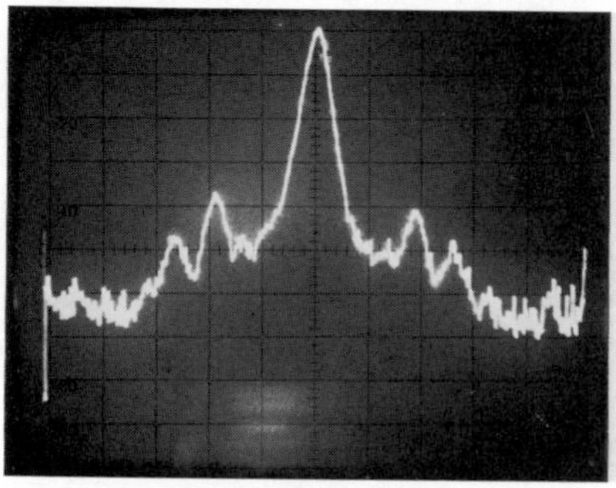

Fig. 8.4
A worse example of modulation noise

amplitude modulation of the recorded tone: this is a direct result of minute regular variations of oxide coating thickness. These variations incidentally appear to be caused by rollers and cog wheels in the manufacturing process.

Modulation noise also includes scrape flutter and varying head-to-tape contact effects caused by irregular back tension. As tape passes over the heads and through the capstan, the length of tape passing has a natural resonant frequency. In high quality recorders this is damped by either an anti-scrape flutter roller or very finely machined roller bearings. This factor emphasizes why recordings made on very high quality tape transports are generally cleaner than those made on inferior ones, even if the magnetic performances are identical. Modulation noise can also be increased by too much back tension being employed, and on almost all machines having pressure pads. One other cause of modulation noise in a very severe form is a poor batch of tape having a friction prone surface or being slit too wide. Some cheaper tapes cause severe screaming at the end of a small spool. Fortunately this problem appears to have been resolved by the manufacturers concerned, but engineers should watch out for the problem at the end of a spool, particularly when the machine being used has back tension designed for larger spools.

Spooling capability

It is imperative that master tapes should be spooled very neatly, so that no ridges of tape stick out from the general plateau. A light touch on a ridge of tape can cause irreparable damage, resulting in a dropout on the relevant channel. While the winding performance of tape depends largely on the tape transport used, significant variations in spooling performance occur with different brands and types of tape. Standard play tapes generally spool better than long play, and fully matt backed types will spool well even on comparatively poor transports. Semi-matt backed types spool significantly better than shiny backed and, for this reason, the latter should be recommended for master recording only when good tape transports are employed.

Dropouts and stability

Tape dropouts are characterized by very short term or medium term reduction in output, and are progressively more serious as the recorded wavelength is decreased. They are primarily caused by poor tape transport mechanisms which may score the surface of the oxide or cause minute particles of oxide to be lodged in the record or replay head gaps. Such particles may be lodged only momentarily but, in some circumstances, they can build up on a gap, causing long term loss of high frequencies. The only cure is thorough cleaning of the recorder heads. Some tapes, however, have their oxide coating less well bound than others and any tape causing a build up of oxide on guides and rollers should be suspect. Dropouts can also be caused by using an inappropriate type of tape for a particular transport: an example of this is the all too common use of professional standard play tapes on domestic transports. Such tapes are considerably thicker and less pliable than domestic tapes and thus the head-to-tape contact suffers. The Revox 77, for example, a very popular machine for copying and monitoring work, has been specifically designed for LP tape: it does not like double play, let alone triple play tape since these can cause undue head wear and even capstan wear. Some professional recorders do not like LP tapes which may ride up and down a capstan designed for thicker tape.

Dropouts are also more noticeable on narrow track recorders, since an oxide particle then represents a higher percentage of the recorded track. Even slight ruffling on a tape will cause severe dropouts on such recorders.

Tape dropout caused by variations in the accuracy of the coating itself becomes more noticeable if the tape is underbiassed, since only the surface layers of oxide become magnetized. In this case, a surface variation becomes larger as a percentage of the magnetization layer. Although a high bias tends to degrade high-frequency performance slightly, the dropout characteristics are improved and it is better, therefore, to use too high a bias than too low. Remember also to keep all tape guides in good condition and replace any that have worn edges. Many fixed guides can be rotated to give a longer overall life.

The stability of a tape concerns the consistency of performance, particularly at short wavelengths. Variations and imperfections in coating can cause high frequencies to waver, and imperfect slitting causes tape weave. Weaving causes variations in azimuth, which again can cause changes in short wavelength output from the replay head. These variations can be detected easily by connecting the two outputs from a stereo replay chain to a dual trace oscilloscope switched to chopping mode. Even better, a phase meter will show quite astounding variations of phase jitter at short wavelengths, which is a direct indication of stability and tape weave.

Velour effect
Some oxide coating is done in such a way as to introduce asymmetric performance between the two directions of travel of the tape. In some circumstances the oxide particles are orientated so that they stick up slightly at an angle to the backing. The sensitivity at medium and short wavelengths and the maximum operating levels will be found to vary by up to 2 dB or more. It is recommended that all professional tapes are recorded directly on a new spool of tape, so that the original front leader effectively becomes the front of the recording. Some users spool through all new tapes but, to be consistent, such spooling must be performed in both directions. If tape is intended to be reused occasionally, it is good practice to check the direction of the original recording before erasure, after which the tape should be reboxed in such a way that the new recording will be made in the same direction as the manufacturer originally intended. The velour effect can be checked by recording 1 kHz and 15 kHz at the same record level in both

directions of the tape. Any studio tapes which show a difference of more than a fraction of a dB should be watched very carefully.

Background noise

The basic background noise on a tape can vary appreciably between one type and another and the variations are dependent upon the characteristics of the oxide used. They also depend on the accuracy of the orientation of the oxide and, to a lesser degree, on the variation of oxide particle size. Recording engineers are primarily concerned with the subjective effect of background noise, and so such noise is normally measured by applying a weighting filter which exaggerates the frequencies which are most objectionable to the ear whilst reducing the response of less important frequency bands. Of the many weighting networks used over the last few years, the latest CCIR curve appears to be most consistent with subjective annoyance, and is recommended. Up to several dB difference in weighted noise can be measured between good and poor tapes, and the measurement is normally quoted as the ratio between a given flux level at a specified middle frequency and the noise measurement. For this measurement, incidentally, the unity gain point of the filter must be stipulated; normally it is set at 1 kHz, although Dolby Laboratories have in some cases recommended 2 kHz in order to give lower overall noise level readings. Since users are concerned only with comparisons, it is felt that 1 kHz is more practical. If noise reduction is not in use, the tape's noise performance becomes very significant but, if noise reduction is employed, tape noise should not become a problem unless the noise reduction system is prone to pumping and noise modulation effects. Of the noise reduction systems in use, the Dolby A system is the least prone to such effects, but gives a total weighted noise improvement significantly less than that which can be achieved by some other types, such as DBX or Burwen. One must listen to the noise, however, in different frequency bands during a high level signal. The Burwen system in particular gives virtually no noise reduction at high frequencies when a low frequency peak passes through the system. Noise pumping sounds like fluffiness behind modulation peaks, and can become very noticeable with some types of music. The choice of noise reduction system is a difficult one for, in some applications, more noise reduction than that given by the Dolby A process is desirable.

The tape's basic noise level can be degraded by a number of causes, the main ones being asymmetric bias and DC magnetization of heads and parts of the tape transport. The bias waveform should have low distortion at even harmonics, preferably well below 0·15%. However, odd harmonic distortion does not cause any problem, and bias has been achieved quite successfully under experimental conditions using square waves. To put it briefly, the area above zero of a bias waveform should equal the area below in any time taken as multiples of a complete cycle. Regular demagnetization of all metal parts in the transport is essential, and it is good practice to carry this out every day before any recordings or playbacks are commenced.

Intermodulation distortion

Most tape manufacturers have completely ignored intermodulation measurements in their specifications. Since the effects of such distortion are far more noticeable than those of harmonic distortion, it is of great importance. It is best measured at middle frequencies, by examining intermodulation products developed by recording two tones of equal amplitude at 950 and 1,050 Hz. The main IM products will be at 850 and 1,150 Hz. A wave analyzer or audio spectrum analyzer will be necessary to perform this measurement and, at any given flux level, the measured distortion is many times that of the third harmonic distortion in the same frequency band. At high frequencies, one can use 9·5 and 10·5 kHz and examine the IM output at 8·5 kHz. At typical peak recording levels used in studios, a horrifying 20% IM distortion figure is frequently reached and, at this point, the oxide is nearing saturation. It is of course pointless to measure harmonic distortion at such a high frequency, since the third harmonic will probably be out of the pass band of the replay amplifier. Bad intermodulation distortion at high frequencies gives the sound a very rough quality and, together with the presence of modulation noise, used to be well known to recording engineers as being introduced when singers having considerable high frequency energy in their voices were recorded in the early days of tape. High frequency intermodulation distortion produced at high recording levels, together with the squashing (non-linearity) of high frequencies is one more reason why recording levels should be generally reduced in modern studios: remember that a noise reduction system is not only designed to reduce tape noise, but should also encourage engineers to record at a lower level.

Choice of replay characteristics

While many people feel quite strongly that the IEC 35 μs, 38 cm/sec and 70 μs, 19 cm/sec curves are technically ideal, a situation has now developed throughout the world where the vast majority of users have chosen the NAB recording curve. The NAB replay characteristic of 50/3180 μs for both 38 and 19 cm/sec was originally chosen as a compromise between the two speeds' optimum performance, allowing a single replay amplifier with no equalization switching. So many American recorders have been sold throughout the world which have almost always incorporated only NAB equalization that, to be compatible with the majority of studios, others have more or less had to choose NAB. Some, however, have stubbornly retained the DIN/ IEC standard recommendation and, although this makes sense, it unfortunately makes tape interchange a problem. Practically all the broadcasting organizations in Europe have retained the IEC curves and do not even acknowledge NAB. To avoid confusion and switching errors, most European broadcasting equipment does not even contain replay equalization switching and so tapes presented to broadcasting authorities should always be recorded to the relevant IEC characteristic. It will be necessary to introduce a shelf boost of 3 dB above 5 kHz, together with a slight bass boost of 3 dB at 50 Hz, if a NAB machine is being used at 38 cm/sec for a recorded tape to be compatible for broadcasting in Europe. At 19 cm/sec, however, a shelf cut of 3 dB above 3 kHz should be introduced before recording, with the same 50 Hz boost. In practice, the bass boost can probably be ignored but the treble compensation is very important since an incorrect relationship of high to middle frequencies can make a sound audibly woolly or toppy.

Metering

While VU meters show the subjective volume level being recorded on to a tape, they fail completely to show the peak levels of the programme. Thus a musical programme, having peaks of very short duration and with fast rise times, will give an indication on a VU meter well below the real level being presented to the tape. Since the tape's performance depends upon the real levels and not the average levels present, peak programme meters of one type or another are essential if distortion is to be predictable on any particular recording. There is possibly a case for having both types of meter, since VU meters can under-read by as much as 10 dB on certain types of programme. The most common types of material that are over-recorded include muted brass, speech, choral and vocal music, and percussion. Conversely some types of music are frequently under-recorded by unskilled engineers, who make too much allowance for VU meter under-reading: the most obvious example of this is church organ music.

Head wear characteristics

Some tapes have had the reputation of producing more head wear than others and, while it is difficult to make measurements objectively, it is worth mentioning as a guide that matt backed tapes tend to cause more wear on heads than non-matt backed types. On examining the tensions recommended for 25·4 and 50·8 mm tape machines, it will be seen that the tension per millimetre width of tape is reduced for the larger tape widths and thus head wear should decrease slightly with wider tapes. While various studios have always had their favourite tapes, rumours concerning head wear characteristics are possibly exaggerated. Since a multitrack head should not cost any more per track than a 6·25 mm head, studios possibly over-estimate the importance of head wear. Most studios have reached a reasonable compromise in using semi-matt backed tapes. Shiny backed tape incidentally tends to skew a little more than semi-matt types and its use may be judged inadvisable because of the phase errors that can be produced across the tape width by skew action. Tapes having poorer wear characteristics also tend to wear tape guides quite badly, and frequent examination of such guides will indicate an unsuitable tape for a particular machine.

Erasure

High output tapes are usually more difficult to erase than normal types and, before ordering quantities of high output types, one should check that all the machines in a studio complex can erase the tape adequately. Some strange effects have been noticed over the years, when tapes have been bulk erased. On occasions, traces of previous recordings have returned after a storage period or when the tapes have been used a second time. On most machines the erase current can be varied, but on some the erase head itself will not be physically capable of erasing certain tapes and this will naturally affect a tape choice. Bulk erasing is advisable and, in this context, the best erasers have a very intense magnetic field internally, while the external field is held to a minimum. Remember that some bulk erasers should be left on for only a few tenths of a second at a time, since their induction windings will overheat badly and cause severe damage if left on for more than a minute. When using open bulk erasers, switch the eraser on first and then bring the spool up to the machine with a continual rotating hand movement. After a few rotations, turn the spool over whilst continuing to rotate. After four or five complete turns at a speed of about two seconds per rotation, withdraw the spool while continuing to rotate and turn the eraser off only when the spool is at least 50 cm away from the eraser. If once-per-revolution low frequency 'bonking' is to be avoided, the user will have to acquire a knack and the aforementioned instructions should be closely adhered to.

The final choice

When choosing a tape type, both the technical and financial aspects have to be borne in mind, for high quality tapes cost appreciably more than lower quality ones. Tape background noise, if a noise reduction technique is in use, becomes of minimum importance but the distortion at Ampex operating or DIN level is probably of greater importance than maximum operating level at middle frequencies. The intermodulation distortion at high frequencies is of great significance and there are quite major differences between different tapes. Print-through has been ignored for many years by too many studios, and so many tapes that have first given an extremely good impression fail badly in this respect. Economics may require a studio to choose a good 'cooking' tape rather than a very expensive one, in order to avoid two tape types being in use on the same equipment. As a final recommendation, it is safe to say that a user should look at all the properties of a tape and select one that is good in all ways, rather than one that is outstanding in one or two parameters but significantly below average in others. There is, however, a case for choosing a tape for the job, provided the user is prepared to set up his machines appropriately. Most tape suppliers have technical departments which are pleased to assist with technical advice.

Although most professionals stick to standard play tape for studio recordings, the advantages of semi-matt backed LP tapes should not be ignored. In some cases they actually give a better performance than their standard play counterparts for, although the distortion is usually marginally higher at middle frequencies, there is often considerably less intermodulation distortion at the high end, thus making them eminently suitable for recordings using the IEC curve at 38 cm/sec and the NAB one for 19 cm/sec. When recording live concerts on location, the extra playing time is a distinct advantage since most classical works can be accommodated on one reel. Semi-professional decks will usually give a better performance on LP tapes anyway, and a matt backed type should be quite easy to edit. The writer has successfully used 12·5 mm LP tapes on a quadraphonic recorder for almost all his quadraphonic recordings, and no trouble has been caused, even when editing. Naturally more care is required in spooling and even more notice should be taken of print-through characteristics, which are usually inferior on LP tape. Double-play tapes cannot usually be recommended for serious professional use, particularly because of spooling difficulties. In general, to achieve a sensible playing time on a portable recorder with small spools it becomes almost essential to choose matt backed LP tape.

One short warning, however, about the use of thinner tapes; the actual speed of the tape through a fixed speed tape transport will usually be slightly different because of the difference of pressure on the capstan. A speed inaccuracy can thus be found of a few tenths of 1%, in the worst case, between one machine and another, which is worth noting.

CHAPTER NINE

Tape Machines

Angus McKenzie

Although tape recorders can be categorized in many different ways, it is most convenient to place them in one of four basic quality brackets. The first is purely domestic and will be disregarded in this chapter; the second is semi-professional, the third professional portable, and the fourth includes the professional console or transportable types which are in general of far higher cost than those in the other categories. Semi-professional machines are capable of giving a performance which is almost equal in many respects to machines in both the higher categories. Their basic differences are that the input and output facilities are domestically orientated and the machines are not designed to withstand hours of daily use, month after month, with the reliability expected by the professional user. Furthermore, such machines usually have domestic type volume controls and metering, which cannot approach the standards of those found on fully professional recorders. Only rarely is it possible for engineers to perform regular lining up with ease without taking the equipment out of the box and, since tape can vary from batch to batch, this can be very annoying. Despite the reservations, there is a definite use for semi-professional equipment in studios, since it is easily portable and frequently contains useful facilities not found on a professional recorder. Many high quality LPs have been cut from master tapes recorded on machines such as the Revox model 77 and the newer Revox model 700. This recorder's tape transport is particularly fine and any reservations relate to the lack of robustness and professional type controls, which can hardly be expected on a semi-professional machine.

Professional users frequently have need for high quality machines which are small and easily transportable. The usual requirement for such a machine is that it shall have fixed gain inputs and outputs, give a very high standard of performance in all respects and be thoroughly reliable under all conditions. A secondary factor which usually applies is that it must not be too heavy. Portable equipment should also have very easy access to all the record pre-set controls, since a good engineer will always want to line up a machine *in situ*.

Although the top class machines are necessarily robust, and thus very heavy, they are usually available in both transportable and console versions, and are designed to work virtually full time under the most demanding conditions. Some console machines, for example, installed at the BBC continuity suites at Broadcasting House, are in use up to 18 hours a day, seven days a week, and they must give of their best all the time. Their reliability must be such that they require only a routine service relatively infrequently, although they would naturally be lined up before any recording session. They usually contain mechanical facilities not present in lower priced machines, in order to speed up the various operations necessary in recording, spooling back, and replaying under session conditions.

Some machines in this class include a built-in memory which allows the beginning of a take to be found automatically, when the rewind button is depressed. Alternatively, an engineer can note down footage or timing points and programme the recorder to commence playback at any of these desired points. Multitrack recorders are in yet another category, which will be dealt with later, as are battery operated portables.

The different performance parameters will now be explained, together with their significance in operation, so that users may have a clearer idea of the differences between machines of various types and in different price categories.

Mechanical considerations

1. Robustness. Whereas most semi-professional recorders have fairly thin chassis and employ plastic panelling, professional machines usually have a thick diecast chassis with very rugged supports, thus forming a rigid outer framework for the machine. Most machines are constructed in such a way

Fig. 9.1
Bias Electronics tape machine

that mechanical adjustments, servicing, and part replacement can be performed fairly easily and quickly. The Bias Electronics machines for example (Fig. 9.1) are particularly easy to service, the entire deck plate being hinged.

When looking at a new tape recorder, then, examine its construction closely and make sure that the entire body work is physically strong and stable. Continued transportation can cause a weak frame to become deformed and this can seriously affect the accuracy of the tape path. Also check the manner in which any printed circuits are fixed into position. Some circuit boards are fixed at one end only and, after a while, the strain on the edge connectors can become so great that intermittent contact and even track breakages can become a problem. Since the capstan and reel motors are usually rather heavy, they should be very substantially mounted or suspended from the main frame. Check that this mounting is really adequate.

Fig. 9.2
Ferrograph Studio 8 recorder, showing the tape guidance system

2. The tape transport. A typical tape transport is shown in Fig. 9.2 and the complete path that the tape passes is from the left hand reel, through the tension control levers, round roller guides, across the heads, through the capstan and on, via another roller bearing and tape guide, to the right hand spool. When evaluating a machine, the angle round which the tape must turn at any point in the transport should not be excessive if the guide in question has a small diameter. Many machines have caused severe oxide shedding and back tensioning problems because the tape passed through an angle of as much as 90° round a guide with a radius of only a few millimetres. Such poorly designed guides can actually harm tapes quite badly, and will often cause tape jitter and flutter since minute variations in the thickness of the tape will momentarily vary back tension. All the bearings over which tape passes must be of high quality and users should check that these bearings are very smooth. High precision ball races are provided on machines such as the Stüder A80 and must be maintained regularly, since experience has shown that wear in them can degrade flutter badly. The replacement of such parts is normally necessary only after many years of use; by this time, manufacturers may well have discontinued normal availability and charge a high premium for supplying the necessary spare part. It is therefore good practice to check availability of spare parts when choosing a particular professional recorder.

Most machines used on the continent of Europe run 'oxide out', which means that the oxide side of the tape is towards the operator and the heads face away from him. In the United Kingdom, however, very few such machines are in service since the alternative oxide configuration is felt to be much more convenient operationally. Most European models are made, therefore, in oxide out or oxide in versions and the user should be careful to stipulate his preference. Although United Kingdom users undoubtedly prefer oxide in, there is a lot to be said for the alternative: in particular, the oxide side of the tape does not physically contact so many metal parts and thus tape scoring is kept to a minimum. If an oxide out machine is employed, the user should always order tape wound oxide out, since twists can cause serious problems in spooling and wow and flutter. American tape manufacturers are not keen to supply oxide out, but European manufacturers make such tapes readily available because of the considerable demand for them in Europe.

3. *Tape tension*. When professional machines first became available, both the back and forward tensioning were controlled purely by reel motor energization and thus a considerable variation of tension could be noticed at different parts of a reel. Variations at worst could exceed 2:1 on large reels and 3:1 on small reels and, for this reason, quite bad wow often resulted towards the end of a recording, when the left-hand reel was almost empty. Several manufacturers have solved this problem by introducing mechanical systems which alter the braking on the pay off motor, thus relieving the back tension produced by the motor at a small diameter, whilst it is revolving without energization. The back tension in such systems is usually held within limits

of $\pm15\%$ or so, which is satisfactory in most cases. A better system employs electronic control of motorized back tension by measuring the tension in one way or another and applying feedback through logic circuits to the motor. This feedback system can be mechanical (gradually switching in more and more attenuation to the motor's current supply) or it can be fully electronic, using photo-electric or other devices, or a combination of both. Some machines overcome the problem by employing dual capstans in which an actual tape drive capstan is moving radially very slightly faster than the back tension capstan. This allows constant tape tension to be achieved over the heads. The adjustment of dual capstan mechanisms is extremely critical and, in most cases, a common motor drives both directly or the direct drive on the main capstan has a belt drive to the back tension capstan. Provided a dual capstan machine is correctly adjusted, the system works well, but if LP tape is likely to be used the machine's performance should be very carefully checked.

Forward tensioning, although not so critical, again benefits from being under constant control. General adjustment can be quite critical, since too high a forward tension can cause snatching and tape stretching, whereas too light a tension can cause loops to be thrown when the machine is started. Many machines increase the tension for the first second or two after the transport is engaged. A relay then cuts in, restoring the forward tension to its normal running value. Machines having damped tension control lever bearings, such as the Revox 700, can operate extremely well and give very low figures of wow and flutter. Constant forward and back tensioning also allows spools of different diameter to be used and such machines do not normally have a spool size tension set switch, since this is already governed by the logic. Other machines, however, such as the Philips PRO 36, Telefunken M15, Stüder B62 and Revox model 77, have switches selecting large or small reel tensions, the smaller spools, of course, requiring a lower average torque. There are many points in favour of mechanical tension control and, in particular, there is less to go wrong, although electronic logic systems give more predictable and accurate results.

4. Wow and flutter. If the speed of the tape past the heads varies continually, an effect is produced which is called wow and flutter. Relatively slow variations in speed (wow) are usually caused by uneven tensioning problems or by large diameter bearings rotating unevenly. High speed variations (flutter) are primarily caused by fast rotating, relatively thin capstans or by the capstan motor itself. It can also be caused, surprisingly, by anti-flutter bearings being incorrectly adjusted or worn and as a secondary effect from uneven back tension, causing the tape to vary in its pull on the capstan bearing.

The bearing may then rock slightly backwards and forwards, or up and down, and this movement actually generates the flutter.

Over the years, different types of wow and flutter measurement standard have been advocated and used, but it is now clear that the DIN peak weighting standard has been accepted throughout the European recording industry. While some manufacturers quote very realistic specifications for their equipment, usually maintaining a performance about 30% better than the specification, others quote a relatively poor figure and consistently achieve performance only one third of the stated value. This has led to a ridiculous state of affairs in which some domestic machines are specified as being better than the finest professional ones. As a guide, it is suggested that at 38 cm/sec a machine should be better than 0·035% in practice, to give playback in which no speed variations can be heard. A machine having a measurement in excess of 0·06% will have wow and flutter which is fairly audible to many listeners, whereas over 0·1% will cause considerable distress to anyone. The performance of a machine in this respect will usually be better with standard play tape than LP tape, and frequently the latter can be as much as 30% inferior.

Some typical causes of wow and flutter will be outlined as a guide for maintenance. Machines having brake band back tension can produce bad wow if the band is worn unevenly. Instabilities in the mechanical or electronic logic can also produce the same problem. Rotating bearings can produce trouble if they are oiled when they should not be, or not oiled enough when they should be, and reference to the instruction manual here will be helpful. Check also that the spool platforms are at the right height. Tape coming off or on to a spool in contact with the edges, either permanently or intermittently, can cause a problem. This can be corrected only by adjustment of the platforms, or the relevant tape guides and rollers, so that the tape can travel evenly and at the same height throughout the entire transport. Capstan bearings usually do require oiling, and once again the manufacturer's instructions should be strictly adhered to. A badly worn pressure idler wheel can cause trouble, and an analysis of the wow or flutter speed will usually indicate the rotational speed of the part causing the main component of variation.

Unfortunately footage counters can introduce wow on many machines, particularly if their mechanism is not oiled sufficiently. They are usually belt driven from a large roller bearing, and sometimes the cogs inside the counter mechanism tend to stick. This can cause variations in back tension on the belt and thus uneven running of the tape transport bearing. A wow and flutter meter should be provided for maintenance staff to check equipment at regular intervals.

5. *Scrape flutter.* As the tape passes across the heads, it can resonate on the record head if the length of the tape between the left hand roller bearing or main guide and the capstan roller is not sufficiently damped. The resonant frequency of this length of tape depends both on the tape type and the amount of back tension employed. In some cases, where back tension is not maintained at a fairly constant level, it increases towards the end as the pay-out spool empties. Some types of tape start vibrating against the record head and cause what is termed scrape flutter, which modulates the sound of the recording by adding a screaming noise, which of course renders a recording useless. The effect can be emphasized if any of the tape guides are underwidth, or if the tape is slightly overwidth, is badly slit, or has a higher than average co-efficient of friction. Telefunken/AEG introduced scrape flutter bearings on their head blocks over 20 years ago to eliminate the problem, consisting of a rotational bearing with extremely low friction lightly touching the tape between the record and replay heads. Several other manufacturers (e.g. Ferrograph, Stüder, Scully) have adopted the same technique, although in some instances the bearing is between the erase and record heads. While this system greatly reduces scrape flutter effects, bearing wear must be watched. If bearings become worn, they can introduce flutter proportionate to their speed of rotation. The provision of such bearings leads to cleaner recording and reproduction of high frequencies and is therefore highly desirable.

6. *Footage and timing counters.* Nearly all recorders used professionally are equipped with tape timing devices of one form or another, and usually they indicate the time in minutes and seconds that has elapsed between the set zero point and any particular point on the tape. They are usually set to indicate at 38 cm/sec, although some three-speed machines, having 19 cm/sec as the centre speed, quote timing at this speed. Almost all types of counter derive their readings from the rotation of one of the tape guide rollers and, although inaccuracies can creep in on some machines because of slippage, many others are surprisingly accurate, even down to a few seconds in half an hour. If the driving roller is rubber lined, inaccuracies will creep in if the roller becomes worn, and this is exaggerated by the property of worn rubber to become very smooth, thus causing slippage. Some counters indicate the length of tape in feet or metres but this becomes extremely annoying, as continual calculations are required.

When an entire taped programme is to be timed by using a counter, the tape should be wound through at an even, moderate speed, and the chosen winding speed should be approached relatively slowly to avoid slippage when the spools are accelerating. If this is done carefully, most counters should read to an accuracy of 1% or so, and some machines can reach an accuracy of 2 or 3 seconds in a full NAB reel. It is worth checking wow and flutter with and without the counter belt disconnected, as some counters unfortunately degrade wow performance. On a few modern machines an electronic counter makes allowances for tape speed, so that the correct timing is shown for any speed in use.

7. *Capstan drive and speed accuracy*. Many types of capstan drive have been employed. One of the earliest, the EMI BTR1, actually used a capstan shaft with a motor at the bottom of the machine rotating the shaft which was about 75 cm long. Telefunken in their M5 machines employed rubber idlers, engaging different diameters on the motor capstan, and gearing these down to different diameters on a heavy flywheel underneath the main tape drive capstan. This technique worked fairly well but was exceptionally difficult to maintain, it being recommended that occasional maintenance should be done by the factory, which meant unsoldering many connections and unbolting the entire assembly. A mechanical variable speed control was provided, which worked by applying an adjustable degree of friction on the large diameter flywheel. A neon stroboscope allowed precise setting of the nominal speeds. Many machines extend the motor capstan vertically to become the actual tape capstan and, whereas some have anti-vibration bellows or couplers, others have a continuous motor/capstan shaft. The Telefunken M28 and M15 machines have a belt drive from the main motor flywheel assembly to a very substantial capstan flywheel. This permits the capstan motor to be mounted further away from the head block and substantially reduces hum induction and transmission of flutter from the main drive motor.

   Drive motors are of many different types, the most important ones being: (a) synchronous mains types in which the number of poles in use is switched for the different speeds, (b) hall effect motors as used in the Telefunken M15, (c) asynchronous motors as used in the Revox 77 with feedback logic circuits to control the AC voltage applied to the motor, and (d) DC motors with feedback to stabilize speed. Motor logic can be extremely complicated and some circuits, such as those made by Stüder, employ discriminators and DC amplifiers which are fed by frequencies evolved from waveforms generated by toothed wheels, around the capstan motor for example. Extreme speed stability can be obtained from this type of mechanism, which is not affected by mains voltage or frequency. Some motors, such as those used on the Philips PRO 36, can be locked to the frequency of an external oscillator which can produce very wide speed variations if required.

   It is important for professional recorders to run with a speed accuracy better than ±1% and most achieve better than ±0·5%, the accepted standard in Europe. This accuracy is demanded by broadcasting organizations requiring very precise timing of programmes, although recording studios would normally need such accuracy only if recordings from different machines are to be edited together at precisely the same musical pitch.

Several test tapes include a very accurate frequency band for speed measurement. Their tolerance is usually closer than their guaranteed ±0·2%, and the BASF 38 cm/sec tapes would seem to be better than 0·1%. The most accurate way of measuring speed is to connect the output from the machine to a frequency counter, note several frequency readings over a period and then calculate the average. The reference level at the beginning of the test tape should be played through in both directions, so that the variable effects of back tension can be checked. It is good practice to wind the test tape on to the beginning of a full NAB spool of unrecorded tape, so that speed can be checked at the beginning of a NAB reel and then at the end in reverse. The speed should be maintained within ±0·2% on a high quality recorder.

If the speed is incorrect, it could be due to inaccurate mains frequency, maladjustment of logic circuits or wear on the main tape capstan, especially if the latter has a fairly small diameter. Too great a forward tension can also cause pulling and, of course, affect speed but adjustment of tensions should put the matter right. Also remember that thin tapes will often pass through a transport at a marginally different speed, and this should be watched. When checking speed with a reference tape, it is advisable to use the same tape for determining all the speeds and, if the tape is selected for the highest speed of the recorder, it becomes advisable to integrate speed over 10 seconds rather than 1 second to achieve sufficient accuracy. A 19 cm/sec test tape, however, can be used with a 1 second gate at the higher speed with perfectly accurate results.

8. Spooling and braking. Whereas some machines have only one spooling speed in each direction, others have a choice of spooling speeds or are provided with continuously variable controls. Recorders such as the Tele-funken M10 and M15 have fast and slow spooling speeds in each direction and also two idling positions, allowing very slow spooling to be achieved with a form of freewheeling action. Other machines, including the Philips PRO 36, Bias Electronics, and later versions of the Stüder A80, have continuously variable spooling. Unfortunately most models have only one speed in each direction, which is to be deprecated, since it is not advisable to spool a master tape with many edits at full speed. A badly made edit could cause almost complete destruction of the master if the edit were to fail. Good, smooth spooling requires a very high quality tape transport. Machines having spooling arms which are either spring loaded or oil damped tend to give better spooling than machines allowing the tape to go straight on to the spool from a fixed guide. The spooling motor spindles should be very accurately ground, so that they are perfectly concentric and vertical. Any slight bend in these spindles will cause a spool to whip up and down, while it is rotating, thus causing a very uneven wind. Ideally the tape should wind on to the centre of the spool without touching either flange: matt backed tapes always spool better than shiny backed types. Sometimes a tape that normally spools badly will spool more evenly if a 180° twist is made at both ends of the transport, and the spooling speed is reduced. Bad spooling is usually caused by air becoming trapped when the tape winds on to the previous layer on the spool. A twist in the tape before it actually makes contact with the previous layer reduces the probability of such air trapping. Great caution should be taken, however, and the technique cannot be recommended for use with very fast spooling machines. The tension employed in spooling should never be too great or a tape may be stretched, particularly at the inside diameters. If plastic spools are used, high tension spooling can even result in the spool becoming cracked. This effect is particularly noticeable when LP or double-play tapes are spooled and in general thinner tapes should be spooled at slower speeds than standard play ones.

Fig. 9.3
Telefunken Magnetophon 15 recorder, showing the use of single sided spools

Many European organizations deliver tapes, almost invariably matt backed, on NAB hubs without flanges. This practice must be strongly deprecated as an unskilled operator can cause a calamity by allowing the centre hub to fall out when attempting to load the machine. Many continental studios employ single-sided spools (see Fig. 9.3) and these should be used only with matt backed tapes, for which they were designed, unless very slow spooling speeds are employed. Most manufacturers can supply backing plates, with special adapters to allow tape pancakes to be loaded. These backing plates are available with diameters to suit all requirements, although all sizes may not be stocked by an importer. Routine spooling should never be performed with the tape in contact with the heads, and most professional recorders include a lever or push-button to permit the tape to be in or out of contact with all the heads, or just the replay head, during spooling. Spooling against the heads seriously increases head wear, since very considerable heat is developed on the gap. Such heat can also cause gap fatigue or strain.

Often a machine's brakes are inadequately maintained and, in such circumstances, spillage can result if brakes are applied when spooling fast. Check regularly that the braking is even and, if necessary, try spooling from a NAB reel to a smaller one in each direction to make sure that the transport stops evenly and without generating a tape loop at either side of the transport. Clutches and brake bands should be watched for wear and need regular replacement. If your machine is no longer in production, or is shortly being discontinued, make sure that you order an adequate supply of spare parts before the price rises dramatically. Another useful hint is to clean regularly any surfaces against which a brake band tightens. Such cleaning can remove any foreign particles or oil that may be increasing the wear or causing problems with the brake bands.

The Ferrograph Studio 8 (see Fig. 9.2) has the spooling speed logic controlled so that when a predetermined speed is reached it is maintained until a required stopping point, when the spooling automatically reverses, and the brakes are applied only when the tape is then at rest. In addition, a facility is provided in which the required spooling-back tape time can be predetermined by using the counter appropriately.

When testing a new machine, it is worth checking to see what happens if the mains lead is suddenly disconnected during fast spooling. A good machine will automatically apply the brakes, but a bad one will create a complete tape mangle! Some very well known machines are badly designed in this respect and it is so easy for someone to switch off a recorder accidentally, a fuse to blow, or a sudden mains failure or power cut to occur.

Various different models of spool adaptor are available and types applying a firm lock by rotation are to be strongly recommended over the cheaper types. Most machines have a spring loaded cine spool clamp, which is very effective. Always ensure that any spool is clamped satisfactorily before spooling, since an unclamped spool can ride up and down.

9. *General mechanical noise*. The actual mechanical noise level audible when a machine is switched on can be very important, since a machine which is noisy can produce considerable irritation if it is in the same room as the mixing console and monitoring equipment. Mechanical noise may seem low relative to the background noise level in a particular room, but a continual drumming noise, for example from a capstan motor, can become very tiring. However, many engineers can put up with this if all other parameters of a machine are excellent. Yet it is clear that machines should not be noisy and this point is often overlooked by tape recorder designers.

10. *Editing facilities*. Various editing facilities are provided on different professional recorders. Some include built-in editing blocks and these should be checked to ensure that they allow both 45° and 90° joints. The best editing blocks have a concave slot for the tape, having edges that are slightly wider at the bottom than at the top. This allows the tape to sit securely in the block and so an edit can be made quickly and accurately. The Stüder A80 and some Telefunken machines are provided with built-in tape cutting scissors and these can be very useful, since they give an accurate and predictable cut. The A80 also includes an optional automatic tape edit marker pen, most useful when a considerable amount of editing is to be done.

If a machine is to be used frequently for editing, check that the static tensions of any swing arms do not cause too great a pull on the tape if it is cut *in situ*. Some machines have edit buttons, which remove the brake bands from contact with the drums under the spool platforms. This allows the tape to be manually swung backwards and forwards to select an editing point. Many professional recorders do not have a safety switch to disable the erase and bias circuitry if the record button is absentmindedly depressed. This facility is extremely important and should be provided in all professional recorders.

Great care should be taken to ensure that all the metal parts of a recorder are adequately demagnetized: when two pieces of tape are joined together, and one piece is slightly magnetized, a click or plop may become audible. All tools used in editing should be non-magnetic or regularly demagnetized, for the same reason.

One final hint in editing is to watch that two pieces of tape are not edited together when one has low frequency rumble in a different momentary phase to another. The sudden change of phase can introduce a click. If an edit in such a place is essential, both tapes should be carefully copied with rumble cut added and the copies then edited. Better still, always use a 20 Hz cut in virtually all microphone channels when recording in locations with rumble present.

11. Head block and heads. Virtually all professional recorders incorporate three separate heads, the first for erase, the second for recording and the third for playback. Some machines have erase heads that are split track, allowing recording on all or only selected tracks. Many studio machines incorporate sync facilities, which allow individual tracks of the record head to become replay tracks either through the normal playback amplifiers, or through separate sync replay ones. The quality obtainable from a record head replay is never to the same standard as that of the proper replay head, and should be used only when recording on some tracks, whilst playing back a previous recording in sync. The playback response is usually lacking in top, because the record head gap is much wider than that of a normal replay head. Furthermore, if the normal replay amplifiers are used, the playback level will usually be between 10 and 20 dB lower, because the record head inductance may be about one tenth of that of the replay head. This can be corrected by using a step-up transformer.

Erase heads are of single or double gap configuration, and are available either with full-track or split-track gaps. Split-track heads vary in the amount of unerased tape between the tracks and should never be used for erasing full-track recordings: otherwise the original recording may break through on replay. Some erase heads do not have a very effective earthing system, and some types of tape can cause electrostatic discharges which in turn cause spits to be audible on replay. The best solution to this problem is to change the erase head for a better type having the same inductance, which will usually be between 1 and 2 mH, although machines with high bias frequencies sometimes have appreciably lower inductance erase heads.

The erase efficiency of the head should be checked by recording at an extremely high level on a high output tape, and then erasing it on the same machine. The erase field should be such that the original recording is reduced in amplitude by at least 75 dB. As a final check, play the erased tape back after a week to make sure that the oxide has been thoroughly erased all the way through. Some erase heads do not give a sufficient field for complete erasure, and increasing the erase current or changing the frequency will not necessarily improve results, since the head may be saturating.

Record heads have many different track configurations, and some of these are dealt with in Chapter Eleven. Such heads usually have an inductance between 500 μH and 7 mH and are available in a number of different materials; ferrite types normally give considerably lower distortion at high levels than mumetal types. Typical measurements have shown that a very high output tape, having a measured third harmonic distortion at 1 kHz of 0·4% with a mumetal head, can give readings as low as 0·1% with ferrite types. Ferrite heads, if treated with care, can last appreciably longer than mumetal types but are much more expensive. Unfortunately they can be very easily damaged and some of them have been known to chip along the gap edges. They are nevertheless to be recommended with caution and it is true to say that improvements in manufacturing techniques are likely to make them more robust and reliable.

Ferrite heads are available with far closer tolerance gaps than mumetal ones and thus are particularly recommended for producing recordings, such as test tapes, with a very even level of magnetization across the tape width. In the past, record heads have often had gaps as wide as 20 microns but nowadays most manufacturers supply 7 micron gaps. The penetration at low frequencies is partly dependent on gap width but the employment of wide gaps, even with very accurate edges, tends to affect high frequency performance. Narrower gaps usually give better performance at HF but slightly at the expense of LF performance. The accuracy of the gap edge also determines extreme HF performance.

Most replay heads now have an effective gap below 4 microns, although older types are still available as spares having a 6 micron gap. A wide replay gap, whilst giving greater output on medium wavelengths, has reduced output on short wavelengths, thus requiring more extreme HF boost.

The construction of tape recorder heads and their characteristics are so specialized that it is probably advisable to accept manufacturers' recommendations, apart from the choice of ferrite/mumetal and gap width. Head blocks are in some cases fixed permanently to the deck, while others are detachable. Normally they sit very firmly on the deck and are clamped by at least two screws. To test the rigidity of the head block mounting, it is recommended that the replay head is azimuthed very carefully to a 19 cm/sec test tape and then the head block is unscrewed, withdrawn, replaced and the azimuth again checked. If there is any significant change, the head block is not seating firmly enough and the manufacturers should be asked to comment.

When a machine is switched to record, the overall tape noise should be absolutely smooth when the machine has been demagnetized. On some models a form of cockling or burbling noise is audible, even when the bias supply has been proved to be perfect. This effect appears worse on thicker matt backed, standard play tapes. It is produced by incorrect tape wrap round the record head, and re-orientation may be necessary to increase the wrap slightly. This should reduce the cockling but will possibly increase tape hiss slightly. Remember, though, that excessive head/tape pressure will exaggerate modulation noise and scrape flutter. Another phenomenon that should be watched is phase jitter and this, when present, gives a random continuous variation of phase reproduced between two tracks at short wavelengths. One channel output should be connected to the Y1 input of a 'scope, to which the instrument is synchronized, while the second track is connected to the Y2 input. The Y2 waveform will vary in position relative to the Y1 waveform, and the amount of variation shows the seriousness of any jitter present. The effect becomes more serious as the tested tracks are further displaced, and the worst case is produced by comparing the two outside tracks of a multitrack recorder. Serious jitter is produced when tape guidance problems exist and, although some machines have this problem inherent in their design, others will show up the problem only if guides are worn or heads have their vertical tilt angle incorrect. Check that the tape is riding evenly round the capstan pressure wheel and not continuously riding up and down. Phase jitter produces azimuth variations and so becomes a most important parameter to watch.

Electrical considerations

The safety aspects of any machine should be checked very carefully to see if they comply with the latest IEE regulations. No mains tag points should be bare under the deck and all mains switches should preferably be two-pole. The machine should be adequately earthed and the mains input transformer should be very substantial.

A check should be made to see if switching on or off produces any sharp pulse in the audio circuits. Some switching transients on professional recorders have been known to damage loudspeakers and amplifiers. A check should also be made to see if any of the other functions introduce clicks. If the machine has a 'drop in' facility, this should be smooth and without any click or whoosh. The deck should not run unduly warm, since this can cause tape warp and encourage print-through to develop, particularly if a master is left on the machine for a period. Adequate ventilation should be provided under the deck.

Any lamps used in logic circuits should be very accessible. Since a lamp failure on a session is extremely serious, the machine should be designed in terms of fail safe, allowing the machine to continue in operation, but perhaps at reduced performance. Small brackets should be included internally, with spare bulbs installed at the factory to allow for this since invariably, when lamp blowing is first experienced by a user, he does not have a replacement.

The Ferrograph Studio 8 employs fibre optics and has an automatic switch-over system, so that a second lamp immediately takes over from a failed main lamp without any degradation of machine performance. A reserve lamp indicator on the front panel informs the user that the machine is in this condition.

Since all motors, mains operated solenoids, and even mains wiring are likely to induce hum, either into the replay head or its associated electronics, the induced hum levels in replay should be checked under all operational conditions. When testing hum induction on replay without tape present, but with the spool motors idling, the hum level will usually be slightly worse than with the spools lightly held to prevent rotation. The latter case, however, is more realistic and any replay noise check with motors running should be carried out in this way.

While some recorders have HT regulation on each separate module, most have their entire HT supply extremely well regulated in the power supply itself. Some machines show a degradation of 100 Hz hum when the record circuits are switched on and this is due to the extra loading of the erase oscillator, etc., on the power supply.

Many machines have an hours-elapsed counter associated either with the general electronics or, more usually, the capstan drive motor. They indicate the number of hours that the machine has been running after its original delivery. If it is to be useful, the machine should not be left switched on but unused for prolonged periods. Many studios keep a log book for each machine, and a note of the hours elapsed at any particular maintenance time can be noted. The counter can also serve as a useful indication to the studio manager of unauthorized use of equipment.

1. Replay amplifiers. The replay chain has to provide considerable amplification of the replay head output, so that the line output stage can be fully driven. The replay pre-amplifier contains basic time constant networks for the different speeds, and any necessary equalization to compensate for replay head losses. Some machines have purely fixed equalization, whereas others have considerable variation available. The Telefunken M15, for example, has equalizers for setting the response at the bass end, the general overall time constant, and the amount of extreme HF boost required to compensate for replay gap losses. The normal replay module allows virtually any replay time constant to be achieved at different speeds, although a switchable NAB/DIN module is available at extra cost. The replay chain also includes bias traps and these should be checked to see whether their null is at the right frequency. The output impedance of the line out amplifier should be checked, and modern recorders should give figures well below 100 ohms, thus allowing many pieces of equipment to be connected to the replay chain without affecting the level. Some recorders have unbalanced jack sockets to monitor the channel output (Scully) and these are particularly useful. If VU meters are provided, they should never bridge an output of higher source impedance than 100 ohms, for distortion can be introduced. If the meters are buffered, however, there should be no problem.

2. Erase, bias, and record head drive. Most recorders now use an erase/bias frequency between 100 and 200 kHz and this is normally fed direct to the erase head circuitry, but attenuated by bias preset capacitors or potentiometers to the record head circuit. A bias trap should always be present between the bias feed point to the head, and the record head audio drive amplifier, thus stopping the bias voltage from blocking the record amplifier. The bias trap should be checked by applying an oscilloscope probe to the output of the record amplifier, and checking that the trap is nulled at bias frequency. Although the record head inductance normally has only a comparatively minor effect on the tuning of the bias trap, the rejection should be rechecked if the head is changed at any time. Split-track recorders frequently employ dummy heads, which are used if a track is not on record, and a check should be made on bias frequency with each track only recording, and then with different combinations of tracks on record. Furthermore a recorder should be given a long soak test on record to check that the bias current through the record head does not change when the machine has been on for some time, and also that the bias and erase frequency does not change.

When the record function is switched on, the erase oscillator should build up to full output within a fraction of a second. Similarly, when the machine is stopped or switched to playback, the erase oscillator should ramp down slowly to prevent any DC magnetization of the record head. This ramping down of the bias and erase is absolutely vital, since too sudden a disconnection can cause asymmetry in the bias power through the heads. Tapes subsequently made on the machine may sound magnetized or have degraded modulation noise characteristics. The earthing system incorporated into the bias/record head circuit is very critical since any poor earth paths can cause bias breakthrough into record and replay amplifier circuits.

When a machine is being used for playback, it is vital that no record amplifier audio current should pass through the record head. Most machines employ a record head mute relay, which short circuits the audio head drive current to earth when the machine is not switched to record. You should check your recorder with a very high level input to the record amplifier, when playing back a blank tape, to ensure that no signal of any kind is recorded in other than the record mode.

3. The record amplifier. This amplifier has to accept the audio input to the recorder and convert it into a constant current drive through the record head, with the equalization necessary to obtain an overall flat response at the different recorder speeds. Equalizers must be provided to allow a choice of tape types and NAB/IEC switching must include a 3,180 μs boost for NAB.

A good machine will give undistorted current through the head at all frequencies and all levels that are likely to be encountered in studio use. While it is easy to provide such a current at low and middle frequencies, the voltage swing necessary to give the equalized high-frequency current through the record head can be very considerable, and some machines incorporate record heads of unsuitable inductance, or the HT line to the record amplifier is insufficiently high to allow undistorted peak-to-peak swing. It is vital that no clipping at any frequency should be present in the record amplifier, so that the head/tape mechanism becomes the only limitation.

Record head amplifier distortion at high frequencies may vary with different equalization settings, since most equalizers rely on variable feedback at high frequencies. Some equalizers, in fact, have more distortion when comparatively little equalization is used, because of the design of the circuit, and this should be watched.

Record amplifier metering is useful and many machines incorporate both input level monitoring and record head current monitoring in addition to a bias metering position. The input impedance of the record amplifier section should be 10 kohms or higher for interconnection with most equipment designed today, but some European recorders are standardized on 5 kohm bridging. Although some recorders include centre taps on their inputs, it is normal practice to leave these floating, since the transformer itself will tend to semi-balance by the capacity of its windings to chassis. Check that no mains hum is induced into the intput or output transformers: if it is, re-orientation may be necessary.

Multitrack recorders
Studios today employ 4-track, 8-track, 16-track and 24-track recorders in addition to machines of various configurations (see Fig. 9.4). While all the previous remarks in this chapter apply to multitrack recorders as much as to 6·3 mm machines, some extra problems arise.

It is much more important for such machines to have electronically controlled back tension, since the weight of tape on the spools is so much higher. A badly designed multitrack transport can cause very bad tape snatching and looping, since the difference in weight between the left and right spools is very noticeable at the beginning and end of a reel. Another problem with multitrack is the accuracy of phasing of all the channels across the tape width. Considerably greater precision is required in the manufacture of multitrack heads, record and replay, and even the finest of these can show serious phase errors between outside tracks. Furthermore any slight movement of tape, up and down or skew, has considerably more effect on phase than that caused by similar motion on narrower tape widths. It is

Fig. 9.4
The 24-track version of the Stüder A80 tape machine

advisable to plan carefully the track locations for the various feeds, so that sounds appearing close in position to other sounds on the final mixdown should be placed close together on the multitrack recording. Severe phasing sounds can be caused by mixing together tracks which have similar information but are widely spaced. In this respect, a highly priced tape transport will usually perform much better than a cheap one and so, when making a choice of machine, bear this particular factor in mind. Multitrack recorders invariably require more powerful motors, and much stronger capstans and bearings, although the average tensions employed per mm width of tape are marginally lower than those for 25·4 mm width. All the guides must be very carefully aligned and a check should be made to see if either edge of the wide tape is in any way being subjected to pressure, which would introduce bowing and poor head/tape contact.

Electronics for multitrack recorders are normally identical to those employed on 6·3 mm machines, with the exception that the erase oscillator and bias amplifiers are more complicated. In some machines, a single erase master oscillator drives slaves for erase and bias for each channel, whilst on others the oscillators are linked together to synchronize their frequency. This is essential if beats are to be avoided between oscillators running at different frequencies. Interlocking systems for multitrack sel-sync operations need to be very complex to allow dropping in and out of tracks at will. Crosstalk in the record head should be carefully examined for any particular application, for this can be a serious problem—in the production of 8-track 25·4 mm copy masters for high speed tape duplication, for example. It is probable that some of the crosstalk associated with stereo 8-track cartridges can be blamed on the 25·4 mm copy masters. It is advisable to record such copy masters only one stereo pair at a time, and in the same configuration as on the cartridge, so that crosstalk will be preserved.

Battery-operated portable recorders
Most studios are asked to make mobile recordings, which are fairly short but which must be made to the highest standard. Some studios refer to them as quickies and they include the recording of brief interviews, commercials, conferences, meetings, and very high quality sound effects. Sometimes a classical music artist will ask for his or her concert to be recorded on location cheaply, thus involving only one engineer. It is convenient in most of these circumstances to use a battery-operated recorder of the highest calibre such as the Nagra (IV-S) and the Stellavox (SP7 and SM7). The Stellavox has been specifically designed for use in the field at one chosen speed and head blocks can be supplied with all the built-in equalization, etc., thus making it necessary to purchase several head blocks, if more than a single speed is required. On the other hand the Nagra, though heavier, provides more facilities. Its microphone inputs can accommodate almost every type of microphone normally used in studios, since several switchable forms of phantom powering are provided. A modification is available which will allow increased gain on capacitor microphones for speech recording and, of the many accessories available, the most useful include NAB spool adapter (Fig. 9.5), line in and line out modules and a Dolby noise reduction adapter, allowing interconnection with Dolby A361 units. Both machines use rechargeable internal batteries, but these can be replaced in an emergency by ordinary alkaline types. The recorders include peak programme meters and monitoring facilities for use with headphones or an external monitor amplifier. Both of them can also be provided with external mixers, which can be interconnected with the high level input circuitry. These machines have remarkably low wow and flutter figures of the order of 0·025% peak weighted DIN. For film recording, the machines can be provided with an independent pilot track for synchronization with a film camera. Naturally there are a few

snags in the operation of portable machines and these include restricted recording time and an exceptionally slow wind-on speed. Furthermore, both manufacturers recommend a user to set up the machine with one brand of tape, and this must be chosen very carefully so that the best results can be obtained. Naturally battery recorders are not as robust as large mains types, so great care must be taken in their use. The entire tape transport

Fig. 9.5
Nagra IV-S portable recorder, with the special large NAB spool adapter in use

should be regularly maintained and the capstan pressure wheel should never be left in contact with the capstan when the machine is not in operation. Miniaturization is extremely expensive, and both machines are very costly, but their very compactness and comprehensive facilities can save many hours of setting up time on simple mobile sessions.

Another machine which has been popular for semi-professional work over the years is the Uher, used by many broadcasting organizations and studios requiring an ultra-lightweight machine, recording to a fair standard. The Uher can accommodate only up to 145 mm reels and the highest speed is only 19 cm/sec. The lead/acid batteries normally sold with the Uher do not appear to last very long and should always be stored in a fully charged state. The more expensive nickel cadmium batteries are much more reliable, will last longer and can be stored in almost any state except completely flat. A flat battery must always be recharged as soon as possible to prevent ir-reparable damage. The speed stability of the Uher may not be sufficient for serious music recording, but the machine's fairly modest price makes it an attractive choice for location speech recording.

Remote and automatic controls

Most machines can be remotely controlled and such equipment should, if possible, operate all normal functions. Many studios have remote facilities incorporated in the control desk. Some machines, such as the Stüder A80, even have a remote tape position indicator. In these days of improving efficiency, remote operation can frequently free an engineer for another job and thus the remote control system can pay for itself comparatively quickly. Some machines can have an external oscillator plugged in to provide a variable speed control for special effects and pitch correction. For these applications, a very stable audio oscillator is required and its stability should be monitored on a frequency counter while in use. One machine, having a particularly useful facility, is the Revox 700 which has an automatic reverse and restart button. To operate this successfully, a tape has to have an extremely long transparent leader at the beginning, and a short one at the end, and all the leaders between should be completely opaque. When operating this function, the machine will play or record continuously, with short breaks for rewinding, and the entire operation is automatic. It thus provides a useful tape loop facility or continuous playback of programme for testing purposes. Extremely short programmes will operate successfully as well as full NAB reels and thus a few seconds at 38 cm/sec or 3¾ hours at 9·5 cm/sec can be accommodated.

The Stüder A80 can be fitted with a mechanism by which a tape can be played from selected points A to B, and will then rewind to A and repeat. Any function can be switched into this mode, thus providing an exceptionally useful facility which allows, for example, a particular tape being reduced from multitrack to stereo to be worked on continuously and automatically with almost no interruption.

Relays and hum fields

Relays can be extremely reliable, but unfortunately some plug-in types are not. They should be checked regularly, and if they are of open construction the contacts should be very carefully cleaned. Sealed relays are normally more reliable, but it is advisable to keep a stock of one or two spares. Some interlocking systems used on semi-professional recorders have unfortunately been designed with faulty logic and, in one well known example, lightly but quickly depressing the rewind button can actually cause the recorder to commence recording instead of rewinding. One other horrifying fault condition on the same recorder is a momentary switch-on of the record head circuit, when rewind is depressed after playback without first going to stop. It is therefore advisable to check all the logic functions when a new type of machine is being evaluated.

Although the way in which a recorder is connected to the mains should not materially affect its performance, reversing the live and neutral mains connections can sometimes reduce hum induction. This shows that almost certainly the live and neutral wiring routing is split, to fuses or mains switches.

If an improvement results, the mains connections to any mains sockets should be checked to see if they agree with the IEE regulations.

Great care should be taken with earthing and, while recorders having balanced inputs and outputs will not normally give trouble, a check should be made to see if connecting or disconnecting the machine's own earth connection changes any induced hum. Machines having unbalanced inputs or outputs can cause very serious earthing problems and, in many circumstances, annoying radio frequency breakthrough can also be produced. With unbalanced equipment, only one point should be earthed to the mains, otherwise earth loops caused by connecting mixer, monitor amplifier, and tape recorder to the mains earth separately can create extremely serious problems. This can be alleviated by using floating balanced-to-unbalanced transformers as input and output circuits. It is probably best when using these to earth the transformer chassis and screens to the mixer, and connect the recorder independently to an earth. Both the input and output transformers should have their windings connected to the recorder completely floating. If the recorder does not have an earth, it is probably best to earth the input rather than the output, in which case a link should be provided to short the bottom end of the input transformer secondary to the chassis, which should already be connected to the chassis of the mixer.

Input and output sockets

When ordering a machine, state clearly the required sex of input and output sockets, where applicable. Most equipment sold in the UK uses female sockets for inputs and male ones for outputs when XLR type connectors are in use. Unfortunately this convention is theoretically wrong, since the plug or socket providing an AC signal should be female, in accordance with recommended AC practice adopted for higher voltages. However it is probably advisable to adopt the common practice, since interconnection between equipment hired or borrowed from another studio becomes easier. If three-pole jack sockets are used, the Post Office type is to be preferred to the stereo headphone type having a large tip. It is essential not to mix these two types, since a stereo jack inserted into the Post Office type socket can harm the latter as well as frequently making intermittent contact. A Post Office type 301 jack inserted into a stereo type jack socket should not cause any particular harm, but will be intermittent.

Most continental studios employ Tuchel plugs and sockets but, unless these are already in use in any particular studio, the more usual types should be demanded. Some smaller studios have chosen locking DIN sockets, and although these are satisfactory for a semi-permanent installation, they become rather unreliable if connections are continually being changed.

When choosing a recorder for a particular application, do not automatically order from the first manufacturer who provides you with details of his models, for an alternative make may suit you better. Ask for a loan of a demonstration machine for a few days. A machine's specification will certainly not tell you all you need to know. Do not forget to check the availability of spares and the competence of the sevicing staff of the manufacturer or importer, since you may have to call on their help in an emergency. If you are spending thousands of pounds on a recorder you must naturally expect immediate service if the machine breaks down. Remember your rights under the Sales of Goods and Trades Descriptions Acts. If you purchase a machine for a specific job, and on delivery it is not 'fit for the purpose', you have every right to refuse delivery or insist on returning the equipment for full credit or refund.

CHAPTER TEN

Mobile Control Rooms

Richard Swettenham

This chapter will consider all the features of large vehicles for multitrack music recording. The points mentioned may readily be adapted to simpler units for direct stereo recording and broadcasting.

For major multitrack operations there are three types of vehicle to be considered. Firstly the rigid chassis commercial box van, using a standard or custom-built body (Fig. 10.1). This offers the greatest flexibility in positioning of doors and windows. There is usually a decision to be made between the type where the rear wheel arches come above the floor and must be allowed for in the internal layout, or a completely flat floor, which will mean a higher construction on the chassis, and thus possibly some limitation on

Fig. 10.1
Rigid chassis mobile recording vehicle outside the Houses of Parliament, London (courtesy Ferrograph Ltd.) — see also Fig. 10.3

internal height to keep the overall height from the road within the maximum that will pass under average bridges. There is an advantage here in the use of a bus chassis whose floor is much closer to the ground, though this type is considerably more expensive than a standard commercial vehicle.

The second possibility is a trailer caravan. This has the obvious advantage that the caravan itself is not subject to the same licensing requirements as a commercial motor vehicle and can be towed by any suitable means. However, as the body is not as heavily constructed as a commercial vehicle, it will not be practical to apply the same weight and rigidity of acoustic treatment. It should also be realized that, when fully loaded with an average complement of multitrack recording equipment, it will need a somewhat heavier vehicle to tow it than might be expected. However, with a suitable choice of caravan chassis and towing vehicle, this can make an excellent combination, particularly as the towing vehicle is always available as a separate means of transport and to carry additional equipment.

The third possibility is an articulated vehicle (Fig. 10.2), either with a suitable fixed body trailer, or with a platform trailer carrying a standard or modified goods container. In this case it is not absolutely necessary for the recording facility to own the pulling vehicle outright. If the unit is to remain for a week or two at one location, it may well be more economical to hire the prime mover from a haulage firm just for the time required to move the unit from one location to the next. This will also avoid a member of the recording crew having to hold the special qualification for driving articulated vehicles. If the recording unit is installed in an international freight container, there is the additional possibility of unloading it for transport by rail or sea. But this is unlikely to be of great use, as a successful and heavily booked mobile unit will require to move from one job to the next in minimum time.

If the unit is intended mainly for the recording of live performances,

Fig. 10.2
The Rolling Stones articulated mobile recording vehicle (courtesy 3M UK Ltd.)—see also Fig. 10.6

where the results are largely to be judged on subsequent playback, the monitoring conditions in the van may be considered to be less important. In this case, considerable economies are possible in the prime vehicle cost; a large box van or military radio type vehicle may well be large enough to contain simply the equipment and the operators, listening on fairly small loudspeakers supplemented by very high quality headsets.

Sound insulation and internal acoustic treatment
In normal studio design it is possible and convenient to consider sound insulation and sound absorption within the control room as separate problems with separate solutions. However, in a vehicle the two become interlinked. It is not possible within the practical weight of a vehicle body to approach the mass required to give the values of sound insulation at low frequencies that are fairly readily achieved in normal building construction. It must therefore be accepted that a certain amount of low frequencies from the monitor speakers will escape through the walls of the vehicle, and that low frequency noises from outside such as heavy motor traffic and aeroplanes will inevitably be heard within. This factor is turned to advantage, however, in the acoustic treatment of the interior to give an even degree of absorption over the whole audio band.

A typical wall construction for a recording vehicle will be as follows. The outer skin of steel or light alloy riveted to the vertical ribs of the body will be lagged on the inside with a mastic compound to a thickness of at least 3 mm. This will minimize the tendency of the skin panels to resonate at specific frequencies. The cavity formed by the depth of the vertical struts will be filled with rockwool or fibreglass and, on the inside of the struts, a plywood panel of say 10 mm thickness will be fixed. Within this, the internal acoustic treatment proper will consist of 25–50 mm thickness of plastic foam covered with highly porous fabric such as hessian, or with perforated metal or hardboard panels.

Such a treatment shows a fairly even absorption coefficient down to the region of 400 Hz, the frequency at which the absorption falls off being determined by the thickness of the foam and the percentage perforation of the covering material. Below this frequency region, the apparent absorption coefficient due to the flexing of the walls increases until it becomes comparable with the absorption provided by the internal treatment at higher frequencies. The two modes of absorption are matched as far as possible in the design of the walls. If it is found that inadequate absorption in the crossover region gives rise to any apparent boominess, this may be corrected by the application of tuned resonant absorbers to other internal surfaces. The ceiling is probably the most convenient location for these, which will conveniently consist of boxes whose depth and surface perforation determines the precise frequency of effectiveness.

As in a custom-built body the overall height is in the designer's hands, the volume of the roof space is naturally the most convenient location for any kind of special absorptive treatment. It is also a possible location for sections of hard reflective surface, should the high frequency reverberation time be considered too short.

Air conditioning

It follows that a recording vehicle with good sound insulation will also be very effectively insulated against the gain or loss of heat from the exterior. The requirements of sound insulation however prevent natural ventilation. It is therefore very necessary in large vehicles to provide effective air conditioning systems. Fortunately this is not difficult to do, and a number of commercially available air conditioning units for medium-size rooms will be found suitable. In selecting such a unit, the following points should be borne in mind:

1. The unit must be so mounted that its motors do not impart vibration to the vehicle body, and the direct noise of these motors is not audible in the working cabin.

2. Carefully designed sound attenuators must be fitted in the air ducts between the air conditioning unit and the cabin, such that neither the noise of the unit itself nor external sounds entering the air intakes are passed into the cabin.

3. The power supplies and incoming mains circuit breakers must be so rated that they are not overloaded by the starting up current surge of the air conditioning equipment.

4. When cooling is in use, it must be so arranged that the thermostats do not turn on and off the cooling compressor. This would give rise to surges and probably electrical clicks which would be picked up on the equipment. The cooling thermostat must therefore operate a by-pass system which allows the compressor to remain continuously running. The heating thermostat must not turn kilowatts of heating power on and off, for the same reason.

Power supplies and regulation

In the vast majority of cases, at least in European countries, it will be found most convenient to use local mains power supplies, whether or not the mobile vehicle is provided with generators. The decision whether or not to provide generators will be based on the following considerations:

(a) Is the vehicle likely to work in any locations where mains are not available?

(b) Are there likely to be any locations in which the mains supply is rendered unusable by violent voltage fluctuations, serious interference on the mains due to high power thyristor lighting, or the danger of supplies being disconnected during a recording?

(c) Is a safeguard against failure of public supply due to breakdown or industrial action sufficiently worthwhile to justify the cost?

(d) Is it practicable and economical to hire generators from an outside source when necessary?

The rating of a generator must take into account the maximum instantaneous demand of air conditioning, lighting, and the recording equipment. Also, when any equipment is being used that depends for its correct speed upon mains frequency, the frequency accuracy of the generating equipment must be firmly guaranteed by the suppliers. Alternatively, if the power requirement of those machines which are dependent on mains frequency is very small (remembering that capstan motors can often be wired so as to be fed separately from the rest of the recorder), it may be more convenient to drive these motors alone from a low wattage source such as an oscillator and amplifier, and employ a less frequency-accurate source for all other purposes.

Generators are available which can be installed underneath the floor of a commercial vehicle body. If operated in this position, there is a probability of transfer of vibration and noise to the body, therefore provision can be made to lower the units on to the ground below the vehicle while in operation. They may be fitted with small wheels so that they can be pushed a small distance away from the vehicle. Another approach, particularly suitable for articulated vehicles, is to mount the generator on an anti-vibration mounting between the driving cab and the vehicle body. In this position, it is always available for operation and, with a suitable sound absorbing enclosure built around it, the noise level radiated can be surprisingly low. But, for generators of large output, the only satisfactory solution is a trailer towed behind the vehicle. This may then be wheeled to a safe distance to prevent any possible noise interference. A decision may be made whether or not the generator shall be taken on any particular recording date. If left at base, it is then available for other purposes such as emergency supply for a fixed studio.

When mains supplies are used, it must be remembered that any fluctuation of the load in the vehicle will cause a voltage variation due to the resistance of the cable, if it is of any appreciable length. It is therefore highly desirable, where possible, that the recording equipment should be fed along a separate cable from that feeding the air conditioning, lighting and utility points. Another consideration in power cable rating is that if any appreciable amount of power cable is left wound on a drum, rather than in free air, the heating effect at its rated current may be considerable. Therefore, from all points of view, the heavier the gauge of mains cable employed, the better.

For the reasons mentioned above, and also due to variations of loads in the premises from which the supply is being taken, it is to be expected that quite large variations of mains supply voltage will occur. It is therefore most desirable to provide either a servo voltage regulator or a constant voltage transformer to feed the recording equipment. Constant voltage transformers must be carefully chosen to ensure that they do not produce serious changes in the waveform of the corrected supply, which may have undesirable effects on the behaviour of AC motors, or produce harmonic components which may pass through the power supplies of amplifiers. The servo-type voltage regulator, which can maintain constant voltage over fairly wide limits, consists of a variable transformer or 'variac' whose moving contact arm is driven by a small motor, from a servo amplifier which compares the output voltage with a fixed reference. The sensitivity of control can be adjusted to maintain constant output within very fine limits.

In addition to this, where the vehicle may be used on local mains supplies outside the normal range, an additional step-up transformer may be installed.

Fig. 10.3
Interior view of the vehicle shown in Fig. 10.1 with sideways mounted control desk and even incorporating a small talks studio

For general purposes this may be an auto transformer but, if possible, the equipment should be fed through a double wound transformer with an electrostatic screen, which has the additional advantage of being a very effective protection against interference pulses coming along the mains supply. The individual power circuits within the vehicle are best fed through separate over-current circuit breakers which, if they are accidentally tripped, may be immediately restored by hand.

Provision will also be made for a mains-operated battery charger, which is on whenever the vehicle is connected to the mains. This will charge a battery to operate the internal low voltage lighting in the working cabin and cable compartment, and also to operate power driven cable drums if fitted. Battery powered outlets for low voltage soldering irons etc. are also useful. It may also be arranged for the charger to give a trickle charge to the vehicle's main battery when the mains are connected.

Interior layout

The positioning of seating and equipment is dictated by the geometry of the vehicle, principally the width restriction of 2·5 metres. Although vehicles have been constructed in which the mixing engineer sits facing across the

Fig. 10.4
The more usual lengthwise arrangement of the control console in a mobile vehicle (courtesy Helios Electronics Ltd. and Island Records)

width of the vehicle (Fig. 10.3), this dictates a very close placement of speakers for stereo, and a listening situation with one's back to the wall is also rather undesirable. Accepting the limitation of width, the preferred listening position is therefore facing lengthways along the centre line of the vehicle (see Fig. 10.4). With typical monitoring loudspeakers, this then gives a distance of about 1·8 metres between speaker cones and an optimum listening distance from speaker to mixing engineer's head of 2·5 to 3 metres.

The area between the console and the speakers is not suitable for listening because of an exaggerated stereo spread and possibly an excessive sound level. This area therefore appears to be rather wasted, and the solution adopted in some vehicles is to raise the floor level over this area so that cable drums or storage can be accommodated beneath.

Control console design for mobile recording varies little from current studio practice except in the need to conserve space. The current requirement for up to 32 input channels in a console mounted across the width of the vehicle, and preserving the possibility of access to the area in front of the speakers for storing loose equipment in transit, means that the main area in front of the operator cannot carry very much besides the actual input channels and master controls, all auxiliaries being located in vertical panels mounted against the side of the vehicle and having minimum depth (Fig. 10.5).

Fig. 10.5
Complex console and vertical auxiliaries panels before installing in vehicle (courtesy Helios Electronics Ltd. and La Maison Rouge)

Fig. 10.6
Interior view of the vehicle shown in Fig. 10.2 with Helios desk, 3M Mincom 24-track and 2-track recorders (a 16-track model is also installed), Revox A77 recorder and Altec 604 8G monitors

Multitrack recorders are unavoidably of the standard studio console construction at present and therefore occupy considerable floor space. In a number of recent mobiles, the multitrack machine has been placed immediately to the side of the operator, to give ease of access for tape changing. However, as it is now becoming very common practice for all multitrack machines to be remotely controlled and to have positional readouts at the console, this now seems wasteful. Positioning the main multitrack machine forward of the console, between the loudspeakers, makes use of space which may not otherwise be used. The mixing engineer also has a better view of the meters on the recorder, and it is no difficulty for a second operator to go forward to the machine when a rapid tape change is required. Stereo tape recorders, and all other such equipment, will be mounted in vertical racks wherever possible. These will be of minimum depth and, because rear access for maintenance is clearly impossible, will be arranged with swivelling front sections.

New facilities
Communication facilities, while not approaching the complexity of television, will be more comprehensive than in the average studio. Circuits will

be included for two-way communication with operators outside the vehicle and, for example, a separate video recording vehicle. One of these intercom circuits may pass through a transceiver for communication with staff carrying walkie-talkie sets. Individual line sending amplifiers with separate gain controls will be provided for feeding programme to various destinations. These may be fed from any of the outputs of the desk, including echo sends and auxiliaries. Provision may also be made for a second multitrack recorder, fed in parallel with the first (see Fig. 10.6) for follow on and standby operation at live performances, though the second recorder may not be carried on board at all times.

An additional facility may be provided in the control desk whereby the individual microphone signals, having been amplified to line level, are then fed out again separately on a multicore connector to feed an amplification mixer, which may be relatively simple and located in the driving cab of the recording van or elsewhere. These signals may be taken off before or after the equalization set up by the recording engineer, but are independent of the settings of the faders in the control desk.

Microphone boxes

In order to minimize setting up time, individual microphone cables run out from the van have largely been superseded by multicore cables typically having ten or more separately screened microphone pairs. At the stage end of the multicore cable, stage floor boxes are provided which carry individual sockets for the microphone leads (Fig. 10.7). The leads from each microphone head need therefore be only about 5 metres long, to reach the box which is placed in the centre of the stage. Phantom power for capacitor microphones will be fed along the main cable from the van, so that individual power supply units will not be necessary.

To cover the many occasions on which microphone feeds must be taken off for sound amplification as well as recording, thus avoiding double miking of artists, each microphone inlet in the stage box has in parallel with it an isolating transformer and pad, or sometimes an isolating buffer amplifier, which leads to an additional output socket feeding to the stage amplification equipment at microphone level. For recording session purposes, there will be a further stage box provided with a talkback speaker, signal lights and sockets feeding signals to headsets and self-amplified studio playback loudspeakers.

Cables and drums

Connection between the stage boxes and their cables will be made by multiway plugs. For maximum robustness, these should preferably be of circular

Fig. 10.7
Stage floor box with socket for multicore cable from the vehicle and individual XLR sockets for the microphone cables

type with bayonet locking rather than screw thread connections. When handling the cables, care must be taken that the end connectors, however robust they may seem, are not dropped on the floor or dragged round sharp corners within buildings. It is better to return to the van carrying the un-coupled end of the cable and then wind it in on the drum, rather than to wind in the cable leaving its connector to trail along the ground. Cable connector protectors may be made by mounting a dummy receptacle on a large circular piece of wood, for example, so that the connector itself will not come in contact with the ground if trailed along.

At the van end, the cables will be wound on drums which may be rotated directly by hand or provided with electric wind-in motors. Such motors will normally be battery operated, so that the mains supply cable itself can be wound in after disconnection. The van end of the multicore cable will norm-ally be captive to the drum and appear on a socket on the side of the drum. Having paid out the required amount of cable, the drum will be locked against further accidental pulling, and a short linking cable will then be plugged into the drum to connect the circuits to the interior of the vehicle.

Where space permits, the drums will be so located that the winding-in operation can be performed from within the vehicle, or under a raised flap or awning. The operator will then be protected from bad weather while winding in and can clean the cables with a cloth as they are taken up on the drums.

The very high cost of multicore cables makes it imperative that they should be handled with great care on paying out and winding in. It is desirable that, when the cables have been paid out, the door to the connection compartment can be locked with the cables passing through in such a way that the connections cannot be interfered with by anyone outside the vehicle.

Non-technical facilities
Beyond the purely functional aspects of a vehicle of this type, the comfort of producers and engineers (often working very long hours in remote locations) must be a factor in the quality of the product. In a recent vehicle designed by the author, it was considered worthwhile to provide as well as possible for the needs of the crew and clients within the space available. We therefore included a washroom with a completely self-contained flushing toilet, wash basin with hot and cold water, and mirrors. There is a galley fitted with a butane gas fired cooking stove for preparing simple meals, a washing up sink, a large capacity electric coffee maker, and a small refrigerator. Finally, in the entrance lobby, there is a small bench with power points for the driver and maintenance engineer to do small repairs while work is in progress.

CHAPTER ELEVEN

Equipment Alignment

Angus McKenzie

When the first professional tape recorders started to be used a few years after the end of the 1939–45 war, engineers tended to line up the record and replay amplifiers rather at random, when seeking to obtain a flat overall response. No accurate test tapes were available and to get reasonable reproduction it was necessary to play back tapes on the machine on which they had been recorded. If they were played on other machines, external equalizers were frequently used to modify the response, so that the tape sounded about right in the opinion of the engineer concerned. For this reason, many of the earliest tape recordings made on machines such as the EMI BTR1, the RGD, and the Philips Magnetophon varied greatly in quality. It was soon realized that to achieve correct interchange of tapes a fixed replay equalization for all professional tape machines would have to be agreed. The early CCIR committee agreed on one set of replay curves for the various speeds while, unfortunately, the NARTB (NAB) in America agreed independently on a different set, thus starting the confusion which still exists today.

EMI at Hayes, BASF in Ludwigshaven and Agfa in Leverkusen all began making test tapes to the European agreed standards, which were at the time adopted by all European broadcasting organizations and most studios. Other British recording organizations, particularly those who had imported American recording equipment, standardized on the American NAB curve, test tapes for which were first produced by Ampex, and then by some other American manufacturers as well.

Before discussing lining-up procedures, it is important to understand the precise differences between the various replay equalizations in current use, and also the complementary equalization necessary in the recording amplifier. The effects of changing the amount of bias driven through the record head along with the audio signal need also to be described.

The replay head and amplifier
Because a replay head is in effect a modified AC current generator in series

with its inductance, the output voltage across the head varies approximately in proportion to frequency within the audio range. At low frequencies, therefore, the head gives an extremely low output voltage, but from a very low source impedance, whereas at high frequencies it gives a relatively much higher output, but from a high source impedance. It is necessary for the replay amplifier to correct for this differential, and therefore all replay amplifiers have an inherent 6 dB per octave bass lift, rolling off at the extreme bass end to prevent transistor flicker noise from causing problems. Towards the high frequency end, the 6 dB per octave slope is terminated at various frequencies dependent upon the characteristic chosen, allowing the response to become approximately flat. The point below which the lower bass frequencies are rolled off is known as the bass time constant, the exact figure quoted corresponding to the frequency at which the response falls 3 dB below the pure 6 dB per octave bass boost curve. Similarly, the high frequency time constant corresponds to the frequency at which the response rises 3 dB above the same line. Figure 11.1 shows the theoretical curves for the usual replay characteristics employed by studios at 19, 38, and 76 cm/sec.

To allow for variations in the performance of replay heads, most professional recorders have replay equalization pre-set controls. At the high frequency end, they may simply alter the high frequency time constant position, or alter the treble boost applied in addition to a fixed replay equalization. Whilst the latter will in general control the 15 kHz response with very little change at 5 kHz, the former alters the entire high frequency response by raising or lowering a shelf. Some machines also have pre-sets for adjusting the bass response, so that head to tape contour effects may be corrected. Pre-set level controls, frequently supplied to control the gain for different speeds, allow any reasonable output level from the recorder to be attained for specific flux levels on a tape. Most machines also have a replay amplifier bias trap. This tunes out any break-through of bias from the record circuit. This rejection of bias in the replay amplifier is most important if accurate lining up of the recorder is carried out at low levels, as is necessary at lower tape speeds.

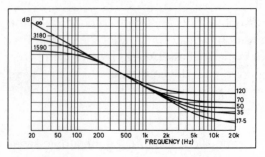

Fig. 11.1
Theoretical curves for the tape replay characteristics in current use

Since the replay head acts as an inductance, it is tuned by the capacity of the lead connecting it to the replay amplifier. Modern recorders running at real time speeds should have the replay head circuit resonating at between 25 kHz and 70 kHz; some older machines used head resonance to improve the high frequency end of the audio range, since early replay heads had greatly inferior gaps to those on modern machines. This resonant frequency should always be at least an octave below the bias frequency, to simplify the design of bias rejection filters. Replay bias rejection circuits should be adjusted by rotating the slug in the inductance component of the circuit where applicable for minimum bias break-through. This can be done easily by using an oscilloscope on the output of the machine to check that any bias break-through present is being reduced to a minimum.

Replay head adjustment

Most replay heads can be adjusted in several planes. Although the most important adjustment is azimuth (alignment of the gap at 90° to the direction of tape travel), several other adjustments are also important. For example, the head must be positioned in the horizontal plane so that the tape passes over the head at the correct approach and recede angles relative to the gap at the front of the head. (These angles should be as near as possible identical on most types of head.) Facilities are usually provided to rotate the head in the horizontal plane for such adjustment, as well as in both vertical planes for azimuth and vertical (fore and aft) tilt. This latter angle, if not adjusted correctly, will cause excessive wear at the top or bottom of the head gap. Height adjustment is also usually provided, to make the head present itself to the tape at exactly the right height, thus scanning the recorded tracks with minimum crosstalk and maximum signal-to-noise ratio.

Mumetal shields are frequently provided in one form or another, to shield the replay head from external magnetic fields such as those from the motors and mains transformers. The screen should be adjusted to give minimum hum when the machine is set to replay with the motors running but, if possible, with no tape present. Care should be taken to ensure that the mumetal screen does not touch the tape during normal running. Note that the hum level may well increase on some machines when the transport mechanism is stopped. This shows that a certain amount of hum bucking is performed by the mumetal shield when the motors are running. Conversely, if the shield is mistakenly adjusted for minimum hum with the motors not running, the recorder may well have an inferior hum level when playing back.

For setting replay head height, BASF make a useful stereo test tape having recordings running alternately on each track. A band of 1 kHz is also recorded along the centre of the tape only. This band should be inaudible on two-track, wide guard band replay heads, and should be only barely audible on narrow guard band stereo heads. Any break-through of the tone should be adjusted so that it is at an identical minimum on both tracks. The same tape also includes a band of white noise and this can be used to adjust the azimuth very rapidly by ear. For really accurate azimuth adjustment, however, particularly at low speeds, it is probably better to use an oscilloscope, and compare the precise phasing between the two channel outputs at middle frequencies. This adjustment can of course be performed at high frequencies, but heads sometimes have unequal gap widths on different tracks and thus require different amounts of replay equalization. Then variable high frequency phase shift may give misleading results when azimuthing by this method. It is probably better to accept errors of phase shift at 15 kHz, with good phase response up to 8 kHz, than have 10–15 kHz reasonably correct while 8 kHz and downwards is incorrect. If any phasing inconsistencies are noticeable when replaying full-track test tapes, careful examination of the replay head may well reveal uneven wear. Head replacement is then the best cure.

Multitrack replay heads
Recorders having four or more replay tracks will almost always present phasing problems which become increasingly noticeable as the number of tracks is increased: 16 and 24-track recorders using 50·8 mm width tape are best azimuthed by observing the outputs of the two outside tracks. The inner tracks can then be checked against the outer ones to make sure that the best compromise has been reached. Test tapes for multitrack recorders are available in two forms from a number of manufacturers. The first type are recorded across the full width of the tape, and are therefore not suitable for very accurate alignment of head height. At very low frequencies, too, and particularly at high tape speeds, some extra induction into each replay track can be produced by parts of the recording on each side of the desired track. A bass rise therefore occurs but should be corrected for only with great care. This is known as the 'fringe effect' and of course occurs on a full-track test tape with a stereo head, etc.

It is usually better to use the second type of multitrack test tape, which has no recording between the different tracks. The magnetization of the different tracks of this test tape may not be quite so consistent at high frequencies, because of the difficulty of aligning the different vertical gaps in the manufacture of the record head. The tape will, however, permit very accurate vertical alignment, and will not present the bass boost problems produced by full-track tapes. Careful alignment of replay heads on any type of machine will produce much better quality from tapes produced by other studios.

The record amplifier

The record amplifier has to convert the voltage at the line input into a current through the record head, such that the replay output using the chosen type of tape, correctly biased, will have as flat a frequency response as possible. The flux produced on the tape by the record head is approximately proportional to the current flowing through it. The inductance of the record head causes it to have a higher impedance at high frequencies, as already explained in connection with the replay head. To produce a constant current through the record head at all frequencies, the record amplifier has to have an output impedance appreciably higher than that of the record head at the highest audio frequency. The correct application of supersonic bias to the record head allows the magnetic particles on the tape to accept the audio part of the magnetic field with minimum distortion compatible with a good tape response at high frequencies. The bias current unfortunately has the side effect of partially erasing high frequencies as the magnetic particles are drawn away from the record gap. Although the replay equalization curve partly offsets this high frequency loss, and indeed almost totally offsets it at the 76 cm/sec speed, nevertheless a degree of pre-emphasis is necessary in the record amplifier to gain a flat overall response. At the higher speeds of 38 and 76 cm/sec the record equalizer may actually have to reduce high frequencies slightly, and this must be borne in mind in design. At lower tape speeds, a fair amount of high frequency pre-emphasis is necessary, but usually not more than a 6 dB per octave boost. It is usually only necessary to vary the turnover point of the curve for the different speeds, and many machines have separate equalizers for each speed. In general, thinner tapes require slightly less bias for optimum performance, and often less equalization. A machine set up for standard play tape, therefore, will usually have a slightly higher boost when LP tape is used without re-equalization. A record gain control is always provided to allow a specific input level to be set to correspond to a given flux level on the tape, which should therefore play back at the same level out of the machine. It is an advantage to have separate record level controls for different speeds, to allow rapid changing of speed, for example when high quality copies are required at different speeds.

Although the professional DIN (CCIR) European replay curves do not require bass pre-emphasis on record, the American NAB curves do. Some 3 dB bass boost at 50 Hz and 7 dB at 25 Hz is required for a flat overall NAB response, and therefore the bass end should be carefully checked in addition to the high frequency end. Although DIN do recognize the NAB recording curve for semi-professional and amateur use at 19 cm/sec, many organizations use the so-called 19H domestic DIN curve for professional work, since the performance of modern tapes is so good at high frequencies that the decreased high frequency noise level produced by this curve is not seriously offset by high-frequency squashing.

Record equalization should be attempted only after the replay amplifiers have been checked and biasing has been correctly set. Equalization can be carried out for 38 and 76 cm/sec at any convenient level up to Ampex operating level for NAB machines, or 8 dB below the DIN reference level of 320 nWb/m for DIN/IEC equalized machines. Equalization should not be attempted at higher levels since a degree of very-high-frequency squash may be noticeable which, if corrected, would cause a treble boost at lower levels to be apparent. At 19 cm/sec and 9·5 cm/sec, equalization is best done at no higher than 20 dB below DIN level, or 16 dB below Ampex operating level, although some tapes will give a flat power response at, say, 10 dB below Ampex operating level. Care should be taken to ensure that the level chosen for equalization is well above any level of bias break-through in the output of the replay amplifier. If an extreme top roll-off is apparent at lower speeds, it is better to have the response reasonably flat at 10 kHz rather than boost it to a considerable degree below this frequency in the desire to have a good response at 15 kHz.

Bias and erase circuits
The bias necessary for the recording process is almost always obtained directly from the erase oscillators. On some machines the bias frequency is an odd harmonic of the erase frequency, allowing a lower erase frequency in the region of 50 kHz to be chosen to give very good erasing action. Placing the bias at a much higher frequency will tend not to produce any serious beats with harmonics of audio frequencies generated in the record amplifier. It is necessary for the bias waveform to have as low even harmonic distortion as possible, to reduce modulation noise and background hiss on the tape. Odd harmonic distortion of the bias is of no consequence, however, since all that is required is that the area of the bias waveform above zero current through the record head must equal the area below it. A perfect square wave, for example (having no even harmonics), is perfectly reasonable for biasing, although impracticable! Some erase and bias oscillators have a symmetry control to allow reduction of even harmonics to a minimum. This can be adjusted by carefully listening to the background noise of the tape on replay during the biasing process. It is best made symmetrical by checking the bias distortion with a high-frequency wave analyzer. Once set, it is not

likely to shift in a correctly designed modern oscillator, but new machines should always be checked after delivery.

The bias current through the record head is usually adjusted by means of pre-set trimmer capacitors or variable series resistors. The bias current path should always present a high impedance to audio frequencies, so that even high frequencies from the record amplifier do not produce crosstalk on to other channels. Since the bias frequency is usually between five and ten times the highest audio frequency that has to be recorded, this is easily done with a low value series capacitor in the bias feed. It is more difficult, though, to keep the bias frequency from blocking the output circuits of the record amplifier, since the bias current through the record head is always very much greater than any audio current. A tunable bias trap is usually located in the output feed circuit of the record amplifier, and this should be adjusted so that the lowest possible HF bias voltage is present on the output of the record amplifier itself. A serious bias break-through at this point can sometimes be passed back through a feedback circuit to an earlier point in the record amplifier and therefore cause serious blocking. This can result in a limitation of output level from the amplifier and, in some serious cases, severe parasitics and distortion can arise at all levels. The bias and erase frequency itself is normally best left untouched, as this can only be set accurately with a frequency counter and is seldom misaligned by the manufacturer.

Setting bias level
The adjustment of bias through the record head is one of the most critical, but necessary, adjustments that have to be regularly made to recorders. The precise setting is always a compromise between optimum performance of the tape at low and high frequencies, and minimum modulation noise and distortion. The adjustment of bias should always be carried out independently from record equalization, and should always be completed before equalization is attempted. It should be stressed that bias adjustment should not be used as a quick form of record equalization, though the response can vary very noticeably at the high frequency end when the bias current is changed.

There are many different effective ways of setting bias current, most of which are reasonably accurate; a fair compromise, when the specific characteristics of the recorder are not well known to the engineer, is to record a 1 kHz tone at approximately 10 dB below nominal peak recording level. The replay level of the recording should be watched critically as the bias current is increased from a low level, while maintaining constant record amplifier gain. As the bias current is increased, the tape output level will also increase up to a maximum. If the bias current is increased further, the output will begin to drop. The correct biasing point on professional machines will normally be when the bias current is slightly in excess of that necessary to achieve maximum tape output for a given input. The output at 1 kHz should have dropped back, i.e. overdropped, approximately 0·25 dB for 19 cm/sec, 0·75 dB for 38 cm/sec and 1·25 dB for 76 cm/sec. Different tapes, however, will be found to have different bias requirements, and manufacturers' recommendations for biasing will usually be found to be reasonably correct.

As the bias level is increased, incidentally, the erasing effect of the bias field produced at the record gap becomes greater, and high frequencies (short wavelengths) are therefore subject to more and more partial erasure. Figure 11.2 shows the changes of sensitivity of a professional tape on a recorder running at 19 cm/sec recording at different bias levels and different frequencies. It will be seen that the effect of bias is far more marked at 15 kHz

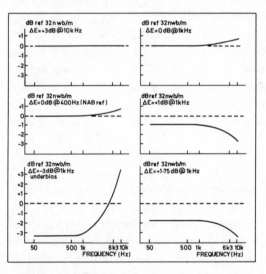

Fig. 11.2
Showing the change of sensitivity, particularly at high frequencies, at different bias levels compared with the value established by overbiasing for a 3 dB drop at 10 kHz

than at 5 kHz, and even more so than at much lower frequencies. Bias setting will also affect the maximum output available from the tape at different frequencies. If the lowest possible distortion is required at middle and low frequencies, without regard to high frequency squashing, a slightly higher bias setting than normal will be beneficial. If, however, the best possible transient power response is required at the high frequency end, then a slightly lower bias setting can be chosen. Figure 11.3 shows the maximum output curve of a typical professional tape at different frequencies at three different bias settings. Remember that, if you choose a very high frequency power response to achieve superb transient recording, it may well be difficult to transfer your recordings to disc without tracking distortion on playback. The performance of some cassette tapes shows how severely this type of tape is affected by over-biasing, since most ferric oxide cassette tapes have relatively poor high frequency performance, particularly when high bias settings have been chosen to give low distortion at middle frequencies.

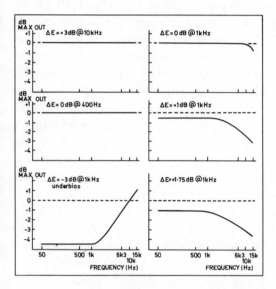

Fig. 11.3
Showing the maximum output level curve of a typical tape at three different bias settings

Many engineers prefer to set bias with an input frequency of 10 kHz. The precise overdrop should lie between 2·5 dB and 4 dB at higher speeds, depending on the record gap, and between 3 dB and 5 dB at lower speeds. Wider gap record heads will normally permit better penetration of the magnetic flux into the oxide coating, whereas finer gap heads will not necessarily record deep into a thick oxide tape. There have been many cases where studios have incorrectly used a thick oxide tape on machines having narrow record gaps more suited to the more usual types of coating. It is not possible to achieve the full performance capability of thick oxide tapes on narrow gap machines. Furthermore, thick oxide standard play tapes may well be excellent at high tape speeds, but relatively poor at slower speeds. It is therefore worth considering the use of different tapes at different speeds, bearing in mind also that copy tapes made at 19 cm/sec may be played back by the client on a semi-professional machine whose heads might become severely worn by continual playing of thick oxide tapes.

Setting up the record head

Adjustments of the record head are normally much more difficult than those for the replay head, since the effect of such adjustments can be ascertained only by monitoring from the replay head. Some machines have the record and replay head wiring fitted with plugs which allow the record head to be plugged in to the replay amplifier. This technique allows much more accurate positioning and, even if plugs are not provided, it is worth wiring the record head in to the replay circuit temporarily. However, no response or level adjustments should be made to the replay amplifier. The outputs should be monitored to obtain the correct head height, azimuth, and output at high frequencies for different tape wrap round paths. Adjustments should be made in the same way as for the replay head. Of course the tests become easier if the record head is fitted with a sel-sync control, allowing tracks on the record head to be switched through to replay. The correct positioning of the record tracks is most important when there is frequent interchange of tapes between studios. Again, if Dolby noise reduction is employed, careless adjustment of the record head may well result in full playback levels not being achieved on other equipment. When adjusting the tape wrap round path over the record head, it should be remembered that too much wrap may exert excessive pressure between the oxide and the record gap. This will create additional wear of the head, often uneven if the tilt angle is not exactly right, and it can also introduce slightly more bias hiss. Scrape flutter can also be introduced by too much tension over the head, and many machines have anti-scrape flutter rollers to prevent longitudinal vibrations of the tape near the head. Any undue wear on the bearings of the rollers can introduce more normal flutter than the scrape flutter that they are intended to remove, however. The tape should barely touch the surface of the roller when in record or replay.

Some semi-professional machines use pressure pads on some or all of the heads. Although this improves the head to tape contact, it invariably introduces scrape flutter and, on some tapes, can create severe modulation noise effects.

The erase head

Erase heads are normally provided with either a full-track gap or separate gaps erasing on different tracks of the tape. They usually have a substantially lower inductance than record or replay heads, and a very considerable erase current passes through them. The adjustment of the erase head is normally not as critical as that of the record head, but it is nevertheless worthwhile checking that virtually perfect erasing action is performed on a tape recorded at a very high level. Some types of professional tape require extremely high erasing flux and, although they may appear to be erased whilst monitoring the replay head output, traces of the original recording may come through after storage. I have even known cases where the application of a small bias current will actually bring back traces of an original recording.

The erase head is usually designed to be part of the erase oscillator's tuned circuit. If the head is replaced at any time, this should be borne in mind. A new head may have a slightly different inductance and so alter the erase, and therefore bias, frequency. To avoid resetting the record and replay bias traps, it is better to observe the break-through of bias from the replay amplifier and alter the erase oscillator frequency by adjusting the slug in the inductance or transformer for the frequency giving maximum replay rejection. Although it is not normally necessary to change an erase head for magnetic performance reasons as the head wears, replacement is desirable at intervals to avoid flats worn across the front of the head, since their edges can produce shedding or scoring of the oxide coating. It is frequently overlooked, but can be a cause of inexplicable drop-outs or uneven tape path across other heads. Again the best way of adjusting the height of a multi-track erase head is to connect two adjacent tracks to replay and play back a multitrack test tape. Azimuth is not particularly important, though erase efficiency is better when the azimuth is reasonably correct. High frequencies will be almost completely absent in the replay, however, since the erase gap is normally very wide.

Noise reduction systems

Most noise reduction systems tend to exaggerate any response or level errors present in a tape recorder. The Dolby system, for example, can be particularly sensitive to response errors above 5 kHz since, in certain parts of the dynamic range, an error of 1 dB can be exaggerated to as much as 3 dB. Although this may not appear serious, the ear can easily hear a shelf boost of 2 or 3 dB and so the importance of accurate alignment cannot be overstated. Since Dolby level corresponds to Ampex operating level, test tapes for NAB machines should have their operating level sections brought back to read 0 VU on the recorder, and the replay amplifiers should give an output to the Dolby units such that, when set to replay, they read Dolby level. DIN test tapes (320 nWb/m) should be played back to read DIN level on Dolby equipment. The tape recorder meter sensitivities should then be set as desired. For recording, the Dolby level output signal should be recorded via tape so that, when played back, the level corresponds to the Dolby level indication which, on older A301 units, corresponds to the NAB mark. The pulsating Dolby level tone which should be present on all recent Dolby processed tapes should, of course, signify Dolby level and not DIN level. Incidentally, A301 units can be fitted with a built-in Dolby tone oscillator, but to avoid confusion they should always be set up for the NAB mark.

Remember that, whatever type of record or playback heads are used, Dolby level at the beginning of any tape, should be brought up on replay to the Dolby level indication. This may well appear obvious, but confusion can arise when a Dolby processed recording, made with a record head having a wide guardband between tracks, is played back on another machine having a narrow guardband replay head. If the original recording was made to the correct Dolby flux level, the replay level on the narrow guardband machine can be as much as 2·8 dB down, which must be corrected on replay. For this reason, many studios are now standardizing on narrow guardband record and wide guardband replay for stereo recordings on 6·3 mm ($\frac{1}{4}$-inch) machines. This completely obviates any problems when tapes are played back elsewhere, or other studio's tapes are played back on the machine. DBX and Burwen noise reduction systems have their own problems.

Guides and rollers

Many machines have adjustable tape guides, some of which may be designed to rotate whilst the tape is passing over them. Fixed guides are often supplied with a screw allowing them to be rotated and, if this is done occasionally, flats where the tape passes across them should not develop. Attention to this type of adjustment, or even occasional complete replacement of guides, will avoid tendencies to oxide shedding and scoring.

Tape speed

The 1 kHz tone at the beginning of BASF and Agfa professional test tapes is normally recorded to close frequency accuracy. It is usually guaranteed to be within ±0·2% (although in practice I have found that the tolerance is ±0·1%). A frequency counter should be employed, driven by the output of the replay channel so that the speed of the tape recorder can be accurately set. Unfortunately, some machines do not have a speed adjustment, and yet I have known professional recorders with speed errors of up to 1·5%. It is most important to have the speed of the recorder accurately set since, if two machines are used on a recording session and it is necessary to edit tapes between them, they must be running at very close to the same speed. Professional tolerances of ±0·25% or better can usually be tolerated, but two machines 1% apart in speed will cause severe problems in editing, particularly for musicians having perfect pitch. Some machines will cause different thicknesses of tape to run at very slightly different speeds through the capstan/pressure idler assembly. Many a slight pitch inconsistency has been tracked down to this phenomenon. It usually arises when two machines are compared in which the capstans make contact on opposite sides of the tape. The machines may run at the same speed with standard play tape, but slightly different speeds with thinner tapes.

The use of test tapes

Before attempting to replay any test tape, it is always advisable to demag-netize all the heads and parts of the tape transport which are ferro-magnetic. Remember to keep the demagnetizing tool switched on until it is drawn away from the parts being demagnetized. Note also that ferrite heads in general require a higher demagnetization flux. The small hand-type defluxers are often not good enough. One should never let the defluxer actually touch the heads, since the 50 or 60 Hz alternating field can cause considerable vibration and might scratch the head or give problems in shifting azimuth etc. Care should be taken, incidentally, to keep any bulk erasers or demagnetizers well away from moving-coil type meters on the front of the recorder, since their sensitivity could be lowered by slight demagnetizing of their magnets.

The level at the beginning of a test tape is defined by the manufacturer, and tapes for 19, 38, and 76 cm/sec have 185, 200, 320, or 510 nWb/m as their stated flux level. NAB machines are usually set up with tapes of American origin, though most continental test tape manufacturers produce tapes for the NAB curves. McKnight, formerly of Ampex, established an Ampex operating level (which is also recognized as Dolby level) and, although this was originally claimed to be 200 nWb/m, it has been remeasured in the last few years, and is now quoted as 185 nWb/m. Thus an error of 0·8 dB is likely to be noticed when comparing tapes of different American origin. BASF and Agfa produce NAB test tapes, but a flux of 320 nWb/m has been established on these, which is most confusing. It has often led to NAB standardized machines being set up to the wrong replay level on the internal VU meters. Continental stereo test tapes usually contain a higher reference level still, namely 510 nWb/m. This level is some 4 dB higher in output from two-track replay heads, when compared with the output of full-track con-tinental test tapes. This was originally introduced to encourage users to employ a higher level when recording stereo, compared with mono pro-grammes, so that two-track stereo recordings played back on a full-track mono replay head for mono broadcasts or dubbing would have compatible playback levels.

Test tapes should always be treated with the greatest care and, unless the tape transport is of the highest quality, a test tape should not be stopped on an actual frequency band. They should always be rewound slowly, if possible, and never in contact with the heads. They should be stored at an even temperature and should never be left on a machine whose deck gets warm in use. Although higher speed test tapes should give accurately calibrated playback for a considerable period, lower speed tapes will often lose output at higher frequencies rather quickly, even if every care is taken. I have noted discernible losses at high frequencies on 9·5 cm/sec test tapes for example, after relatively few plays, and so frequent replacement is advisable. In practice it is a good idea to have a routine test tape in use, checked periodically against one kept simply for checking purposes. When any differences are apparent, the routine tape should be discarded and the check tape can become the routine one, a new test tape being purchased as a standard.

Which make of tape?

Standard play tapes are available today in three basically different types— shiny backed, semi-matt backed, and matt backed. Fully matt backed tapes wind and spool very evenly, even on comparatively poor tape transports. They store well and are more rugged than other types. Most engineers find that they are easier to edit without joins being audible but, unfortunately, they tend to have some severe disadvantages. They are inclined to wear heads rather more quickly than the other types and, since multitrack heads are becoming more and more expensive to replace, such a consideration must become economically important. They also tend to have inferior modulation noise characteristics and most of them have a thicker oxide coating, which is unsuitable for use on many semi-professional, let alone amateur, recorders. Tape guides are also inclined to be more quickly worn and I have even come across slight grooving of capstans. Matt backed tapes are not usually polished as much as shiny ones, and any sharp edges in the tape transport seem to produce a tendency to oxide shedding. Shiny backed tapes are much kinder to the tape transport and heads, but some spool rather badly on any but the finest tape transports. A rapidly spooled master, recorded on a shiny backed tape, can easily produce dropouts if ruffled edges are knocked by a hand. For this reason, many companies have now made semi-matt backed tapes which have almost all the assets of shiny and matt backed tapes, but without most of their shortcomings. Although these new tapes are in general a little more expensive, their use is desirable since, in the long run, they will be found to be more satisfactory. As for the differences in magnetic properties between different tapes, note that some tapes will give a better performance overall when used with NAB curves at higher speeds, whereas others are more satisfactory for the DIN or current BSI and CCIR recommended curves. The distortion performance should be compared at middle frequencies as against the squash point at high frequencies. It is also important to relate the maximum output performance against the measured background noise of the tape. Although most modern tapes have a reasonably low print-through performance for speech recording, particularly when noise reduction is not being used, low print tapes should be used when they are likely to be kept for a considerable time. Print-through can often be reduced, incidentally, by periodically playing through master tapes. To encourage the tape to be wound through before playing, thus helping to reduce print-through, it is good practice to store tapes wound end out.

Summing up

To achieve consistent and good results, it will be seen that care taken in lining up the electronics, heads and tape transport is vital. Standardization with currently available test tapes is of extreme importance since compatibility throughout the industry is necessary. It is always advisable to use a recognized standard test tape rather than one copied as a favour, since any errors present on such a copy will be transferred through to any tapes made on the recorder set up with it. Perhaps the most critical adjustments are on machines with eight or more tracks: 25·4 and 50·8 mm (1-inch and 2-inch) test tapes are very expensive, but are most necessary. Remember that, if your tapes sound wrong when a client plays them back at another studio, you may well lose that client, and a reputation gained after a lot of hard work can quickly be lost.

CHAPTER TWELVE

Maintenance

L. G. Harris

As in all industries, the success rate in sound recording largely depends on the ability of the equipment being used to perform satisfactorily with the minimum of breakdown time. Proper maintenance is even more vital in the recording industry since the end product at a studio cannot be stored and then released when breakdowns do occur.

No supplier of studio equipment is foolish enough to guarantee that his equipment will never fail; he usually states that any loss of studio bookings due to breakdowns are not his direct responsibility. Even if he offers to repair equipment, a time lapse of say 24 hours would mean a substantial loss of studio time. Fortunately, most failures of studio equipment do not mean the complete loss of a session as spare equipment can usually be brought into service. However, a breakdown in the middle of a session can be quite upsetting to the artist concerned, even though one is able to correct the trouble fairly quickly.

Basic requirements

A typical maintenance department would consist of at least four engineers, depending on the size of the studio complex, starting with two engineers for the first studio, and one more engineer for every additional studio within the same building. This would be the minimum staff to provide normal maintenance duties; extra staff can also be added in a training capacity.

To carry out a complete maintenance service, it will be necessary to provide a fully equipped workshop. A second workshop can be useful, especially where extra design and prototype work is envisaged. The main workshop should contain plenty of bench area and storage shelving, to cope with all equipment entering for repair and storage, prior to being returned to studio use. Benches should be wired for 240 and 110 volt AC supplies, together with all the necessary types of outlet socket required to feed the studio equipment in use.

Test equipment used by a typical maintenance department would include the following:

Quantity	Description
1	Dual Beam Oscilloscope 10 mV/cm sensitivity
2	Audio Oscillators, Mains and Battery
2	AC Millivoltmeters, Mains and Battery
2	Multimeters AC/DC
2	Bench Type Variable Power Supply Units 0–50 V
1	Insulation Tester (Megger)
1	Wow and Flutter Meter
1	Distortion Measuring Set
1	Resistance/Capacitance Bridge
1	Set of Test Tapes to suit equipment in use
1	Monitor Loudspeaker Unit and Amplifier.

It should be noted that some items of test equipment are battery operated, this being necessary for normal daily alignment checks in the various control rooms. The audio oscillator and AC millivoltmeter are the principal items and a careful check on the battery condition should be made every time these items are used. This is easily done, since most test equipment has a battery check facility built in.

A good selection of general tools should be kept, together with any special tools required for individual pieces of equipment. Recommended spares for all the major items of equipment are best kept in a separate store or in lockable storage cabinets. It is only by experience that one really finds out which items should be held in store.

All the appropriate service documentation and general reference books should be available to maintenance personnel, not locked away in an office. It is also suggested that the main circuit diagrams and alignment procedures should be duplicated and slipped into plastic envelopes for general bench use, with the main manuals as a back up.

Maintenance procedures

Studio maintenance falls into two main categories, 'running maintenance' and 'routine maintenance'. The former takes care of breakdowns and extra alignments as called for by the studio. It should be carried out between recording sessions or, if the nature of the fault necessitates immediate action, as soon as possible. Obviously a thorough knowledge of all the equipment in use should be acquired by all maintenance staff as quickly as possible. This not only saves studio costs in breakdown time, but also gives the client confidence in the studio and its staff.

Routine maintenance should be fitted in when the studio is not booked for recording sessions. This means in theory that all major items of equipment are tested at least once every day or two. Thus one should discover any faults which are liable to develop and observe the alignment of the electronics and also the mechanical side of all recorders and consoles. This planned maintenance gives one the chance of noticing wear patterns prior to possible breakdowns. There is therefore time in hand to obtain any spares needed from the various manufacturers.

Due to the nature of the recording industry, and the fact that studios often operate a 24-hour day, the job of routine maintenance has to be made flexible so as to fit in with studio bookings. However, this does not mean that routine servicing should be put off for longer than absolutely necessary.

The session engineers and tape operational staff will naturally expect maintenance to be carried out at the earliest opportunity, especially when equipment goes faulty in use. They can report faults directly to the maintenance department, where all faults should be listed in a daily faults book or on a serviceability state wall-board, or both. The other method of reporting will be via the general office where, at the end of each session, the tape staff will make up a session work sheet, stating the hours worked and materials used together with any equipment failures, however minor.

This faults list should be passed to the maintenance department as soon as the normal day shift arrives. The daily faults list should always be examined to see if a major item of equipment is in urgent need of attention. As an example: 'Faulty rewind control on the mono machine in Studio 1': 'Faulty transport logic on the 24-track causing tape to snatch on starting in Studio 2'. Obviously the faulty mono machine should be serviced after the 24-track master recorder.

After everyday studio faults have been cleared, or at least reduced so that the only outstanding items are of a minor nature and can safely wait till time permits, the maintenance department then has to attend to the 'faulty equipment' shelf in the workshop. This will invariably have one or two faulty microphones, faulty console modules, headsets, and a host of different plug-in items.

Every effort should be made to keep this faulty equipment shelf as empty as possible. There will be some items for which spares have to be ordered by the maintenance supervisor: the item in question should be packed up with a label stating the spares required and placed on a shelf marked 'Items awaiting spares'.

Logging of faults

Due to the long hours worked, it is very easy to let faults accumulate without being properly logged. This is where a Daily Serviceability Board comes in very useful, as a simple reminder of outstanding faults. A diary of daily breakdowns, etc., also serves to show how some faults develop and the various remedies tried. As some form of shift system will be worked to cover early mornings and late nights, a record of maintenance staff on duty should be noted in the workshop diary.

The paper work created by other departments in the organization should not be overlooked. This is usually handled by the Maintenance Manager, who is responsible for the smooth running of studio maintenance administration. The daily work rota will have to be drawn up according to the individual studio requirements. This he will do by keeping in touch with the general office to check on the times during which the various studios are being used, and plan how routine maintenance can be fitted into the times between bookings.

The ordering of all equipment and spares, together with progress chasing of third-party suppliers, is also his responsibility and he must ensure that all equipment performs to specification. Any new equipment required will obviously be discussed with the studio personnel to determine reasons for the choice of one type of equipment as against another. If there are several studios to equip, it pays to minimize the number of different equipment types and manufacturers. For instance, all the 6·25 mm (¼-inch) tape machines might be bought from one manufacturer. This means that the maintenance staff can become quickly familiar with six machines or more of the same type, and the stocking of spares is much easier.

The same does not necessarily apply to microphones, which might total as many as 50 or 100. One soon realizes that certain engineers prefer to work with certain types of microphone and this means that the number of different types to be stocked will be at least six. Most microphones will do most jobs, but a useful golden rule is that ribbon microphones should never be placed in bass drums or in front of guitar amplifiers. The failure rate of microphones always seems abnormally high on first inspection: something like ten a week is not unusual. When these are checked out in the workshop, on a test rig designed to accommodate all the different types in use, the main troubles will usually be found to be distributed as follows:

20% no faults found; rejected in haste because there was no time to locate the real problem,
50% faults in leads, plugs, or power packs if used,
20% electronic failure, i.e. FETs or other components,
5% physically damaged beyond normal studio maintenance repair,
5% capacitor heads requiring cleaning.

It will be seen that most of the troubles are due to fair wear and tear in a busy environment. The maintenance staff should instruct the operational staff in the best way to handle microphones, which are more expensive and fragile than is often realized. When not in use, they should be returned to a suitable storage cabinet with foam rubber compartments. If one session follows another, then any microphones not needed for the second session should likewise be placed out of the way. All microphones should be fitted with some form of quick release adaptor. This allows speedy and safe fixing on to any microphone stand with the other half of the adaptor. This type of spigot arrangement means that no screwing and unscrewing is needed and this relieves strain on the lead entering the microphone head via the plugs and socket.

Monitor power amplifiers used in the control rooms will also need routine checking, especially if these are valve types, as ageing causes loss of power and possible distortion. As spare power amplifiers should be available, it is possible to test these thoroughly using a dummy load resistance with an oscilloscope across the load to monitor the output waveform. The power output just prior to sine-wave clipping can be measured in terms of the voltage across the load resistance. The signal-to-noise ratio and distortion figures should also be checked and the amplifier labelled as tested O.K., dated and initialled by the engineer involved. Similar procedures should be adopted for all items of studio equipment serviced by maintenance workshop staff.

The manufacturer's specification should be referred to when testing any equipment, especially power amplifiers. Figures which have been obtained in regular tests should be written into the relevant service logs as a means of identifying any discrepancies which might occur.

Connecting leads

Studio leads should be checked whenever time permits. Studio engineers will agree that there is nothing worse than trying to record a full orchestral session with an assortment of intermittent faults in extension leads. These leads are usually made up in 8 metre (25 ft.) lengths of heavy-duty twin screened cable with a three-pin Cannon XLR plug at one end and socket at the other. The correct assembly of these plugs and sockets must be adhered to, as with all forms of cable connectors. Thus, if pin 1 is screen and pins 2 and 3 in descending order of 'hotness' (the usual convention) then this must be maintained throughout the system. As mentioned previously, 50% of all faults in the studio are related to cables and plugs.

A simple test box can be made up to check all types of extension cable. This should be wired up to indicate continuity or open circuit, perhaps using LEDs as indicators. A studio cannot have too many extension leads; these will include microphone leads, mains extension leads and jackfield/patch bay jumper leads. Numerous adaptor leads will also be called for, to match odd makes of guitar or synthesizer into the standard studio sockets.

On the question of guitars and other electrical instruments, many of the amplifiers used by pop groups do not conform to studio standards of electrical safety. For this reason, all the mains outlet sockets in the studio should be individually fused, through trip type circuit breakers, on several circuits around the studio. Isolation transformers should be available for connection between the instruments and the mains, together with 240/110 V step-down transformers for use with 110 V equipment.

All mains outlets in the studio area should be regularly checked, especially adaptor boxes on long extension leads. The earth wiring to all sockets should be checked, and the proper polarity of Neutral and Live wiring. This is easily done with the aid of a test plug, as used by electrical contractors, which usually has a neon lamp to show whether the wiring is correct or not. The practice of running extension mains leads from one studio to feed equipment in another should be avoided as it is possible for different studios to be on different phases of the three-phase supply feeding the building. It is worth checking all flexible mains extension leads daily: it takes only a few minutes and could mean the difference between life and death.

Standby facilities

As most studios are totally dependent on artificial lighting, the possibility of a mains failure with a full studio of up to 100 musicians and staff makes it essential to have a standby emergency lighting system. This would consist usually of a 24 V heavy-duty battery storage, and a trickle charger, feeding transistor fluorescent light fittings in the main studios and passageways. This will require testing once a month, including a check on the battery distilled water level and a hydrometer test of the electrolyte. As part of the emergency systems, it is almost certain that some form of fire alarm will be installed. This should be checked once a week and any failure rectified at once, either by the studio maintenance department or the company responsible for fire alarm maintenance. All types of fire extinguisher used throughout the studios should be situated for easy access in the event of a fire—and not used as door stops. The only type normally used in the studio and control room is gas carbon dioxide; water types are mainly situated in the passage and stairs. All Fire Exits should be clearly marked and kept clear of obstructions.

If the studio has a standby diesel generator for use in the event of a mains failure, this should be checked once a month by running for at least one hour, on load if at all possible. As with a car, the generator requires a careful check of the oil, water, fuel, and battery prior to being run up. The running log should be attached to the generator, filled in by the person testing and signed, listing any comments about the test run. The electrical changeover from mains supply to emergency generator usually consists of a three-phase changeover breaker switch, so that the generator and mains supply cannot feed the studio building at the same time.

When actually in use, the generator should be regularly inspected to ensure that the oil pressure and water temperature are not outside the normal rating for the engine, and that the electrical load is within the working range of the alternator unit. Most control systems have alarm circuits fitted which can be extended into the maintenance department. Thus, for example, if engine oil pressure or water temperature rises outside the normal limits, an alarm bell will sound to inform the maintenance staff that a fault requires urgent attention.

Test tapes

As alignment test tapes are quite costly, it may be decided not to employ these for all daily routine checks. They would soon become unusable and possibly damaged with such frequent use. Once a fairly new machine has been aligned, using an approved test tape, to achieve accurate record/replay performance figures, it can then be routine checked using a short form alignment tape made for the purpose. This might contain several minutes of 1 kHz and 12 kHz tones, for example, and should be made as accurate as possible, certainly to within 1 dB of the nominal level.

This general-purpose alignment tape can then be used as a quick check by all maintenance personnel, without the risk of damage and wear to the master test tape. The latter should be used only when doubts arise with the general-purpose tape. Before any test tape is used, of course, the heads must be cleaned and demagnetized with the machine switched off.

Some studios will also have 35 and 16 mm magnetic film recording facilities, which opens up another area of equipment maintenance. The projection equipment does not usually call for much attention, but the magnetic film recorders and replay machines need alignment checks as with any tape recorder. The system used to interlock the film recorders and projectors to the film replay machines is always electrical. It may consist of a motor generator which has to run up to 50 Hz and then lock on to the three-phase mains system, or the more recent solid state motor drive, but will certainly require maintenance on a regular basis.

Studio foldback systems may use loudspeaker units for various sections of musicians, though headphones are more usual. These headphones are usually fed from a fairly high power amplifier at low impedance, to allow several pairs to be used in parallel, with a means of protection in case one set develops a short-circuit.

Groups of headsets can be plugged into a junction box on a flying lead, perhaps with a gain control for each headset outlet. The headphones and boxes tend to be left around at the end of a session and are in danger of physical damage. A good idea is to use a stand to hold four sets of phones, which are permanently wired into the top of the stand with gain controls in the base. Each stand can be wired with a 15 ohms resistor in series to protect other headset stands in the event of a shorted line in one stand. A suitable three-pin plug and socket arrangement can be devised so that several stands can be connected in series without the series resistors being additive. The musicians can be encouraged to hang their headsets on the stand when not in use, so reducing the risk of physical damage.

Spare headsets should be readily available, to ensure that a session is not delayed by breakdowns of this fairly fault prone item. Higher quality headsets for control room listening are sometimes requested and arrangements must be made to provide a suitable monitor feed for electrostatic headsets as well as dynamic types.

Studio loudspeakers

Maintenance of loudspeakers generally consists of changing faulty drive units, when it is found that the application of a clean electrical signal produces distorted sound or silence, even after substitution of the power amplifier. Replacing the suspect unit with a new or recently overhauled one is the only quick cure available. Crossover units rarely give trouble, but again substitution is the best way to show if a fault does exist. Loudspeakers are always liable to receive very high levels at times, not only due to high monitoring volumes but also from fader faults or fast winding of tapes.

Spare loudspeaker units should therefore be held in stock at all times for instant replacement, as the repair time by manufacturers can be a month or more. The phasing of speaker leads should be checked when making any substitution of units as the labelling of wiring is not always reliable.

Some control room monitoring circuits include equalization in the power amplifiers or line cards to correct for the room frequency response. In such a situation, the power amplifier or line output cards should be identified in some way so that they are not substituted without the frequency response being rechecked. This problem does not arise in the usual situation, of course, where the line out from the desk and through the power amplifiers has a level response and the desired frequency response has been obtained by careful speaker design, position of the speakers and acoustical correction to the control room itself.

The devices used for artificial reverberation range from spring units and echo plates to solid state delay lines. The more sophisticated reverberation units are normally repaired by service agents, except for simple faults in the plug-in modules. Many studios use a spare recorder to introduce delay before feeding signals to the spring, plate or echo chamber. Such machines run for many hours and so head, capstan, and guide wear is fairly high. Machines which lend themselves to varispeed control are preferred for echo delay and they should receive regular monthly service in a busy studio, with a major overhaul in the workshop every six months.

Apart from the normal maintenance of studio consoles and the associated electronics, a maintenance engineer should attend to the general servicing of many items not directly connected with sound recording. These include all forms of studio lighting, heating systems, and electrical appliances, used within the studio or on mobile recording sessions. The maintenance staff should be able to diagnose the trouble in any of this equipment and, if spares are available, carry out the repair. If the fault calls for an outside specialist, as in the case of air conditioning equipment, the staff should be able to contact and arrange for the services of the relevant company. After any such repair, the maintenance department should ensure that the work has been carried out satisfactorily and the maintenance manager should clear the payment for such services with the accounts department.

TECHNIQUES

CHAPTER THIRTEEN

Speech and Drama

Derek Taylor

At the outset it should be said that all microphone balancing and studio managing is an art or a technique, not a science. It is impossible to lay down hard and fast rules. If you say something must always (or never) be done, the next day some combination of programme requirement/studio acoustic/ equipment characteristic will prove that the only practical solution is the exact opposite. Also no two studio engineers will achieve their results in the same way. The only criterion is: will it sound right to the listener? The only way of being sure is to try something and listen. This however may take time. The following notes are designed to help obtain the desired result more quickly by suggesting well tried methods to use and some of the pitfalls to avoid.

The simplest form of programme likely to be encountered is a single voice in a talk or story reading. The aim should be to produce an accurate representation of the person's voice, not iron out all voices to a standard 'good quality'. It is a good plan with a new speaker to go into the studio and have a short conversation both to put him at his ease and listen to the character of his voice.

The studio should have a reverberation time of about 0·25 to 0·4 sec at all frequencies, with an even decay. Also it should not be too large, something about the size of an average living room. A large studio, even if it is dead enough, sounds wrong. The impression of size is given by the timing of the first reflection; the longer it is delayed, the larger the studio sounds. Acoustic screens can help in such a case. Arranged round the microphone, they may not have any significant effect on the total reverberation time, but they will provide an earlier first reflection and disperse some of the wall reflections falling on them at the rear.

The microphone type is not critical provided it has a smooth frequency response. Avoid bright sounding microphones as they often have resonances in the upper middle and top registers which emphasize sibilance. Some microphones which sound very good on orchestral strings are very unpleasant for speech. At the same time, working too close to a pressure-gradient microphone (i.e. a ribbon or any type with a figure-of-eight polar diagram) will produce a bass tip-up which can alter the character of a voice and reduce clarity. As far as microphone mounting is concerned, the choice is either a table stand or suspension from the ceiling or a boom.

If a table stand is favoured, strict precautions must be taken against mechanically transmitted bumps and rumble. Movements of the speaker may produce very little air-borne noise, but considerable mechanical interference. Also, structure-borne noise can be a problem, such as footsteps in another part of the building or outside sources, traffic or tube trains. The stand should be as solid as possible, to provide inertia, and have no loose joints or spigots to cause clicks and rattles. There should also be effective mechanical decoupling between the stand and the microphone: rubber in tension is a better shock absorber than rubber in compression. Little wire tripods clipped to the microphone body are very troublesome. Flexible swan-necks are however quite effective for light-weight microphones.

It is probably simpler to avoid these problems by suspending the microphone over the table from a boom with elastic cables. However, this does call for a little more patience in positioning the microphone in front of the speaker.

The type of table and accessories, such as script racks, can have a significant influence on the sound quality and ruin an otherwise good studio. Any hard objects can reflect sound into the microphone, but they will only reflect sounds whose wavelengths are shorter than the dimensions of the

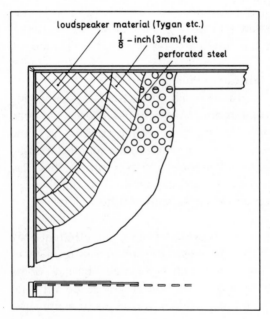

loudspeaker material (Tygan etc.)
$\frac{1}{8}$ – inch (3mm) felt
perforated steel

Fig. 13.1
Construction of an acoustically transparent talks table

reflecting surface. Thus, the bass frequencies are not affected but the higher frequencies are reinforced, with a slight delay or phase shift, and often produce harsh quality.

Tables should be as acoustically transparent as possible; a satisfactory construction has proved to be a wooden frame covered on top with perforated steel (approx. 6·25 mm ($\frac{1}{4}$-inch) holes closely spaced) overlaid with loudspeaker cloth (Fig. 13.1). A 3 mm ($\frac{1}{8}$-inch) layer of felt under the cloth can increase its stability, as the cloth must be fixed only at the edges and any movement on the steel may cause rustling noises. Never glue the cloth down on to the steel, as the whole thing will tighten up like a drum skin with disastrous effects on the sound.

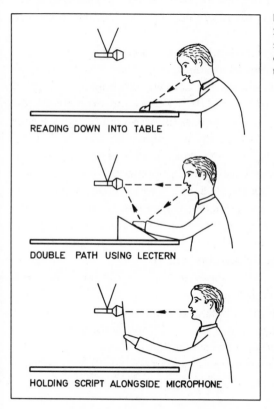

READING DOWN INTO TABLE

DOUBLE PATH USING LECTERN

HOLDING SCRIPT ALONGSIDE MICROPHONE

Fig. 13.2
Showing two common faults in speech recording and the method of holding the script at the side of the microphone

Script racks or lecterns should also be acoustically transparent, but they are a doubtful asset. It is important that the speaker should speak directly into the microphone (Fig. 13.2). A rack may help him to keep his head up and not to read into the table, but the script can also cause HF reflections and the angle of the rack may direct the reflections into the microphone. It is better to encourage the speaker to hold up the script at the side of the microphone, so that he can speak straight into the latter and simply divert his eyes to the side to read.

A single voice

The main factors in the balance of a single voice are perspective and volume, and both are a function of the distance from the microphone. The perspective is the ratio of direct to indirect sound being picked up by the microphone—the further away, the more indirect sound received. However, this is also a function of the polar diagram of the microphone. A figure-of-eight will pick up fewer reflections from the studio walls, ceiling, etc. than an omni-directional microphone as it is live on only two faces. Thus the figure-of-eight will sound closer. (A cardioid would perhaps sound somewhere between the two.)

Very close working for speech should be avoided (except for special effects in drama). The techniques of modern singers who handle microphones like ice-cream cones should be actively discouraged. A good working distance is about 50 to 60 cm ($1\frac{1}{2}$ to 2 feet) and even this is too close for a ribbon microphone, unless the bass tip-up is countered by a filter to roll off the bass. Close working tends to emphasize the mechanical processes of speaking, giving rise to teeth clicks and lip smacking; also the sheer weight of breath can cause blasting and popping of the microphone, especially on the explosive consonants P, B, etc. A wind-shield will help with the latter. If the speaker has a weak voice, it is generally better to increase the gain than to get the microphone too close. It is therefore important that the studio equipment should have the best signal-to-noise ratio possible and that ambient noise in the studio should be kept down to a very low figure, with maximum freedom from traffic noise, etc., and minimum noise from ventilation plant and fluorescent lighting.

Electronic frequency correction is best kept to a minimum. As mentioned, a high-pass filter may be essential when using a ribbon microphone. With a very woolly voice, the addition of a 'presence' hump can improve clarity. Also some reduction of the higher frequencies can help a very sibilant speaker, but discretion must be used.

Two or more voices

The term 'balance' comes more into its own when two or more voices are involved. For interviews it is more natural for the two people to be facing one another and, if their voices are of similar volume and have no unusual characteristics, a bi-directional ribbon microphone placed between them will serve very well (Fig. 13.3). The figure-of-eight polar diagram will accom-

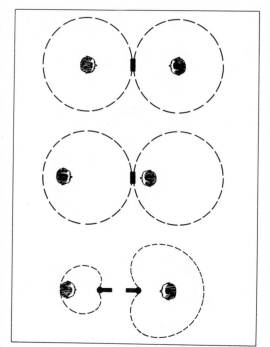

Fig. 13.3
Two evenly balanced voices can use a single bi-directional microphone (top). If one voice is louder, the distances can be adjusted (centre) or separate cardioid microphones used bottom)

modate the two speakers, whilst being dead to the rest of the studio and therefore reduce ambient noise.

If the volumes of the voices are not well matched, however, the microphone can be placed nearer one speaker than the other. There is a limit to how far this can be done, however, as there is the danger of excessive bass on one voice, as already mentioned, and also the perspective will change and, in extreme cases, the two people may sound as if they are in different rooms. In this situation, two cardioid microphones arranged back to back are more satisfactory (Fig. 13.3). The perspectives can be equalized better, as the microphones can be placed at the same distance from each speaker, any bass tip-up is greatly reduced and the compensation for volume can be made electrically. Up to four people can be successfully accommodated on a ribbon microphone—two each side—but more than that requires them to sit uncomfortably close and even lean inwards.

Round-table discussions can be picked up using an omni-directional microphone hanging over the table, but a cardioid will give a closer perspective and reduce unwanted noise. It can either be hung with the dead side upwards, which will reduce ventilation noise from the ceiling, or standing on the centre of the table or in a well. This will reduce script rustles, etc., but of course may be subject to bumps if the table is knocked or kicked.

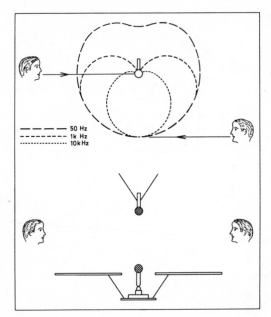

— — — — 50 Hz
– – – – – 1k Hz
·············· 10k Hz

Fig. 13.4
Since the frequency response of a cardioid microphone varies with the angle of incidence (top) it is better to place the microphone well above or below eye level

A word of warning regarding cardioid microphones may not be out of place here: many microphones sold as cardioid are only so over a restricted frequency range. They are frequently omni-directional in the bass and single-sided in the top, getting narrower as the frequency increases. Therefore, if you are going to work round a cardioid, as distinct from into the front, it is better to arrange the microphone either a little above mouth level, if hanging, or below if table-mounted. This avoids working in the areas where the response is likely to vary with frequency (Fig. 13.4).

As with two-voice programmes, a single microphone works well if all voices are of similar volume or if all the speakers are experienced broadcasters; if not, then a multi-microphone set-up is needed. One cardioid microphone per person is sometimes used, and some studios are equipped with this in mind. Studio 3E at Broadcasting House, for example, has a large D-shaped table with room for a presenter and newsreader on the straight part and up to eight contributors round the curve, each with his own microphone. To avoid bumps and rumble, the microphones are mounted on swan-necks fixed to a small steel table or plinth bolted to the floor and standing within the D, but not in contact with the table. This is a rather elaborate solution, and having a large number of microphones open together in a small studio can cause problems of increased ambient noise and phasing, due to voices being picked up by more than one microphone. It is often possible to reduce the number by arranging the contributors in pairs, with one microphone between them (Fig. 13.5).

Fig. 13.5
Use of two ribbon microphones shared between the voices in a round table discussion (courtesy BBC)

Whenever more than one microphone is used at a time, great care must be taken to ensure that they are in phase, otherwise the voice will take on a thin and distant quality. This can cause complications if mixed polar diagrams are involved, as the two sides of a figure-of-eight or hypercardioid are in opposite phase. Therefore, if a cardioid microphone is placed in the field of the back of a ribbon, for example, both microphones will pick up the same voice but out of phase.

Panel games and quizzes before an audience present problems of their own. The main possibilities are either a long straight or horseshoe-shaped table, with the question master in the middle and the team split equally on either side. Or two tables can be used facing each other on either side of the stage, with the question master on one and the team on the other. This is useful if there are guest artists who appear for only part of the show as they can share the question master's table and microphone. For the team, one microphone between every two artists is a practical alternative to every one having his own as in Fig. 13.6.

Picking up questions from the audience is best done with a hand microphone on a trailing cable, or a radio microphone, passed to the questioner by an assistant. Attempting to pick out one person in an audience with a

Fig. 13.6
Use of a separate microphone for each voice in the 'Brain of Britain' programme (courtesy BBC)

rifle microphone is rarely satisfactory. If this technique is contemplated, better intelligibility can be obtained with a cardioid microphone and a parabolic reflector, though this is more cumbersome. A 60 cm (2 ft) dish is quite adequate.

Actuality interviews using portable gear are best conducted by holding a cardioid microphone vertically at about chest level between the inter- viewer and interviewee, somewhat nearer to the latter. The habit shown by some interviewers of holding the microphone first to their own mouth and then thrusting it in the face of their victim for the reply is disturbing to the person concerned, and usually produces a lot of handling noises. This technique should be adopted only in cases where the background noises (traffic, machinery, etc.) are excessive and it is not practical to move to a quieter venue.

Not much work has been done so far in utilizing stereo for discussions etc., but it seems a profitable field for experimentation as it is much easier for the listener to discriminate between voices, particularly if all the members of the panel are talking together. It seems sensible to position the question master in the middle, with the panel ranged either side. This can be done either by placing them in a semi-circle round a coincident pair of crossed cardioid microphones, having natural positioning and studio ambience, or having some other convenient seating layout with one mono microphone per person and pan-potting the microphones to the desired positions on the sound stage. This latter solution does have the disadvantage of having no continuous ambience and sounding somewhat disjointed. If there is an audience, a crossed pair of microphones directed over them can provide a background to blend the other microphones together.

Drama

The balance engineer's job in drama is to provide the actors with a suitable environment which will convey to the listener the impression that the action is taking place in the locations indicated by the plot. This aural scenery is created partially by the acoustics and partially by effects and, within this setting, the actors must make convincing moves.

The most important factors in the acoustics of the setting are the reverberation time and the size of the location. To cope with all types of dramatic productions, the studio needs to be fairly large—around 850 m³ (30,000 cu. ft) and the acoustic treatment varied to give different reverberation times in different areas (see Fig. 13.7) with curtains to shut an area off, if required. A separate, very dead or anechoic room leading off the main studio is very useful for outdoor scenes, but it must be fairly large. Typical reverberation

Fig. 13.7
Typical drama studio with 'The Archers' in rehearsal (courtesy BBC)

times are 0·2–0·3 sec. for the dead end, 0·5 sec. for the normal parts and 0·7–0·8 sec. for the live end. It is a great advantage if the live end has a carpet which can be rolled back for live scenes and laid to deaden it down and give a bigger normal area. Portable acoustic screens, with one reflecting and one absorbing side, can be used to modify the studio acoustics to simulate a larger number of different locations.

In mono drama, the most useful microphone is a ribbon. Its figure-of-eight polar diagram means that actors can face each other, which is more natural and comfortable for them than standing side by side. Also, having two dead sides means that the studio can be made to give the impression of much greater size than its physical dimensions dictate. The reason for this is that our judgement of distance is determined by the ratio of direct to indirect sound; the more indirect, the further away the source appears. Thus, anyone standing even quite close to the microphone in the dead area will not be picked up, except by reflection from the studio walls, and will sound very distant. If he then backs away from the microphone and circles round to the live side, he will appear to have made a long straight approach. To produce the same effect on an omni-directional microphone would require three or four times the studio space. For normal speech, the actors do not work closer than about arm's length from the microphone, and they step back or turn off slightly when using a very loud voice. However, for very intimate scenes or 'thought' voices, they may work much closer, down to 75–100 mm (3–4 inches), but in this case it is essential to work across the microphone instead of straight on to it, to avoid popping and blasting.

Omni-directional microphones (or cardioids suspended with the dead side upwards) are often used for scenes involving a large number of actors, especially in fairly live acoustics such as courtrooms, etc. This gives much more room to work, and very long approaches and recedes are not usually required.

Artificial reverberation or 'echo' may be required and an echo room is preferable to a reverberation plate as plates tend to sound metallic on speech. The variable reverberation time of a plate or other device is not so much of an advantage for drama and, in any case, the reverberation characteristics of a room can be modified to some extent by introducing screens near the echo microphone.

A good microphone technique, giving the widest possible dramatic range and yet keeping the volume within the restricted dynamic range generally employed in broadcasting, requires a great deal of control and discipline by the actor and is usually developed only after long experience. The transition from stage to studio is not easy, and even experienced radio actors cannot always judge the volume to use since they cannot hear the mixture of

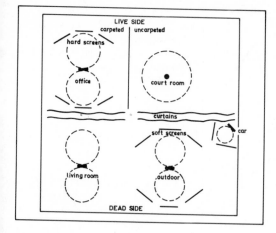

Fig. 13.8
Typical layout for mono drama in a live end/dead end studio with movable screens

effects and music to voices which the engineer is hearing. They are therefore very reliant on his skill and clear advice.

A typical set-up is shown in Fig. 13.8. The requirements of the script are: living-room, outdoor, car interior, office and courtroom. For this a figure-of-eight microphone on the dead side of the studio will suffice for the living-room. The outdoor scene must be as dead as possible and is therefore on the same side of the studio, but surrounded by soft screens for more absorption. Low frequency sounds have a wavelength longer than the width of the screens and so the latter do not have much effect on bass. This bass colouration can be reduced by using bass cut in the outdoor microphone circuit. There is no need to use screens on the dead sides of the microphone, and those on the live sides must be angled so that any reflections from them are directed into the dead studio and not back at the microphone. Also, no two screens must be parallel, otherwise standing waves will be set up (see Figs. 13a and 13b).

The car interior must sound small and boxy. As mentioned before, the size of a location depends on the timing of the first reflection; therefore there should be a reflecting surface very near the microphone. A good plan is to screen off a corner of the studio and place a ribbon microphone with one live side close to the wall (but not quite parallel to it) and the actors standing side by side on the other face. The cramped space will also help to keep the actors on microphone, as long movements in a car would not be appropriate. The office would be on the live side of the studio, with hard screens to reduce the size of the location. If this proves to be over bright, then soft screens should be used. The courtroom could occupy most of the live area, with a suspended cardioid or omni-directional microphone. If added reverberation is required, it is a good idea to try a second microphone hung high above

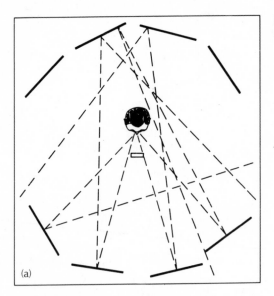

(a)

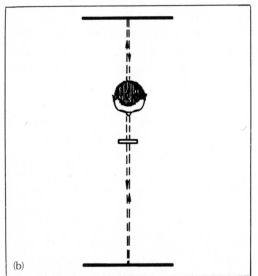

(b)

Fig. 13.9
Screens should ideally be non-parallel as shown in (a). If screens are parallel, as in (b), standing waves will cause colouration

the acting area and add artificial echo to this and not the main microphone.

The reverberation times achieved will almost certainly not be those found in real locations, but they should provide suitable contrasts to give the right impressions to the listener. The addition of background effects will heighten these impressions, especially on outdoor scenes; however, too much reliance must not be put on them. The technique of using only one acoustic and adding different background effects is very unconvincing and distracts from the action of the play.

Sound effects

Effects are divided into two groups: recorded and 'spot'. Spot effects are those performed in the studio during the action of the scene, e.g. doors, crockery, pouring drinks, telephones, etc. Recorded effects are backgrounds and sounds which cannot conveniently be accommodated in the studio, e.g. express trains! At one time, spot effects were used to simulate sounds of all kinds—lead shot on a drum for sea-wash, the thunder sheet, wind machine, etc. but, with the reduction in size and weight of mobile recording gear, there is less necessity to fake effects. Also, with the improvements in transmission and reception quality, it is more difficult to pass them off on the listener.

There may be a temptation to use only recorded effects, or even dub them in afterwards. It is much better for the actors, and much easier to get per-spectives right, if spot effects are used when appropriate. The timing of an effect is vital and can turn high drama into farce if it goes wrong. A good spot operator works with the actor and positions himself in the same per-spective. A separate spot microphone should be avoided if possible as it tends to alter the studio acoustic, distort perspectives and divorce the operator from the action. Its use should be confined to effects which are cumbersome or otherwise difficult to get near to the main microphone, e.g. footsteps, water tanks, doors, etc. If there are many actors in the scene, it may be more practical to put a small spot table on the dead side of the main microphone and hang a cardioid over it.

Doors can be difficult. If they are built into the wall for the sake of solidness, they are nearly always in the wrong perspective. They sound wrong too as there is no room beyond them. (If the door is a good fit and the cavity behind small, holes must be drilled in the door to let the compressed air through, otherwise it will be impossible to slam it.) Portable doors, on the other hand, are much more convenient and easier to get into correct perspective, but tend to sound flimsy.

The choice of recorded effects depends largely on the time (and therefore money) available and one's resources. Given access to a good library of recorded effects and only a limited time to complete a programme, the choice is obvious. However, if effects can be recorded specially for a particular programme, the end product should be superior. Again, where time is important, effects recorded on disc have an advantage. Given gramophone decks with good groove location, it is much quicker to find a particular spot on a disc than to spool through a reel of tape. Storage of large quantities of material is also easier on disc. Of course the background noise is better from tape unless the discs are changed very frequently.

Cartridge or cassette systems have a great appeal in theory, but not much use is made of them. This is largely due to the length of time required to make up a set of cartridges for an individual production, and the mammoth storage problems. One 175 mm (7 inch) $33\frac{1}{3}$ rpm disc may easily contain 20 or 30 possible starting points: if each cartridge has to start from the beginning, this means 20 or 30 cartridges.

Whatever system is employed, it must be flexible and fast enough for the effects to keep pace with the action. It is no good having all the effects in a rigid order and duration if the cast have to wait for cues to allow the effects to happen. The whole flow of the play will be lost.

Stereo drama

Much of what has been said about mono drama also applies to stereo but stereo does bring its own problems. Most of these are in production rather than technicalities, especially when the programme must be mono/stereo compatible. This compatibility is very important in broadcasting as it must be assumed that, for many years to come, the majority of the audience will be listening in mono. Even when there is full stereo coverage over the country, many people will be listening in situations or circumstances where stereo is not practicable.

The transmission system used is compatible in that the stereo listener hears two channels (A-left and B-right) while the mono listener hears one carrying both sets of information (A+B). This is achieved in simple terms by modulating the main carrier with A+B, or M as it is usually called, and a sub-carrier with A−B (or S). Thus, the mono listener hears the sum of both channels but his receiver does not respond to the sub-carrier. The stereo receiver, on the other hand, detects both signals and by suitable matrixing reconstitutes A and B.

If a sound is central in the stereo picture, it will be equal in both channels and thus add to form M (in practice 3 dB up) and, when subtracted, will cancel completely and produce no S signal. A sound fully left or fully right will produce equal M and S signals. On the other hand, an out-of-phase signal will not produce any M and be inaudible to the mono listener. Thus the system is compatible but the programme material may not be. Sounds which are perfectly audible, but perhaps not well located, in stereo may be lost in mono.

This explains one of the reasons for the preference for coincident pairs rather than spaced microphones in broadcasting. The spaced pair relies largely on phase shift for its effect. Any sound other than dead centre has a different path length to the two microphones and therefore a time-of-arrival difference or phase shift. With the coincident pair, all sounds arrive at the same time (in the horizontal plane anyway) and the stereo effect is produced purely by volume differences and is therefore potentially more compatible.

The working angles for coincident microphones of different polar diagrams are shown in Fig. 13.10. It will be seen that a pair of crossed figure-of-eights gives an acceptance angle of 90°. A sound on the X axis will be picked up only on the A microphone, as it is on the dead side of the B microphone, and vice versa on the Y axis. A sound in the centre is picked up equally on both and, in other positions, more on one microphone than the other. However, if the sound source is moved round to one side (beyond the 90° acceptance angle) it will be picked up on the front of one microphone and the back of the other, and so be out-of-phase. Normal stereo will be produced in the back 90°, but the left and right directions will be reversed. Working in the out-of-phase angles must be avoided, as this will produce cancellations in mono and unpredictable location in stereo.

Crossed cardioids have no back lobes and therefore there is no out-of-phase area. The useful angle is shown as 180°. This is the full extent of the stereo picture from one loudspeaker to the other. Using the greater angle of 270° approximately will give perfectly acceptable quality, but no more width; the level will fall off, the further round one goes. The area at the back will give a very distant perspective and the sound is liable to jump from one side of the picture to the other rather suddenly. Hyper-cardioids give an acceptance angle somewhere between figure-of-eight and cardioid; about 130°.

The different angles can be very useful and so variable polar diagram capacitor microphones, with two capsules in one case, such as the AKG C24 or Neumann SM69 are favoured. The fact that the stereo effect is dependent on the polar diagram means that the two capsules must be very accurately matched at all frequencies. This, of course, makes the microphones expensive and, even with good microphones, the angles should not be taken on trust, but should be checked.

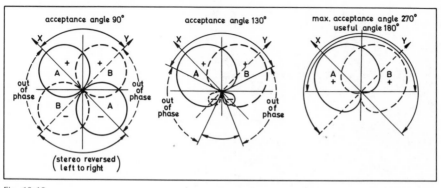

Fig. 13.10
Polar characteristics of coincident pairs of figure-of-eight, hyper-cardioid and cardioid microphones at a mutual angle of 90°

Coincident pairs must always be lined up, whether they are in one case or separate mono microphones mounted close together. To ensure that the gains are equal, the microphones are set up to face the same direction and, whilst an assistant is talking in front of them, one listens to the S signal (that is both outputs on one loudspeaker, but out-of-phase with each other) and adjusts the gain of the two channels for the null point. Then the monitoring should be restored to stereo (in phase) and, with the microphones still facing the same direction, the assistant should walk slowly round the microphones talking continuously. His voice should stay in the centre of the stereo picture. It will become more distant as he passes through the dead side but, if it moves from side to side, the polar diagrams of the two microphones do not match.

With the microphone axes then set to 90°, it is as well to check at what angles the voice becomes fully in each loudspeaker. The angle found on crossed cardioids may well be greater than the theoretical 180°, due to inaccuracies in the cardioid pattern. This does not matter as long as the actors are aware of the limits of their stage; it is a good idea to stick strips of white tape on the floor to mark them (see Fig. 13.11). Alternatively, with variable polar diagram microphones, the angle can be narrowed by setting them towards the hyper-cardioid condition.

Fig. 13.11
Use of a coincident pair of microphones for stereo drama, showing the floor marked with tape as a guide to positioning for the actors (courtesy BBC)

In drama, the crossed cardioid is the most often used configuration as it gives the maximum working area. The main thing that the actor has to remember is that to move in a straight line across the stage he has to walk in a semi-circle, keeping at the same distance from the microphone pair.

Working in stereo is more demanding in terms of the studio itself. Much more room is required for approaches and recedes, since the dead side cannot be used as in mono. It is very difficult to get a good open air sound, as the stereo microphone reproduces the studio acoustic much more accurately: therefore large, dead studios are required, with no ventilation or outside noises. Such a studio is seldom found in practice and the best has to be made with what is available. The actors can help a lot to simulate distance by pitching their voices, as if projecting from a distance, but not using much actual volume. Turning away from the microphone and talking into a soft surface will also help.

Great care must be taken with spot effects to ensure that they are in the same position and perspective as the associated voice. Footsteps may prove more difficult than usual as coincident microphones are usually mounted one above the other, and sounds from the floor reach the bottom one before the top. This produces a phase shift which gives the footsteps a slight offset. It may be better to do them in a distant part of the studio on a mono microphone and pan them, or pre-record the steps with the microphones at ground level and make sure that the actor follows the same path. Generally speaking, the greater discrimination given to the listener by stereo means that greater realism is need for all sound effects.

Recorded effects should ideally be stereo, but this may not always be practical and there are methods whereby mono recording can be made to produce a reasonably convincing result. One device is a 'spreader'. This produces varying phase shifts at different frequencies and is sometimes used by recording companies to convert old mono recordings to synthetic stereo. Instead of simply spreading the higher frequencies to the left and the lower to the right, as is usual, the frequency spectrum is divided into several bands spread alternately left and right. This works quite well with effects which have a wide frequency range but, if the range is narrow, they tend to move more to one side than the other. If an effect, say a crowd, does not sound well through a spreader, good results can be obtained by the rather more laborious process of pre-recording and taking several copies of the same crowd, starting them from different points in the duration of the effect and panning them to different places across the sound stage. Obviously, the more copies the better but, if there are holes in the crowd, it can be copied and the mono effects mixed in again, panned to the gaps and so on.

With stereo effects, care must be taken to get the width in correct scale with perspective. For example, a horse and cart passing in the far distance would be a point source and a mono effect panned across would be quite appropriate. In the foreground, however, the horse has two pairs of feet and the cart two sets of wheels and so it should take up most or all of the sound stage. With spread effects (or stereo effects used in a different perspective to the original recording), width and offset controls are required on the stereo channel to enable the effect to be narrowed and moved. Alternatively, two mono channels can be used, one for the A side and one for B, and the width and movement controlled by pan-pots. By spacing the positions on the pan-pots, the width can be set accurately. In fact, an effect can start distant and narrow on one side, come closer and wider in the centre, narrow down and fade out on the other side, but this does require more than the usual complement of hands! Foot pan-pots have been tried but were not popular. A slider fader combined with a rotatable knob for the pan-pot would seem to be a better solution.

At the time of writing, experiments in quadraphonic drama are taking place, but are still in a very early stage. So far, the microphone arrangements have been four cardioids at 90° to each other (see Fig. 13.12), with quadraphonic pan-pots for mono sources. A 'surround sound' is fairly easy to achieve, but it is more difficult to bring the action in close to the listener and

Fig. 13.12
Use of four cardioid microphones for quadraphonic drama ('Oedipus Rex', January 1973). Note the use of live music (courtesy BBC)

make him feel part of it. If this can be done, it will be a great asset to producers, since stereo tends to put the action back behind a proscenium arch and the listener is less involved than in mono.

In Germany there is renewed interest in artificial head stereo, especially for headphone listening. This can give some remarkable perspective effects but there are reservations regarding fore and aft positioning along the centre line, speech quality, and compatibility for loudspeaker listening. In short, sound radio is still experimenting and progressing.

CHAPTER FOURTEEN

Classical Music

Tryg Tryggvason

It would be pretentious to suggest that an account of recording techniques could be in any way definitive. Quite apart from the fact that the variables involved are so manifold as to defy detailed analysis, the results are judged by aesthetic standards upon which there is, at best, agreement in only statistical terms. Furthermore, there is disagreement upon what the ultimate aim of the balance engineer should be. On the one hand, there is the viewpoint that a performance should be transcribed as nearly as possible to the original—that is, the sound as heard by a listener at a certain point in the original location. On the other, it is suggested that a certain degree of artistic licence is permissible, provided that this results in an improvement in sound quality, impact, or whatever.

These are necessarily vague terms and, in fact, there is a range of approaches from one extreme to the other; there are occasions nowadays, for instance, when a composer writes with technical innovations in mind that can only be achieved artificially during recording. Nevertheless, for the most part, 'serious' music recording is concerned with traditional music, for which there is equally a sonic tradition, and it is this aspect of recording that will be dealt with here.

There are essentially two different circumstances in which such music recordings take place; with an audience present and without. In the first case, the performance is presented, whether on record or broadcast, as a unique *event*, and there is a psychological tendency for the listener to identify with the audience and occasion. For this reason, it can be expected that the listener will not judge matters of balance too harshly, in exactly the same way that it is not reasonable to condemn a performance because of the odd musical mishap. This is perhaps as well, as the engineer's control over positioning, microphone layout, and other factors is extremely restricted. It is natural that the listener should expect the perspective of the balance to reinforce his identification with the audience, and the effect of his involvement in the occasion in terms of his expectations of sound quality should not be underestimated.

However, these observations do not apply equally to recordings made under session conditions. For the listener, the performance tends to assume an abstract, timeless flavour, and the actual location may well be unknown to him. When he selects and plays a record, the performance is for him alone, in his listening room, and there is no atmosphere, such as audience sounds, to encourage an identification with the audience in a concert hall. The direct result of this is a more critical attention to aurally perceived detail, and a heightened sense of dissatisfaction with any imperfections, particularly with repeated playing. For these reasons, there arises the need to transcribe the performance in terms of the recorded medium, with the objective of idealizing the sound quality in the hall, *under listening room conditions*.

The mere fact that nearly all recordings nowadays, including those made with coincident stereo microphones, are made with the assistance of spot microphones is itself demonstrative of the fact that there is general agreement on this principle, and it follows that any attempt to evolve an ideal microphone technique *theoretically* is quite irrelevant to the business of making records.

Microphone systems

As the usual technique of music balancing is to obtain an overall stereophonic sound image from the main microphones, and to reinforce this as necessary with spot microphones, it would be as well to examine the two commonly adopted systems. These are the familiar coincident pair, and the less well-documented spaced microphone system, both of which can yield sound of very high quality.

The coincident pair, or stereo microphone, relies on two directional microphones angled respectively to the left and right, to reproduce the sound waveforms that would have impinged upon the ear, at a certain point, from the left and right directions. In spite of the fact that the two signals are reproduced via two loudspeakers, thus introducing significant cross-talk, the stereo image produced is excellent, and positional definition outstanding. Provided that they are used at a reasonable distance from the performance area, all sources are evenly and realistically picked up, and the close proximity of the two capsules to one another results in negligible phase discrepancy between them, which accounts for the positional stability. Any polar response may be used, subject to certain limitations, but obviously an omni-directional characteristic results in near-mono; some stereo microphones are equipped with infinitely variable polar characteristics, which may be changed remotely from the mixer. The two capsules may be angled with respect to one another and this angle can be chosen to give the desired stereo width or angle of cover.

The sum and difference signals may be separated electrically, and the magnitude of the difference signal varied with respect to the sum. By using this technique, the capsule mutual angle may be set to around 90° to 120° and width, as well as polar patterns, may be remotely controlled. The larger angle reduces the risk of degeneration of centre sources as a result of microphone non-linearities off-axis. These facilities make the stereo microphone invaluable for the recording of live performances in particular; it is unobtrusive and, apart from its initial placement, all manipulations may be effected from the mixer.

It is not proposed to deal extensively with stereo microphone parameters here, as they are adequately dealt with in Chapter Thirteen. A cursory glance at the effective parameters for an included angle of 90° will suffice to illustrate some observations on their effectiveness in recording.

The polar diagram for the figure-of-eight position is illustrated in Fig. 13.10. The available angle of cover is 90° at the front. The side quadrants are out of phase, and therefore not useful. The rear 90° quadrant is useful for reverberation pickup but is in antiphase to the front signal.

In the cardioid position (also shown in Fig. 13.10) the available angle of cover is 270°, but is generally restricted to the front 180° to avoid any off-axis non-linearities. The rear 90° is insensitive.

The hyper-cardioid pattern gives a covered angle of 130° at the front; the side 70° angles are out of phase, and the rear 90° quadrant is not really useful as the rear hyper-cardioid lobe is small.

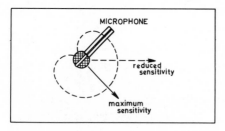

Fig. 14.1
Showing how the changing sensitivity of a directional microphone (a cardioid in this example) can be used to discriminate between forward and rear sections of the performance area

It will be clear that changes in the microphone position, as well as its polar response, will affect both the stereo width and the reverberation content in the signal. Furthermore, as the figure-of-eight pattern has the rear quadrant in antiphase to the front, there can be a certain cancellation of bass reverberation components, which is undesirable. For this reason, that pattern is not favoured and the remaining patterns, of course, discriminate to some extent against natural reverberation.

Remembering that polar patterns should be thought of as solid, obtained by rotating the pattern through 180° on its own axis, a certain degree of discrimination between forward and rear sections of the performance area may be obtained by tilting the microphone, as shown in Fig. 14.1.

The interdependence of the parameters, together with the fact that the entire performance area is covered by only two microphones, effectively means that little control over details of balance within the performance area is afforded the engineer, and it can be difficult to optimize one parameter without adversely affecting another. It could also be argued that the discrimination against reverberation may compel the engineer to work at a greater distance from the source than he would wish, or to reinforce reverberation with separate microphones for this purpose.

On occasions, when recording larger ensembles, the main pickup image may be reinforced with two omni-directional or cardioid microphones on the left and right flanks.

Spaced microphone systems

In this approach we are effectively sampling the sound at various points across the stereo stage, and recreating the wavefronts between the loudspeakers by panning each microphone to a position corresponding to its physical location. A typical system is illustrated in Fig. 14.2.

Complaint is frequently heard that such a system results in unacceptable phase ambiguities and, while there is a certain amount of truth in this, a careful attention to the geometry can minimize the effect, and positional definition can be very good. The microphones used are omni-directional types, but they should nevertheless be carefully angled towards the area that they are intended to cover since most omni-directional types are, in fact, quite directional at higher frequencies. The central three microphones are the most important, and should be thought of as a single stereo system; a correct balance between them must be maintained, as this is fundamental to correct overall balance and any fader adjustments required are therefore made equally to all three. The extreme left and right microphones are used only as a reinforcement of the outer wings of large ensembles.

There are several major advantages offered by this technique. The omni-directional polar pattern results in a higher and more natural reverberation pickup than is achieved by directional types; it is interesting to note that

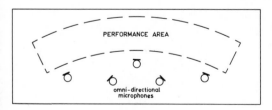

Fig. 14.2
Use of spaced omni-directional microphones for stereo

these pressure sensitive transducers function on the same principle as the ear itself, unlike the directional family. This enhanced reverberation sensitivity effectively means that it is possible to work closer to the source than with cardioids, for the same reverberation content, resulting in clarity without excessive immediacy; indeed, the relatively close working distance of 3 to 4 metres (9 to 12 feet) is essential to take full advantage of the high frequency directional characteristic. It also offers the added benefit that level differentials, between similar signals received by more than one microphone, tend to swamp any phase ambiguities. The fact that the microphones are separated permits quite subtle but worthwhile adjustments to suit each occasion. Layout is rather critical and unique to each situation, much of the work being done in placing the instrumentalists themselves, after which the precise microphone placings may be attended to.

These, then, are the two systems in general use; each has its own applications and merits but, for the purposes of records, the spaced system appears to offer important advantages. Were the coincident system able to offer higher sound quality than this technique, the loss of control could be tolerated, but there is no evidence that this is the case; even if the positional definition is marginally superior, it is considered that the sound quality of the omni-directional microphones, together with the creative flexibility of the spaced system, far outweigh this. It is, in any case, open to serious question whether the integrity of the coincident system can be preserved at all when spot microphones are used in addition to them.

In the examples which follow, the spaced technique is used exclusively, but most of the discussions remain valid if a stereo pair is substituted for overall pickup.

Preparations

It is of great value to study the material to be recorded thoroughly before the actual session, with a view to forestalling any technical problems which might arise. The manner in which a piece is written can provide valuable information as to the optimum placement of musicians for stereo, and it will be found that the usual positions taken up by the musicians in performance are by no means always ideal for stereo recording. Clearly, it will be important to create a stereo image in which there is a reasonably balanced activity across the sound stage, and an examination of the score can often suggest a suitable layout. Furthermore there may be artifices required, particularly in opera, which require substantial technical preparation. Fader work may also be necessary at certain points, for which a cue would be very useful, and such areas of likely difficulty may be noted in the score, so enabling the producer to give the necessary cue during the session.

The criteria by which a suitable location for a recording is chosen will not be dealt with in detail here. It should be stressed, however, that a good and complementary acoustic is the most fundamental requirement for music recording, without which all subsequent operations are necessarily compromised. Finding a really good hall, which does not suffer unduly from noise or other problems, can easily be the single most time consuming factor with which the recording team must deal; a useful source of information, in an unfamiliar area, can often be the local fire service, who will be able to point out the halls of any size that could be suitable.

Usually, a great deal may be learned of a hall's acoustic qualities by ear, with the aid of a few judicious handclaps and shouts. Most traditional music appears to be best complemented by an acoustic having a reverberation time of between 2 and 2·5 seconds, with a reasonably even decay throughout the frequency spectrum. Figure 14.3 shows the reverberation/frequency curves of an excellent recording hall; the increase in reverberation time

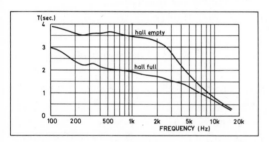

Fig. 14.3
Reverberation/frequency curves of a typical hall often used for recording

towards the bass end is a recurring characteristic of the better halls. Naturally, it is important to ensure that there are no unpleasant slaps, caused by standing waves between parallel surfaces in a hall.

Much thought must be given to the question of space and layout as, with multi-microphone techniques, clarity and separation can be obtained only if it is possible to locate musicians in such a manner that crosstalk between microphones is minimized; a large, unobstructed floor area is therefore important. In the case of large scale recordings involving orchestra, chorus and soloists, accessible balconies and a stage of some kind can be most helpful, as a set-up of this kind could become extremely cluttered if all the musicians are at the same level; in particular, contact between sections could be very problematic.

Turning to the question of microphone types, it must be said that this is largely a matter of individual preference. Microphone technical specifications, although valuable, tell us nothing of their sound quality, and microphones with not obviously dissimilar specifications can sound markedly different. The main microphones are naturally the most important; in the case of stereo types, many possibilities exist as, of course, any pair of directional types may be used. The quality of the Neumann SM69 is excellent, as is that of a pair of AKG 414 types. For the spaced system, the Neumann M50 is an old favourite, and the KM83 is also very good. Other types may well yield convincing results, but it is important that they should become somewhat directional at high frequencies.

Spot microphones must usually be cardioid, in order to achieve separation, but omni-directional types may sometimes be used if well separated from other performers. The Neumann KM84 is an excellent general purpose microphone, and some engineers favour also the AKG 451. For some percussion instruments, the Neumann KM88 appears to offer an appropriately incisive quality. Sometimes it may be necessary to compromise to some extent in the choice of microphone because of limited availability; if this is necessary, it is obviously best to do so in some minor area, where the effect of the particular microphone is minimal.

For the most part, capacitor microphones are used but occasionally moving coil or ribbon types are selected, either because an engineer has a particular preference for such a microphone in a certain application, or where one is pressed into service for a detail effect, in the absence of a capacitor type.

It is essential that all microphones are connected in the same phase, and a convenient way of checking this is to use an oscilloscope Lissajous display. The 'scope is switched to 'external X', and an oscillator applied simultaneously to the X and Y inputs, to establish the phase of the instrument itself. Some oscilloscopes will display a line sloping upward from left to right, but many indicate the opposite slope, upward from right to left. Whichever is displayed represents the in-phase direction. The X and Y sensitivities should be adjusted to give a 45° slope. The instrument can then be connected with the left signal to the X input, and the right to the Y input.

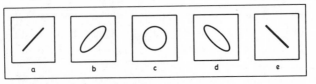

Fig. 14.4
Types of oscilloscope display produced by different amounts of phase shift

If we assume the in-phase display to be as in Fig. 14.4a, any in-phase signal monitored will be thus displayed. Progressive phase shift of one channel with respect to the other causes the display to change as in Figs. 14.4b, c, d and e, according to the degree of shift, providing that sine tones are used.

Thus we have a visual display of relative phase between left and right, which gives an immediate indication of stereo image width and phase.

Naturally, a stereo music signal will be indicated as a 'splash', but this should be discernibly ellipsoid in the in-phase direction, as in Fig. 14.5. If it is ellipsoid in the other direction, then this indicates an out-of-phase connection at some point. If the signal is panned towards mono centre, the 'splash' will narrow in width until finally it becomes a straight line.

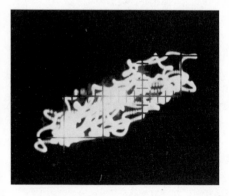

Fig. 14.5
Ellipsoid shape of oscilloscope trace during music with microphones properly in phase

It will be evident that the relative phase of a pair of microphones may easily be checked, using this instrument, by placing them close together and observing the display. In addition to this, however, the instrument gives a visual display of many parameters simultaneously; apart from left-right balance, phase and stereo width, excessive use of spot microphones and frequency dependent phase problems, resulting from poor layout, are immediately obvious. It is therefore worthwhile to have a Lissajous display available throughout a recording session, by connecting an oscilloscope to the left and right signals as described.

We have so far examined some of the more important aspects of recording in very general terms, and can now proceed to an examination of some particular examples. The only justification offered for the approaches described is that they have been used successfully, and the results have withstood the test of general critical scrutiny.

Solo performers
There is little difficulty in recording most solo instruments, as there can be no conflict of interests in the choice of microphones or placement. Microphones of any characteristic may be chosen, according to taste, and used in pairs to render the random phase reverberation stereophonically. Whilst a coincident pair may perfectly well be used, there is really no need to angle the two microphones at all; for example, a pair of omni-directional microphones placed a foot apart, and both pointing at the source, can produce a richly stereophonic image, as a Lissajous display will show. As the significant

stereo information is contained in the reverberation, the phase difference at the two points is accepted by the ear as stereo information, and the direction from which it emanated is unimportant; in these circumstances, there is a good case for keeping the source on the microphone axes. Omni-directional types would normally be chosen for their natural quality and, if it were necessary to resort to directional types, this would tend to imply that the acoustics were not really suitable.

There may be occasions when it is desirable to create an atmosphere of space in a solo recording; for example, a solo vocalist may be required to sound in a rather operatic perspective. This may be achieved by placing a main microphone system at some considerable distance from the per-former, and obtaining focus by the use of a pair of spot microphones, rather as though the main system were placed to cover an imaginary orchestra.

Singers, generally, are extremely variable in their vocal power and the differences in the optimum distance from the microphone can be very considerable. Unfortunately, the closer that it is necessary to work, the greater become the dynamic variations from the microphones, particularly between low and high notes, when there is any tendency to dynamic un-evenness in the voice itself. There are vocalists who, on certain notes, peak perhaps 6–8 dB above their average level, and it may be exceedingly difficult to focus the lower registers without being in constant danger of sudden overmodulation. In the worse cases, the only answer may be a pair of limiters with a fast attack time, but matters are rather serious if one is forced to this resort, which is always to be discouraged. In most circumstances, the voice is followed on the faders, with the assistance of cues from the producer, and a good memory!

Some vocal qualities benefit from gentle equalizer assistance, particularly the rather 'edgy' quality encountered with some voices, but it is important not to turn too readily to equalizers to solve problems, when better solutions might be found in other areas. It may well be, for instance, that a slightly different microphone placement, or the choice of a different microphone, will provide a superior improvement.

The piano is notoriously difficult to record, but again an omni-directional pair is recommended. Tastes seem to differ widely here, and very different qualities of sound may be obtained, both by placement of the microphones and the position of the instrument itself. Experience has shown that different artists playing the same piano, under identical conditions, may require different microphone placement to be adopted, and changes in repertoire often suggest complementary balance changes. Furthermore, the sound quality of individual instruments, even of the same manufacture, is enormously variable.

All these factors should be borne in mind when seeking a balance, and a constantly experimental approach is likely to be the most successful. It can also be very helpful to keep a note of the serial numbers of the various instruments encountered, and their individual tone quality, so that it may be possible to obtain one that is known to be good, for subsequent recordings.

Figure 14.6 illustrates recommended microphone positions. Towards the middle of the piano case, the sound quality is quite bright and it generally becomes warmer towards the tail end; the exact position between these extremes may be varied according to circumstances. Worthwhile improvements may be obtained by moving the microphones only a few inches one way or the other and, by exercising a little diplomacy, most artists may be persuaded to co-operate in allowing sufficient balancing time without becoming too impatient.

It is a simple matter to arrange alternative types of microphone simultaneously, in closely grouped pairs, to evaluate the differences in their sound qualities, and it may even be found that two pairs, of different types, offer some enhancement of quality when used simultaneously.

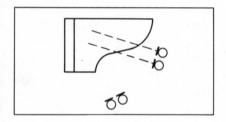

Fig. 14.6
Alternative positions for a pair of microphones for the piano

Chamber music

There are, of course, very many different kinds of ensemble under this heading, and a beginning can be made by considering the string quartet or quintet. As with any relatively quiet music, one of the greatest problems is finding a location which is both acoustically appropriate and free of excessive ambient noise. Really good halls are, in any case, hard to find and one is fortunate indeed if there is no difficulty with extraneous noises such as traffic, trains, or aeroplanes, to name a few regular offenders. Even in relatively secluded locations, there may be a great deal of noise from wind, rain, or even birds. When assessing a possible hall, therefore, any such noises should be listened for and investigation made of the feasibility of eliminating them at source. Low frequency noise may be reduced to some extent by the use of steep cut bass filters, provided that care is taken to ensure that they do not significantly affect the recorded sound quality.

There is little point in placing microphones on individual instruments, as it is usually important to preserve the intimate character of this kind of

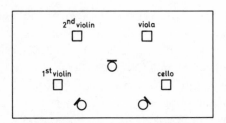

Fig. 14.7
Use of three omni-directional microphones for a string quartet

music and to avoid any suggestion of sensationalism. The stereo trio of microphones described earlier can be arranged to cover the group, at a height of between 2·5 and 3 metres (8 and 10 feet), and the instruments arranged around it as shown in Fig. 14.7. Finer points of balance may then be dealt with by moving individual instrumentalists rather than microphones.

In practice, the best grouping may be rather more widely spaced than is usual for performance, to obtain clearly defined positional information in stereo; the difference is not great and most musicians adjust comfortably to it.

In the case of music involving a piano with other instruments, it may be difficult to control the powerful piano sound in relation to the other instruments. If there are several other instruments, such as in a piano quintet, the arrangement shown in Fig. 14.8a is safest, presenting the dead side of the piano to the omni-directional trio on the strings. If, however, there is only one other instrument, the arrangement in Fig. 14.8b is more satisfactory. It is possible to use a pair of cardioid spot microphones on such an instrument, discriminating against the piano to some extent. With a little care, adequate separation may be achieved, the omni-directional pair on the piano providing most of the bloom. Thus an intimate, integrated sound can be obtained, whilst at the same time preserving the all-important aural contact between the musicians.

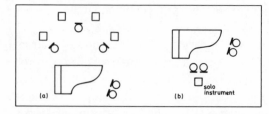

Fig. 14.8
Possible arrangements for chamber music with piano: (a) a piano quintet, and (b) a solo instrument sonata

One factor which is not always considered is the quality of the piano itself. Apart from the differences between those of different manufacture, there may well be a case, in some circumstances, for using a rather smaller piano than the usual full-sized concert grand.

Early secular music can turn up a very large range of instruments, many of which are very quiet, and there may be little relevance in attempting to create a concert balance; much of the material is very intimate and personal, and not greatly enhanced by reverberation. The usual omni-directional trio may therefore be used at a considerably lower height, and very close spot microphones may be required on some instruments. In such cases, difficulty may be experienced with finger noises on plucked instruments, or breathing noises, and optimum microphone positions may be found by standing near each instrument whilst it is being played, and listening at different points. The very high degree of amplification required for some instruments can make the slightest ambient noise obvious, but this is offset to some extent by the fact that bass filters can be used at higher cut-off frequencies than is possible with the more modern instruments.

Orchestral music

As with chamber ensembles, a good physical layout is of fundamental importance and the recording team should set out all seats and music stands before the arrival of the orchestra. A typical layout is shown in Fig. 14.9.

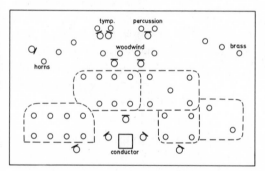

Fig. 14.9
One possible arrangement of micro-phones for a symphony orchestra

Note that the individual string sections are well defined, and the omni-directional main microphone system arranged so that each microphone has a definite duty area for which its placement is optimized. It is very important to provide depth as well as width in the layout, as this will be reflected in the stereo sound, giving a natural perspective to the orchestra and a good body of strings in the central area, as well as at the sides. The basses are best kept well back from the main microphones, and provided with their own omni-directional spot microphone to locate and clarify them.

The woodwind layout may be varied according to numbers, and it can be advantageous to arrange them in two rows, if they are many. It is not a good thing to place them too far back, as they should be well represented through the main microphones, whilst some control over their relative balance may be achieved, without destroying their perspective, by means of a fairly high pair of cardioid spot microphones, as shown in the diagram.

Incidentally, it is worth noting that the use of spot microphones in pairs, wherever possible, affords the opportunity of creating stereo images for sections, rather than relying on a conglomeration of mono panned signals.

The positions of the horn and brass sections, still farther back, may be interchanged as musically appropriate, but the left position for the horns is usually chosen as, in this position, their bells are pointing away from the rest of the orchestra, reducing the risk of their sound quality 'swimming'. The use of cardioid microphones, focussed on the bells from the rear of the players, can enhance the quality of their sound but they should be used discreetly in order to avoid distorting their perspective. The brass section, being comparatively powerful, can often be placed in such a manner that spot microphones are unnecessary; their sound quality is entirely dependent upon an adequate and focussed main microphone pick-up, and details of balance may often be dealt with by asking the players themselves to change their dynamics.

Percussion and timpani may be placed more or less as desired at the back and sides of the orchestra, the arrangement shown in the diagram being one commonly adopted possibility. In the case of timpani, a pair of cardioid spot microphones may be better than one, if there are more than two instruments used, and a suitable position is above the skin, but not over the centre where the sound quality is not particularly good. A recurring problem is a certain thick quality in the timpani sound, which is more a consequence of the omni-directional technique than anything else. Nevertheless, matters can often be greatly improved by asking the player to use harder sticks. It is in cases like this that an ability to relate amicably with musicians is of paramount importance. Co-operative players may often take an active interest in their recorded quality during a session, and adjust their technique accordingly, should this be beneficial.

Similar considerations apply to the rest of the percussion section; the dynamic latitude in recording is not as great as in performance, and any corrections necessary must be made by the musicians. Provided that the dynamics are kept low enough, good detail control over the sound quality and dynamics should be available, using spot microphones. A further useful observation is that percussion instruments are frequently bunched together, to keep them within the reach of a single player. It may be more appropriate, for stereo, to spread them more, and it may be necessary to be aware of this well in advance, so that additional percussionists can be made available at the time of the session.

One aspect of recording technique which is well worthy of attention is the choice of orchestra size. While composers sometimes specify this precisely, and in other cases it is governed by tradition, it should be remembered that these directives relate to live performance. In the recorded medium, an orchestra can often sound far larger than it actually is, depending on the acoustics, and numbers should be chosen with this in mind; authenticity is of little value if the quality of the end result is degraded by the thick quality characteristic of excessive numbers.

Harpsichord continuo presents an interesting problem; correctly balanced, it is barely audible—it has been said that one should not hear it but, if it were missing, one should miss it! For this reason, it is best positioned towards the rear of the strings, possibly near the basses with which musical contact is often important. A cardioid spot microphone, placed under the body of the instrument, can be used for fine control of quality.

Concertos, naturally, demand that the solo instrument be placed at the front, close to the main microphones; a pair of cardioid spot microphones can be used to focus the instrument, although omni-directionals can be effectively used if desired, provided that they are well separated from the orchestra. It is as well to give consideration to the question of what degree of soloist dominance is required well before the session, in conjunction with the producer and artists. Some concertos are very soloistic, with the orchestra in very much an accompanying rôle, whereas others are more symphonic in structure; such differences should be reflected in the balance, and can be adjusted by means of alterations to the soloist's proximity to the orchestra, and appropriate use of his spot microphones.

In conclusion, then, the fundamental balance in orchestral recordings should be obtained through the main microphone system by means of sensible positioning and internal balance; any attempt to correct a deficiency in these areas by means of spot microphones is a certain recipe for disaster.

Opera

A few observations were made at the beginning of this chapter about the fundamentally different listener conditions pertaining respectively to the recorded medium and live performance. It is in modern opera recording techniques that these principles reach their highest development, in terms of traditional music, for it becomes the clear duty of the recording team to utilize every available technological artifice creatively, to compensate the listener for the absence of the visual element, and the consequently depleted dramatic impact. There are nearly always stage movements in the action which must be convincingly rendered in stereo; in addition, there may be various effects, such as off-stage events, which require imagination and meticulous preparation if they are to succeed without the aid of the visual factor.

The cost of recordings on this scale can be enormous, and the scheduling extremely tight. Artists are ever-increasingly internationally mobile, and plan their commitments sometimes years in advance; key singers may be available only on a very few specified sessions, during which their performances must, at all costs, be safely recorded. As a consequence, it is always vitally important to ensure that no time is unnecessarily wasted. The producers and engineers normally spend lengthy sessions in consultation, long before the recording, planning the technical and artistic approach to each session. Often, apart from the main producer, a second producer will remain on the stage during the recording, co-ordinating the activities of the soloists, with the aid of a marked-up score and telephone contact with the control room; there may well be two balance engineers also, one dealing with the orchestra, and the other the voices. Clearly, a good working relationship between all involved is of primary importance.

Technically, in order to provide a degree of insurance against balance imperfections, a multitrack master is taken simultaneously with the stereo, with such areas as orchestra, soloists, chorus and off-stage locations on separate pairs of tracks; this also enables the engineers to meter the individual sections as required. However, the aim is to obtain a stereo master

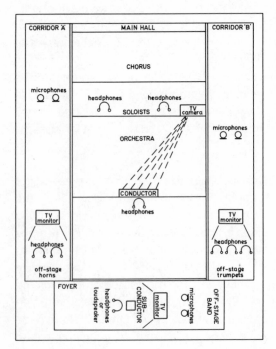

Fig. 14.10
Opera recording in an outside location where three off-stage sub-areas are used, helped by TV cameras and headphones or speakers

in the first instance, and it is therefore this signal which is monitored. Any reductions which might be required can then be edited, as necessary, into the stereo master which remains mostly first generation.

Remembering that the recording may be spread over several weeks, or even months, and that it must be possible to inter-edit the tapes, the entire technical arrangements must be meticulously logged, so that they can be reproduced exactly at any subsequent time. In particular, for any session subsequent to the first, the tape machines should be lined up to the frequency run made during the first session, rather than the standard alignment tape; this is of paramount important when noise reduction systems are used.

It has already been mentioned that good recording halls are hard to find and, in the case of opera, this problem is further augmented by the large numbers of performers involved and the consequently high sound levels. The absorption of the performers themselves, together with the enormous climaxes which occur in some works can result in acoustic saturation of the hall. This, of course, degrades the apparent reverberation time and adversely affects the stereo perspective.

In order to overcome these problems, in the absence of more suitable halls, it has become necessary to exploit existing locations to the utmost, with the aid of the increasingly sophisticated machinery available.

Figure 14.10 illustrates a set-up in which the available resources of a location have been exploited in this manner. Three off-stage locations are used, all of which are in contact with the conductor by means of closed-circuit television; the musicians are able to hear the main orchestra by means of foldback feeds from the mixer. Artists may become somewhat alarmed when these arrangements are suggested, but usually they will co-operate happily once the advantages are clear to them. While it may be perfectly possible to achieve the effect required by means of suitable placement within the main hall, the distance between the off-stage groups and the main orchestra may well lead to ensemble difficulties as a result of the time taken for sound to travel between them; the foldback arrangements, of course, allow all the musicians to hear the main microphone signals. In addition to this, it is likely that the television picture of the conductor will be a good deal clearer than the view an off-stage musician might expect to have in a cluttered hall.

The recording benefits are, of course, enormous; full attention, in terms of microphone technique, may be paid to each group, without the problems of crosstalk between microphones, and full advantage can be taken of the acoustics of the individual locations. Each group may be recorded on separate tracks of a multitrack machine, to provide for any balance alterations which may be required later, and their individual autonomy permits the engineers to place them, spatially or in perspective, in any manner of their choosing.

For larger off-stage bands, it has proved more efficient to use a sub-conductor to control the ensemble of the group, relaying the main conductor's beat with the aid of closed-circuit television and foldback; it is usually quite in order to use a small loudspeaker in place of the headphones, if this is prefered by the artists.

In the main hall, the orchestra may be laid out more or less as described earlier, and the stage and chorus sections placed typically as shown in Fig. 14.10, at some distance, and with their own spot-microphone arrays. While separation is obviously important, it should not be sought to an extreme degree, as the sound quality of both the stage and chorus sections is dependent upon their adequate representation through the main microphones; their spot microphones are used to clarify and focus them, but should never dominate. It is usually helpful, in the interests of musical contact, that all the vocalists should be raised relative to the orchestra and, to this end, it may well be necessary to have temporary stage areas or extensions built for the recording.

The question of stage movements requires some thought and, while it is possible to achieve this to a certain extent by means of the pan-pots, it is a rather dangerous method, as the electrical positioning may conflict with the information given by the main microphones. Usually, the necessary moves are noted in the stage producer's score, and he can thus prompt the soloists to make the moves physically at the correct time. The main producer should, however, simultaneously prompt the balance engineer, in order that he can track the moving voice on the faders.

Occasionally, dynamic changes in the vocal quality of a singer might be required—usually taking the form of a recession into the distance, or vice versa. Sometimes this kind of change can be satisfactorily achieved by arranging that the singer moves in relation to his spot microphone, but frequently, an echo chamber or plate, used exclusively on the particular voice, can be the most effective solution.

It falls to the producer to co-ordinate the activities of the large number of participants, in various locations, and this task, in itself, can be formidable in view of the inevitably high ambient noise between takes. By providing comprehensive talk-back and telephone communications to all locations, from the producer's desk, this problem can be greatly eased and, where the facilities are available, closed-circuit television monitoring of the various locations can be of enormous benefit. A further communication refinement is the provision of talk-back facilities from the conductor to the stage and chorus areas, in order to improve the clarity of the conductor's directions to them.

At the mixer, the orchestra section provides the basic sound field, and this is therefore usually attended to first. Subsequently, the various other locations and sections can be balanced separately within themselves, before an integration of the overall image is attempted. A really good understanding between engineers is essential, if fader creep—the process of always increasing the level of the weaker section rather than reducing the excessively strong one—is to be avoided.

One of the great benefits of using multitrack machines is the possibility of adding new material subsequently to the main recording. The very considerable scheduling problems have already been mentioned, and there is the ever present risk that an artist might fall ill at the crucial time when he is required, and re-scheduling may well be prohibitively expensive. However, it is quite possible to record the main material in the absence of the indisposed artist and, at any convenient time later, record the missing information on a vacant pair of tracks on the multitrack machine. The previously recorded orchestral tracks may be sent, via the sel-sync facility, to a pair of headphones or a small loudspeaker, and the artist is thus able to synchronize his performance to the main material. It is by no means easy to record the orchestral tracks in such a way that 'space' is left for the new part, and care is also necessary to avoid imparting an unnatural prominence to the overlaid voice. Any shortcomings in this respect will sound offensive, quite apart from completely giving the game away! The microphone technique adopted for superimpositions of this kind requires a little thought; in order to render the artist as he would have been recorded had he been present at the original recording, it is necessary to simulate the crosstalk between microphones that would have occurred. It is therefore important to set up the main microphones, in roughly the position that they would have occupied had the orchestra been present, in addition to the usual soloist's microphones.

Naturally this technique need not be used solely as a buffer against illness and other disasters; there may well be reasons for using it to achieve a particular brilliance and clarity on an instrument, where the scoring is such that a worthwhile improvement over normal recording technique can be effected. This is sometimes the case with percussion instruments, when they are used in a particularly dramatic or soloistic manner; it can be difficult to obtain a really incisive quality when such instruments are picked up excessively by the main microphones.

There may be cases when material of some kind must be superimposed on the original, but no spare tracks are available on the multitrack machine. Whilst it is perfectly possible to make an immediate reduction to stereo simultaneously with the superimposition, this may not necessarily be desirable, as no subsequent remixes would then be possible. In such a case, an

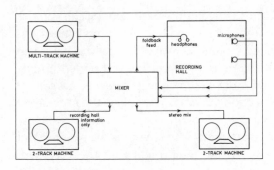

Fig. 14.11
Arrangement for superimposing a new recording on a multitrack original and recording a trial stereo mix, without affecting the original

arrangement as shown in Fig. 14.11 may be used; the multitrack machine is connected through the mixer as for a normal reduction, and the synchronization tracks sent to the artist in the hall by means of the mixer foldback circuits. The replay heads are, of course, used in place of the sel-sync system mentioned earlier. Thus, a stereo reduction is produced at the time, incorporating the new part, but the new recording is also preserved independently on a second stereo machine. Should further remixing be necessary, it is only necessary to obtain the same stereo and multitrack machines, and align the tapes for synchronization; good machines can be relied upon to hold synchronization for at least a few minutes, which is quite adequate for most superimpositions.

The techniques which have been outlined here serve to illustrate the increasing complexity of large-scale recordings and, with the imminence of quadraphony, both techniques and machinery are likely to become still more sophisticated. It is perhaps pertinent, in conclusion, to observe that while great fluency in the manipulation of machinery is essential to the balance engineer, the most gifted engineer will invariably subjugate his technical fluency and facilities to the needs of the music; any technical innovation is worthwhile, provided that it serves this master alone.

Acknowledgement
I should like to acknowledge the co-operation I received from James Lock of the Decca Record Company in the writing of this chapter.

CHAPTER FIFTEEN

Synthesized Music

Tristram Cary

Successful synthesis of a musical sound (or any sound at all) depends on accurate control of all the parameters which made up the original. If we are trying to make an electronic copy of a particular note on a clarinet, for example, or a mixed orchestral timbre, we must first find out and analyse every detail of the acoustic prototype. The term 'synthesis' is also taken to cover the creation of new sounds with no instrumental equivalent and, for many composers using electronic methods, this is a much more important aspect of synthesis than the imitative one. In the latter case, of course, there is no model to analyse, but the same methods of construction apply.

The idea of the composer controlling his own sound sources and dispensing with the need for intermediary interpreters goes back almost a century. It is not so much that composers have scant regard for the ability of musicians to play their ideas, but it does signify a desire, at least some of the time, for the independence enjoyed by painters, who can disappear into their studios and emerge some time later with a work of art completely ready to put before the public. This was not by any means the only motive for the development of electronic music, but it was one of them, and pioneers like Russolo and Varèse, in the teens and twenties of the century, predicted a time when electric machines would be able to produce any sound the composer could think of. In the event, the machines produced quite a lot of sounds the composers had *not* thought of, and this led to various avenues of research into the subjective effects of sound, closer analysis of what actually went on in a musical note, etc. What synthetic methods can do is extend a given parameter into areas not covered by normal instruments, often with surprising results.

Acoustics has always been the Cinderella of physics, and the understanding of aural phenomena, along with the development of sound sources including musical instruments, was very haphazard until Helmholtz showed that it could be scientifically studied—and Helmholtz still remains the most important acoustics textbook even after more than a century. Long before this, of course, composers had dreamed of a 'total' instrument, and the history of the organ is a parallel to the dream of personal realization by electronic means. Organs tended to get larger and larger: more stops and all manner of ingenious facilities were added as engineering arts advanced, and underlying some of this development was the concept of the ultimate sound machine. In both cases, that of the organ and of the synthesizer, the tendency has lately been to abandon this impossible notion and to concentrate on limited specifications for designated special purposes—a Baroque-type organ, for example, or a live-performance orientated synthesizer. But in fact how difficult is acceptably accurate synthesis?

Basic requirements for synthesis

To absorb a listener, music must be interesting in sound as well as structure and content, and interest means constant change. Continuous unvarying sound is very boring, and no practical musical instrument survives unless it offers variability of spectrum, either controlled or random. The 'plainest' note one can think of in terms of unvarying sameness is probably an organ flue stop driven by constant air pressure, but even here there is a very important random element caused by air turbulence. Consider the most important parameters of a single note, regarded as a musician would regard them and also as an engineer must in order to analyse them:

	Musician	Engineer
1.	Pitch	Frequency of fundamental
2.	Timbre	Spectral content
3.	Dynamic Outline	
4.	Articulation (Attack)	Envelope
5.	Duration	
6.	Vibrato	Frequency modulation
7.	Portamento (from the last note and to the next)	Slew rate of frequency staircase
8.	Tremolo	Amplitude modulation
9.	Bow scrapes, hand attacks, breath sounds, etc.	Nature of noise content

Now if we imagine this for example as a violin note which we wish to synthesize, every one of these parameters is interdependent and continuously changing. The pitch (1) is not constant because vibrato (6) is being

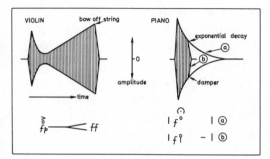

Fig. 15.1
Comparing two typical musical envelopes

applied to it, also portamento (7) at the beginning and end of a note. The timbre (2) is continuously changing as the bow is moved, and depends too on the dynamic level (3). Articulation is also a factor affecting dynamics, typically an attack or short-term period of high amplitude at the beginning of a note. Duration (5) of a sound would seem to be the most determinable parameter, but a slow diminuendo may disappear below noise thresholds in a way that makes it very difficult to state exactly where a note ended. The engineer can construct a time/amplitude curve which describes the last three parameters together as Envelope, and Fig. 15.1 shows two typical envelopes, with approximate musical instructions.

The violinist's bow is in constant control of the sound, enabling a large variety of envelopes to be played. A pianist, on the other hand, loses control of a note the moment it is struck, and from this point the sound will decay exponentially to silence, unless shortened by a damper.

Vibrato (6) is applied by the shaking motion of the left hand, and in a real violin is irregular, varying typically from 5–7 Hz and around ¼-tone on each side of the note. To the engineer this is frequency modulation of the main pitch.

Portamento (7) is often part of a violinist's style of playing, particularly when his left hand is changing position, but some portamento is inevitable in any instrument with continuous pitch variability. (Equally, of course, it is impossible on a preset instrument like the piano.) If one regards successive notes as a pitch staircase, immediate arrival at the next pitch would analyse as an infinite rate of pitch slew. Portamento can be expressed as a rate—octaves per second. The staircase is another form of frequency modulation (usually slower than vibrato).

Tremolo (8), when applied with the bow, is fairly rapid amplitude modulation of the note, superimposed on the main envelope. Often a player will apply vibrato and tremolo at the same time, at different frequencies.

Item (9) covers all the odd noises, such as the scrape of the bow, the attack sound at the beginning before the string is vibrating properly, the sound of left hand fingers striking the strings to press them down, etc. These small sounds are extremely difficult to analyse and synthesize because, being transient phenomena, they cannot easily be displayed or measured. Nevertheless they are vital to the character of instruments, and the first few milliseconds of a note, which contain more of these noises than any other part, also hold the main clues to the identity of the instrument. An experiment anyone can do is to record a number of instrumental tones and then remove by cutting the first ½-second of each sound. If you play the tape to someone else, even a musician, it is very unlikely that he will identify all the instruments correctly.

I have described one sound at some length, to give an idea of the difficulty of correct synthesis of even a single note, and the most important thing to remember is that all the contributing factors are changing during the whole course of the sound; therefore, even to attempt accurate synthesis, we must have a means of controlling every relevant parameter continuously. Even then, with circuitry which makes the synthesis theoretically possible, the mathematical analysis of what is required is extremely complex.

A practical synthesis (or equally the creation of a 'new' sound) can be attempted at many different levels, depending on the requirements of the final user of the sound, and the technical means have of course changed dramatically with concurrent advances in the science of electronics. For example the provision of a real-time, live performance synthesis in the form of a playable musical instrument obviously involves compromises which are not necessary in a research situation, and in the end it is the economic factor which often decides how far a process can go. In the case of electronic organs, there has also been some preconditioning by years of experience with pipe organs; when you draw a stop marked 'Flute' or 'Trumpet' you do not really expect it to sound like these instruments—you accept it as a 'Flute stop' or 'Trumpet stop' sound.

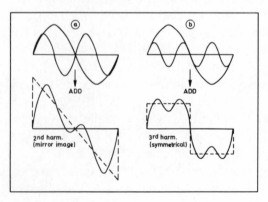

Fig. 15.2
Comparing the addition of second and third harmonic waveforms to the fundamental (in phase)

Subtractive synthesis

In practice, the simplest way to achieve a reasonably acceptable musical timbre (thinking for the moment of a single 'note'—one fundamental + harmonics) is to take a rich waveform of known harmonic content and use filters to remove unwanted portions of the spectrum. This method, used in most electronic organs, involves generating a waveshape which contains either a complete series or, for some instruments (e.g. clarinet), an odd harmonic series. The most easily generated 'complete series' waveform is the sawtooth, and any symmetrical waveform will contain either no harmonics (sine) or odd harmonics only (typically square or triangle). A characteristic of even harmonics is the mirror-image type of waveform, and Fig. 15.2 shows 2nd and 3rd harmonic shapes (in-phase in this instance) for comparison.

The dotted lines show the tendency of the shapes if further even or all harmonics are added to (a), and odd harmonics only are added to (b) (at decreasing amplitude with increasing pitch). The resulting known spectra can be modified by filtering to produce an approximation of the required instrumental timbre. This process is made easier by the fact that instruments exhibit a 'formant' pass band whose frequency limits remain the same throughout the range of the instrument—i.e. the filter need not be tuned as well as the oscillator. However, dynamic timbre control, which as we have seen is vitally necessary to proper synthesis, is not normally part of an organ design.

Apart from some kind of shaping circuit for timbre, and keying circuits to make sure that attacks are smooth and click-free, even the most modest organ will contain two other signal modifiers—vibrato (applied to oscillator frequency by another—sub-audio—oscillator), and 'sustain', which is a means of allowing a note to die naturally after the finger has been removed from the key, instead of being brutally cut off.

The better and larger organs are much more generously specified. For example, an effect of 'dynamic' timbre can be achieved by two free running oscillators in unison, because they will beat slowly and cause phase shifts. Noise generators may be used to add aperiodic components. Instead of using tone generators for the topmost octave only, and dividers for the rest, an expensive instrument may have an oscillator for every note. Some organs use electro-mechanical generators, which never need tuning.

But, with the advent of electronic music on tape, composers became more interested in subtler signal manipulations, and were prepared to trade the convenience of real-time performance for better control of the sound. Since they could realize their music on tape, they could take as much time as was necessary to get it right. In any case, the music itself might be quite unsuitable for any type of keyboard instrument, because composers were beginning to think of electronic music in quite a new way. Rejecting the organ, they began again from basics, and some even limited their sources to sine generators *only*, since this is the fundamental building brick of all sound. But, when it became clear after a few years of *ad hoc* studios, that electronic music had come to stay, engineers began to think of designing 'packages' of matched devices specially orientated towards the electronic music composer.

Thus was born the 'synthesizer', and the first ones (e.g. the RCA Synthesizer in New York) were formidable arrays of equipment. The RCA machine did in fact look forward to present-day developments in having a digital input, but the devices themselves were analog. In general, to distinguish them from computer-like mechanisms, synthesizers of this type are called analog synthesizers.

The idea was to assemble as many source and treatment modules as possible, route them through a patch for changing the configuration, and control them, in the first instance, manually. Sources included both ends of the spectral possibilities (sine and white noise) and a selection of known periodic spectra in between. Treatments included filters of various sorts (e.g. bandpass, band reject, $\frac{1}{2}$ or $\frac{1}{3}$-octave, high and low pass, resonating, etc.), dynamic contour generators (envelope shapers), reverberation, modulators (multipliers), etc. But as long as all changes had to be made manually accurate synthesis, requiring as we have seen multiple and continuous variation of at least five or six parameters, was impossible. Composers did their best by carrying out as many operations as they could simultaneously, and proceeding by successive recording generations, using tape as a secondary source and treating its output further (apart from mechanical manipulations of the tape itself). The greatest difficulty was the accumulation of tape and system noise over successive recording generations.

The RCA machine was the first to be fully automated, using a wide punched paper roll input based on 4-bit words (hole = 1, no hole = 0) giving 16 choices per word. These instructions were routed to massive relay trees which operated the devices. Multitrack sync on tape was achieved by using a tape recorder pulse to start the paper roll. This very expensive, and in a way marvellous, device still exists and can be seen at the Columbia Princeton Electronic Music Center in New York. Even in 1959, it cost well over $100,000.

The voltage controlled analog synthesizer
In the middle 1960s Robert Moog published practical designs for a Voltage Controlled Oscillator (VCO) and a Voltage Controlled Amplifier (VCA) with acceptably low distortion and predictable law. By now the transistor revolution was also in full swing, and in a very short time a completely new, much smaller and cheaper type of synthesizer came into being, based on

the above two devices, from which all other VC devices could be quite easily derived. Voltage control made possible, without continual manual adjustment being necessary, the multiple parameter control essential to a subtler approach to synthesis. Furthermore, a much smaller number of actual devices could be used because, instead of being dedicated to one job, a single circuit could be used for a variety of purposes; for example a VCO could be used (1) as an audio sine source, (2) as an audio source of some other waveform, (3) as a control source at audio frequencies (FM or AM of a VCO or VCA), (4) as a control source at sub-audio frequencies. For slowly changing phenomena, a new requirement was for oscillators capable of working at frequencies as low as 0·01 Hz (100 secs/cycle). Used to control an audio oscillator, a triangle output at this frequency will produce a very slow glissando or, used to control a VC filter, it will cause a slow timbre change. From the electronic point of view, a synthesizer must be direct coupled throughout or these versatilities are not possible.

Manual control is still there, but it is used more to set variables than to alter fixed parameters. Manual and voltage control are used together—e.g. you might manually set a mean vibrato of 6 Hz, but also add a random voltage control to give it a frequency locus of 5–7 Hz. Although the control may appear very simple (e.g. a keyboard producing a voltage staircase) the influence it can exert may be multiple. For example, as well as controlling pitch, a keyboard might be programmed so that it causes progressive timbre changes, slower/faster vibrato, more reverberation, etc., according to a nominal 'pitch' programme—indeed the control of pitch itself may not even be involved. In cases like this, an apparently normal notation may be used, but the 'notes' stand for certain prepared groups of mean values.

An 'instrumental' type of VC synthesizer patch might be as shown in Fig. 15.3. This is a fairly elaborate patch for producing a 'single' note, but it gives control of nearly all the parameters in our initial list. Starting at (2) in that list, timbre has three controls, a randomly varying one from VCO4, a dynamically dependent one and an envelope dependent one (a dynamic or velocity dependent output from a keyboard is obtained by using two contact sets and measuring the time between successive closures). The dynamic outline (3), preset as an average, will also change according to the dynamics sent from the keyboard, and the attack (4) is part of the envelope setting, the shapers being triggered by a pulse from the keyboard. Duration (5) is a matter of envelope (controlled as above) plus reverberation, which will get shorter at higher notes ('pitch' voltage controlling direct/reverb ratio). Vibrato (6) comes from VCO3, and will vary in speed with dynamics. Portamento (7) is a built-in variable staircase slew in the keyboard, and will increase in speed with 'loudness'. Tremolo (8) goes in at the output VCA from VCO5. This

VCA could also have been controlled by the keyboard 'dynamic' output but, in this patch, an absolute loudness control is deliberately omitted because the other effects caused by low 'dynamics' would not be heard if the output level were reduced to pianissimo at the same time. Dynamic *contour*, as opposed to general loudness, is of course taken care of by the envelope shapers. Noise content (9) is added through a second envelope shaper, the two shaper outputs being suitably mixed.

I have left (1) till last, because I have shown in the diagram, as well as the subtractive effect of the filtering, a degree of additive waveshaping before the filtering takes place. I will deal with this different principle in a new section.

Additive synthesis

All sounds are composed, in the end, of separable sinusoidal components, so it has always been obvious that the 'purest' method of synthesis would be to take as many sine sources as were necessary and mix them to produce the required sound. In practice, however, this is very difficult to do. Not only must you know exactly what frequencies are required, and at what amplitudes and phase relationships, but you need a large number of very pure (and therefore expensive) sine generators—purity being necessary because any impurity adds unplanned harmonics and detracts from the accuracy of

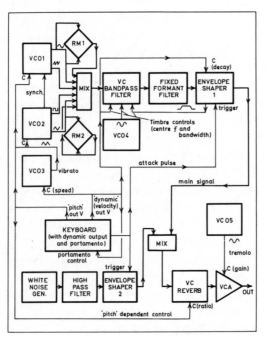

Fig. 15.3
Example of the patching of a voltage controlled synthesizer for a single note

the mix. In addition, free running oscillators will always drift slightly, so it is impossible without synchronizing arrangements to establish and maintain a phase relationship. Additive synthesis is not normally attempted, therefore, at the technical level of an analog synthesizer except in the very limited way shown in Fig. 15.3.

Here VCO1 and VCO2 are tuned an octave apart and synchronized. They will not only track together an octave apart but remain in phase. VCO1 offers sine and sawtooth, and the sine is taken to a ring modulator in frequency doubling configuration (difference $f = 0$, summation $= 2f$). VCO2 has a square and a triangle output, and the triangle is taken to the frequency halving configuration of a second modulator—its output will be an odd harmonic series on a fundamental one octave below. The resulting six outputs are all locked together and can therefore be additively mixed to produce a complex wave of calculable shape. Since we have four fundamentals spanning three octaves, each with a known harmonic content, we can exercise considerable control over the shape (and therefore the sound), and it is possible to use this method without any filters to produce subtle timbres. But the limitations in this context are fairly severe (no VC control of timbre—no possibility of random timbre variation), and the full potential of additive synthesis is normally realized only when it is possible to use computers.

Computer additive synthesis

The general methods described in this brief survey are subject to numerous special variations, and it is not possible to describe individual developments in detail. Thus there are many designs of analog VC synthesizer, the specifications varying according to their intended use. Ready made machines are available from a number of firms, among them EMS (London), Moog, Buchla, and ARP. There are now also some construction kits for the home builder. In the field of computer synthesis, however, where the hardware is more expensive, the main work has been done in particular places, usually universities or industrial research establishments.

The principle is very elegant, and dispenses altogether with music devices as such—in this form it is called 'time domain additive synthesis'. You describe to a computer the mathematics of what you require, and the computer generates the digital equivalent of the sound you are looking for. Any waveform can be converted to a series of amplitude samples (see Fig. 15.4).

It is necessary, of course, to sample at a rate which will allow the highest frequencies to be represented in the number series and, in general, since the minimum information for a single cycle is one positive and one negative sample, the rate of sampling has to be in the order of twice the highest frequency required. In this way the computer can store a *sound* as *numbers* and, conversely if you know the mathematics of the sound, the computer can generate numbers corresponding to it. The sampling process above takes place in an Analog-to-Digital Converter (ADC). By the opposite process, Digital-to-Analog Conversion (DAC), you can change the discrete samples back into an integrated continuous function and listen to the result. Treatments like filtering become merely part of the total concept of the sound. Even echo and reverberation, essentially delay mechanisms, become subroutines of the digital process. In theory a total synthesis method should be the best: the only analog device needed is the final tape recorder on which the result appears (digital tape recorders are also used, of course, but within the computer system).

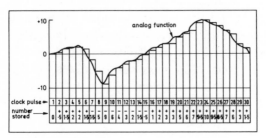

Fig. 15.4
Showing how an analog waveform can be converted to a series of amplitude samples in an analog-to-digital converter (ADC)

The difficulties in practice are considerable and, although current research is rationalizing the methods by which it can become a normal compositional technique, the fact remains that pure synthesis has so far been the province of specialized workers with large resources at their command. The mathematics is formidable, and the slow processing time (e.g. conversion of input to punched cards) makes it an awkward medium for practical composition. One of the biggest problems is that most computer programs use a machine language better fitted for accountancy than music, and nearly all adaptations of these languages involve the composer in hundreds of exact parametric decisions—all of which must be made or the program will not run. Long lists of figures tend to have limited appeal to composers and, when the computer asks, for the *n*th time that day, 'what timbre do you want?', he may feel inclined to reply 'let's hear a few and see if I like them'. In fact programs which allow just this kind of dialogue are being developed and, with the increasing speed and efficiency of digital systems, it is likely that future synthesis will use variants of this method at all levels. But it is certain that only a computer can deal adequately with the problems of additive synthesis, because the amount of data requiring rapid handling is very large if parameters are constantly changing (and we have already seen that they are).

What the composer wants from any synthesizer is real time interaction between himself and the machine, and most research programmes are at least aiming in this direction. Up to now, though, the most practical way of achieving real time synthesis using a computer is not to attempt full scale additive synthesis but to hybridize digital and analog methods.

Digital/analog hybrid synthesis

The main drawback of the straight VC analog synthesizer is the difficulty of exactly repeating a programme, and hence of designing a meaningful notation. You may realize, empirically, the sound you have in mind by delicate setting of the interactive controls, but to repeat this exact sound on a later occasion, or to notate it precisely for someone else, is virtually impossible. Dozens of knobs may have been set by ear, and the interactions are such that, unless you reset them in the same sequence and to an accuracy of minutes of angle, the chances of recapturing that exact sound are very slim indeed. So in a number of current designs an acceptable compromise is found by combining the accuracy of digital control with the flexibility and immediacy of analog music devices. In a typical hybrid system you decide how many choices are necessary for a particular parameter. For example 60 or so discrete values of amplitude are quite enough for nearly all practical purposes, which means that you can describe amplitude using not more than 6 bits (64 choices). If you need 60 pitches within an octave (10th-tone increments) and a range of 7 octaves, the discrete voltages required to interface a VCO are $60 \times 7 = 420$. You will need a word length of 9 bits (512 possible choices). The on/off, yes/no type of decision can of course be controlled by one bit.

Digital/analog synthesis can be applied at a modest level (e.g. a digital sequence generator operating a small analog machine—as in the EMS Synthi AKS). At medium levels a more elaborate digital sequencer can be given editing facilities and made to handle several simultaneous streams of data (like 'voices' in musical counterpoint). At computer level the processor is specially interfaced for direct control of the analog system, and one has all the advantages of the machine's arithmetic and storage capabilities. Some music devices can be designed as digital in the first place—e.g. a digital oscillator, where frequency is controlled by numbers, and where the specification of a frequency by number must always result in correct tuning. Various languages have been devised for composers using hybrid computer studios, and in most cases the software is developed along with the hardware of the studio. Among these languages are 'Musys', developed by EMS of London, and 'Groove', designed by Max Matthews of Bell Telephone, New Jersey.

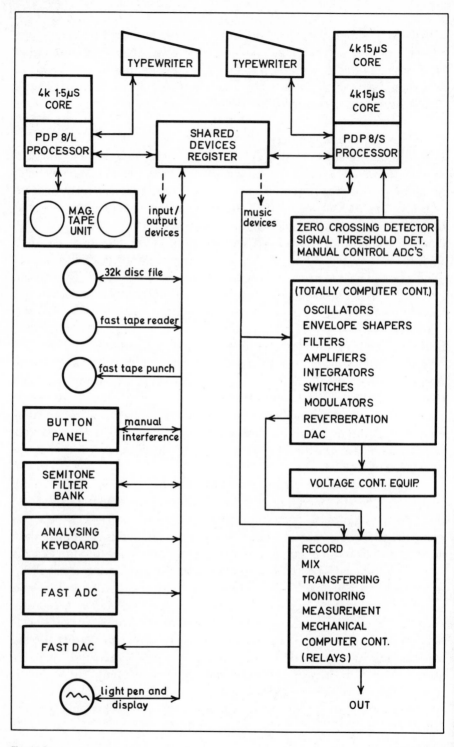

Fig. 15.5
Block diagram of the basic hardware in a modern hybrid computer studio (the 'MUSYS' system by EMS, London)

A great advantage of hybrid systems is that, because the computer does not have to calculate actual waveform data, but only control devices (plus, of course, the data concerned with the music itself), quite modest word lengths and clock rates can do a great deal of effective work. Large and expensive processors are not necessary, and a low-cost mini-computer, with special inputs and outputs and probably some extended storage, is all that is normally necessary. Figure 15.5 shows in block form the basic hardware of the EMS Musys system, as it was in 1974.

The PDP8/L mini-computer, on the right, looks after the Text, edits it, compiles it and issues 'bus lists'—i.e. it deals with the mathematical side of the problem. The PDP8/S, which is a slower processor, is interfaced with the other computer by a 'shared devices register' and with the music hardware. It can even carry out mechanical operations such as starting and stopping tape recorders, giving cues to musicians, etc. Real time interference by the composer is possible at any stage, and his *ad hoc* decisions can become permanent ones at will.

Some other methods of synthesis

We described above the general principles of time domain additive synthesis, and some of the drawbacks. One of these, that the composer is expected to make, unerringly, a large number of parametric decisions, can to some extent be avoided by statistical procedures, since an element of randomness is very important in music in any case. If the composer has some idea of the limits within which the 'right' sound will lie, and with experience he should, the computer is instructed to choose random numbers within those limits, and the composer can either accept the result, ask for another selection, or make an exact choice by gradually reducing the random element to zero. Some fascinating work on frequency modulation as a general method has been done by John Chowning at Stanford, California, and a variant of this method has been developed by Barry Truax at Utrecht, achieving quite complex pure synthesis on a comparatively modest computer—PDP15.

In Stockholm, Stiftelsen EMS and Swedish Radio have built a digital studio using not mathematical synthesis but digital music devices. Playback is directly from the digital system rather than from analog tape. Daphne Oram in Kent developed a system (Oramics) some years ago using graphic inputs drawn on film to control analog devices, and a visual input certainly has great appeal to some composers. Miss Oram's machine is still at the development stage and, like all the systems here briefly described, is unique and exists in one studio only.

EMS in London have devised a new system which starts from the completely different principle of frequency domain instead of time domain synthesis.

A spectrum is considered as a large number of frequency locations and, instead of time/amplitude samples of a waveform, the computer takes frequency/amplitude samples of a spectrum. This spectral data can be analysed and stored with much greater efficiency than can time domain data, and small, economical storage systems can therefore be more effectively used. As an analyser it works, in fact, rather like the human ear. Called DAOB (Digital Analyser and Oscillator Bank), this system is very much orientated towards real time dialogue with a composer, and has an important second rôle as a speech data compressor, making possible the transmission of large quantities of intelligible voice information at bit rates far below those possible with conventional pulse code modulation (bit rate= bits/second, a measure of the product of word length and sampling rate, which roughly assesses the handling capacity of a system).

With the reduction in size and increased efficiency of small digital devices which we have recently seen (witness the tiny calculators now in all the world's shops), much active work is going on in music synthesis to produce comparatively low cost systems which will have at least some of the features of the complex and very expensive time domain synthesis methods so far developed. A variation of time domain synthesis is phase-summation synthesis, in which two complex waves with mutually variable phase relationships are mixed. The second waveform will cause dynamic timbre changes in the first, and very subtle but predictable control is possible. This method is being developed by Anthony Furse in Australia (Creative Strategies Pty. Ltd.), whose synthesizer also features a 'progressive structure' synthesis where a bank of prepared harmonic structures can be used, rather as an orchestra is a large collection of known sounds whose exact combination is organized by the composer. In fact any computer system can be used in this way because the composer will build up a library of precalculated sounds which he can call on as required.

Conclusion

If the foregoing seems to present a confusing number of alternatives, this is only because those alternatives actually exist. At the present moment the connotation of 'synthesizer' in 95% of cases is 'array of analog voltage controlled devices with variable patching facilities'. In recent years it is increasingly common to find some digital control devices as well. Specifications vary a great deal, but the general principle of such machines is subtractive—i.e. generating rich waveforms and filtering to taste. But small digital machines, of much greater predictability in use, are being actively developed, and digital/analog hybrid studios have now reached a high level of performance. Pure digital synthesis, without conventional analog waveform sources, is also moving from the exclusive and expensive area to a user-orientated, more compact and less costly one. In less than a decade from now, the digital synthesizer will probably have completely supplanted the VC analog machine.

The future lies as much with musicians as designers. It is certain that any sound you can reasonably think of will be *possible* to synthesize, and imitations of voices and instruments more or less indistinguishable from the real thing will be commonplace. Whether we will want to use these techniques, or whether the artists will call for a different sort of tune, it is not possible to predict. But electronic synthesis is here to stay, and has not so far shown any sign of ousting the human musician from his traditional perch. Indeed, as time goes on, and the first shock wears off, the instrumentalist begins almost to welcome the presence of the synthesizer in his midst—particularly as so many instruments have 'gone electric' in any case. In the many live electronic pieces now being written, active co-operation between the musician and the machine is opening up new possibilities for composers and new paths in music.

CHAPTER SIXTEEN

Location Recording

Robert Auger

The recording of music outside normal studios, or 'on location' as it has come to be known, falls broadly into two categories: formal sessions and public performances. Although it might appear at first sight that, from the engineer's point of view, both categories present similar problems, in practice the working conditions in each case are greatly dissimilar, and require an entirely different approach; so for the purposes of this chapter it is proposed to consider them separately.

Formal sessions

There are several reasons why a producer may decide to arrange for a formal session, or more likely a series of formal sessions, to be recorded on location rather than in a studio. The first and most obvious is that he may have to undertake the recording of a large-scale work and does not have, or cannot get, a studio large enough to contain the performers (see Fig. 16.1). A work does not have to be all that large to make location recording preferable; there are only one or two studios in this country which can accommodate a full symphony orchestra, and the fact that a given studio can physically contain a certain number of musicians does not necessarily mean that an artistically acceptable result can be obtained when it is filled to capacity.

A second reason for recording on location is that the work may not sound as it should when it is performed in a studio acoustic, and it is significant that even record companies with large studios of their own prefer to record the majority of their repertoire in halls or churches selected for their concert hall acoustics. A suitable acoustic is probably of even more importance to the artists than it is to the engineer for, with reservations that will be mentioned later, an agreeable sound can often be produced by processing the tape after recording; but musicians, especially singers, cannot give of their best in an acoustic unsuited to the work in performance.

Thirdly, a producer may choose to record on location to escape from the economic pressures of the studio and allow the artist or artists more freedom in regard to hours of work and rest. It would be a great pity, for instance, to

Fig. 16.1
A typical large scale location recording (for Schoenberg's 'Gurre-Lieder') with Pierre Boulez conducting the BBC SO (157 players) and BBC Choral Society (augmented to 350) in the West Ham Central Mission (photo by Clive Barda)

have to stop recording a quartet with the musicians in top gear, simply because their time had run out in a busy studio.

1. Choice of location

In an ideal world, the choice of location for an outside recording would depend entirely on its acoustic suitability for the work to be performed, but unfortunately in this country, and in London in particular, the first problem is one of outside noise. Consequently one's priorities become reversed: the first question one asks is 'Is the location quiet enough?' and the second 'Are its acoustics good, or only adequate?'.

Nowadays it is becoming increasingly difficult to find locations that are easily accessible to performers and are at the same time reasonably free from traffic and aircraft noise. For some years I have held the opinion that far too much publicity is given to the noise problems of people living and working near our major airports, compared with others who are supposed to be more fortunate living ten to twenty miles away. Road traffic noise too has increased enormously over the last ten years; one of my favourite locations in North London is now untenable since the electric buses were replaced by diesels.

Even a venue which is free from these hazards, and which on a first visit appears to be ideally quiet, may subsequently prove to be adjacent to a source of noise not evident at the time: a printing works which suddenly erupts into life, or a building site which has appeared since the first visit was made. A change of weather too can lead to unexpected complications; traffic noise, which on a dry day takes the form of a low-frequency rumble that may be filtered out without much difficulty, can on a wet day become a mid-frequency hiss caused by wet tyres which no filtering can satisfactorily remove.

Electrical interference is another possible nightmare which may not become evident until late in the proceedings and, if the performers have already arrived, it will be difficult for the engineer to obtain the quiet he needs to locate the source of interference, whether it be mains-borne or picked up in the microphone cables. Such setbacks and other unpredictables may even lead to a session having to be abandoned, and the producer who attempts to plan a location recording to a very tight schedule lays himself open to frustration.

There is, however, an interrelation between the type of material being recorded, the acoustic required and the amount of external noise that can be tolerated, and in this respect the producer will be greatly dependent on the engineer's experience and ability for advice. A level of traffic noise which would prevent the recording of a string quartet in an open acoustic might cause no concern during a close-microphone session with a jazz group; such considerations are not capable of quantitative evaluation and can only be decided by personal judgement based on experience.

2. Acoustic considerations

Assuming then that we have a choice of locations quiet enough to record in, we now come to consider the acoustic requirements of the buildings themselves. Here the major established recording companies have a great advantage over the smaller ones in that they are able to schedule their releases a long way ahead and can thus reserve the more ideal venues in good time, or even make exclusive bookings with church and local authorities. Because only selected locations are used, specialized microphone techniques can be evolved. The great mass of halls large enough to accommodate a full orchestra, but which suffer from all kinds of heating and noise problems, can be rejected by the majors but may have to be used by the smaller record companies and independent producers.

Consequently many LPs are made in churches and halls which are far from satisfactory for the purpose; it is up to the ingenuity of the engineer to get round the problems by whatever technical means and expertise at his disposal. Often this means working with microphones closer than one would like, and excluding the use of omni-directional microphones altogether; the effects of these enforced techniques then have to be modified during dubbing to obtain a satisfactory perspective.

The first requirement of the hall is that the reverberation time shall be long enough to put a pleasant ambience on the music; the second is that the reverberation shall not be coloured in any way. Unevennesses, for example boominess, or a mid-frequency 'honk', can be recognized by experience when taking a walk round the hall and, in my opinion, it is preferable to record in a room which is fairly dead but has an even frequency response than one which is nicely reverberant but uneven to the extent that it either rings or booms. A dead recording can have artificial reverberation added to it later; this can be done in a tasteful way so that it cannot be noticed that the reverberation is artificial and indeed many of today's LPs are treated in this manner.

3. Control rooms

The engineer will indeed be lucky if he has much choice as to where his control room is to be; almost certainly its acoustics will be far from adequate and room colouration can do terrible things to a standard monitor system.

The monitoring level is probably the first thing to be affected. A very dead control room, say a cloakroom lined with clothes and drapes, will cause the engineer to drive his monitor system far harder than normal, even to the point of distortion. A very live room like a church vestry can cause the opposite to happen, with monitor levels being reduced to a point where the sound becomes subject to an apparent middle and treble lift. It is therefore important that the engineer should work with equipment which he knows and is well used to; he will then be able to judge fairly reliably the effect that the room is having on the sound. The person in difficulty will be the producer who, without previous experience of the particular equipment being used, may take some time to adjust to the surroundings and even ask that the balance be altered in a way that he will subsequently regret. The same consideration applies to artists coming into the control room for a playback, and the engineer must not only be very sure of his equipment and his judgement, but also be possessed of qualities of tact and persuasion if serious errors are to be avoided.

An engineer of my acquaintance has a quick method of evaluating monitoring conditions which has much to recommend it. For this he uses a test tape made up in two sections. The first section is a straightforward music recording which he engineered himself and knows well; the second is a 'wobble tape' made up of short bursts of tone at various frequencies interspersed with similar bursts of 1 kHz reference tone. By playing the whole tape through the monitor system, any colouration becomes quickly apparent.

Alternatively, but perhaps less effectively, suspected room colouration can be checked by comparing the sound through the monitor loudspeakers with that produced by a pair of good quality earphones of known performance.

4. Communications

For solo recitals, or small groups such as a string quartet, a simple talkback loudspeaker is normally sufficient; the artists will be close enough to a microphone for the control room to hear what they are saying. In these circumstances it is preferable for the monitor loudspeakers to be dimmed rather than muted when the talkback key is operated, enabling easy two-way conversation to take place.

For larger combinations, from chamber orchestra upwards, it is desirable to have a telephone link with the conductor as well. Such an arrangement is not only convenient but also has psychological advantages: the people in the control room can probably hear what is happening in the studio better than the conductor can, and it may be more tactful to refer to individual shortcomings over the telephone than to announce them over the talkback for all to hear.

In the case of a full symphony orchestra, where more microphones are in use and are probably strung up higher, it is usual to put an additional microphone in front of the conductor to enable the producer in the control room to hear what he is saying. There is however a danger, if this microphone is routed through the main mixer, that it may inadvertently be left open during a take, so its output should be routed separately to its own amplifier and loudspeaker in the control room.

Closed-circuit television is very useful and can save a lot of worry. If, for example, a singer's voice suddenly disappears during rehearsal it may only be because he or she has moved away from the microphone for some reason; an engineer who cannot see this will perhaps assume that a fault has developed and start to take action accordingly. When recording a jazz group, television is really indispensable, as front-line jazz musicians are accustomed to walking about while they play, leaving the engineer with the alternative of keeping all his microphones open or guessing where the musicians may happen to be.

5. Recording opera

Procedures for recording formal sessions on location are broadly similar to those employed in the studio, but because opera tends to be recorded more often on location than in a studio it may be appropriate at this point to say something about its particular problems.

There are two basic ways to set about recording opera; their difference is rather more the concern of the producer than of the engineer, but the engineer has to be able to deal with both of them. The first is the system pioneered by John Culshaw in the 1950s of putting the singers behind the orchestra on a chessboard stage with a line of five or so cardioid microphones along the front. The number of the square in which the singer should be standing at any particular moment is marked on his or her score; this affects not only the left-to-right position but also the back-to-front, so that various perspectives can be obtained. This method has proved to be enormously successful. It requires a great deal of planning, a lot of intelligence and much work at the actual time of recording; additionally it requires the services of a stage director in telephone communication with the producer. Its disadvantages are that it is expensive and puts a great strain on the conductor, who may not be able to hear the singers across the wide expanse of orchestra. This is what I would call the 'grand' way of recording opera and, if all its requirements can be met, the result is very good indeed.

The second method involves far less preparation and has the singers grouped on either side of the conductor facing into the orchestra. The microphone outputs—one per singer, or pair of singers—are recorded on separate tracks; balance and panning are subsequently effected in the mixdown. Cardioid microphones must be used for the orchestra as well as for the singers, to maintain separation and make it possible to pan a singer from one side of the orchestra to the other. This system makes it possible to work much faster: less preparation time is needed and the sorting-out can all be done afterwards rather than during the session itself.

6. Recording facilities

During the last few years, the gap between the technical requirements for recording popular music and those for classical music has narrowed appreciably. Up to the late 1960s, classical music was invariably recorded in two-track stereo, or at the most in four-track, just to separate the soloist and accompaniment for later mixing at a dubbing session. The advent of quadraphonic recording, and the appearance of so many different matrix and discrete systems for the final presentation to the public, has caused the major companies to hedge their bets at the recording session and record on multitrack equipment, each track containing a section of the orchestra for subsequent mixing into whatever master system is eventually used. In other words, the companies are now storing information on the session for archive purposes. Had this attitude been adopted over the last 25 years, many great performances would now be available in real stereo and not have to be electronically processed.

'Light' music however has always been quick to benefit from continual technical development of facilities since the early 1950s. The advantage of recording instruments and soloists on separate tracks soon became apparent, especially when different balances were required for mono and stereo LPs. The American guitar and vocal duo, Les Paul and Mary Ford, were making eight-track multiple recordings in the early 1950s and the New York studios of Atlantic Records were recording one microphone per track, without mixing on the session, by 1960. Perhaps one reason why the classical people were slower to use multitrack was the inherent tape hiss which became audibly noticeable when the tracks were mixed for the master tape used for disc production. This problem was largely solved by the professional Dolby A noise reduction system in 1966. Tape hiss and print-through are now virtually things of the past, so far as tape masters are concerned.

Multitrack equipment, Dolby units, and closed-circuit television have, however, greatly increased the work and physical effort in today's location recording, and it is not unusual to employ two or three tons of equipment for recording an opera or a live pop concert (see Fig. 16.2).

Public performances

As a result of the many improvements in recording equipment and techniques outlined above, producers are becoming increasingly attracted to the recording of public concerts and other events where the reaction of the audience to the performers (and vice versa), as well as the general ambience, can create a sense of occasion unobtainable in a formal session. Such events include pop shows, concerts by international stars, stage productions, and jazz concerts, as well as classical performances requiring musical forces so large that they can only be assembled once.

For the engineer, the principal consideration that distinguishes this kind of recording from the formal session is the limited amount of time available to him. Public halls, arenas, stadiums, and the like are let on a 24-hour basis; during this period the engineers will have to set up as many as fifty microphones, test, balance, record, strike, and get away again. For this reason it is usual nowadays to use a mobile control room for concert work, and many recording vehicles contain not only comprehensive technical facilities, but also more mundane comforts for the crew in the form of showers and toilets, not to mention the all-important refrigerator (see Chapter Ten).

1. Setting up

I remember with affection a magazine article published many years ago giving some hints and tips for amateur recordists. In the middle of the page was a box containing the statement 'It often pays to have the microphones set up before the musicians arrive'. The relevance of quoting this in the present context is to state the rule that, when setting up, one should always work from the microphones back to the control room and not the other way round.

The procedure is to get the microphones rigged, with their cables connected, and make sure that everything in the space that the artists are going to occupy is installed first. In the control room, first connect the microphone lines to the mixer panel, then connect the monitor output from the mixer to the loudspeakers. Connections to the tape recorder can wait until later; they will not be wanted until last.

Fig. 16.2
Control room equipment at a modern location recording can be very complex. Here two control consoles are in use, with multitrack recorders, Dolby units and full-size monitor speakers (courtesy Unicorn Records)

Then follows the routine of identifying the microphone channels, or 'scratching out' as it is often called: the undignified business of an engineer going round the microphones and saying, for example, 'This mike is on the first violins' and scratching it for identification on the mixer. It is a crude practical test, but there is no better method. In the quiet of a church hall on a formal session, it presents no problems as the control room can easily communicate with the recording area over the talkback, but in a large stadium this is impossible and the only satisfactory communication is by a two-way radio link.

2. Splitting microphone outputs

When the performance being recorded already requires the use of microphones for public address purposes, there are three possibilities for the recording engineer: to instal another complete set of recording microphones, to use the public address microphones to feed the recording mixer, or to replace the public address microphones by recording microphones and use the latter to feed the public address system. The solution adopted will depend on the circumstances and, in particular, what kind of agreement can be reached with the public address engineer.

It is not unknown for a pop group to use 30 or 40 microphones of their own, as one man may play as many as five or six different keyboard instruments, each with its own microphone or microphones; to duplicate them all could result in having 60 or 80 microphones on stage. There are therefore considerable advantages in splitting the outputs from one set of microphones; but also there are problems. The way *not* to do it is by putting in a junction lead so that each microphone output feeds both systems direct; this is open not only to hazards of mismatching but to problems of earthing, with the public address system putting hum into the recording mixer and vice versa. The clean way of doing it is to use a hybrid transformer with the microphone output on the primary feeding two secondary windings, one for the recording system and one for the public address. If a phantom-powered capacitor microphone is used, arrangements must be made for the powering to be applied to the primary of the transformer.

For performances which rely on the use of public address systems, then, splitter boxes must be regarded as part of the normal equipment of the recording engineer. I have recently engineered a concert where we had splitters on 48 microphone channels, giving 96 feeds out; each feed had its own on/off switch for earth so that, if hum arose in any part of the system, we could check the earth on every leg of every split. It cost a lot of money to make but was very efficient.

3. Theatre performances

The same considerations apply to theatre performances that depend on a public address system but, if we are recording what might be termed an 'acoustic' show, we have to think of the audience who will not want a whole lot of microphones blocking their view.

The stage director will undoubtedly have clear opinions about what he will or will not permit (usually the latter), and the engineer's problem is how to observe these restrictions yet at the same time achieve complete coverage of the whole acting area, in depth as well as width, with something like the same presence usual on a commercial record. Surprisingly good quality can however be obtained by putting microphones in the footlights very close to the stage, or even on the stage itself. Such positions will of course pick up a fair amount of footstep noise, but this will not matter unduly if the recording is intended to sound like a live performance; otherwise one would hope to be allowed to instal narrow microphones at approximately knee-height, and to hide a few more on the stage in various parts of the set. Considerable advance planning is necessary, and one would not expect to be able to record a stage show without seeing it first to plot the action in detail.

Opera is easier to record, as the singers are accustomed to projecting their voices and suspended microphones can be used, though microphones in the footlights will still be necessary. Phasing must be carefully watched, as strange cancellation effects can occur when singers move across the stage; these can be eliminated only by observing them during rehearsal and moving microphones to positions where such effects are absent. Multi-miking will probably be necessary for the orchestra. The final result should be accurate and convincing, but will usually sound less cramped if a small amount of artificial reverberation is added.

Unquestionably the greatest hazard when recording in a theatre is electrical interference from the stage lighting dimmers, particularly thyristor dimmers. The interference is usually picked up on the microphone lines and takes the form of a nasty, fizzy, wide-band buzz which is almost impossible to filter out. It is worth taking a lot of trouble to arrange with the chief electrician for a complete run-through of all the lighting changes which take place in the performance and check that no interference is picked up. If it is, it will then be necessary to experiment with different microphones and cable routes to find a combination which will cause the minimum effect.

4. Presentation of concert recordings
In the case of band or jazz concerts, it is now possible with the use of multi-track equipment to record the individual sections of the band on separate tracks and not only adjust the overall balance at the dubbing session, but also alter the audio presentation as a whole.

When a concert is recorded in a small club, for instance, there will be a total lack of room reverberation on the original tape and this may cause the recording to lack sparkle. The deadness will affect the brass section in particular and can cause even the most powerful of bands to sound tired and uninteresting. A small amount of artificial reverberation introduced during the dubbing of the final master tape can make all the difference, without making the overall recording sound artificial.

Of course it may be that the producer will decide to go even further and totally re-create the sound picture during dubbing. This might mean introducing large amounts of equalization to the individual tracks, various degrees of different types of reverberation, electronic phasing, and the whole gamut of normal permanent studio gimmicks. This style of treatment is quite common with LPs of live pop concerts.

What is important, of course, when the word LIVE is printed across the album cover, is the audience reaction and, whilst most producers keep this to only five seconds or so between musical items, it must sound enthusiastic at the right time. Although applause and general reaction are recorded on a separate track during the show, it is not unknown for 'booster' tapes from another show altogether to be used with discretion during dubbing. I have a reel of four different-sized audiences rendering applause at varying degrees of appreciation which has stood me in good stead for the last ten years; I suppose I shall have to make up a quadraphonic version soon.

CHAPTER SEVENTEEN

The Rôle of the Producer

John Culshaw

The qualities needed by a good producer are many and include, in no particular order: musicianship, imagination, economic and budgetary awareness, psychological judgement, and at least a degree of technical knowledge. It was not always so, for until fairly recently the classical record producer was an uncredited and unidentifiable being. His contribution to the process of record making was accepted, though sometimes with reluctance, by the industry itself and by the artists with whom he worked; but to the record-buying public he did not exist. This anonymity was an inheritance from the days of the 78 rpm record, when technical limitations restricted his activities to checking that the notes were correct during the course of the performance, since there were no playback facilities in those days; and if he had any title at all, he was known to his employers as a 'musical supervisor' and to the engineers as a 'dot reader'. Doubtless, many conformed with that. They left the sound to the engineer, the interpretation to the artist and the budget to the management; and all *they* did, at the end of a four-minute 78 rpm take, was to comment on the musical cleanliness or otherwise of the performance.

Yet there were others who felt a greater responsibility and even sensed a challenge; and they were the genuine original uncredited producers. What they did was to seek a close relationship on the one side with the artists and on the other with the engineers. They began to think that sound quality as such was at least part of their concern; and they were not beyond discussing and sometimes changing points of musical interpretation with artists whose confidence they had gained. They sensed that most artists are much more nervous in the studio than appearance suggests, and they took trouble to create relaxing conditions. They were both catalysts and pioneers.

Technical revolutions

All the same, the real opportunities for creative production in classical recording did not arise until three technical revolutions within a decade provided the facilities. The first, at the end of the 1939–45 war, was the expansion of the recordable frequency range. This was launched by Decca as 'ffrr' (full frequency range recording) and was greeted with a great deal of scepticism by those who had not heard it or who did not know how it was done, and with enormous enthusiasm by those who felt that they were hearing everything from a full orchestra to a harpsichord recorded accurately for the first time. For the still anonymous producer it meant that at last, in close conjunction with the conductor, he could come to grips with uncompromised orchestral balances and colours; he could even record a proper bass line. Precisely because of a technical development the scope for artist, producer, and engineer broadened beyond recognition. Other companies quickly followed suit with their own versions of the same thing; yet from every point of view there was still one serious limitation, and that was the format of the 78 rpm record.

The launching of the LP record in the United States by CBS in 1948 was the second breakthrough; and its equivalent at the studio end was the introduction of magnetic tape which could be played back and edited. The repertoire explosion began. Complete operas, which had been cumbersome beyond belief in the 78 rpm format, began to pour off the production lines: La Bohème on four sides, Carmen on six and Parsifal on twelve; and from CBS came a brilliant Porgy and Bess, brilliant not just because it was a good performance, but because it conveyed as never before on records the perspectives and dramatic action of an opera. It carried a significant credit: Produced by Goddard Lieberson, and produce it he certainly did.

The coming of stereo in the 1950s was, from the production end, the most exciting development of all. By that time most of the bugs attending the birth of the monophonic LP—recorded level, end-of-side distortion, the new generation of light-weight pickups, consumer unfamiliarity with the microgroove format—had been at least identified and to some extent eliminated. Stereo gave the producer no option but to produce, for at the very simplest level he was faced with a spatial requirement: it made no sense at all, or indeed it was downright comical, to record a love duet in which the characters were audibly several feet if not several yards apart. The producer and his imagination finally became a determining factor in the effectiveness of a record, which was a development not altogether welcomed by the industry: there were enough problems with temperamental and demanding artists without the added burden of staff producers who sometimes went over-budget in their first attempts to grapple with the new medium. Yet it was a burden that the industry had largely brought upon itself, for had it in earlier years granted its producers a degree of recognition and, had it been less' paranoically secretive about budgets, it would have developed more rapidly a generation of men equipped to handle both the imaginative and economic issues involved.

Today the situation is very different. Any producer handling a major project will either know the allocated budget in advance or will indeed have been required to work out the costs and submit them for approval. An awareness of the money involved does not, or should not, compromise the producer's work. He will allocate his resources carefully, and above all he will have the authority to talk to his artists about the most economic way of scheduling a major work. The record producer today is not just a man who handles the studio: he is, or should be, the man in charge of casting, costing, and planning at the start of the operation, and of editing and approving the final dub at the end.

He cannot, however, work in isolation; he is neither as creative nor as authoritarian as a film director. He must inspire confidence in the artists and technicians with whom he works, and he must think long and hard about the possible effects of current technology on whatever piece of music he is recording. As recently as 20 years ago this aspect of his responsibility scarcely existed, since what was recorded at the time of the sessions was inevitably—give or take a bit of equalization—that which ended up in the record groove. That is no longer the case. For some years now, multitrack tape machines of seemingly boundless versatility have made it possible to re-mix and re-balance the sound to such a degree that, at an extreme, the end product may have little resemblance to what was actually played in the studio. The validity of this approach in pop music is no longer seriously disputed, but even a partial application of the technique in the classical field inevitably causes a few raised eyebrows. Like everything else, it is a matter of degree—the multitrack facility can be used or abused; but to claim, as have some musicians, that its very existence is an abomination is to display either ignorance or stupidity, or perhaps both.

An example may be useful. In the days when the producer had at his disposal nothing more than a two-track machine, he had no means of correcting a moment of faulty balance other than that of asking the artists to perform the offending passage again. Yet there are a hundred reasons why the balance can go momentarily wrong in a complex ensemble like the opening of Verdi's *Otello* or the third act ensemble in the same opera. In rehearsal the artists will almost certainly have been conserving their voices and the conductor will not have asked the maximum of the orchestra. A skilled producer working with a good balance engineer will allow for such things—indeed, he will be disappointed if the actual master performance is not considerably more powerful than the rehearsal. Even so, something can happen—a vital vocal or instrumental line can suddenly become obscured because something else has suddenly become disproportionately loud. If the performance has been recorded only on two-track, the producer and the artists have to choose between leaving it as it is—including the faulty passage—or recording at least part of it again. But, if the performance has been recorded on four or more tracks, then in most cases it is a simple task to make the correction outside session time by adjusting the balance between the tracks.

Effects in opera

A similar principle applies to effects and positionings in operatic recordings, and to the multiple perspectives demanded by works like Britten's *War Requiem*. I continue to believe that it is a good idea to try to get them right in the studio and not to depend on multitrack salvation every time; but there are cases where it would be lunacy nowadays not to apply multitrack from the start. To return to *Otello*: the exhausting opening scene can be ruined in the first 45 seconds if Verdi's cannon is a fraction early or late, or fails to go off at all. In the past you had to risk putting it on along with the music, and you were bound to stop the take if anything went wrong. Today it would be added afterwards, outside session time, and with unlimited opportunities to get both the timing and the perspective right. The producer must therefore decide in advance what can best be done 'live' and what can with advantage be post-dubbed. There is no golden rule about this, though there is a cautionary thought which suggests that, if the performers and the performance will be helped by a 'live' effect, then the risk is worth taking. For example, it might seem to make economic sense to track the off-stage chorus and band in the final scene of *Carmen*, but it would be artistic madness.

Relationships with others

The existence of such versatile facilities calls for a very close understanding between producer, engineer, and artist if the result is not to be an untruth, which means an artificial performance 'created' through the process of multitrack recording and the subsequent editing. There is now virtually no aspect of performance that cannot somehow be altered in the post-recording phase, even to the point of changing a tempo without any perceptible difference in pitch; and the temptation to use a facility just because it is available presents a constant challenge to judgement and musical sensitivity. A good producer should never forget that his own ears are finally the most valuable equipment in the studio.

Psychology also matters, in the sense of creating an atmosphere in which artists can work comfortably and within the allocated time. This covers a multitude of things which may seem superficial on paper but which are essential for the proper handling of a studio. If, for technical or experimental reasons, a different orchestral layout has been devised, it must not be forgotten that whatever the microphonic advantages the players need to be able to hear one another and to see the conductor. They must also be comfortable, which really means that they must have enough room to play. It may not matter if the trombones have their backs towards a semi-absorbent surface, but it would ruin the sound of horns. Removing the lid of a grand piano may improve the sight lines in a set-up for a piano concerto, but it may seriously affect the tone. These, and dozens of similar considerations, come into an area involving both the producer and the balance engineer, since a purely musical solution may be unacceptable technically, and vice versa.

Clearly, there are overlapping functions. A good producer needs a degree of technical knowledge but he does not need to know how to repair the mixer if it blows up; equally, a good balance engineer should have at the very least an enthusiasm for music but he does not have to know how to read transpositions. In some countries—notably Germany—the functions of producer and balance engineer are sometimes rolled into one and the result is someone called a *Tonmeister*. Precisely because so many of the functions appear to overlap, this seems at face value to be a good idea; but there are many professionals who dismiss it as wholly impracticable. For a start, it is *physically* impossible to read a full score and watch at least two meters at the same time; furthermore, a classical producer uses a score as a tool of his trade and has no inhibitions about making pencil markings as he goes along (wrong notes, faulty entries, misplaced or mispronounced words, poor intonation, weak ensemble, and so on) which is something he cannot possibly do if his hands are on the faders of a multi-channel console. It is precisely because of the overlap in the functions of a sensitive producer and a good balance engineer that all the qualities required are unlikely to be found in one person; and in any case the system is likely to function more fluently if the responsibilities are divided.

At the end of a take it is the balance engineer's job to check *at once* anything which may have struck him as technically suspect during the recording, just as it is the producer's job to get in touch *at once* with the performers in the studio. Nothing is more demoralizing, for artists who have just performed to the limit, than to be left in a silent studio with no word from the control room. 'Thanks—I'm coming out' or words to that effect is what the producer should say and indeed do, and while he goes over any musical or production points with the artists his technical colleagues can verify the tape. It is not utterly impossible for one man to perform both functions but, at a time when session costs are rising rapidly, it is undoubtedly uneconomic because it requires more time; and psychologically it is at least dubious because artists as a rule will tend to take direction better from a fellow musician than from even the most distinguished hybrid. These observations are not to be taken as an attack on the *Tonmeister* degree courses now being offered by several universities; on the contrary, it is admirable that graduates should emerge with a thorough grounding in both music and technology. However, in the classical field at least, the chances are that they will have to decide professionally to go in one direction or the other.

Job opportunities

Job opportunities are depressingly limited. Even the large companies employ only a handful of classical producers and—unlike the pop world—the opportunities for the freelance are virtually non-existent. Nor is the work particularly well paid unless or until the producer is promoted to managerial level, at which point ironically he is forced to do less and less of the very job which has gained him the promotion. At that stage he will from time to time make appointments as vacancies occur, and he will be looking for particular qualities in any candidate.

A university degree is useful but by no means essential: it simply means that a certain area of knowledge is covered. Fluent and accurate score reading is a first essential; languages help; and the candidate must at least show signs of being, or becoming, the sort of person capable of handling highly-charged personalities in difficult circumstances. But beyond all this, the potential producer needs to have a concept of what records are about, or for; it is on the whole true that most of those who have become successful producers over the past 50 years started simply as record enthusiasts, whatever other qualifications they may have had. The worst choice of all is the artist *manqué* because, no matter how hard he tries, the conditions of studio work will merely increase his frustrations: a good producer can discuss delicate musical points with conductors, pianists, and singers precisely *because* he is a professional producer, and not a failed conductor, pianist, or singer. He must have nerve, but he must also have tact. He should learn quickly how to work out the cost-per-minute of any given session, if only because it is one of the quirks of the profession that almost all the agonizing decisions occur in the last fifteen minutes of a session, and overtime is a very expensive luxury.

The prospects for those who manage to get through the door have probably never been better: recorded music has ceased to be a luxury or even a hobby; in one form or another it has become virtually a necessity. It is one of the very few consumer products to have gone *down* in real price over a period of 25 years and, precisely because technical innovation has been gentle, a good recording remains a good recording almost irrespective of its age. It is by now hard to think of any musical work of substance that is not available somewhere on records, with the exception of the bulk of contemporary music: and the question of substance in that area depends either on the verdict of posterity, which if favourable will inevitably result in a recording, or in the more immediate enthusiasm of a producer who will persuade his company to invest in a particular work or composer. Beyond that, the classical world is at last beginning to catch up with the world of pop, and several important magazines on both sides of the Atlantic have taken to naming producers and apportioning credit or blame accordingly.

The day may still come—though I cannot myself see it for some time yet— when it will be possible for an independent specialist producer to earn a living by concentrating on those composers and works which mean the most to him. Meanwhile, the staff producer must expect to have to cope with Johann Strauss in one week, a late Beethoven quartet in the next, and the prospect thereafter of a completely unknown contemporary work. Versatility is therefore another essential; but the biggest essential of all is imagination, both in terms of recorded sound itself and in the recommendation of repertoire to be recorded. As in every other field, it is the degree of imagination that marks the difference between a routine and a great producer.

CHAPTER EIGHTEEN

Popular Music

Peter Tattersall

For the purpose of this chapter we will go through the procedures for a standard group line-up consisting of drums, bass guitar, lead guitar, acoustic guitar, vocals, and various percussion.

Setting up the session

It is a good idea to spend some time with the producer before a session to plan the course of action. A good producer will have a fair idea of how he wants the finished product to sound, and will have given some thought to overdubs etc. If it is at all possible, one should plan in advance the track layout for the majority of overdubs. This will save headaches later on and indicate the amount of track jumping which will be needed to accommodate all signals.

It is very important to establish and maintain a congenial atmosphere to bring out the best performance from the musicians. Therefore one should try to be as helpful and friendly as possible to producers and musicians alike.

Studio layout (see Fig. 18.1)

It is good practice to group the musicians as close together as possible, as

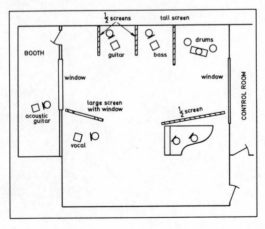

Fig. 18.1
Typical studio layout for basic small pop group

they play with more feeling if they are together, instead of being shut off in separate booths or heavily screened. The drums can be conveniently set up in a corner near the control room window, with the bass guitar amplifier next to the drums, facing the wall, and a screen between the drums and amplifier. The lead guitar amplifier may be near the bass, with a small screen between. Opposite the drums can be the piano and the acoustic guitar will normally be placed in a booth, if available. It is usual to place the vocals somewhere in the middle of the group and lay down a guide vocal on a spare track. This helps the rest of the group to get the feel of the number being recorded and is also very helpful for overdubbing.

Microphones

It is quite impossible to lay down precise rules for the choice and placement of microphones but a typical scheme will indicate the basic approach. Another engineer in different acoustics might choose something quite different.

On the drums, one might use the following:

Snare Drum	—	Beyer 201
Hi-hat	—	Beyer M160
Tom-toms	—	Beyer M88s
Bass Drum	—	AKG D25 or D202
Top Cymbals	—	Neumann U87 (two)

The above microphones are suitable for drums because they have a good cardioid response and they can take high acoustic levels which is important with close working. For the remainder of the group one might use:

Bass Guitar	—	AKG D202
Lead Guitar	—	Beyer M160
Acoustic Guitar	—	Neumann KM56 or KM86
Piano	—	Neumann KM86 (two)
Vocals	—	Neumann U47

The KM86 and KM56 microphones are a good choice for the acoustic guitar because they produce a pure sound and enable one to obtain a good full tone from the instrument. The reason for using a U47 on the vocal at this stage is that, even though it is only a guide vocal, it may add a little presence which can be extremely useful on the final mix. Two microphones are commonly used on the piano whether a stereo piano is needed or not. Obviously one is placed at the bass end of the piano and one for the treble, near the hammers, usually an octave above middle C.

Grouping of channels

The balance engineer will adopt a scheme of allocating instruments to channels which makes for the best working conditions, e.g. all drum channels together, then bass, guitar, piano, etc. One possible arrangement might be as follows, starting with the drums:

Channel 1   —   Snare Drum
Channel 2   —   Hi-hat
Channel 3   —   Top Tom-tom
Channel 4   —   Floor Tom-tom
Channel 5   —   Bass Drum
Channel 6   —   Top Cymbals and kit left ⎫
Channel 7   —   Top Cymbals and kit right ⎬ Stereo
Channel 8   —   Top over-all
Channel 9   —   Bass Guitar
Channel 10   —   Electric Guitar
Channel 11   —   Acoustic Guitar
Channel 12   —   Piano bass end
Channel 13   —   Piano top end
Channel 14   —   Guide Vocal

Routing of channels to tracks

Every engineer has his own preferences in regard to track layouts, but there are one or two points to watch. The edge tracks (1 and 16) are most vulnerable to damage or misalignment and so it is not normal to put rhythm instruments there (bass and drums). The outer tracks are best used for overdubs, say guitar riffs or piano runs, etc. A fairly standard final track layout for a group might be as follows:

1. Electric Guitar riffs
2. Drums left   ⎫
3. Drums right   ⎬ Stereo
4. Snare Drum
5. Bass Drum
6. Bass Guitar
7. Acoustic Guitar 1
8. Acoustic Guitar 2

9. Piano top   ⎫
10. Piano bass ⎬ Stereo
11. Lead Guitar solos
12. Lead Vocals
13. Backing Vocals ⎫
14. Backing Vocals ⎬ Stereo
15. Tambourine
16. Any extra percussion or synthesizer

The sequence of stages in laying down the tracks will follow a regular pattern, starting with the rhythm.

Stage One. Tracks 2–5—drums as above. Track 6—bass guitar. Track 7—acoustic guitar 1, and Track 16—guide vocal.

Stage Two. Overdub acoustic guitar 2 on to track 8 and perhaps lay down piano at the same time on tracks 9 and 10.

Stage Three. Lead Vocals on to tracks 14 and 15, then re-record (jump) both together to track 12.

Stage Four. Backing Vocals. We will suppose that the members of the group are going to sing a three-part harmony, doubling the first harmony and single tracking the top and bottom harmonies. Then all the harmonies are to be placed into a stereo perspective on tracks 13 and 14.

First harmonies on to tracks 15 and 16, top harmonies on to track 1, bottom harmony on to track 11.

The track jumps would be as follows:

Track 15 to 13

Track 16 to 14

Track 11 to Tracks 13 and 14, in stereo half left and half right

Track 1 to Tracks 13 and 14 equally

They should end up in the stereo perspective shown in Fig. 18.2.

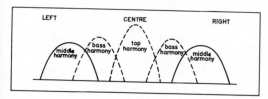

Fig. 18.2
One possible stereo arrangement of the musical parts in a pop mix

It is important to check phasing at all stages of multitracking vocals and track jumping.

Stage Five. Overdubs. Electric guitar riffs on to track 1, solo guitar on to track 11, tambourine on to track 15 and any further overdubs on to track 16. Notice that, as the tracks are gradually built up, they are placed in the stereo perspective as planned. This is extremely useful for the final mix.

Special facilities

There is no point in using limiting and compression just for the sake of it; they should be used positively but discreetly. An obvious use of compression is to keep a vocal at a constant level without a serious limiting effect. Some units incorporate an expander, limiter, and compressor, and these can be used to give really good presence to a voice and almost appear to lift it out of the track.

1. *Equalization units* are quite often used on drums, especially the snare drum. If the engineer has already obtained a good drum sound in the studio by tuning and padding, then adding just a touch of EQ can give just that little extra which makes the difference between a good snare sound and a

brilliant one. The main point to watch is not to over-equalize. When this happens, the only course left is to start again from scratch. Some engineers prefer to record flat, then add all the frequency effects on the final mix. It all comes down to the individual taste of the engineer and producer concerned.

2. *Phasing* used to need two tape recorders, with tracks running slightly out of sync, but there are now quite sophisticated electronic phasing units on the market. It may be said that phasing is a gimmick, but any gimmick which helps to improve the effectiveness of a recording is worth using. Phasing is most effective on guitars and voices, but it can be used on almost any instrument as long as the signal is fairly constant. It is especially interesting on a hi-hat. Auto-phasing is a favourite technique as the signal is phased in time with the track. A trace of phasing on a backing vocal can also produce an interesting sound. Again the rule is not to overdo it; a track in which half the sounds were phased would be very boring.

3. *Tape echo* can be used on almost anything. On a vocal it can obviously be introduced to obtain an old Rock and Roll effect or, with a tape recorder which runs at 76 cm/s (30 ips), a single repeat will give the double tracking effect. Again, tape delaying a signal before sending it to an echo plate makes the reverberation much warmer and natural. If tape echo is being used on a guitar or saxophone, one should try to make the musician play along with it; this nearly always produces a much better sound.

The Cooper Time Cube is an interesting piece of equipment. It gives 14 or 16 milliseconds delay, or it can be cascaded to give 30 milliseconds. On a vocal it is possible to feed the original signal half left in stereo and the delayed signal half right. This produces a definite double-tracked voice. It will also give unusual effects on a bass guitar.

4. *Gain expander units* or noise gates, such as the Kepex, can be used during recording or mixdown or both. Their main uses are to cut out tape hiss, amplifier noise, or studio background noise. On an acoustic guitar microphone, for example, there may be a fair amount of studio noise or spill from other instruments. So long as the unwanted level is significantly lower than that of the desired signal, the noise gate can be adjusted to reject it.

If used correctly, the expander can be invaluable and can also be used to great effect in recording electronic music effects. One interesting example is to introduce a fake bass drum by feeding a 60 Hz tone through the unit and key it with the bass guitar. This will sound like a bass drum being played in perfect timing with the bass guitar.

Sounds

Now that we have dealt with studio layout, track selection, and special facilities, we will get down to the main functions of console operation, producing the sounds.

1. The drums. The drum kit can cause many problems of microphone balance (see Fig. 18.3) and choosing a drum sound is an extremely personal matter. Unfortunately the sound liked by the drummer and the producer may differ considerably. The first thing to do is to listen to the drum kit in the studio and reduce the range of live sounds to manageable proportions before starting to build up the desired sound electronically. Let the drummer play for a while to warm up and ask him to hit the kit as hard as he intends to during the takes.

Drummers in groups tend to prefer a thick sound and this is possible to achieve by reducing the middle and top frequencies. However, this can leave the drums sounding rather dead and it is preferable to work on the kit itself. The snare drum will probably create the biggest problem. No doubt it will ring too much, and an easy way round this is by careful taping and re-tensioning of the snare without necessarily re-tuning it. A thin duster taped over the top end of the snare, away from where it is played, can make a big difference (see Fig. 18.4). It may also be necessary to put some tape over the snare itself. A great deal depends on the condition of the snare drum and, bearing this in mind, it is useful to keep some spare drum keys in the studio. The amount of equalization to use on the snare will depend on individual taste, the microphones being used, and the acoustics of the studio but a good starting point, after the necessary taping etc., is about +8 dB at 10 kHz, middle around 2·8 kHz and bass at about 200 Hz.

The bass drum nearly always presents a problem as most producers prefer a dry thud. The easiest way to achieve this is to remove the front

Fig. 18.3
A top view of the drum kit

Fig. 18.4
The snare drum

screen and place a blanket inside the drum (see Fig. 18.5). Take care to remove all fittings that screw or clip off, or you will have some strange noises occurring during a take. It is not always wise to EQ the bass drum by adding too much bass as this will invariably be lost in the final mix. It is usually better to have a middle to top sound.

The tom-toms do not normally present many problems. If they have been tuned correctly, only a small amount of taping should be necessary. Cymbals can cause quite a few headaches, depending on the type. If the drummer has a good set of cymbals, they will usually produce a good sound on their own and need very little frequency correction. Cheap cymbals will always sound like cheap cymbals, so a little bit of masking tape and EQ may be used to remove the tinny ring.

Fig. 18.5
The bass drum

Fig. 18.6
The acoustic guitar

To recap on drum sounds: make sure that the kit is properly tuned and all loose fittings have been tightened up. Let the drummer play for a while before recording a take, and always check the drum sound between each number because the sound will often change as the session progresses, due to changing atmosphere in the studio.

2. Bass guitar. This is another instrument which can involve some time in achieving the correct sound. The guitarist may use a plectrum or his fingers. The plectrum is easier to record since 'picking' a bass guitar gives a slightly percussive sound and is much clearer and cleaner than a bass played with finger or thumb. The bass can be recorded either from the amplifier speaker unit or by direct injection to the mixing console, or a combination of both. The bass amplifier is the one which gives the most problems, as the group will be used to playing at high level on stage and the bass amplifier will probably buzz or rattle. The only way around this is by careful control of the volume of the amplifier and the amount of bass lift the guitarist is using.

One can always add bass at the desk if it has been taken off at the amplifier speaker.

With direct injection you will have none of the above problems but the sound will possibly be too pure and not have enough guts. A mixture of direct injection and straight bass can be very effective. Make the direct injected bass slightly bassy and the normal bass middley (not too clicky) by balancing between both sounds, and adding top to one and bass to another. Remember that the bottom two strings will sound more boomy than the top two, and be prepared to compensate for this with equalization. Using both signals on the bass will also give more flexibility; for instance, it would be possible to limit one and put a small amount of reverberation on the other.

It is a good idea to check the bass sound through small speakers, to make sure it is not being lost, as normal studio monitors can tend to give a much better sound on the bass than the usual domestic record player or hi-fi.

3. Lead guitar. Like the bass guitar, the lead guitar can cause a few problems via an amplifier. It is quite amazing how many sizes of amplifier find their way into a studio. The most popular amplifier is a compact one with a good sound and sturdily built so that it tends to show few defects. The bigger amplifiers do not necessarily produce the best sound. A great deal depends on the guitarist, how he looks after the amplifier, the state of the strings, etc. The accessories used with the guitar sometimes need a fair amount of attention. Some guitarists use a combination of fuzz, wah-wah, and sustain pedals all linked together and quite often there is a mismatch between them. Also many such accessories are battery powered and very few guitarists seem to have spares: so it is a good idea to keep some batteries in the studio. The guitar sound used on a track may vary from a tight rhythm

Fig. 18.7
A stereo approach to guitar balance

Fig. 18.8
The piano

sound to a sustained fuzz solo. Solos are generally overdubbed and the first track laid down will be a rhythm.

This will normally be a fairly thick sound, making use of middle and bass, but of course it depends on the arrangement and on personal taste. Once again, one should use a combination of guitar tone and amplifier settings to achieve the desired sound in the studio, and improve it on the desk.

Guitar solos are usually trickier, depending on how much sustain, fuzz, room echo, etc., is wanted. Sustain is controlled by the guitarist, but it can be helped with a small amount of tape delayed reverberation and boosting of mid-frequencies. The solo guitarist usually needs more foldback than normal and one method is to feed the foldback through a speaker at high level, which enables him to turn up his own amplifier and put more feeling into the solo. This helps to create the effect of playing the solo with the group around him.

4. Acoustic guitar. The backbone of the rhythm track is often the acoustic guitar, normally double tracked to obtain maximum effect. The microphones used are mainly capacitor types like Neumann KM86, angled towards the top strings (see Figs. 18.6 and 18.7). An acoustic guitar tends to have a slightly bouncy sound which needs taking out, usually around the 60–200 Hz range. Also the squeaking sound, made by the fingers of the left hand in changing chords, may need to be eliminated. This usually happens with new strings. Certain acoustic guitars have pickups, and an interesting sound is to record the guitar with a microphone in the conventional manner and simultaneously direct inject it from the pickup, splitting each signal on to a separate track. When an acoustic guitar is double tracked, it is obviously sensible to EQ each track differently and add different amounts of echo.

There are numerous ways of balancing an acoustic guitar. For example one microphone in front, angled towards the top strings, can be mixed with one placed behind. Placing a microphone inside the guitar is also possible but it needs to be a very good instrument.

5. Piano. It is normal to use two microphones on a piano, one placed near the bass string and one near the hammers about an octave above middle C (see Fig. 18.8) and to split them in stereo (if the tracks can be spared). If the piano is good and well in tune, there should be no problems at all. The top microphone is normally placed near the hammers to obtain a hard percussive sound, but this depends on the type of sound needed for the recording. To achieve good separation on the piano, if it is being played at the same time as other instruments, the lid will have to be low and the microphones slung in below. This tends to restrict the sound and it will have to be helped with a fair amount of EQ and echo. Obviously the best sounds are achieved by having the lid up and the microphones further back, making full use of the sound board and reflections from the lid.

6. *Electric piano.* There are quite a few makes of electric piano and these are of two types: the stage piano, which is just a keyboard and requires an external amplifier, and the complete model which has its own amplifier. The second is best for recording: a good stereo effect can be obtained by placing a microphone on each side and, when vibrato is used, the sound switches from speaker to speaker. Any kind of microphone can be used for an electric piano, as the principle is similar to picking up a guitar amplifier. The type of EQ depends on whether a hard percussive sound is required or a soft bassy one.

7. *Vocals.* This is where the type of microphone and EQ become very important, as the vocal is the one sound which will invariably be heard above all others. Capacitor microphones are normally used and amongst the most popular are the Neumann U87 or the newer U47. Sibilance is one of the problems. It may seem obvious to roll off some top end response but this may affect the overall vocal sound and make it too dull. A way round this is to ask the vocalist not to over-pronounce the letter 's' and to sing across the microphone on sibilants. This also applies to the letters 'p' and 'b'. Over-emphasizing these is known as 'popping' and can be very annoying but, by careful use of EQ and some thought by the singer, this problem too can be overcome.

Limiters are often used on vocals to level out the signal and keep it constant, but it is important not to overdo limiting. There are all types of vocalists —from quiet ones who sing very close to the microphone to real rockers who can be heard at the other end of the studio, and each requires special treatment. It is necessary to make the vocalist at ease in the studio by giving him the correct amount of foldback and monitor echo.

Reduction

Many engineers prefer to reduce multitrack tapes on the day after the recording. This is a very good idea as it gives one time to settle down after the recording, put ideas into perspective and, after a few hours break, be more constructive about the recording.

Reduction can conveniently start with the rhythm, firstly the drums. As mentioned earlier, the drums will already be in stereo. So channels 2 and 3 can be split hard left and right, with snare and bass drum in the middle. Now is the time to add further EQ on the bass drum, for instance, to make it cut through on small speakers (middle frequencies usually do this) and perhaps some extra bass on the snare to give it depth. The bass guitar is the next to be treated. It has obviously to blend in with the drums (except when there are bass runs) and quite often it is a good idea to balance between the bass drum and bass guitar to give the rhythm a solid feel. The type of EQ to add to the bass guitar depends on the style of playing, whether it is picked or played with the fingers, but remember that too bassy a guitar will become lost in the final mix.

Acoustic guitars are next and, as there are two, they would be placed in stereo, possibly panned half left and half right. Once there is a fair balance between drums, bass and acoustic guitars, one can start on the vocals, lead vocal first. The level of vocals depends on the producer. He may want them sunk back in the track or well out in front. He may even split the double tracked vocals slightly left and right in the stereo picture, though this is unusual. There are many effects which can be asked for on vocals, including various types of echo, plate or tape delay, limiting, etc., or it may be that the vocal sounds better very dry. Whatever is needed, it is always worth experimenting with various levels and sounds.

The backing vocals have already been placed and recorded in stereo, so it is just a matter of level between them and the lead vocal. The same goes for the piano and tambourine. The guitar riffs and solos can be placed anywhere in the stereo picture, together with such interesting effects as having the main signal mostly left and the echo from the right.

Once all the channels are connected up and one is placing sounds into their appropriate places, an engineer's expertise really comes into its own. Mixing is just as important as recording and the beauty of multitracking and reduction is that one can try as many mixes as one likes until the final one with that 'something extra' is achieved.

During all stages of reduction it is wise to check the phasing, play back through small speakers as well as the large studio monitors, especially if the record is a single, and also check mono and stereo compatibility and adjust as necessary.

Tape machine operation

Most multitrack machines today are extremely sophisticated and have auto-locate systems. This means that the operator can zero the tape at the start of the number then, at the finish, simply press the locate or reset button and the machine will automatically rewind to zero. Also, some auto-locates allow one to punch out a new locate position in the middle of the take and this is very useful when doing drop-ins.

A tape operator's job is made easier by this type of machine, and this is a good thing as it enables the operator to be of more help to the engineer, as well as watch what he is doing, and therefore learn more about the engineer's problems.

Before each session, the machines should be lined up and the heads cleaned and demagnetized. In fact all the machines and consoles should be kept as clean as possible.

Tapes should be properly looked after and always wound tail-out after the session. It is normal practice to leader each number, which helps to locate the numbers easily when it comes to the reduction stage and also shows a degree of professionalism. Tapes which have been correctly leadered and timed are much appreciated by any client. All information relating to each take should be clearly marked on the tape box or edit sheet and nothing omitted, as a take which did not seem right at the time may nevertheless be used on the final mix.

CHAPTER NINETEEN

Popular Electronic Music

John Keating

The most memorable moment of my early career was when I took a song and a band arrangement into a studio in Edinburgh to make a record. To this day I still find the recording studio the most stimulating medium for making music. At that time, in 1946, the technique of recording by means of magnetic tape had not been perfected and so one recorded directly on to a master disc. It was impossible to hear the master at recording time, because to play it was to ruin it. One eagerly awaited the release of the pressing and sometimes this was a moment of great disappointment.

Magnetic tape soon changed all this and, coupled with increasingly complex electronic techniques, offered the producer of pop or electronic music almost unlimited possibilities by the early 1970s. Confining ourselves to the technological possibilities, the most relevant are:

1. Multitracking
2. Extensive overdubbing
3. Synthesized sound
4. Quadraphony.

It is these four innovations which I would like to discuss in the following section. Instead of attempting to describe the separate operations, which are already covered in Chapter Eighteen, I shall outline the way these techniques were employed in some record albums.

The new methods

I approached multitracking (eight tracks or more) and overdubbing with a certain scepticism, suspecting the motivation behind their development. This prejudice arose perhaps from the knowledge of clandestine overdubbing indulged in by inferior pop singers, whose activities were frowned upon by professional performers and formally banned by the Musicians Union to protect their members against exploitation by more unscrupulous employers. With regard to multitracking, any fears I had were quickly dispelled at my first multitrack recording session. This used an 8-track machine to record an album of TV themes with the London Symphony Orchestra. Because the orchestra was divided into eight parts, the inherent flexibility of balance was immediately apparent, even with a rough mix during the first playback. The many advantages of multitracking were further displayed at the subsequent re-mix stage. The clarity of orchestration was greatly enhanced, and the rôle of the conductor could be continued even though the musicians had left, making the employment of large forces, such as a symphony orchestra, a more economical proposition. Middle market products, such as the TV themes album, rely on a good string sound and, despite countless attempts to prove otherwise, the plentiful use of echo. There is no substitute for weight of tone and good quality players are always desirable; they become more essential in inverse proportion to any reduction in their numbers.

A follow-up album—'250 Years of Film Music'—proved the legitimacy of overdubbing. The first title to be recorded was for strings and organ, and during the rehearsal the electronic organ developed a fault and could not be used. The session continued minus the organ, leaving the eighth track free for overdubbing later. The rubato nature of the composition made overdubbing a problem but, compared with the alternative economic disaster of re-booking the entire orchestra, this was negligible.

The next album—'Space Experience'—involved the recording of electronic music, using a 16-track tape recorder. A band of between 25 and 30 musicians was employed, consuming 10 tracks, leaving 6 tracks for various synthesizer overdubs. The repertoire consisted of titles with space connotations such as 'Upon Another Earth' and 'The Unknown Planet', and the fusion of electronic music via the synthesizer and pop music, played on conventional instruments, seemed appropriate. The synthesizer was used to function as a melodic voice in the general orchestration and to create electronic music sounds for space effects. As yet there is no standard procedure for notating pure electronic music, and so a first class performer is essential, with good communication between producer and player and a keen sensitivity to the composer's intentions. The recording of the synthesizer was by direct injection (no microphones), eliminating all leakage problems.

I then received a request for a quadraphonic release on both SQ matrix disc and 4-channel discrete tape cartridge. Research into quadraphony revealed a state of affairs amounting to total confusion and a general feeling of apathy towards the medium.

It must be stated that quadraphony is not simply double stereo. This implies two front sources of sound with an illusion of centre, and a similar distribution of two more channels at the back. Quadraphony is at least more than this; it makes possible the use of two other centres, namely between front left and rear left, and front right and rear right. With the SQ matrix, experiments had revealed that any signal which was sent to the two rear speakers, so creating an illusion of rear centre, would on transfer to disc move to the centre of the complete square when played on stereo equipment, and vanish on monophonic playback. This incompatibility had to be recognized if we were to release a disc which could be played on all equipment, quad, stereo or mono. To do one quad re-mix for both SQ disc and discrete tape would be to sell short the more exciting possibilities afforded by the latter, so it was necessary to do a separate re-mix for each medium. The set-up for both systems was similar, except for those instruments which were spread over both the rear speakers in the discrete tape mix and had to be assigned to one or the other for the SQ disc version. The artistic approach was to apply directional stereo to quadraphony, resulting in a greater emphasis on the positioning of solo passages, and a general spread of block sounds such as strings, creating new dimensions previously impossible. Extensive pan-potting was utilized and the composite effect was one of vibrance, coupled with liveliness caused by the periodic interplay of solos, and the vigorous movement of effects. Alternating between playbacks of discrete tape and simulated SQ versions verified the superiority of the former.

The remainder of this chapter will be devoted to describing some of the problems confronting the record producer, recording artist, composer, conductor, and arranger. Rather than choose these at random, four albums recorded between July '73 and September '74 will be used to demonstrate specific problems as they actually occurred, and the subsequent solutions found for them.

Some problems and their solutions

Example 1. 'Songs of Love'

The first album for analysis is 'Songs of Love', in which the London Symphony Orchestra was used to accompany a voice (Thelma Keating) in sophisticated settings of well-known folk songs. The recording was made on an 8-track machine. One song dispensed with the orchestra, being an *a capella* setting for eight voices, all sung by the solo artist. Four of the songs were sung in foreign languages and so we engaged a language coach to supervise the finer points of accent and pronunciation.

Most of the music was free flowing and, as this makes overdubbing more difficult for the artist to synchronize, having no constant beat to follow, plans were laid to record the orchestra and artist simultaneously with the intention of minimizing the subsequent overdubbing problems. Some overdubbing would be inevitable, and so it was necessary to leave at least one spare track. For most of the musical arrangements the orchestra was allocated six tracks, divided as follows:

Track 1   —   1st and 2nd violins
Track 2   —   violas
Track 3   —   cellos and basses
Track 4   —   woodwind
Track 5   —   french horns
Track 6   —   percussion and miscellaneous additions
Tracks 7
and 8   —   reserved for the voice.

The positioning of the orchestra was similar to that for a concert hall performance and the singer, although in close proximity, was isolated in a small booth behind the conductor, who wore a headset throughout. Little or no sound from the orchestra was picked up by the vocal microphone, and so leakage problems were minimal.

The first title opened with a full verse sung unaccompanied. A large studio filled with 70 or so musicians sitting silently created a particular ambience which was virtually impossible to simulate at a later overdubbing session. The original opening verse was retained but, for lyric reasons, the second verse, which included the orchestra, had to be overdubbed. This presented the real problem of voice matching and, despite the ingenuity of the engineer, a slight difference in voice sound was noticeable. The human voice is the most temperamental and changeable of all musical instruments, and is always difficult to record. Regardless of the number of edits and interchanging of performances from different tracks, it is well to remember that the definitive version will usually be drawn from material recorded on a single day, where the same conditions prevailed.

For one song, the accompanying chamber group comprised 6 cellos, 4 violas, and 2 basses. The orchestration was contrapuntal and, with stereo and quad in mind, good physical separation of the players was attempted. But a chamber group playing rhythmic music in a large studio, with long reverberation, was not successful. A closer regouping of the players was necessary, with the stereo separation considerations becoming secondary to artistic necessity.

In another song, a solo Spanish guitar part was allocated one of the voice tracks, and left to the overdub stage. The opening bars of the music contained only long-held notes in the basses and cellos, with the guitar strumming soft chords at the tempo set by the conductor. No problems were evident at the original recording session but later, when overdubbing the guitar part, synchronization became troublesome. The conductor, although setting a tempo for the first few bars, continued to make subtle accelerandos and ritardandos and the guitarist, with no real guide, was left in a position similar to walking a tightrope. Much time was spent before the task was completed satisfactorily, underlining the fallacy that overdubbing is the cure for all situations. Being left with only one track for the voice overdub brought its own restrictions. No composite performance could then be made from different tracks, and language difficulties put extra strain on the singer to complete the performance in one take. It is true to say that dropping in and out for the odd phrase is possible, and sometimes necessary, but this practice can be hair-raising at times and occasionally adds clicks to the tape.

The harpsichord is a most difficult instrument to record. Its voice is quiet and necessitates close miking and extra level boost, which invariably picks up the noise of the pedals, in constant use for making changes of register. Even in the finest recorded examples of the harpsichord these are often apparent, and the quieter pedal clicks, like the finger slides encountered in many Spanish guitar recordings, are accepted as inevitable. Where two harpsichords were employed (the second overdubbed) the problem was increased and at times became intolerable. However, by utilizing two extra performances recorded on spare tracks, to allow a shift from a noisy track to a quieter one, the worst of these bumps were eliminated.

One setting presented the singer with a more than usual variety of problems. This has no rhythm section or conductor for tempo guidance; eight voice parts with no orchestral accompaniment on which to rely for pitching; seven parts to be recorded while listening on headphones or a monitor speaker at low level; the parts themselves to be performed with a vocal discipline usually reserved for experienced choir singers. Nevertheless, the artist welcomed the challenge and it was felt that the outcome would more than compensate for the inherent difficulties in the process. The tempo dilemma was solved by a metronome set at the desired speed, and recorded for the necessary number of bars on track 1. The texture was a basic three-part harmonic structure, with the same three parts echoed in canonic form at the distance of two bars. To combat the pitching difficulties, these six parts were recorded by piano on to tracks 2 to 7 inclusive and, after the singer had recorded the first main melody on track 8, the equivalent piano part on track 2 could now be eliminated to make way for the second main melody, which was in fact a harmony line. This process was continued until all six voices had been recorded. It only remained to add the final two voices, which were included to bump up the lead voices of both the antecedent and the consequent (formal terms for a melody and its canonic echo). The eighth voice was recorded on track 1, and so it was sung without the aid of the metronome, which by this time was unnecessary. All seemed well with this song until remix time, when it was discovered that leakage from the headset had resulted in metronome clicks being picked up by the microphone. These were present on several tracks in varying degrees of dynamic level. Luckily, most of them were quiet and easily removed by various processes of fading. The more persistent clicks were finally eliminated by using a noise gate, an electronic device for filtering out unwanted low-level sounds. With choir singing, the inherent problem of a profusion of sibilants, which mars even the finest choral recordings, can be avoided by allocating those sounds to a small number of voices and having the majority of singers articulate the offending words minus the sibilant letter. This technique is both difficult to handle and psychologically disturbing, as it draws attention to technicalities, thus debilitating, if not completely destroying, the dramatic impact of an otherwise emotional passage. In the 8-part song just described, the letter 's' was left out by five or six of the voices.

The album was finally remixed for stereo, using a spread string sound, with horns on the left, woodwinds on the right and solos coming from either the left or the right, dictated by the artistic demands of the individual arrangements. The solo voice was placed in the centre throughout. For the quad remix, the strings were spread over the front speakers, with woodwinds rear left and horns rear right. For the singer, the signal was sent to all four speakers and so appeared to come from the centre of the square (or inside the listener's head).

Example 2. 'Hits in Hi-Fi'
With the invention of the small synthesizer, music synthesis by electronic means became readily available to the creators of pop music. Although these instruments can supply an infinite number of new and simulated sounds, their usefulness for live performances is limited. Too much time is required to patch each desired sound and, of course, the technical know-how needed is discouraging, at least to the average rock player, whose main requirements are for fresh sounds in conventional surroundings, rather than involvement in pure electronic music. The demand for the live performance synthesizer led to the manufacture of several pre-patched instruments, with varying selections of instantly available programmed sounds. The time-saving factors inherent in these instant synthesizers enhanced the credibility of an economical all-synthesized band, and was the inspiration for the creation of 'Hits in Hi-Fi', a middle-of-the-road album with a repertoire consisting of pop songs drawn mainly from the best-selling singles of 1973. The album was recorded in April 1974 using a 16-track machine. The size of the orchestra to be simulated was equivalent to 4 trumpets, 3 trombones and tuba, 4 french horns, 3 or 4 woodwinds, a 5-piece rhythm section, a choir, strings, and a few miscellaneous instruments. Except for one passage of white noise, the music is conventional throughout and so traditional notation was used in scoring.

The first three recording sessions were used to lay down the rhythm tracks for each title. In a pop band the rhythm section is of paramount importance and, by allocating a separate track for each rhythm instrument, the utmost flexibility can be obtained. The rhythm section included two guitars playing mainly rhythm, a bass guitar, one drummer miked for stereo, and a rhythm keyboard man playing a variety of instruments. For the opening of one number, two wah-wah pedals were used in conjunction with a Fender Rhodes electric piano, which has a stereo output. Therefore two tracks were needed and, as one guitarist was tacet during the introduction, his track was borrowed temporarily.

With the completion of the rhythm section, the task of recording the first synthesized pop orchestra was begun. With no precedent for guidance, it was decided to choose one family of instruments and record every title in which they were involved before moving on to another instrumental group. Not all the synthesizers were completely programmed, and some time was necessarily spent in setting up each sound. By the method adopted, we avoided the constant patching and re-patching of the same instrumental sound. This proved to be a valuable time-saver. As the french horns were involved in most titles, they were a natural choice for the first overdubs. The best horn sounds were obtained from a combination of three different types of synthesizer. The four notes required were recorded two at a time on tracks 7 and 8. When completed, to avoid the embarrassment of eventually running out of tracks, these were bumped on to track 9, while the patches were set up for the next group of instruments. Bumping (also called 'jumping') could be described as an interim mini-mix, or reduction, and involves the playback from the record head (sync) of the relevant signals which are sent to the mixer, balanced accordingly and simultaneously recorded on to a spare track or tracks, as required. By this process, tracks 7 and 8 were now available for recording and, on an overdubbing project of this magnitude, every track is precious.

Almost the opposite thinking was applied for recording the strings, whose sounds were simulated by one type of synthesizer for high and middle register violins, and another for the lower violas and cellos. This involved the technique of automatic double-tracking (ADT) which effectively doubles the number of strings without actually having to record the passage twice. The technique requires a second tape recorder, with variable speed control. The high string signal on track 7 was taken from the record head of the 16-track and fed into the second machine, running at a pre-selected slightly slower speed. Then, via the playback head, this was returned to the mixer and recorded on track 10. By automatic double-tracking, an extra track was swallowed up, but the violin sound had doubled and the musicians' time saved was spent patching the next overdubbing section of instruments. Incidentally, it was felt unnecessary to apply this technique to all the arrangements.

Before leaving the string section, it should be mentioned that the introduction of one number opened with a very rapid passage for violins. Although this was a fairly normal piece of idiomatic string writing, it became practically impossibly to play when transferred to a keyboard. The solution was found by slowing down the tape machine to 19 cm/s and recording the troublesome run at half speed and down one octave. On playback at 38 cm/s, the music was then raised to its original octave and the proper tempo. The whole string introduction was then phased by a technique similar to automatic double-tracking, utilizing the variance of speed afforded by the second machine.

The sounds of the heavy brass (trumpets, trombone and tuba) were synthesized by three devices, including one of the few polyphonic brass synthesizers available. This speeded up the recording process and economized on track consumption. With some bumping, the completed brass passages finally accounted for three more tracks.

The woodwind sounds, such as flute and bassoon solos, were played on a single synthesizer. The other woodwind sounds used a group of synthesizers, taking up two of the three remaining tracks. Track 16 was reserved for most of the solo work. A Mellotron 400 took care of the choir, timpani and cymbal crashes and was recorded on any track that was temporarily available, likewise the various organs and electric harpsichord.

On one number, a particular sound for the harpsichord was obtained by tape delay with controlled feedback during the remix stage. The signal was sent from the mixer to a second machine and then taken immediately from the replay head of the second machine back to the mixer. This signal was then fed back to the second machine again and again at a controlled level, producing a number of repeats. (If the send level is set too high, of course, unstable feedback occurs.)

With the exception of the two organs and harpsichord, all overdubbing took place in the control room. Every instrument was recorded by direct injection and playback was via the control room speakers at a good listening level, so that a real feeling of live participation was imparted to the player. Much time was saved by hearing exactly what was being recorded, in relationship to the texture of the orchestration and the music as a whole, and so no running back and forth between the studio and control room was necessary. In fact this is the most artistically rewarding way to approach the inherently mechanical process of overdubbing.

When setting out a stereo distribution at remix time, I do not attempt to retain static positions for any solos or groups of sounds throughout the entire album. But, paradoxically, at the outset several instruments are allocated positions which are conserved for every title, although often for convenience only.

In 'Hits in Hi-Fi' the basic plan was: 1st guitar left, 2nd guitar right, with bass and drums in the centre. Strings, horns and choir were spread over both speakers. All other sounds were distributed according to the needs of the individual arrangements in terms of good balance and lively dialogue between speakers. Panning occurred only once, in an electric harpsichord passage which was recorded at 19 cm/s and became particularly effective when speeded up and panned continuously from side to side.

With a track for each member of the rhythm section, and every other sound overdubbed and leakage-free, the number of permutations possible for quad remixing are infinite. The nature of the simulated sounds dictated the basic distribution. Reverberant instruments were allowed to spread and the dryer directional sounds kept in isolation. Using the numbering system of front speaker left—1, front speaker right—3, rear speaker left—2, rear speaker right—4, the orchestra was distributed as follows: 1st guitar—1, 2nd guitar—3, bass and drums front centre (1 and 3), stereo Fender piano—2 and 4. When the acoustic piano, clavinet and electric harpsichord functioned as rhythm instruments, they were allocated one or other of the rear speakers. In varying degrees the strings signals were sent to the four speakers, creating an all encompassing surround sound. The horns and choir on 2 and 4 filled the rear area. Various other colours were spread between the front speakers. Effectively the combination of these elements provided a rhythmic and harmonic backcloth for all the solo activity. When a soloist was heavily featured, the signal was sent to all speakers, creating the illusion of being in the centre of the square.

Separate mixes were undertaken for SQ disc and discrete tape. The disc has a better sound quality with less hiss, and the advantage of choosing any track at will, but the four-channel cartridge is undoubtedly better separated quadraphony.

Example 3. 'The Electronic Philharmonic Orchestra'
The desire to conduct and record more classical music, and the pleasure derived from performing on 'Hits in Hi-Fi', led to the idea of creating a completely synthesized symphony orchestra—the Electronic Philharmonic Orchestra. For the EPO's first album, the choice of repertoire was a simple matter and the editing, arranging and rescoring of the material was completed before facing the technical problems of recording such a mammoth project. It was presumed that extensive bumping would doubtless take care

Fig. 19.1
A corner of the author's studio showing some of the synthesizers used to simulate a full symphony orchestra

of the many overdubs involved. The large collection of synthesizers available would surely cope with simulating the sounds of the instruments of the symphony orchestra (see Fig. 19.1) and, despite the keyboard virtuosity demanded by the scores, technical expertise in sound synthesis and affinity with classical music, the capable musicians, although few in number, could be found. The X factor lay in the conducting sphere. Having no previously recorded rhythm section tracks with which to synchronize the overdubs, and as the click track method utilized in the film industry, with its strict metronomic beat, was totally alien to the nature of classical music, it will be realized that even the conductor would find it impossible to synchronize his beat with the first or any track previously laid down. In the search for the solution, many avenues were explored, including the use of video, but again the problems of synchronizing the video machine with the recording machine ruled out this possibility. It was evident that, to preclude visual communication with a conductor, the only alternative was to invent some means of oral direction. Many hours were spent assessing the requirements for this and future EPO albums, and eventually I approached an expert to solve the musical problems by electronic means.

Delivery was duly taken of what I now call my 'electronic conductor's baton'. The basic idea of this machine is that there are three metronomes housed in one box, each with a variable speed knob and an individual stop and start button. This means that, by simply pressing a button, three tempos are always available. Any two can be altered while the other is functioning, and so new tempos can be obtained *ad infinitum*. All gradations of tempo change are possible by rotating the variable speed knob in the appropriate direction, thus allowing the conductor to make many accelerandos and rallentandos. An adding device keeps a count of the number of bars and displays these through a small window. A separate switch facilitates changes of metre from 1 to 8 beats in the bar. The scores were carefully scrutinized, all the desired tempos and changes were translated into metronomic speeds and the appropriate directives marked in the scores. The entire album was recorded in the control room. In contrast to 'Hits in Hi-Fi', the recording of each composition was completed before moving on to the next title. For every composition the conductor's beat, via the metronome, was carried on track 1 and, with few exceptions, retained throughout the countless overdubs despite the dire shortage of tracks, notwithstanding the use of a 16-track machine.

For this album, 'John Keating Conducts the Electronic Philharmonic Orchestra', faithful reproduction of the works in accordance with the composers' wishes was the main objective. Most of the compositions were of short duration and recorded in their entirety, with neither additional parts nor deletions. (For Wagner's Prelude to Act III of 'Tristan and Isolde', some white noise was added to create an atmosphere of surrounding sea and rocky cliffs.)

To start the overdubbing, french horns were again chosen. During the remix stage of 'Hits in Hi-Fi', the recording engineer experienced great difficulty when balancing the french horns. Somehow the edge had disappeared from the tone quality, and extensive equalization was necessary to compensate for this loss. The answer to this sound phenomenon lay at the very roots of sound synthesis by electronic means. Due to the limited number of waveforms used to produce the sound, electronic instrumental passages contain many of the same characteristics and this reduces definition. Endeavouring to simulate a true french horn sound, for example, by using the same synthesizer to do so, produced a unique similarity of sound for each part, particularly when in unison, resulting in a tendency for the parts to cancel each other out. When recording the EPO, the problem was easily solved by utilizing different synthesizers for like sounds, or by a slight change in timbre in the next overdub when using the same instrument. When the horn parts were completed, bumping reduced them to two tracks. An overall bumping plan was adopted to permit a four-part division of each of the three main groups of a symphony orchestra (strings, brass and woodwind). This would allow for a quadraphonic distribution of any one family, but a more exciting prospect was a possibility of a tutti passage in which every section was divided into four parts, resulting in an unprecedented distribution of the elements of the symphony orchestra. To simulate this effect in a live performance by a traditional symphony orchestra would require the musicians' seating arrangements to be completely reshuffled, a situation which is impracticable, if not unthinkable.

No real technical problems were experienced in the recording of the album, but performance difficulties were in abundance, due mainly to the unidiomatic keyboard passages occasioned by the necessity to transfer parts from other instruments, especially strings. During the recording of Khachaturian's 'Sabre Dance', the fast tempo made it practically impossible to play some of the bare off-beat parts. The situation seemed hopeless before the recording engineer offered a technical solution. The principle was based on the knowledge that, if the offending off-beats were made to appear as on-beats, the playing difficulties would be eliminated. This necessitated a precise shift in the position of the conductor's beat (the click track). The distance between the record and playback heads of the 16-track machine was insufficient and a second machine, with a variable speed control, was brought into operation. When the signal from the 16-track, via the playback heads, was fed to the second machine and returned via *its* playback head, the distance was now too great. The speed of the second machine was gradually increased until the exact position was located—Eureka! The distribution of the elements for the stereo and quad remixes was very much an individual affair. The textural complexities of each composition were carefully examined and these considerations above all finally influenced the settings.

Example 4. 'In Search of Atlantis'
The fourth and final album for analysis is a progressive one. It is a concept album of all original material with no individual tracks and is called 'In Search of Atlantis'. It contains a mixture of progressive pop and pure electronic music, and is performed by a rhythm section, some percussion, a number of keyboard instruments and several synthesizers. The recording was made using a 16-track machine. The music was recorded in stretches and, at the

remix stage, most of the joins were crossfaded. Unlike 'Hits in Hi-Fi' and the EPO, where the simulation of conventional instruments was the main objective, we set out purposely to create interesting new sounds and generally experiment with fresh ideas. Two drummers were present in a six-piece rhythm section and, as usual, these rhythm tracks were recorded first, leaving 10 free tracks for overdubs. The guitarists made extensive use of individual phase boxes, octividers, controlled fuzz units, wah-wah pedals, etc. The keyboard instruments were fed through sound rotators, Lesley speaker units, and even the grand piano was 'prepared'. An electric harpsichord passage was played backwards. This was accomplished musically by playing the harmonic sequence in the reverse order, and technically by inverting the tape for the recording on track 1, which became track 16 when played back in the normal manner. Several segments were recorded at half speed, and many other gimmicks were employed before the recording stage was finally completed.

The stereo remix proved to be most complicated. All the mixes were finished before any crossfading or editing was tackled. A few passages were panned and some subjected to tape delay with controlled feedback. The finale of the composition involved a technical practice worth mentioning. A previously recorded, all synthesizer, version of the Bach/Gounod 'Ave Maria' was required for insertion at a given point in the finale, which was a long stretch of pure electronic music occupying eight or nine tracks. The two-track reduction of 'Ave Maria' was copied on to the 16-track machine. One normal version was fed straight to the 16-track and occupied tracks 11 and 12. Simultaneously, the same two signals were sent to a synthesizer having stereo facilities and were ring modulated before being recorded on tracks 12 and 13. When remixing, the ring modulated version was required first and faded in accordingly. As the music was reaching its climatic point, the normal version was slowly faded in, while the ring modulated version was faded out. At the highest point, the pure electronic music was faded out completely, leaving only the 'Ave Maria' now in full blast. As the climax subsided, the reverse procedure was adopted; first the return of the electronic music, the slow switch from the normal 'Ave Maria' to the ring modulated version, which in turn slowly disappeared, leaving only the electronic music. This too was slowly faded, as the composition drew to its close.

With the main reductions completed, the final task was to link the various stretches of music to make the composition continuous. Most of the dovetailing was done by the crossfading technique. This required the use of three machines; for example, when crossfading segment A into segment B, new and separate reductions were made of the last few bars of A and the first few bars of B (the easiest editing points having determined the specific number of bars). The machine carrying A was started, sent to the mixer and recorded on to a third machine. As this music was being faded out, the other tape recorder was started and segment B faded in. When this process was over, the portion of tape was edited on to the original mixes and the now redundant segments discarded.

After many years in the recording business, as I said at the beginning of this chapter, I still find the recording studio the most stimulating medium for making music.

MANUFACTURING PROCESSES

CHAPTER TWENTY

Disc Cutting

W. H. Livy

Amplitudes, velocities and recording characteristics

The master gramophone record is made by moving a sharp-edged sapphire stylus radially across the rotating surface of a lacquer-coated disc so that a spiral groove is cut and a continuous small thread of lacquer is removed. Older monophonic records entailed the stylus being moved by the modulation in a line at right-angles to the direction of the groove, but always in the plane of the disc. With stereophonic discs, the cutting stylus must be capable of moving in any direction within a plane perpendicular (nominally) to the direction of the groove.

The mechanical relationship between the amplitude and velocity of the motion of the stylus due to the modulation is shown in Fig. 20.1. It can be seen that sinusoidal waves having the same maximum velocities (which occur at the zero-crossing points) have maximum amplitudes which are inversely proportional to the frequency:

$$\text{Amplitude} = \frac{\text{Velocity}}{2\pi \times \text{frequency}}$$

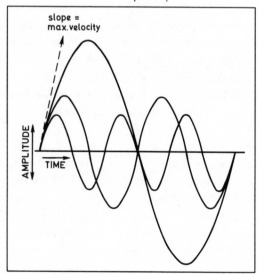

Fig. 20.1
The relationship between amplitude and velocity for sinusoidal waves of different frequency

If we were to record modulation using a constant velocity characteristic over the full audio range, then at low frequencies the amplitudes would become very large and use a lot of disc space. In order to reduce these large amplitudes, the constant velocity characteristic is changed to a constant amplitude characteristic at low frequencies. Also, at high frequencies, in order to improve the ratio of signal to groove-noise, the constant velocity characteristic again changes to constant amplitude. The internationally standardized recording characteristic is shown in Fig. 20.2. It will be seen that the extremely low frequency characteristic again reverts to constant velocity. This is to avoid the necessity of providing the reproducing characteristic with continuously increasing gain right down to the lowest recorded frequencies. This could cause trouble with turntable rumble and vibration.

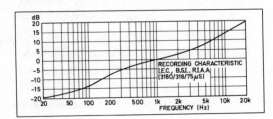

Fig. 20.2
The international standard recording characteristic (RIAA etc.)

The lathe

The master lacquer disc is cut on a lathe which rotates the disc horizontally about a vertical axis, the cutting stylus moving radially across the disc by means of a lead-screw, cutting a spiral groove as it goes. The turntable is driven by an electric motor, which in one widely used design is a very heavy, multiple-winding, multiple-pole, slow speed synchronous motor with its shaft flexibly coupled to an oil-damped high inertia turntable which filters out any small irregularity in the motor drive. Another make, now not in production, used a heavy high-speed motor with multiple belt reduction loops to a flywheel and heavy turntable. Another recently introduced lathe uses a heavy turntable directly driven by a crystal reference servo-controlled DC motor which maintains constant rotational speed independent of the cutting load.

The cutting stylus, in its cutterhead, is mounted in a suspension unit on a carriage traversed across the disc by the lead-screw which is driven from a separate voltage servo-controlled motor. The rotational speed of the lead-screw can be varied by adjusting the proportion of the generator voltage fed back into the servo-amplifier. The generator voltage, and hence the lead-screw speed, can be monitored by a meter calibrated in grooves/inch (grooves/mm). A control is provided for setting the minimum groove spacing required.

The stylus cuts a V-shaped groove in the lacquer, the angle being nominally 90° with a very small bottom radius. For stereophonic recording, the drive systems are designed to modulate the left and right groove walls independently, the driving action being accurately set to 45° to the disc surface and hence at 90° to each other (Fig. 20.3).

Since the left and right modulations usually differ, the appearance of the two walls of the groove will also differ, but there are some special cases which are of interest. These are shown in Fig. 20.3 from which it can be seen that monophonic recording is only a special case of stereophonic in which the left and right modulations are identical and in phase.

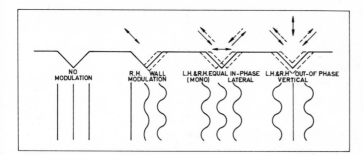

NO MODULATION　　R.H. WALL MODULATION　　L.H.&R.H.EQUAL IN-PHASE (MONO) LATERAL　　L.H.&R.H. OUT-OF PHASE VERTICAL

Fig. 20.3
Showing how the stereo groove is modulated by the resultant of two stylus motions at 45° to the disc surface

Figure 20.3 also shows that the overall width of the groove depends upon the modulation amplitude, more particularly on the vertical component of the modulation, and also that the necessary spacing between grooves depends on the lateral component of the modulation together with the average depth of the groove. In order to conserve disc space, means are provided for automatically adjusting the average groove depth and groove spacing, so that the grooves may be set as close together as possible and give maximum playing time. So as to provide sufficient space for higher levels of modulation, the groove spacing must be opened up and the depth adjusted in time to accommodate the greater signal amplitude when it occurs. This means that information must be supplied in advance of the signal being recorded, and this is usually obtained from an extra replay head on the tape machine in advance of the normal replay head.

By means of switches actuated by the movement of the lathe carriage, the cutterhead can be lowered into the lacquer at a predetermined diameter, and lead-in spirals, concentric finishes and other functions carried out automatically. The thread of lacquer (or swarf) cut from the disc is carried away from the cutting point by means of a suction tube, and is collected in a jar since it is extremely flammable. The cutting stylus is wound with a heating coil and it can ignite the swarf momentarily and cover the stylus with fused lacquer and carbon, as well as spoiling the lacquer disc. It is therefore essential

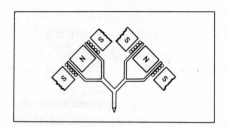

Fig. 20.4
The basic Westrex and Neumann stereo cutter drive system

that the swarf be removed immediately in a continuous thread from the stylus.

The lacquer disc, if simply laid on the turntable (over the centre peg), would slip relative to the turntable as soon as the stylus began to cut. So some means of clamping is required. The method which is now universally used is to hold the disc to the turntable by suction, applied through small holes in its upper surface.

Cutterheads

All high quality cutterheads use moving coil drive systems which have good linearity, but there are two basic methods of coupling the left and right channel drives to the cutting stylus.

One method is shown in Fig. 20.4, where the two channel drives are mounted at right-angles to each other. The drive rods connect directly to the stylus holder, which is restrained by a cantilever tube along the direction of the groove. The other method (Fig. 20.5) has the drive systems mounted side by side and connected to opposite ends of a connecting bridge, at the centre of which the cutting stylus is attached.

In practice, these cutterheads can give substantially similar results when used with their respective amplifying systems. Cutterheads for professional quality work all use feedback loops, covering the driving power amplifiers and the electromechanical transducer. Since any cutterhead has a mechanical resonance, where it requires a minimum of power to make it move, this resonance is deliberately arranged to occur near the middle of the audio frequency band in order to conserve power requirements. At frequencies above resonance, the stylus motion is controlled by the mass of the moving

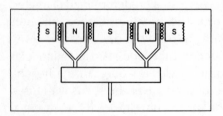

Fig. 20.5
The basic Ortofon system

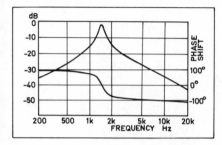

Fig. 20.6
Typical cutterhead response to constant current input

system; below resonance it is controlled by the stiffness of the restraining springs (Fig. 20.6). Feedback coils are fitted to the drive system, as close as possible to the cutting stylus so that the voltages generated in these coils are virtually directly proportional to the stylus velocity. Elaborate copper screening rings are used between the drive and the feedback coils, to ensure that no direct magnetic coupling exists and that the feedback voltage is due only to mechanical motion.

This feedback voltage is fed back into the drive amplifier in antiphase in order to flatten the overall frequency response (Fig. 20.7). It also helps to reduce still further any distortion products which may be present. The amount of feedback which can be safely applied depends on the feedback voltage being negative except where the loop gain has dropped to less than unity. This phase relationship is much more difficult to maintain over an amplifier plus cutterhead than for the amplifier alone, owing to the $\pm 90°$ phase shifts introduced by the main resonance, in addition to phase shifts due to unwanted mechanical resonances at high frequencies (Fig. 20.6).

In practice, the feedback usually changes from negative to positive in the 10 kHz region and increasing the feedback gain will result in an increase of level at high frequencies, rather than a decrease. The amount of feedback recommended by the manufacturer is usually such as to flatten the overall response at high frequencies, whilst maintaining at least 4 dB of loop gain in hand before instability and high frequency oscillation occurs.

The feedback voltage is a good indication of the cutterhead frequency response, except at the highest frequencies where differences occur due to the feedback coil not being right at the stylus tip. This voltage is used for monitoring the cutterhead performance during recording and calibration. The degree of feedback permissible may not be sufficient to flatten the frequency response completely in the bass, but this fall-off can be restored by an appropriate bass lift in the drive amplifier. Frequency correction to the IEC recording characteristic is provided prior to the feedback loop.

It is extremely useful to check the performance of the cutterhead electrically by energizing the drive coils and measuring the output from the feedback

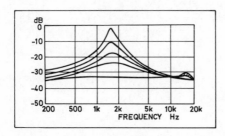

Fig. 20.7
Effect of feedback on cutter overall response

coils. By this means it is possible to detect changes due to physical damage, ageing of springs, dirt in the magnetic gap, etc., which show up as changes in resonant frequency, loss of sensitivity, or non-linearity of output level with change of input level.

Vertical cutting angle

Since all commercial designs of stereophonic pickups have the effective pivoting point of the stylus tip located above the surface of the disc, it follows that the plane in which the stylus moves is not actually vertical, but is inclined at an angle (Fig. 20.8a). If the plane of movement of the cutting stylus tip does not coincide with that of the pickup, then the pickup output will be distorted (Fig. 20.8b). The plane of the cutting stylus has therefore been standardized at $20° \pm 5°$ to the vertical, and stereophonic pickups should all be designed to operate in this plane.

Different mechanical designs of cutterheads have different planes of operation, and the actual plane may not coincide with what appears to be the obvious one, but all cutterheads are fitted with inclined mountings which ensure that the stylus tip moves in the required plane. If the cutting stylus were mounted in the cutterhead so that its length were in this plane, the level which could be cut would be restricted by the back angle of the stylus (Fig. 20.9) and this has meant that the mounting of the stylus in the cutterhead is at an angle so that it contacts the lacquer disc vertically (Fig. 20.10).

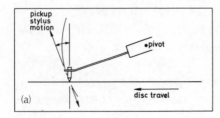

(a)

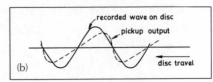

(b)

Fig. 20.8
(a) Showing that the plane of motion of a typical pivoted pickup stylus is at an angle to the vertical;
(b) distortion due to vertical tracking error

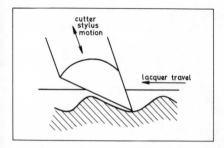

Fig. 20.9
Restriction of level would occur if the cutting
stylus were mounted at an angle

In practice, the distortion caused by small differences between the cutting
and pickup planes is generally considered to be negligible.

Cutterhead suspension

The cutterhead is mounted in a suspension unit attached to the moving
carriage of the lathe. If the surface of the lacquer disc were perfectly flat,
then the cutterhead could be mounted rigidly and it would cut a groove of
constant depth. However, no lacquer disc is sufficiently flat for this purpose
and so the cutterhead is pivoted so that the stylus can follow, to a certain
extent, the rise and fall of the disc surface. The cutterhead is partially counterbalanced about the pivoting axis and the depth of cut is adjusted by means
of a spring. One heavy type of cutterhead uses a sapphire ball which glides
on the surface of the disc just ahead of the cutting point, and the depth of
cut is adjusted by altering the pressure of this ball (Fig. 20.11).

The effective mass of the cutterhead and its pivoting arm form an oscillatory system in conjunction with the stiffness of the suspension and of the
lacquer under the cutting stylus. This oscillatory system would produce a
regular vertical modulation of the groove, which would be seen as a regular
radial or spiralling pattern on the disc surface, becoming more apparent
the closer the grooves were spaced. In practice, this vertical oscillation is
virtually eliminated by mechanically damping the motion with an oil-filled
dashpot. The oil used is preferably of the silicone type, in order to nullify
the effects of temperature change. The degree of damping can be optimized
by adjusting apertures in the dashpot plunger, so that a reasonable com-

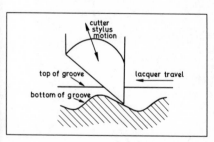

Fig. 20.10
Vertical position used in practice

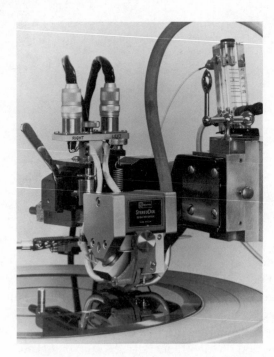

Fig. 20.11
The Westrex cutterhead with advance ball, on a Scully lathe

promise is obtained between patterning, due to insufficient damping, and excessive damping preventing the stylus from following surface irregularities (Fig. 20.12).

Some lathes use a form of servo-mechanism on the depth control, one using a position-controlled servo (Fig. 20.13), whilst another uses a pressure servo-mechanism, which should ideally assist materially in maintaining a constant groove depth. With most suspensions, alterations in the depth of cut are obtained by varying the current passing through a coil attached to the cutterhead pivoting arm, and moving in a magnetic field, but one system uses the method of passing direct current through the cutterhead drive coils in addition to the modulation signals.

One of the great difficulties in achieving a long playing time is the practical limit on the closeness of groove spacing due to the inconstancy of the

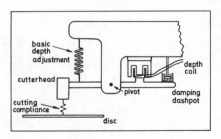

Fig. 20.12
Use of oil damping in cutterhead

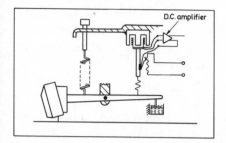

Fig. 20.13
Ortofon depth position servo

groove depth caused by slight variations in the flatness of the lacquer, no matter what type of suspension system is used. One factor which controls the degree of this inconstancy is the position of the pivoting axis of the cutterhead suspension. Setting the pivoting axis higher above the disc surface will reduce the groove depth fluctuations, but at the expense of increased frequency modulation of the recorded signal due to the forwards and backwards movement of the cutterhead along the groove as it rises and falls. A compromise setting must be arrived at depending on the flatness of the lacquer discs in use and the audibility of the frequency modulation.

The suspension unit normally incorporates facilities for automatically

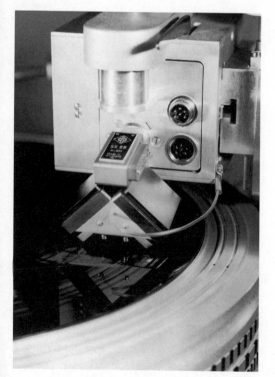

Fig. 20.14
Neumann cutterhead with suspension unit

lowering the cutterhead on to the disc at the correct diameter for the start of the lead-in spiral before the actual music grooves, also for lifting the cutter-head from the disc at the end of the recording after the lead-out spiral has completed its terminating concentric groove (Fig. 20.14).

Cutting stylus

In the days of soft wax recording, the cutting sapphire stylus had its cutting edges ground and polished as sharp as possible, and this gave an extremely quiet and smooth groove when using the warm, thick, wax blank. However, the electroplating process for wax introduced appreciable noise and, when the microgroove LP record was introduced, lacquer-coated aluminium discs were adopted which could be processed much better. Sharp cutting styli on lacquer produced unacceptably noisy grooves until wear of the cutting edges became evident; friction of the dulled edge partially swaged the groove walls as the swarf was removed and gave a good polished appear-ance. Unfortunately, the worn cutting edges prevented high frequencies from being cut properly (except at very low level) and also produced con-siderable mechanical loading on the stylus. This varied with the cutting radius and caused a loss of high frequencies towards the centre of the disc.

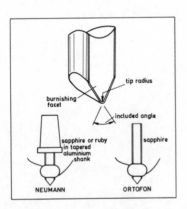

Fig. 20.15
Showing two types of heated stylus and the dulled cutting edge (burnish-ing facet)

   To overcome this trouble, a coil of wire is cemented on to the cutting stylus close to the tip (Fig. 20.15) and is heated by passing current through it. This momentarily has the same effect on the groove walls as the older dulled edge stylus. With this heating, the stylus can now be given an almost sharp cutting edge which produces very little mechanical loading on the stylus and negligible top loss across the disc. Cutting styli are now made with a slightly dulled cutting edge (or burnishing facet) approximately 2 microns in width and, with the optimum heating current, should show a loss of level at 16 kHz of not greater than 2 dB when cutting at 33⅓ rpm between the maximum and minimum music diameters.

The actual heating current used will depend on the individual cutting stylus, its burnishing facet, the depth of groove and the type and age of the lacquer disc. It is necessary to make no-modulation test cuts with a range of heating currents in 0·05 steps between 0·4 and 0·8 amps, and to select the quietest operating value (see Fig. 20.16). It will be found at low currents that the hiss is high but will become lower as the current is increased. After reaching a minimum, it then changes to a low spluttering which becomes worse as the current is increased further. Excessive current will not only cause unnecessary noise but may even cause the coil to become red-hot with the attendant probability of a lacquer fire.

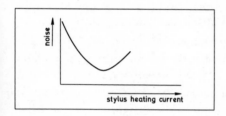

Fig. 20.16
Variation in noise level with stylus heating current

The life of a stylus depends on two things: firstly on physical damage, which can be caused by careless handling or by the tip being chipped or broken by a small piece of solid material on, or in, the surface of the lacquer; secondly by wear. As the groove is being cut, it gradually wears the cutting edges of the stylus, making the effective burnishing facet wider and also broadening the tip radius. Both of these effects can cause trouble, the first by increasing the top loss at the centre, and the second by the possibility of the replay pickup stylus contacting the bottom of the record groove. In practice, the 16 kHz top loss test is sufficient to check the wear on both the edges and the tip. When the acceptable loss is exceeded, the stylus should be changed even though the surface noise may be excellent.

Cutterhead drive amplifier

The response curve of a typical cutterhead shows its velocity sensitivity against input level. Without feedback, it is typically very high at the resonance, but falls to a low value at the extremes of the audio band (Figs. 20.6 and 20.7). Although feedback will flatten the response curve, it does not alter the velocity/coil-voltage requirement; the flat response is obtained because the feedback increases the power supplied to the coils at the extreme frequencies, and reduces it at resonance. To these power requirements must be added the high frequency increase due to the IEC recording characteristic which, at present day recording levels, involves the use of high-powered drive amplifiers to allow for cases where the programme contains appreciable high frequency content such as loud cymbal or muted trumpet passages.

In order to cope with the increasing demands of wider frequency response at high levels, the expansion of multitrack facilities with closer microphone techniques, and the use of electronic synthetic instruments, cutterhead drive amplifier power has been rapidly increased. Whereas 60-watt amplifiers were adequate up to a few years ago, 500 and 600-watt amplifiers are now common. The use of such high powers has been made possible only by the use of new materials in cutterheads which can withstand the higher temperatures generated in the drive coils. A few years ago the maximum safe temperature was 100°C, but now the limit has been raised to 250°C.

The internal temperature of the cutterhead and the coils depends on the rate at which the heat can be dissipated by conduction from the outside case, which depends mainly on the conductivity of the air inside the cutterhead. It has been found that this rate of heat dissipation can be appreciably increased by replacing the air inside the cutterhead with hydrogen or helium, which have thermal conductivities about six times that of air. In practice, helium is used rather than hydrogen, owing to the danger of ignition when using the latter. Cutterheads are now provided with a small bore inlet tube through which a trickle of helium is passed, being metered with a gas flowmeter. A medium sized cylinder (1,246 litres (44 cu. ft.)) of mineral helium should last several weeks, provided the plastic tube connectors are gas tight. This should be carefully checked, since helium is very volatile and even the smallest leak will quickly empty the cylinder. The use of helium means that, for the same temperature rise, the recording level can be increased by about 3 dB or, alternatively, the factor of safety is increased for the same recording level.

Some form of cut-out is incorporated in the drive amplifier to prevent amplifier overload, or the cutterhead being damaged by excessive current. For many years these cut-outs were based on a maximum permissible voltage applied across the drive coil, with some allowance for signal duration, or else by a simple drive coil fuse. These earlier cut-out devices were not very satisfactory since neither the voltage nor the current is a specific indication of probable failure of the cutterhead. Modern cut-out devices are controlled by the actual temperature of the drive coil, which is continuously checked by measuring the change of its resistance in a bridge network. This is a much more realistic safety system and has the added advantage of easy addition of meters which show the actual coil temperatures. Thus any build-up of dangerous signals can be identified and, if necessary, modified.

Groove spacing and depth control

To obtain the longest possible playing time, the width of the groove is made as small as possible (25 μm (0·001-inch)), consistent with the need for the pickup stylus tip to contact the groove walls and not to rest on the top of the groove. Also, in order to prevent a ragged groove top which would cause trouble in electroplating, a small but definite space should separate adjacent grooves (say 5 μm (0·0002-inch)). When the programme modulates the groove walls, the grooves vary in width and depth and it is necessary to increase the basic spacing and groove depth to accommodate these variations, yet still maintain the necessary minimum groove width and clearance between grooves.

With a knowledge of the programme material and very long experience, control of the spacing and depth can be done manually, but this is extremely difficult without making a mistake which could render the lacquer useless. Therefore, to ensure the best conditions for long playing time together with accurate repeatability during possible recutting, the process is made automatic.

This automatic operation is based in a small computer in the lathe which is fed by signals from the left programme channel, together with both left and right channels, from an extra replay head on the tape machine. The extra head (called preview or advance head) is fitted at a tape distance equivalent to just over the time for half a revolution of the lathe turntable (say 1·1 secs. at $33\frac{1}{3}$ rpm) in front of the normal programme head. These signals are passed through equalizers, the outputs of which are proportional to the amplitude excursions of the cutting stylus. From these outputs, the lateral amplitude components of the left programme channel and right preview channel are derived while, from the difference between the preview left and right channels, the vertical amplitude component is obtained together with the extra lateral spacing component needed due to the increased mean depth (Fig. 20.3).

The required increase of mean groove depth, being derived from the preview channels, gives time for the change of depth to take place smoothly by the time the programme modulation is to be cut. As soon as the vertical modulation stops, the mean depth is allowed to revert smoothly to normal.

The groove spacing required by the lateral components of the programme differ between the left and right channels (inner and outer groove walls respectively). For right channel modulation, the spacing must be increased in time to permit the stylus excursion to occur without overcutting the previous groove; therefore the control is taken from the right preview channel. This new spacing must continue until the right programme amplitude is reduced, when the spacing can quickly reduce to the new appropriate

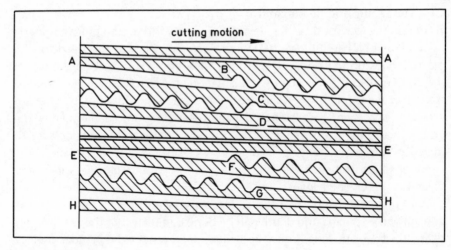

Fig. 20.17
Unwound portion of record to show opera-
tion of automatic groove spacing and depth
control:
A. Depth increase [from L and R preview]
    Spacing-for-depth increase
B. L programme starts
    Spacing increases [from L programme]
C. L programme stops
    Depth and spacing for depth reduce
    Spacing for L programme maintained

for 1 disc revolution
D. Spacing normal
E. Spacing increases [from R preview]
    Depth and spacing-for-depth increase
    [from L and R preview]
F. R programme starts
G. R programme stops
    Spacing due to R programme reduces
    Depth and spacing-for-depth reduce
H. Depth and spacing normal

value. With the left programme channel (inner groove wall) there is no
previous groove for the modulation to overcut, so the spacing information
is taken from the left programme channel alone. The spacing increases so
that the succeeding groove has sufficient clearance not to cut into the
modulation. This spacing must be retained for one complete revolution
after the modulation amplitude has been reduced, after which it can revert
smoothly to its new appropriate value (Fig. 20.17). To these left and right
groove spacing controls is added the extra groove spacing necessary to
accommodate the increased mean depth of cut.

The length of playing time achieved, whilst retaining adequate groove
separation, depends upon several factors of which those under normal
control of the user are as follows:

1. The frequency responses of the programme and preview channels of the
tape machine should be very closely matched, particularly at low frequencies
where disc amplitudes are significant. Above about 4 kHz the amplitudes are
normally very small and the preview channel responses need not be so
closely controlled; but at low frequencies a difference of 1 dB between the

programme and preview channels can cause about 10% difference in groove spacing, which may easily result in loss of playing time, intercutting, or insufficient groove width.

2. The same accurate matching applies to any level or response changes used to modify the programme material for artistic or technical reasons. It necessarily follows that any changes made in the programme chain must be matched with a closely equal change in the preview chain. If these changes take place while cutting, the preview alteration should be made first and the programme change the time of half a disc revolution later.

3. The cutterhead low frequency response must be very carefully adjusted to the IEC characteristic, so that the amplitudes cut on the disc do not differ appreciably from the amplitude signals fed to the spacing and depth computer. Only when these conditions have been met will it be possible to cut very long playing discs consistently.

Programme control console

Ideally, recorded tapes presented for disc cutting should require only level control before being fed to the drive amplifiers but, in practice, this ideal seldom occurs and most tapes need some adjustment of tone balance, dynamics and level. Most disc-cutting consoles have controls for such modifications, and the more facilities that are provided, the greater the possibility of improvement. The photograph of a modern sophisticated console (Fig. 20.18) illustrates the facilities which have been found advantageous.

Input selector for four different inputs, RH channel poling switch, LH and RH channel transposing switch, input level controls, channel level balance control, 90° phase shift, and mono combining switch.

Tone controls for each channel, comprising four independent frequency bands, each band with five switched frequencies and each frequency with five different shapes up to ±10 dB in 1 dB steps.

Compressor/Limiter with output level, hold and recovery controls.

Filter unit with switched variable high-pass and low-pass filters and also a presence filter with eight frequencies up to ±10 dB in 1 dB steps.

High level switch which increases the level in 1 dB steps up to 8 dB to the drive amplifiers, without changing the meter or speaker monitoring levels.

Groove space control which varies the groove spacing in 1 dB steps from +6 to −4 dB.

Spreader which opens or closes the stereo angle in 1 dB steps up to ±5 dB.

Vertical amplitude limiter which limits the low-frequency amplitudes over the range of +3 to −6 dB referred to 35 microns.

Fig. 20.18
Disc-cutting programme control console (courtesy EMI)

Faders in programme channels only, with continuous tracks.

Oscillator which gives stable output at thirteen frequencies, with level control of 20 steps of 2 dB and continuous fine control; switchable to inputs, check units and, via 75 microseconds de-emphasis, to drive amplifiers.

Correlator which indicates phase relationships between channels.

Noise meters indicating noise levels in circuits.

Disc replay unit switchable to inputs or to monitor.

Meter unit which uses VU meters with +10 and +20 dB switchable extra sensitivity.

Quadraphonic matrix decoder switchable in monitor unit.

Dolby replay units switchable in input unit, only in programme channels.

Left and right channel controls are ganged where appropriate.

All programme channel controls are duplicated for the groove spacing and depth control channels except where stated.

With such a console, tapes which would originally have been rejected as impossible or unsuitable to cut may possibly be turned into outstanding successes.

Tracing distortion correction

Probably the greatest cause of distortion inherent in replaying disc records is the fact that the pickup stylus tip has a finite tip radius, whereas the groove is cut with a relatively sharp stylus. This form of distortion is known as tracing distortion and is a combination of phase and non-linear amplitude distortion which becomes worse as the diameter becomes smaller (Fig. 20.19).

A number of systems have been introduced with the object of reducing this distortion by adding a complementary distortion to the programme signal. Thus the recording on the lacquer is predistorted in such a way that, when replaced with a stylus having a specific tip radius, the distortion is cancelled out (Fig. 20.20). These systems have met with varying degrees of success since the theoretical requirements are stringent and require cutter-

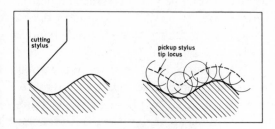

Fig. 20.19
Tracing distortion: note that locus of stylus tip does not follow the recorded waveform correctly

heads and drive amplifiers which have smooth and stable frequency and phase responses up to double the normal frequency range. If these require-ments are not maintained, the complementary distortion may give rise to worse results than without the addition. A further difficulty arises in the not unusual circumstance of the recorded level being such that the pickup stylus is unable to maintain constant contact with both groove walls. Under such conditions the theoretical analysis breaks down and the overall effect is unpredictable.

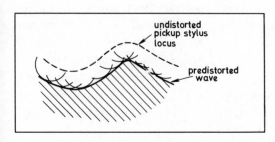

Fig. 20.20
Use of predistortion to reduce tracing distortion

With these points in mind, despite the evidence of specific frequency tone tests, it would be a reasonable precaution for the user to make com-parative tests of the type of programme material concerned, recorded at the required level with and without the predistortion system, in order to deter-mine whether any detectable improvement is obtained when played back with pickups having a range of stylus tip radii.

Quadraphonic disc cutting

Quadraphonic disc recordings, using a number of different systems, are being issued commercially by many record companies. Unlike quadraphonic 4-track tapes, the disc has only two basic channels and the difference between the various systems concerns the manner in which the four channels of information are encoded into two and, on replay, decoded into four.

These various systems can broadly be divided into two groups, namely matrix and discrete, which have very different technical requirements for the disc-cutting equipment. The matrix systems involve some method of combining the original four channels into two without alteration of the original normal bandwidths. Therefore the resultant two encoded channels each occupy only the normal bandwidth and can be recorded in the same way as any ordinary stereophonic programme. There exists only one small disadvantage when cutting these encoded matrix discs and that is the likelihood of increased out-of-phase signals, caused by phase shifts which are an integral part of the system. This may entail an increase of groove spacing and hence some loss of playing time.

The principal discrete system puts two channels on to each groove wall by having one channel covering the normal audio band, plus a higher frequency band consisting of a carrier at 30 kHz frequency modulated by the second channel, so that the overall bandwidth extends to 45 kHz. Although cutterhead responses have been extended to about 27 kHz, this range is not sufficient to record directly at normal speed. It is therefore necessary to cut at half speed ($16\frac{2}{3}$ rpm). The 4-track tape machine must also operate at half speed and, in addition to the normal preview head for groove spacing and depth control, there is a second preview head which adjusts the carrier level on the disc according to the programme level. This carrier level has also to be increased as the recording diameter is reduced, and this appreciably increases heating problems in the cutterhead. At present, the disc-cutting operation involves a considerable degree of trial and error, besides the disadvantage of half speed working. However, if further cutterhead development can extend the response sufficiently for normal speed cutting, then the time factor may be improved.

Cutterhead calibration

When setting up a cutterhead according to the manufacturer's instructions, the basic criterion of accuracy of the recording characteristic of the system lies in the degree of flatness of the feedback monitor output when the drive amplifiers are fed with constant voltage. The instructions usually state that this check should be made by using a special 'calibration' condition of the drive and feedback amplifier equalization. This switches out the high frequency pre-emphasis and thus avoids the possibility of dangerous cutter currents caused by high levels at high frequencies.

This method of calibration is generally quite satisfactory, but it does depend upon the 'calibration' condition of drive and feedback equalization having the correct values. Should the responses of the amplifiers change at any time, the engineer may be tempted to readjust the feedback setting to realign the response, with the possibility of oscillation and burnt-out cutter coils. For this reason it is a wise precaution to check the actual frequency response on the disc itself. There are several methods by which this can be done, of which the eaiest is by comparison with one of the standard IEC recording characteristic test discs issued by major recording companies (e.g. EMI TCS 101).

The light-bandwidth method is more refined and has the advantage that the response can be inspected visually on the lathe turntable, or can be measured more accurately with comparatively simple equipment. Inspection of the light-bandwidth must always be made with a small filament lamp situated at the focus of a large diameter (say 75 mm) convex lens, so that the incident rays are virtually parallel and strike the disc at 45° to the disc surface. The viewing angle must also be 45°. With stereophonic cutterheads, these 45° angles are essential since any appreciable divergence can cause large changes in light-bandwidth (Fig. 20.21).

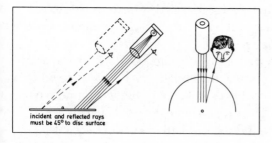

Fig. 20.21
Light-bandwidth method of checking frequency response

incident and reflected rays
must be 45° to disc surface

The width of the reflected light-band is proportional to the velocity of the modulation, and with sinusoidal signals measurements of the width can be converted to velocity from the expressions:

$33\frac{1}{3}$ rpm   1 cm/sec. rms (at 45°)=0·572 cm LBW
45 rpm   1 cm/sec. rms (at 45°)=0·424 cm LBW.

For lateral only recording (monophonic) the velocity of the modulation is the addition of the horizontal components on each wall, which means that the lateral velocity is 1·41 cm/sec rms for the light-bandwidths quoted above.

It is better, particularly at low frequencies, for the lacquer disc to revolve slowly on the turntable so that the extremes of the light-band are clearly defined.

Hints on practical disc cutting

1. Stylus. The large front facet must always be at right angles to the groove to avoid high frequency loss, particularly at the centre of the disc. The special stylus microscope made for this by the cutterhead manufacturer is of great assistance.

The cutterhead/suspension-unit mounting must permit the stylus to move radially across the disc as the carriage travels. If not, there will be top loss and distortion at the centre of the disc.

The stylus must always be vertical when it is cutting the lacquer.

Never lower the cutterhead on to a stationary disc when the disc amplifiers are switched on, since some cutterhead/amplifier combinations with a small stability margin may go into oscillation, causing overheating or mechanical damage.

To ensure good swarf collection, high suction can be used as the point is lowered, but it should be reduced when the swarf is picking up satisfactorily. Too high suction can transmit noise and vibration to the cutting stylus and to the groove.

If the swarf is not taken away by suction, it will pile up under the stylus and eventually touch the heating coil, melt, and volatilize. The stylus should always be removed from the cutterhead and soaked in acetone to dissolve the encrusted lacquer, or permit removal by a soft brush. In obdurate cases a sharply pointed orange stick may be used.

An excessively deep cut may go through the lacquer down to the aluminium base of the disc, and the cut will show a bright silvery line at the bottom of the groove. The stylus will probably be chipped or broken, or more often a small particle of aluminium will be swaged on to the front face of the stylus. This may not be removable, and the stylus will then be unserviceable.

A clean, quiet groove can be cut only if the stylus is absolutely clean. It should be cleaned before and after each cut, no matter how short in duration, by gently pushing it into a piece of soft pith dipped in acetone.

2. Groove jumping. This is a serious trouble which may not be discovered until the record is on the market. It is due to older, or cheap mass-produced players with pickups which are in poor condition, having high mechanical impedances which cannot follow the level of modulation on the disc and throw the pickup stylus up the groove wall and sometimes out of the groove. Test lacquers and pressings should always be tried on a range of such poor instruments to check this possibility. If it occurs, the lacquer should be recut at a slightly reduced level and, if possible, with a deeper overall groove.

3. *Pre- and post-echo.* This is found on processed discs, but seldom on lacquers, unless intercutting has taken place (or is on the tape due to print). The most objectionable echo is pre-echo since it cannot occur in nature. The incidence of this defect cannot be predicted, but it can be reduced by wider groove spacing when a quiet passage is followed by a loud sound, e.g. at the start of a loud band in an album. Most lathes now have a push-button to increase groove spacing to a pre-determined value when this is expected.

References

Standards	BSI 1928–1965 with amendments
	IEC Publication 98 with amendments
Cutterhead Calibration	Axon and Geddes. *Proc.I.E.E.* Vol. 100. Part III No. 66. July 1953
	Bastiaans and van der Steen. *Philips Tech.Rev.* Vol. 23 1961/62. No. 3
Cutterhead Suspension	Davies. *J.I.E.E.* Vol. 94. Part II No. 30. July 1947
	Hansen. *Radio and Electronic Engineer.* Dec. 1965
Vertical Cutting Angle	Bastiaans. *J.A.E.S.* Vol. II No. 1. Jan. 1963.
Tracing Distortion	Olsen. *Audio* Nov. and Dec. 1964
	Braschoss. *J.A.E.S.* Feb. 1971
	Ohkawa, Kuriyagawa and Makino A.E.S. 39th Convention Oct. 1970 (Preprint No. 747-F-7).
Groove and Depth Control	Braschoss. *International Broadcast Eng.* July 1967
	Hansen. *Radio and Electronic Engineer.* Dec. 1965

CHAPTER TWENTY-ONE

Disc Manufacture

E. B. Pinniger

The mass production of commercial disc records is a very specialized process. Basically it consists of the production of large numbers of thermoplastic mouldings from negative matrices electroformed from the original disc recordings. Electroforming is in essentials the same as electroplating but, instead of the very thin films of metal used for protective and decorative plating, a substantial deposit is made which can be detached from the original cut master and used in turn to produce second and third generation electroforms.

The thermoplastic moulding takes place in a specially constructed hydraulic press, the dies of which have a rapid cooling and heating cycle. The records may be produced by either compression or injection moulding.

Terminology

The industry has produced its own special jargon or terminology which had better be defined at this stage:

Lacquer Recording Blank: An aluminium disc of the required dimensions for processing, the surface of which is coated with a specially lubricated and plasticized nitro-cellulose lacquer suitable for cutting.

The Original or Master Lacquer: This is the cut disc made on a master lacquer recording blank by means of a disc-cutting lathe.

Master: The metal negative obtained by electroforming on to the surface of the Master Lacquer.

Positive or Mother: A metal positive obtained by electroforming from the Master; in effect a copy of the recording in metal which may be played for purposes of quality control.

Stamper: A metal negative obtained by electroforming from the Positive and intended for use as a mould for the production of pressings.

Matrices: A generic term used to cover all the generations of electroforms.

Pressing: The thermoplastic moulding produced by heat, pressure, and subsequent cooling from a pair of stampers in a suitable record press.

The first disc records date back to Emile Berliner who used a glass blank coated with a paint-like substance into which a spiral track with lateral modulation was cut. Subsequently wax-coated metal blanks were used; the trace cut could then be etched and the metal positive thus produced used for the production of stampers from which copies could be impressed and the first true gramophone records made.

A brief history

It may be as well to give a brief history of the technique of processing at this stage before proceeding to consider processing as it is today. All the early disc records were recorded on wax blanks and the metal used for the electro-forming process was copper. The wax was specially compounded from montan wax, stearine, lead oxide and sodium hydroxide by melting the ingredients in a large, oil-jacketed, gas-heated vessel. The molten wax was passed through a filter press and cast into blanks in aluminium moulds under carefully controlled conditions. These waxes were 33 cm in diameter and 6·4 cm thick and were rough turned on a conventional lathe. The final polish of the recording surface was produced in a special machine with a horizontal faceplate, the polish being achieved by shaving the surface with an agate blade. The resulting swarf was removed by suction. A polished wax had a very delicate mirror surface and was packed in a strong circular box, the recording surface being protected by means of central and peripheral felt pads in the base of the container. Before a recording session, the wax was warmed in a special cupboard in the studio for several hours to a temperature of 25–30° C. At this temperature the blank was in a suitable condition for cutting.

Electroforming on to a wax surface presents difficulties. The method employed in the production of printing plates was to brush the wax surface with graphite powder to produce a conducting film. This method was adapted by the record industry, a specially prepared grade of graphite being used. However such a film consists of discrete particles and the method of application reduced the polish on the surface of the wax. The resulting graphite film had poor electrical properties, with the result that the production of the initial copper film was a long and hazardous process. A very low voltage and current density were employed to avoid overheating the surface being covered. In an effort to obtain better conductivity, 'Bronze' (copper) powder was used in place of graphite and supsequently a process was developed in which the mechanically applied copper was chemically converted to silver. Silver cyanide solution was applied to the copper surface and silver deposited by simple replacement. This silver film could be further intensified by treatment with solutions of silver nitrate and pyrogallol. All the processes had the disadvantage of relying on a conducting layer applied in powder form. In the early days high surface noise was acceptable, but with the development of electrical recording general quality improved and changes in processing techniques became desirable.

Attempts were made to use the known process for the silvering of mirrors but the range of wetting agents now available had not then been developed, with the result that efficient wetting of the surface of the wax was a difficult process. Air bubbles were retained in the sound track and, although a wet silvered master had a lower basic surface noise, the number of random plops increased alarmingly. Attempts to vacuum-coat waxes were more successful, either gold, silver, or palladium being used. This process, known as cathode sputtering, was employed by the larger companies until lacquer-coated blanks came into general use.

As stated earlier, all the electroforms produced from wax originals were in copper. The electrolyte used was a conventional copper sulphate, sulphuric acid solution with copper anodes. This was a comparatively trouble-free process and the masters and positives were deposited to a thickness of around 0·9–1·0 mm, the process taking several hours. Stampers were either deposited solid, and the backs turned level on a vacuum chuck, or a thin shell made which was subsequently soldered on to a heavy copper backing plate. A nickel chromium layer formed the pressing surface of the stamper. This was first achieved by nickel plating the face of the copper shell but, as this involved adding a layer of metal to the actual surface of the sound track, the 'direct nickel' process was soon developed. In this method, the nickel surface of the stamper was deposited on to the face of the positive and then copper plated on till it reached the desired thickness. This resulted in a stamper in which the working surface had been deposited in intimate contact with the surface of the recording. The layer of chromium was merely a flash and was added to avoid sticking of the pressing, and also to reduce wear on the stamper surface; the pressing materials used for 78 rpm records were very abrasive.

The development of the lacquer-coated disc by the late Cecil E. Watts in this country in the late 1930s, together with similar developments in both Europe and North America, was one of the factors which led to the end of the use of wax as a recording medium.

The broadcasting authorities were interested in the so-called direct recording disc because of its ability to be played back without further processing—a great advantage in the days before magnetic tape had been invented. Also, the fact that discs could be cut easily at normal temperatures, were light and much less easily damaged than waxes, made them very suitable for mobile work. The direct disc soon became firmly established with such manufacturers as MSS and EMI in this country, Pyral in Europe, and Presto in America. Glass-based discs, and coatings other than cellulose lacquer, were produced experimentally but the product soon stabilized into a form very similar to that in use today. As the disc came into general use with the broadcasting authorities, private recording studios began to be opened and there was a demand for processed copies of the direct recordings. This was the main factor in the start of the private label and custom pressing business.

The writer was directly involved with the early experiments on processing lacquer-coated discs. Reasonable results were obtained by using one of the processes developed for the production of silver mirrors on glass in order to obtain the initial conducting film. Lacquer surfaces are fairly readily wetted and, as the deposited silver was very fine grained, a satisfactory signal-to-noise ratio was obtained on a master made from a properly cut master disc.

These experiments were taking place at about the same time as the introduction of the first vinyl resins suitable for thermo-plastic moulding. It may come as a surprise to learn that a 12-inch experimental record rotating at 33 rpm, containing three musical items on each side and pressed in unfilled vinyl compound, was manufactured as early as 1937. The improvement in signal-to-noise ratio and general quality was striking when compared with the then current shellac pressings. However, it was not until the lightweight pickup was introduced that such pressings became a practical commercial proposition.

Metallization

The recording blank in general use today consists of an aluminium disc coated on both sides with a specially formulated cellulose lacquer. This lacquer contains castor oil and is relatively soft at normal temperatures, enabling it to be cut cleanly without any pre-treatment. The presence in the lacquer of a considerable amount of volatile matter raises serious problems if any attempt is made to metallize the surface using a vacuum coating system such as sputtering. It will be appreciated that, as the lacquer is a non-conductor of electricity and the master has to be electroformed on to the recorded surface, the application of a thin metallic film is the first requirement in processing a disc. Before metallization, silver being the metal normally employed, the sound track on the master disc must be chemically clean and perfectly wetted. Pre-cleaning is normally done by careful use of chemical cleaners and detergents, rinsed with generous amounts of de-ionized water. When clean, and showing no water break, the surface of the disc is sensitized by the application of a dilute solution of stannous chloride. This sensitization is essential for a uniform and clean silver mirror to be produced (see Fig. 21.1).

Fig. 21.1
Inspecting a silvered lacquer (courtesy EMI)

The silver may be applied in the form of two solutions poured by hand on to the surface, the lacquer disc being contained in a shallow dish, or preferably by means of a spray gun with two or three nozzles for the appropriate solutions. The jets from the spray gun are so angled that the mist blends on the surface to be metallized and a mirror is rapidly formed. The whole process may be automated; in this case a bank of jets delivers the various cleaning, sensitizing, silvering solutions, and rinse water in the correct sequence, which is controlled by timing devices. The disc is normally rotated to ensure even distribution of the spray over the whole surface to be coated. The basic metallization process relies on the reduction of an aqueous ammoniacal solution of silver nitrate by means of a glucose formaldehyde solution. The formulation of the solutions varies a little in different factories. In some cases a small amount of sodium hydroxide is also added to the silver solution to increase the sensitivity.

Plating
The silvered lacquer is normally pre-plated at low temperature and current density, before being transferred to a tank for deposition at the normal speed. A relatively low solution temperature is essential to avoid distortion of the recorded surface and possible 'sweating out' of the oil. A low current density

is needed until the initial layer of metal is thick enough to be able to carry the high currents encountered in high speed plating.

At this stage it is important to stress that, although the silver metallization process is basically quite a simple reaction, i.e. the reduction of a silver nitrate solution in order to deposit a film of the metal, this stage and the preplating have a profound effect on the final product. If the cleaning, rinsing, silvering, and initial plating are not undertaken with extreme care and rigidly controlled, however good the subsequent processing and pressing may be, the results will not reach an acceptable standard.

When nickel sulphate is dissolved in water, it ionizes. If two electrodes are immersed in this electrolyte, the positively charged nickel ions are attracted to the negative electrode or cathode, while the negatively charged sulphate ions tend to migrate to the positive electrode or anode. If the anode material is nickel, it gradually dissolves and combines with the sulphate radical, replenishing the nickel sulphate in the solution which has been used in the operation of plating. Thus the process results in nickel being transferred from the anode, through the solution and deposited on to the surface of the cathode.

The nickel electrolyte formerly used in the record industry was known as the Watts solution and contained nickel sulphate, nickel chloride, and boric acid. The operating temperature was 50–60° C and the pH about 4–5. This process produced ductile deposits, but with a moderate internal stress resulting in a tendency for the deposit to curl. An electrolyte containing nickel sulphamate in place of nickel sulphate, but otherwise similar to Watts solution, produces deposits with a very low internal stress. The use of relatively high concentrations, up to 450 g per litre of the sulphamate, makes possible high current densities, with the advantage of rapid deposition of metal. Anodes take the form of oval bars or, if contained in titanium baskets, may be small 25 mm cubes or rounds. For the successful use of such an electrolyte, strict pH control, constant filtration and avoidance of contamination either metallic or organic are vital.

The matrices deposited from sulphamate solutions are normally fine grained, ductile and with low internal stress, but the presence of small amounts of organic matter may cause the nickel to be deposited in a brittle condition with high internal stress. These faults will result in splitting of the stamper under pressure. Nickel anode material contains small percentages of metallic impurities, principally in the form of iron and copper. The process of plating lacquer discs causes organic contamination. Under these circumstances constant filtration, low voltage plating out, and periodical treatment at high pH with hydrogen peroxide and activated carbon are desirable, if a consistent product is to be maintained.

In its simplest form, a plating unit consists of a steel tank with a hard rubber lining containing provision for initially heating the solution, either by means of a low pressure steam coil or an electric immersion heater. In a still solution, air agitation is desirable to enable reasonable current densities to be used. A central anode bar along the length of the tank, with two parallel cathode bars, one on either side, are connected to a suitable control panel and fed by a transformer rectifier unit. The cathodes are mounted on jigs and suspended from the cathode bar, and a number of nickel anodes, the

Fig. 21.2
Vertical spindle nickel plate vats for the production of masters, positives and matrices (courtesy EMI)

total area of which must be at least equal to the cathode area, are suspended from the central bar. A potential of 6–8 V DC is applied and, at a current density of 500 to 750 amps per square metre, a usable shell will be deposited in three to four hours. An improvement on the static system is the provision of a rocking motion to the cathode bars. This enables higher current densities to be used. However, in any system where the cathode does not rotate, there is inevitably some variation in thickness round the periphery of the electroform. In the case of masters and positives this is not important but, with stampers, a fair degree of uniformity is desirable.

Fig. 21.3
An alternative design of plating vat
(courtesy Europafilm)

Rotary plating units can be arranged in banks in a large tank with a common electrolyte but with separate controls for each cathode. However, in most of the types in current use, a small tank or module is used for each cathode (see Figs. 21.2 and 21.3). Each disc has its own controls, ampere-hour meter and anodes. The electrolyte is supplied, already filtered and at the correct temperature, to the face of the cathode and exhausted from behind the anodes, thus ensuring that any fine particles or sludge are removed before they can cause roughness on the deposit. The solution is constantly circulated by the filter pump. At high current densities, some heating effect takes place in the electrolyte and, to maintain a constant temperature, facilities for both heating and cooling are necessary. The cathode is rotated by means of a small electric motor mounted on the lid of the module, the disc clamped by a Perspex mask and electrical contact made through the centre spindle. When the lid is shut, the disc is able to rotate in the horizontal plane in a face downward position. If the inter-electrode distances are carefully controlled and suitable baffle plates used, very uniform stampers can be deposited.

The great advantage of the rotary system is that rapid deposition is possible, together with accurate control of thickness. The rectifier units deliver up to 20 V DC at 250 amps, giving a possible current density of 2,500 amps per square metre and producing a stamper in 45 to 50 minutes. Up to ten electroforming tanks, each pair being mounted over a common storage tank, can be used with an electrolyte, circulation and filtration system common to all. Provision is made in most systems for 'plating out'; this is a method of purification involving deposition, at 2 to 3 V and a very low current density, usually on to a corrugated cathode. The process takes place in a separate small tank. Alternatively, dummy loads at low voltage may be used in the normal plating positions, as certain metals plate more readily at these low current densities and may consequently be removed from the electrolyte with the minimum loss of nickel.

Fig. 21.4
Stripping the master from the lacquer (courtesy EMI)

To summarize, the processing of metal parts consists of the following stages: the disc is metallized, made cathode in the electroforming tank, and the required thickness of nickel deposited. At the end of deposition for the required number of ampere-hours, the lacquer disc is removed from the tank, rinsed and the master stripped from its surface (see Fig. 21.4). The master is inspected and any slight roughness at the edges removed. Before further processing can take place, the surface must be carefully cleaned and thoroughly wetted. For the successful separation of the next stage from the master, it is essential for a barrier film to be formed on the surface. Immersion in a solution of an organic colloid, or a very dilute solution of potassium dichromate, results in the formation of a separation film about one molecule thick. The second stage electroform may now be deposited to the required thickness in the same manner as the master, and then stripped to form the positive or mother. The positive is capable of being played for purposes of quality check and, when it has been examined and passed, stampers can be produced. As in the case of the master, a separator must be applied to the surface of the positive before the stamper is deposited. These stampers are usually thinner than the previous stages, being only about 0·25 to 0·38 mm (0·01 to 0·015 inches) in thickness.

All the matrices (the general term by which processing electroforms are known) have a mirror surface and are objects of quite considerable beauty. It is fortunate that they are capable of reproducing the most minute details of the soundtrack through all the stages of processing, otherwise the mass production of records would be impossible.

Preparing the stamper

Even though all the electroforms are of solid nickel, careful handling is vital. At the negative stages, the minute bottom radius of the groove is very easily damaged. All matrices are carefully examined for blemishes and the stampers are finally trimmed to size and provided with an exactly central pilot hole. This is achieved by viewing a small area of the soundtrack through a projection microscope while it is rotated on a faceplate. The faceplate is adjusted for centre until the image of the spiral runs steadily towards the centre of the disc without any trace of swing being visible on the screen. The stamper is then clamped in this position and the central hole punched. The thin nickel plate is then coined in a special forming tool to provide the contours of an LP record with raised edge and centre. In the case of a 180 mm (7-inch) stamper, the anti-slip serrations may also be embossed at this stage. The stampers have a smooth satin finish on the back, and it is usual to polish this surface with fine abrasive before mounting the stampers in a record press.

Processing as outlined above may be taken as typical of practice today, though plant design varies a good deal and details such as cleaning techniques are not standard. In some plants the edge and centre of the recorded disc are roughened with abrasive to prevent premature separation of the master. Opinions also vary on the desirability of using the positive as a means of quality control. As emphasized before, all chemical and electrolytical processes need careful analytical control and a high degree of care and general cleanliness. Plant must be kept in good order and efficient filtration of solutions is vital to success.

Faults

Faults in electroforms may be of several types. In plating, rough deposits can occur through contamination of the electrolyte by dust, sludge or fine anode particles. Shielding of the anodes with suitable anode bags and thorough filtration are the remedy in such cases. Gas pitting is another fault which can occur, particularly with the sulphamate solution; this consists of minute hydrogen bubbles adhering to the surface of the deposit. In extreme cases these produce pinholes but in any case may show on the surface as undesirable sinks. The remedy again is in efficient filtration, strict pH control and thorough solution agitation. In some plants a wetting agent is added to the electrolyte to overcome this problem. The objection to this last remedy is that the anti-pit agent may in time break down to produce organic contamination of the solution, and its removal usually involves treatment with activated carbon. Damage may occur at all stages of process unless great care is taken in stripping. High stress in the deposited nickel will result in premature separation of the electroform and brittle nickel. This again can be controlled by additional agents, and in fact tensile stress may even be rendered compressive by this method. However, as satisfactory nickel may readily be produced from solutions in which a high degree of purity is maintained, I regard this as the preferable method.

Future developments

Nickel sulphamate solutions have almost completely superseded the straight sulphate solution in nickel electroforming and it is difficult to predict further developments. There is no doubt that higher current densities than those at present employed could be used but, as the accent is on quality rather than speed, it is hard to see that much advantage would result.

Metals which might offer advantages over nickel are not obvious. Iron deposition has been tried with some success but suffers from the serious disadvantage of needing immediate protection against corrosion, usually by means of a thin layer of chromium. This process was used for a time during the serious nickel shortage of a few years ago. Tin nickel alloys can be deposited; the metal is wear and tarnish resistant, but is unfortunately much too brittle for electroforming purposes. It might be possible to use a thin facing of the alloy backed with the conventional deposit of ductile nickel from a sulphamate electrolyte.

No doubt the type of plant in current use is capable of further automation but, as each master is treated as a one off job, there is little point in the application of batch treatment techniques. There is also a good deal of resistance to change, as well tried methods are not readily abandoned in a process where even slight changes can result in failure.

Pressing materials

Whereas development in the field of processing has been gradual, the major changes being the transition from wax to lacquer masters and from copper electroforming to nickel, the changes in pressing materials and techniques have been much more revolutionary and dramatic. Shellac (78 rpm) pressings were produced by experienced operators with the temperature and time cycle of the press under manual control. Nowadays pressings are frequently made completely automatically and, where press operators are employed, they merely load and unload the press, the moulding cycle being entirely controlled by electronic timing devices.

The composition of the shellac record really had little or no bearing on the development of the long-playing record. The change to the formulation of the vinyl-based record was a complete break with previous methods of record production. Even the early vinyl mixes contained very little in the way of mineral fillers, in contrast to the shellac based material which had a filler content of about 60%. Many plastics were tried in the search for the ideal pressing material. Cellulose acetate, polyvinyl acetal, acrylics, polystyrene, and vinyledene chloride were the subject of extensive tests. In some cases, records were produced and marketed in one or more of these materials. A series of resins made by the copolymerization of vinyl chloride and vinyl acetate proved to possess most of the qualities required for the satisfactory moulding of records.

The type of copolymer at present in general use is of low molecular weight and made by a suspension polymerization process. The polymer particles are spherical in shape and have a very dense particle structure. The vinyl acetate content is only 15% but it has a profound effect on the properties of the material. Records made from straight PVC by conventional moulding techniques would be quite useless. A typical LP vinyl-base record compound could have the following formulation:

Vinyl Copolymer	100 parts by weight
Stabilizer (a metal soap such as dibasic lead stearate or barium cadmium laurate)	1 to 2 parts by weight
Pigment (carbon black)	0·5 to 1 part by weight

The ingredients are thoroughly blended in a high-speed powder mixer, producing a dry blend which in itself may be suitable for direct use in some types of screw compounders. In order to produce the usual granules or dice, the compound is extruded in the form of slab or laces and may be cut at the die face of the extruder according to the form of pre-heating to be used. In addition to the copolymer, small amounts of homopolymer are sometimes added to the batch in order to modify the flow properties of the final material.

On the historical aspect, it may not be generally known that as well as the early fine groove records made in the 1930s, the pre-war Talking Books made by the National Institute for the Blind were specially recorded long playing records revolving at 25 rpm. These discs were pressed in vinyl acetal with a 25% superfine filler content and incorporated a special lubricant in order to cope with the very high stylus pressures in use at the time.

The pressing cycle

The first stage in the manufacture of a record consists in preheating the material to a suitable degree of plasticity, and in a pre-form of suitable weight for the actual operation of moulding. The mixing and extrusion of the pre-form or puck usually takes place nowadays in a specially designed unit which will handle either granules or dry blend. In the past, hot air heaters or infra-red heating units have been frequently employed, using the material in the form of dice.

The thermoplastic moulding, which is the gramophone record, is produced from two stampers by the application of heat, pressure and subsequent cooling. A basic record press consists of top and bottom plattens carrying record dies, which in turn hold the stampers forming the mould. The daylight or space between the plattens is closed by applying hydraulic pressure to one platten while holding the other firmly locked in position. The dies must be capable of being heated and cooled at the correct points in the pressing cycle.

In its simplest form, the record press consists of a four column structure with a fixed head and portable dies mounted on slides. The bottom half of the machine contains the main hydraulic cylinder and piston in an up stroking press. In the open position, the dies are supplied with steam for heating. Insertion of the dies into the press completes an electrical circuit, bringing into operation a process timer which controls the application of hydraulic pressure and the subsequent cycle. After a few seconds of heating under pressure, the steam valve shuts and cooling water is circulated through the dies. When the record is cooled to a temperature suitable for extraction, the cooling water is in turn shut off, the hydraulic pressure released and the press opened ready for removal of the record (see Fig. 21.5).

The usual type of press used for making 300 mm (12-inch) records has a counterbalanced pivoted head and is known as the 'tilting head' type. In this case the dies are permanently fixed to the plattens and the whole manufacturing sequence, including the lowering and locking of the press head, is controlled by the process timer.

The actual moulding cycle is very critical, particularly with stereo pressings. The stampers must be at the correct temperature at the commencement of

Fig. 21.5
A bank of compression moulding record presses (courtesy DGG)

each moulding operation. A typical example of such a pressing sequence could be* as follows. Open press time for preheating and loading the dies with labels and the heated preform of material—14 seconds; heat under pressure—2 seconds; water cooling—12 seconds. Allowing for extraction of the moulded record, this gives a total pressing time of a little under 30 seconds, making the production of over 100 records per hour quite feasible. As, during the brief period of the moulding cycle, the temperature of the die face may range from 26° to 160° C (80° to 320° F), it is obvious that efficient steam and water circulation are essential together with rapid heat transfer to the actual mould surfaces. The weight of material used in compression moulding a record always exceeds that of the finished pressing. This results in a ring of flash round the edge, and the trimming away of this flash is the only operation needed to finish the record.

A very obvious feature of a gramophone record is the label. This should be attractive in design and well printed. The paper and printing ink must be capable of withstanding the high temperatures encountered in the moulding cycle. Every trace of moisture must be expelled from the label before use and special ovens for treatment of large batches are used for this purpose. If moisture remains in the paper, it will boil during the heating cycle and the printed surface will be destroyed. No adhesive is necessary, or desirable, as the labels are moulded into the record material and cannot be subsequently removed even by prolonged immersion in water.

The stampers are positioned and retained in the dies by means of clamping rings at the edge and steel bushes at the centre. There is a fixed pin in one of the bushes which forms the centre hole in the pressing. The other bush also carries a pin for correct location of the label but this pin retracts under pressure. These pins must be of such diameter that they mould the correct size hole in the record, but the hole in the labels must be slightly smaller in order to grip the inverted top pin. Setting up the stampers in the press calls for great care, as the centre of the recorded spiral must coincide exactly with the centre of the pin, otherwise the record will be off centre or, as it is commonly known, 'a swinger'. The die face and the back of the stamper must also be perfectly clean during setting up, otherwise the surface of the pressing will be marred by sinks and bumps which will certainly ruin the appearance and may produce audible thumps on replay.

As they are moulded, the records are stacked in special containers having a central spindle. Periodically they are collected from the press room and stored for a time at constant temperature to stabilize before being passed to the examination and bagging department. After inspection, the records are placed in the inner bags and finally in printed sleeves before being packed into boxes ready for despatch.

The first pressings from each set of stampers are sent to quality control for careful checking and, at regular intervals during the production run, further samples are taken and similarly checked.

Injection moulding

The above account may be taken as typical of the manufacturing sequence for a long playing record produced in a semi-automatic plant by compression moulding. Large numbers of 180 mm (7-inch) records are now made by a process of injection moulding (see Fig. 21.6). In this method the pre-plasticizer is an integral part of the press, which is constructed as a horizontal machine. Closure of the dies results in injection of the soft plastic into the mould cavities. Production speeds can be much higher than with compression methods, as double impression dies producing two records per cycle are usual.

A further production development resulting from the use of injection moulding is the elimination of the paper label from 180 mm records. The application of labels tends to present problems in fully automated systems but, by substituting for the conventional centre bushes, engraved plates carrying the label information, a pressing in which the coloured areas of the label are moulded in relief can be produced. If, after pressing, coloured ink is

Fig. 21.6
G. K. N. Windsor injection moulding machine for production of 180 mm records (courtesy EMI)

applied to the central area of the record, the effect of a label with black lettering on a coloured ground is achieved. The whole operation, including inserting the finished record in the paper bag, can now be performed by the press without the need for an operator. An added benefit from the use of the engraved label is that scrap and reject records can be completely reclaimed and valuable material saved for recycling. With record scrap, normal procedure is to remove the central area of the record before re-processing. In the case of 180 mm records with paper labels, this is so wasteful of material that the resulting scrap hardly justifies the cost of removing the centres.

The application of the technique of injection moulding to the production of 300 mm records presents problems which, at the present time, appear to have prevented any large-scale manufacture by this method in Great Britain. However, successful systems of automation for the compression moulding of 300 mm records have been developed and the new factory built by EMI at Hayes would seem to have taken the process almost as far as possible. From the delivery of the polymer to the finished record, the whole material compounding and pressing operation is controlled from a master control system. Even the monitoring of the amount of dry blend material in the hopper of each record press is carried out automatically at regular intervals, and the amount of attention needed by press personnel is minimal.

Adequate services are essential for the efficient running of any pressing plant. Taking the widely used Alpha press as an example, the following supplies are needed; steam at 12 kg/cm² (170 psi), cooling water at 10–12 kg/cm² (140–170 psi), hydraulic liquid at 200 kg/cm² (2,850 psi), compressed air at about 6–8 kg/cm² (85–115 psi) and electrical power 150 VA single phase 50–60 Hz, 110–250 V.

Consideration of the equipment to supply these services is rather outside the scope of this book, but it is necessary to bear in mind that such plant must be reliable and well able to cope with the maximum demands likely to be made upon it by the pressing machinery.

Pressing faults

Faults in pressings can take numerous forms, an off-centre record or 'swinger' being a common example. This may be due to incorrectly set or distorted stampers, or even wear in the locating pins of the dies. Wear on the fixed pin will result in record pressings with centre holes which are a tight fit on the spindles of record player turntables. Foreign matter in the vinyl material, particularly if it is abrasive in nature, can lead to damages on the stamper and result in pressings with repeating clicks. Slight contamination of the record material will result in generally noisy surfaces. Lack of care in the cutting of the master, or its subsequent processing, can lead to ghosting in the form of pre- or post-echo. 'Stitching', which is a moulding fault often encountered where there is a large vertical component in a stereo cut, is due to incomplete moulding of the record surface and takes the audible form of a muffled ghost preceding a loud signal. Careless stamper setting, resulting in dust particles between the die face and the stamper, leads to depressions or 'sinks' on the surface of the pressing, causing faint thumps in the recorded signal.

The cure for most if not all of these troubles is strict control of materials, care in setting stampers in the press and strict quality control in order that large numbers of reject pressings should not be produced.

Foil sampler records

One form of record has not yet been considered; this is the PVC foil sampler record, widely used in publicity because of the ease of mailing. These records are not moulded but embossed. The stampers used are similar to those in a conventional record press but need to be very uniform in thickness, as no flow takes place in the material used. If for this reason pressure is not uniform, areas of track which are not properly formed will be evident. This type of record has limitations, but is capable of surprising results and can be produced in mono or stereo in both single or double sided form.

It has been suggested that future developments may take the form of even longer records. Such extensions of playing time are in theory possible, by the use of a slower speed of rotation or a finer groove and groove pitch. All of these modifications are liable to lead to a gramophone record which is much more easily damaged because of the minute dimensions of the sound-track. They also require replay styli which are more costly to produce and much more liable to accidental damage.

The standard of care, or lack of it, accorded to his records by the average record buyer results in rapid deterioration of the quality of the reproduced sound. Developments such as those mentioned would require a drastic change in the whole attitude to the care of records.

Electroforming: Facts and Formulae

Disc silvering
Priming solution: a freshly prepared solution of stannous chloride, concentration between 5% and 10% with a slight excess of hydrochloric acid.
Reducer solution: Glucose 4–8 g. Formaldehyde 40% solution 1·5–5 ml. Water to 1 litre.
Silver solution: 8–12 g. Di-ammine silver nitrate. Water to 1 litre.

Nickel sulphamate electrolyte

Nickel sulphamate	300–400 g/l
Nickel chloride	7·5–22 g/l
Boric acid	25–45 g/l.

Operating conditions pH 3·0–4·5
   Temperature 60°C
   Cathode current density up to 3,000 amps/m^2.
   Constant filtration and adequate solution flow essential.
All processing solutions should be made up using distilled or de-ionized water. In plant recently developed, the cathode is rotated at an angle of up to 45° from the horizontal and current densities up to 4,000 amps/m^2 are employed, resulting in the production of stampers in 30 minutes.

References

The Gramophone Record by H. Courtney Bryson published by Ernest Benn. An early book, long out of print, it is interesting historically.

The Processing of Gramophone Record Matrices by C. H. Rumble: Trans. Inst. Met. Finishing, 1956, 33, 141–160. A paper giving a fairly detailed account of the chemistry of the process.

Nickel Plating from Sulphamate Solutions by R. A. F. Hammond: The International Nickel Company (Mond) Ltd. Publication No. 2420 A, 1964.

Nickel Plating by Robert Brugger: published by Robert Draper 1970. A very comprehensive book on the theory, practice, properties, and application of all types of nickel plating.

Electroforming by Peter Spiro: published by Robert Draper 1968. A full account of the subject including a description of the production of gramophone record shells.

British Standard Specification for Processed Disk Records and Reproducing Equipment. BS 1928: 1965 and Amendment Slip N.1. 1972. AMD 856. A document giving the dimensional and other characteristics necessary to secure interchangeability.

CHAPTER TWENTY-TWO

Tape Duplicating

John B. Schefel

The compact cassette and the 8-track cartridge have become the two major sound-carrying systems in general use for stereo reproduction from magnetic tape, since their conception in the mid-1960s. In essence, the cassette (Fig. 22.2) is a reel-to-reel bi-directional system offering two 'twin-track' stereo recordings, with the side 1 pair of tracks recorded in one direction and the pair for side 2 in the other. Except for a few auto-reverse playback machines, the cassette has to be turned over to play the second side. The cartridge, however (Fig. 22.3), is an endless loop uni-directional system offering four 'twin-track' stereo recordings, with all tracks recorded in pairs in the same direction for each of the four programmes. The ends of the loop are joined by a metallized foil which marks the start of each programme and activates the switching mechanism of the cartridge machine.

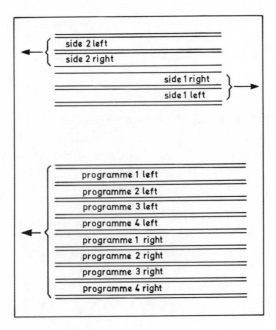

Fig. 22.1
Track layouts for Compact Cassettes (above) and 8-Track Cartridges (below)

Fig. 22.2
Assembly of typical cassette

This moves the 'twin-track' playback head in line for the next programme pair of tracks.

The cassette contains a 3·81 mm (0·15 in.) wide magnetic tape, which is transported by the capstan-pinchwheel drive of the playback machine at 4·76 cm/s ($1\frac{7}{8}$ in/s), between two freely rotating hubs located inside the cassette. The cartridge by comparison has a 6·25 mm ($\frac{1}{4}$ in) wide magnetic tape transported by a different type of playback machine at 9·53 cm/s ($3\frac{3}{4}$ in/s). The cartridge contains a pinchwheel which engages the tape with the capstan drive of the playback machine, which withdraws the tape from a freely rotating hub-platform inside the cartridge and passes it around the outer wind of the stored tape resting on the platform. Both systems are easy to use and can provide a high standard of sound reproduction when employing high-quality playback machines. Figures 22.2 and 22.3 show a typical inside view of the two systems, while Fig. 22.1 shows their soundtrack layout in accordance with IEC requirements (IEC publications 94A and 94B).

The manufacture of cassettes and cartridges can be divided into the following production activities: Tape Mastering; High Speed Tape Duplicating; Tape Tailoring and Winding; Labelling and Packaging.

Tape Mastering
The source material is usually a 6·25 mm ($\frac{1}{4}$ in) stereo master tape recorded at 38·1 cm/s (15 in/s) to either the NAB or the IEC recording curve (IEC publication 94). The master tape is played back after using its level and azimuth reference tones to set the left and right channel balance, high-frequency output, stereo/mono phase compatibility, and to set the replay level when decoding a Dolby A encoded recording. The sound quality of the master is assessed by the sound engineer together with the title timings. The title running order may have to be rearranged so that the two cassette sides, or the four cartridge programmes, can have equal or similar playing times. Edits, cross-fades, and silent run-offs are kept to a minimum to maintain artistic continuity of the repertoire.

Fig. 22.3
Assembly of typical 8-track cartridge

Once the title running order is established, it is convenient to make a Dolby A encoded 6·25 mm ($\frac{1}{4}$ in) stereo interim master tape at 38·1 cm/s (15 in/s) to either the NAB or the IEC recording curve (IEC publication 94). The interim master will possess the cassette or cartridge title order and all the sound adjustments for the final tape medium. The present state of the art is to achieve the best signal-to-noise ratio, low distortion and good sound balance within the dynamic capability of the duplication tape. Recent advances in recording technology such as improved gamma ferric oxide (γFe_2O_3) and chromium dioxide (CrO_2) tapes, with the Dolby B process, have enhanced the overall sound quality performance of both cassettes and cartridges.

From the interim master, a running master 25·4 mm (1 in) wide is made at 19·05 cm/s ($7\frac{1}{2}$ in/s) to the NAB recording curve (IEC publication 94), and this can be Dolby B encoded if required for the final tape product. Since 25·4 mm (1 in) tape can accept up to eight sound tracks, four for the cassette format and eight for the cartridge format, the running master can be considered as a larger version of the final recorded tape.

High speed tape duplicating
The running master is loaded into a loopbin storage chamber (Fig. 22.4) which is 25·4 mm (1 in) deep and rectangular in shape. As the tape is loaded into the bin, loops of tape are formed across the width of the bin parallel to the exit and entrance sides. The cassette master is loaded in 'start' first, unlike the

cartridge master which is loaded in backwards or 'end' first, so that the tape pancakes are duplicated the correct way round for the appropriate tape tailoring and winding stage. Each 'end' of the master is joined with splicing tape to one end of a short length of 25·4 mm (1 in) cue tape containing a 6 Hz signal, which completes the loop. The master is run at 32×19.05 cm/s = 609·6 cm/s ($32 \times 7\frac{1}{2}$ in/s = 240 in/s) over the playback heads of the master machine which is adjacent to the loopbin.

Fig. 22.4
Master playback machine and loop-bin storage chamber

Each slave recorder is loaded with virgin tape in the conventional reel-to-reel manner. The cassette slave recorders are able to accept C60 and C90 thickness tapes, while the cartridge slave recorders are set to handle back-lubricated long play and extra-thin play tapes. The nominal lengths of these tapes can vary from about 1,100 to 3,300 m (3,600 to 10,825 ft) depending on the manufacturer. In order to preserve the 1:1 speed ratio with the master running at 609·6 cm/s (240 in/s), the cassette and cartridge slave recorders are run at 32×4.76 cm/s = 152·32 cm/s ($32 \times 1\frac{7}{8}$ in/s = 60 in/s) and 32×9.53 cm/s = 304·96 cm/s ($32 \times 3\frac{3}{4}$ in/s = 120 in/s) respectively. The real time recording curves of these slave recorders meet the IEC requirements.

It is interesting to note that the master playback machine and the slave recorders have to deal with frequencies 32 times greater than that of a normal speed audio recorder and, as a result, the recording bias frequency has to be increased to between 2 to 10 MHz depending on the recording heads used.

It is usual to have one master playback machine feeding the cassette slave recorders and another to feed the cartridge slave recorders for production. Figures 22.5 and 22.6 show two kinds of tape duplicator used. When the final tape product is required to be Dolby B encoded, the concept of 'Dolby Level' is established throughout the whole process, both when recording the running master, and during high speed playback and duplication of the master on to the slave tape.

Fig. 22.5
Cassette tape duplicating

Since the master is a continuous closed loop, each duplicated tape pancake contains a series of copy recordings of the master separated by the 6 Hz cue signal. To check the sound quality of the recording, the duplicated tape pancakes are replayed against the running master, or interim master, at real time speed.

Tape tailoring and winding

Each cassette tape pancake is placed on the supply-drive carrier of a tailoring and winding machine, and the end of the tape is laced through the machine

Fig. 22.6
Cartridge tape duplicating

and twisted around the take-up drive shaft. Both drives are then rotated at high speed, winding the waste end of the tape on to the take-up shaft, until the first cue signal is sensed by the magnetic head situated next to the splicing unit. The machine stops and reverses, lining up the cue signal on the splicing unit where the tape is cut. The waste tape wound on the take-up shaft is then discarded.

Fig. 22.7
Cassette tailoring and winding machine

An empty cassette pack, called a C-zero, containing a leader tape attached to the two hubs, is placed into position so that the take-up shaft passes through the centre of one of the hubs. The leader tape is looped out of the pack on to the splicing unit, where it is cut in two. The leader tape attached to the hub on the take-up shaft is joined to the cut end of the tape pancake with splicing tape. Both drives are rotated again, winding the tape from the pancake into the pack at high speed. When the second cue signal is sensed, the machine stops, reverses as before, and cuts the tape at the cue signal. The end of the wound tape is then joined to the other leader with splicing tape, and is removed from the splicing unit and wound into the cassette pack. The loaded cassette is replaced by another C-zero pack, and the whole process is repeated until the last cue signal is sensed, and the remaining portion of the tape pancake is removed from the supply-drive carrier which can then accept the next pancake.

Cartridge tape pancakes are treated in a similar way, except that the tape is wound on to a hub-platform from a capstan-pinchwheel drive, which has only a forward direction cycle. The hub-platform containing the wound tape is put into a cartridge pack base, and the two ends of the tape are lifted out and placed on the splicing unit, where they are joined on the magnetic coating side by a metallized splicing foil. The tape join is removed from the

Fig. 22.8
Cartridge tailoring and winding machine

splicing unit and wound on to the hub-platform, taking up the excess loop of tape. Finally, the top of the cartridge pack is snapped into the cartridge base and the loaded cartridge is rewound to the start.

The first packs loaded from each type of tape pancake are checked for mechanical performance, sound quality and repertoire content. Typical tape tailoring and winding machines for the two products are shown in Figs. 22.7 and 22.8.

Labelling and packaging

The cassettes are placed on the input conveyor of a labelling machine, so that side 1 of each cassette faces the side 1 label dispenser. Each side label is picked up by a transfer roller which wipes the back of the label against an adhesive coater, moistening the non-printed side of the label with adhesive. The two side labels are then rolled on to the cassette as it passes through the machine. The labelled cassettes are fed into the packaging machine, which contains a supply of plastic library boxes and inlay cards. As each cassette arrives at the packing point, a library box is opened at the same time as an inlay card is folded; then the inlay card is inserted into the library box with the cassette. The library box is closed with the packed cassette and inlay card, and the complete package moves on to where it can be wrapped in a plastic film, before passing on to the exit conveyor.

Cartridges are handled in a different manner. The cartridges are put into the stack feeder of a labelling machine, with the back of each cartridge facing upwards. Each back label is moved over a heater plate, which activates the adhesive on the non-printed side of the label. When a cartridge moves

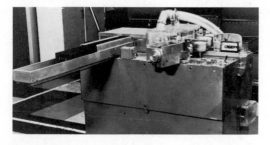

Fig. 22.9
Cassette labelling machine

Fig. 22.10
Cartridge labelling machine

into position, the heated label is placed over the back of the cartridge and pressed on to the surface of the pack. The front cartridge label is applied using the same technique. The labelled cartridges are then wrapped in an individual plastic film and slid into a separate cardboard slip carton. The slip carton is labelled to match the cartridge, and the whole package is wrapped again in another plastic film. Figures 22.9 and 22.10 show the machines used for labelling cassettes and cartridges, while Fig. 22.11 shows a cassette packaging machine. A final quality check is made prior to packing and despatching the order.

Fig. 22.11
Cassette packaging machine

ALLIED MEDIA

CHAPTER TWENTY-THREE

Sound Broadcasting

Glyn Alkin

The techniques for broadcasting are very similar to those of professional recording, in fact most commercial recordings are destined to be broadcast at some time or other. However, two particular aspects need to be considered in relation to broadcasting.

1. Broadcast material has to be contained within practical limits as regards volume range and, to some extent, frequency range. This is because it has to be routed between studios, switching centres, and transmitters via land lines or radio links and, on arrival, must be suitable to modulate high-power transmitters correctly to maintain a proper service area without causing overload or a low signal-to-noise ratio.

For the benefit of the listeners, the material must slot smoothly into the run of programmes that precede and follow it. This usually means the exercise of restraint in terms of overall volume range and consistency of approach, except in some particular circumstances where contrasts are justified for artistic reasons. In these cases, steps should be taken to link successive programmes or items in such a way as to prepare the listener for the change of approach. Much depends on the network into which the programme is being fed and the type, if any, of automatic volume compression or limiting being employed in the system—to protect the transmitter or increase the average modulation level and thereby the service area.

2. Although a large proportion of broadcast material is pre-recorded, a good deal must be produced 'live' or recorded in circumstances where repeats are impossible, which amounts to much the same thing as far as technique is concerned. This can include the whole gamut of programme material from speech, possibly audience participation 'phone-ins', to all types of music. Music balance, even for a relay from a public performance where facilities are very restricted, must bear direct comparison with good quality commercial records as they are heard by the home listener in the same conditions, possibly using the same equipment.

The broadcasting network

The method by which the programme signal reaches the transmitter or transmitters depends on the scale of the operation. It can vary between a simple console feeding a single transmitter with recorded programmes, interspersed with 'live' announcements and interviews, to a full-scale broadcasting network feeding a large number of transmitters.

In a large broadcasting organization with national and regional commitments there may be a number of transmitters for each programme service. These can be linked together to transmit a common network contribution, or 'opted-out' to provide a separate service for their local community with programmes originated in their local Regional Studio Centre.

The links between them can be divided into two types: *contribution circuits* which carry the programme from the originating studio centre or outside broadcast location to the switching centre or continuity suite, where programme switching takes place, and *distribution circuits* which carry the programme selected for the network to the regional switching centres and thence to the appropriate transmitters.

1. *The continuity suite* is an area where 'on air' programme switching is accomplished, linking announcements made and standby arrangements are on hand to fill in and maintain the service in the event of failure of a contribution. Complete programmes, involving no more than pre-recorded material linked with live announcements and possibly interviews, can often be undertaken in these areas. The equipment usually consists of a simple mixing console capable of selecting and fading between the various contribution sources, which in many cases will have been pre-selected and tested by an adjacent switching centre. Comprehensive 'pre-hear' facilities are provided to enable the operator to check the identity and level of a programme source before fading it up for transmission. In some continuity suites, notably those used for television, the operations are performed by the announcer, using a microphone slung over the desk. In areas where more complicated operations are required, and from which whole pre-recorded programmes are transmitted, it is more usual to employ a separate operator in an adjacent room with a glass partition between them.

The suite will include tape and disc reproducing equipment, comprising at least two of each to enable one to be set up while the other is playing. Many continuity operations use cassette or cartridge tape reproducers with automatic cue facilities to play in 'jingles' (i.e. short recorded musical phrases used to identify recurring items) and pre-recorded announcements to relieve the announcer from the necessity of working 'live' during a complicated programme junction. Continuity suites used for 'pop' music presentation by 'disc-jockeys' require special compressors. These are in-serted in the music circuits but have their compressing action (i.e. their side-chain) controlled by the output of the announcer's microphone. The effect of this is to pull down the level of the music automatically to back-ground level, whenever the announcer (disc jockey) speaks. This process is similar to that used in the early days of film newsreel and is known as 'ducking'.

2. Transmission links. The links between centres may take the form of land-lines or radio links. Sometimes transmitters use a receiver to pick up the broadcast from another transmitter earlier in the chain, and then rebroad-cast it. This is not a very reliable arrangement, due to the risk of co-channel interference, but it is a convenient method of providing a standby in case of failure of the main link.

For all programme circuits the aim is to achieve a sensibly flat amplitude/frequency response from 50 Hz to 10 kHz and, if possible, 15 kHz with good noise separation and freedom from 'crosstalk' (interference from other circuits) and harmonic distortion.

The links may operate at 'baseband', i.e. audio frequency, using balanced-pair cable, as used for telephone circuits, repeatered (amplified) at regular intervals and 'equalized': i.e. the signal is passed through an electrical circuit with a complementary response to that of the line, to produce a flat overall response.

Alternatively, the audio signal may be translated into a higher frequency for transmission over a common-carrier telephone system. This so called 'music-in-band' system takes the place of three telephone circuits (in practice it takes up a whole 48 kHz group) and allows a bandwidth of 10 kHz, but requires the use of sophisticated noise-reduction techniques (com-panding) to achieve a satisfactory noise performance.

Pulse code modulation

The problems of transmitting high-quality analogue audio signals over long links are formidable, even for monophonic reproduction, to maintain fre-quency response, signal-to-noise ratio, consistency of level, etc. Stereophony adds the very considerable problem of maintaining matching phase between the two circuits.

Most of these problems can be overcome by a system of transmission called 'Pulse Code Modulation'. In essence this is a system in which the analogue waveform of the audio signal is converted into a code composed of pulses, all at full modulation amplitude, which represent in binary form

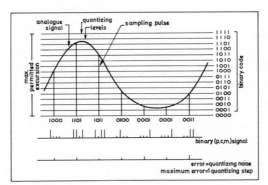

Fig. 23.1
Examples of sampling and coding of an analogue signal using a 4-bit code, which allows only 16 levels of measurement (quantizing levels). For high quality PCM broadcasting, a 13-bit code is used which provides 8,192 quantizing levels and a signal-to-noise ratio as high as 78 dB

a series of values that describe the amplitude of the waveform at each moment in time. (This is also referred to in Chapter Fifteen.)

The process at the sending end can be roughly divided into three basic functions: sampling, quantizing, and coding (see Fig. 23.1). A similar complementary function is used to retrieve the analogue signal at the receiving end.

1. Sampling. The process begins by taking samples of the instantaneous value of the analogue waveform of the audio signal. These samples are taken at a fixed rate which must be at least twice the highest frequency that it is desired to transmit. Each sample is held in a store while it is measured to a certain degree of accuracy and this value converted into a code.

2. Quantizing. The process of measurement involves comparing the sample against a scale consisting of a number of discrete values, called 'quantizing levels', each one of which is assigned a reference number to represent its value.

As the analogue signal can have values continuously variable over the whole range of measurement, it follows that the actual level and the quantizing level will seldom coincide exactly. The greater the number of quantizing levels the more accurate will be the measurement.

Differences between the sample amplitude levels and the quantizing levels cause errors in the reproduced signal which can be heard in the form of noise. This takes the form of 'white noise' on large amplitude signals and 'granular distortion' (resembling non-linear distortion) when the signal falls to an amplitude where only a few quantizing levels are in use. As the error is proportionately greater with fewer quantizing levels, the noise tends to become more objectionable at low levels.

3. Coding. In practice, the number of quantizing levels that can be used depends upon the coding system used to describe them and this depends upon the available bandwidth for the resulting signal.

There are a number of different methods of converting analogue to digital signals, including pulse amplitude modulation, pulse time modulation (pulse duration or pulse position) and pulse code modulation which is the one chosen. The code used is binary, i.e. the numbers representing the quantizing levels of the signal are described by groups of digits in binary notation in the form of pulses of full amplitude which are either on, representing logic (1), or off, logic (0). Such a system makes the transmission of PCM signals extremely rugged as the receiving terminal has only to recognize all above 50% modulation as (1) and all below as (0). Therefore, provided that the noise level is less than 50%, the transmission should be completely unimpaired and the original analogue signal can be reconstituted as good as new. In fact this process can be repeated several times and, provided the noise level of each section is within limits, it will be virtually wiped out with each transition instead of being cumulative as in analogue systems.

The number of quantizing levels (assuming they are linear steps) required for high quality reproduction would normally be in excess of 1,000. A binary code composed of 10 digits (called 'bits') will provide 1,024 (2^{10}) quantizing levels with a peak signal/peak quantizing noise ratio of 60 dB. A 13 bit code would allow 8,192 levels with a signal-to-noise ratio of 78 dB.

4. *Bandwidth*. The freedom from noise problems and amplitude and phase distortion that PCM provides is not achieved for nothing; it is traded for bandwidth. As stated earlier, the minimum sampling rate must be at least twice the highest frequency it is required to transmit (in practice 2·2 to 2·3 times) so that, for a high quality system with an audio range of 15 kHz and a high signal-to-noise ratio (using a 13 bit code), the total bit rate would be $15 \times 2·2 \times 13 = 429,000$, which suggests a bandwidth of 429,000 kHz.

Various methods can be used to reduce the bit rate and hence the bandwidth without sacrificing too much signal/quantizing noise ratio or, conversely, of improving signal-to-noise ratio without increasing bandwidth. They include:

5. *Pre-emphasis and de-emphasis*. As the high frequency component of quantizing noise tends to be the most obvious, there can be an advantage in pre-emphasizing the high frequency components in the analogue signal and then de-emphasizing it after the PCM process. Unfortunately this advantage only holds provided that the HF content of the programme material has less amplitude than the LF but (as explained in reference to FM transmission), this assumption, usually true in real life, does not hold with modern sound reproducing practice. If the overall level has to be reduced to avoid HF overload most of the advantage is lost.

6. *Companding*. This is a method of compressing the signal volume variations at the sending end and applying the complementary expansion at the receiving end. As the noise in PCM systems tends to be predominantly high-pitched, it is not readily masked by the main power of the sound. There can, therefore, be an advantage in dividing the audio frequency spectrum into bands and treating each one separately (somewhat in the manner of Dolby) or more simply by giving special treatment to the high frequencies by applying pre-emphasis before the compressor, and de-emphasis after the expander.

Various other methods can be employed to reduce any residual noise, and systems of error detection and concealment (involving the use of 'parity bits' to provide a logic check). In general, the system is very rugged and provides almost perfect transmission over long distances; but, due to the simplicity of the (1) or (0) logic system, there tend to be no half measures and, in the event of excessive noise or disturbance on the lines or failure of the terminal equipment, the effect is disastrous. The signal is either almost perfect or it is replaced by silence or, more likely, a very unpleasant noise, despite the use of cleverly designed muting circuits which minimize this possibility.

7. *Multi-channel links*. It is possible to transmit up to 13 separate PCM channels plus a data channel on a single link of the type designed for 625-line monochrome television transmission (5·5 MHz bandwidth) using a system of time-division multiplex. The data channel can be used for various 'housekeeping' functions such as passing link status and transmitter switching information.

Television sound in syncs
A PCM system similar to the one described above can be used to transmit the sound element of television in association with the picture waveform over landlines and radio links. A time-division multiplex system is used in which the sound is allotted the only periods that are not fully occupied by vision information, i.e. during the line synchronizing pulses (see Figs. 23.2 and 23.3). In the case of a 625-line system, the line sync pulses occupy 4·7 μs of which 4 μs can be made available for the coded signal without upsetting the synchronizing information (see Fig. 23.2). These pulses occur at a rate of 15,625 per sec. Remembering the requirement, mentioned earlier, for the sampling frequency to be at least twice the highest frequency it is desired to transmit, it is evident that the obvious choice for high quality is 31·25 kHz (twice line frequency). This provides for an audio bandwidth of about 14 kHz. A 10-digit code is used allowing a theoretical signal-to-

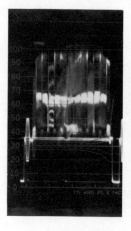

Fig. 23.2
Two oscillograms of one line of a
colour television picture. In each case
the 4·7 µs line sync pulse can be seen
at the right hand end, the first having
a simple pulse and the second with
the pulse-coded audio signal added

noise ratio of 65 dB. (There is also a 'ruggedized' version of SIS, used for
local link applications where music is not involved, which samples at line
rate and uses a nine digit code.)

The standard system of SIS employs 21 pulses (see Fig. 23.3). The first is a
marker pulse which occurs just after the leading edge of the video synchronizing pulse. This is followed by two sets of 10 digits (pulses, or the
absence of pulses) representing two consecutive samplings of the audio
waveform. These have been taken at twice line frequency, alternate samples

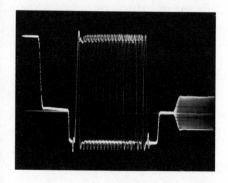

Fig. 23.3
Enlarged view of the sound-in-syncs
pulses showing how they fit into the
line sync pulse period

being delayed by half a line, inverted, i.e. logic (1) exchanged for logic (0) and
vice versa, and their pulses exactly interleaved between those of the preceding sample. Both sets of pulses are rearranged in reverse order so that
the least significant digit appears first. This ensures that those digits that are
subject to most variation due to changes in the sound signal are furthest
from the leading edge of syncs, where they might cause vision problems.

The signal/quantizing noise ratio is improved by the use of a frequency-
dependent compressor (as described previously). Because the compression

is so severe, amounting to limiting at the top end of the scale, insufficient information is available at the expander for it to be able to reconstruct the original signal accurately. This is overcome by the addition of a pilot tone of a frequency higher than the highest audio frequency transmitted. The amplitude of the pilot tone becomes modulated by the action of the compressor and, when extracted from the signal at the far end, its level is used to control the gain of the expander so as to maintain the overall gain constant.

Technical quality

In considering the matter of technical quality in broadcasting, it is necessary first to draw a distinction between what goes on at the point of origin and what happens to the signal subsequently.

At one time it would have been true to say that the aim of most broadcast engineers, other than those engaged solely in long-distance communication, was to produce a reasonably flat amplitude/frequency characteristic response throughout the entire system from microphone to receiver. Nowadays considerable use is made of frequency response shaping filters at the originating end, but this form of distortion is carefully applied for artistic purposes. It is still no less important that the entire equipment chain should have an immaculate response, so that the final result can be properly judged. To maintain this condition, it is necessary to conduct frequent checks by sending a full frequency run (50 Hz to 15 kHz) and measuring noise separation and harmonic and intermodulation distortion throughout the entire network out of transmission hours. Some of these checks are made by automatic means.

Automatic monitors

Many of the transmitters in use nowadays are unattended, or combined so that a number may be housed together under the control of a small engineering staff who are not able to check or monitor each one continuously. Automatic monitors are therefore employed which detect abnormalities in the signal, or loss of signal after a specified period of time.

The principle of the automatic monitor is to compare the level of the programme signal at the input of a system with the signal at the output. If the difference is significant, i.e. is sufficiently severe and consistent in duration to be detrimental to enjoyment of the programme, the device can be used either to give an aural or visual alarm or to institute automatic executive action, such as the re-routing of the circuit concerned or the interchange of equipment.

There are basically two conditions for automatic monitoring.

1. Where the input and output are both accessible at the monitoring point, e.g. when comparing the input to a transmitter with the output of a receiver tuned to it.

2. Where the signals to be compared are separated by some distance, as in the monitoring of programme distribution lines.

Local comparison

In the first, simpler, case what is required is to pick up a 'listen' output (i.e. a connection that does not break or otherwise affect the normal circuit) of both input and output of the equipment to be tested. These are fed into integrating circuits where their respective amplitudes are measured with respect to a reasonable time scale (to obviate the effect of unimportant instantaneous differences of a transient nature). The signals can be made to light lamps which are arranged in vertical rows, one for the input and another row for the output. The lamps light in ascending order to represent particular values of signal parameters. The input row would have three lamps representing low level (below -35 dB), medium level (between -35 and -9 dB), and high level (above -9 dB).

In practical terms it is not expected to work to an accuracy greater than ± 3 dB, and this is allowed for by giving the output indication five lamps representing (1) -38 dB, (2) -38 to -32 dB, (3) -32 to -12 dB, (4) -12 to -6 dB and (5) above -6 dB.

If the levels of the input and output sources agree, the lamps, lighting in sequence to follow the programme level variations, will appear to follow each other in a more or less level manner; but, if one has greater amplitude than the other, the lamps will light in a more diagonal formation, indicating which way the discrepancy occurs.

The signals are also fed into a comparator which compares their levels and, if a discrepancy of more than 3 dB exists for a significant length of time, lights another lamp (usually yellow) as an indication of the fault condition. If required, and usually after the fault has persisted for a specific length of time, automatic changeover of equipment can be instituted, or alarms given.

Remote comparison

If it is not possible to compare the input and output of a system directly, as in the case of programme distribution lines, arrangements must be made to measure the instantaneous value of the signal at the input and the output separately. The input measurement can be used to produce a signal which can be sent over the circuit with the programme. Then, when it is decoded at the far end, the instantaneous values represented can be compared with the measured values of the output by means of lamp signals and an automatic comparator as in the previous case. Executive action could also be instituted in the same manner.

To achieve this, it is necessary to curtail the bandwidth of the programme circuit by 1·5 kHz to make room for the level measurement signal. It is possible to indicate the four states required for the input assessment by means of two tones, A and B. Low level is indicated by tone B, medium level by tone A, and high level by tone A+B. Typical values for the tones would be 10·6 kHz and 10·8 kHz respectively.

The fact that tone is sent for all levels, even in the absence of signal, can be used as a continuous check on the tone system as well as the link, failure of the tone being indicated by a red light, or other warning device. If the two ends of the system are very far apart (e.g. over 200 miles) the difference in signal phase between the sending and receiving end will vary with frequency and can have a significant effect on the comparison. It is therefore necessary to introduce quadrature circuits to make the necessary correction.

Modulation range

Brief mention was made earlier of the need to exercise control of modulation range. The matter has already been discussed in relation to recording technique, but there are certain aspects of broadcasting that make it particularly critical.

Except for certain very specialized channels, it must be assumed that the listeners will expect to be able to listen for long periods of time, embracing a wide variety of programme types, without having to adjust their volume controls. In practice this is practically impossible to achieve, no matter how much care is taken to unify the levels, and the more varied the programme material the less the chance of success. This is due to various psychological factors which affect the listener's volume level preference. For example apparent loudness is related to programme appreciation. Unwanted sound (noise) sounds louder than an equal volume of wanted sound. A jarring discord sounds louder than a chord because of the irritation it creates. What listeners really want, if the truth were told, is not that all programmes should sound equally loud but that those elements in which they have a particular interest should sound louder than the rest. Obviously as peoples' preferences are varied it is impossible to please everybody.

The subject which usually leads to more complaints from listeners than any other is the relative level of speech and music. Although, in real life, music is many times louder than speech, listeners tend to expect broadcast speech to be at least equally loud. This is partly due to the need to maintain full intelligibility of speech at average listening levels (which are usually much less than real life) and the nature of music which tends to be more continuous in character and therefore contain more energy for a given peak amplitude. Again psychological factors enter into it. For example, the listener who has neighbours separated from him by a thin partition wall will tend to worry about creating a disturbance much more where music is concerned than speech, because he assumes it will be louder, although in fact the overhearing of unintelligible speech can be much more irritating. On the other hand, the serious listener who has adjusted his set to enjoy a concert at something approaching realistic volume will be upset by unnaturally loud announcements.

The only way to avoid giving offence is to analyse the interest of the audience in terms of the substance of the programme and allow the major volume emphasis to those aspects that are most relevant.

Some 'pop' enthusiasts, who normally use radio as a continuous background, expect very little variation in volume or character of the sound so that it forms a sort of acoustic 'wallpaper'. The sound created by the highly compressed technique used in this type of broadcast tends to stand up well to reproduction through miniature portable radios.

Listeners to car radios generally prefer speech levels to be louder than music in order to maintain intelligibility against a high level of ambient background noise. Apart from artistic considerations, the practical limitations of the transmission system must be taken into account, particularly as regards the transmitter where small audio signal voltages eventually control systems of enormous power in the modulation process.

There are basically two types of transmitter in general use, one type is amplitude modulated and the other frequency modulated (see Figs. 23.4 and 23.5).

Amplitude modulation (Fig. 23.4). With amplitude modulation the transmitter radiates at a fixed radio frequency (the carrier wave) the amplitude of which is varied, i.e. modulated, by the audio frequency waveform. The practical limits of the system are set, at the low end of the scale, by the need to maintain a reasonable service area for the transmitter in terms of signal-to-noise ratio as the radiated power is directly controlled by the amplitude of the audio signal. At the high end, it is governed by the overload point of the transmitter or, in practice, the limiter protecting it. (Anyone who has sat at a transmitter and watched the voltages in the later stages shoot up by many thousands on a high peak will appreciate the need for protection—and for careful control.)

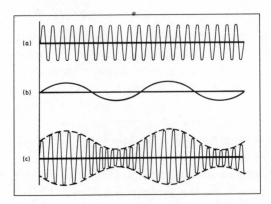

Fig. 23.4
Amplitude modulation of the radio frequency carrier (a) by the audio frequency signal (b) produces the modulated wave (c)

Limiters used to protect amplitude modulated transmitters must act very fast, i.e. have very rapid attack times, to prevent the risk of physical damage to the components caused by excessive voltages. To reduce the harmonic distortion this type of limiting can create, it is usual to give the limiters fairly slow recovery times. They can therefore appear to saturate after a heavy peak, and a short sharp sound like a pistol shot can severely depress the sound level for a considerable time afterwards. This is a very undesirable effect which is not apparent at the originating studio.

Frequency modulation (Fig. 23.5). With frequency-modulated transmitters the amplitude of the audio signal varies the frequency of the carrier wave with respect to its nominal radio frequency. The maximum variation, or 'deviation' as it is properly called, is determined by the bandwidth allowed. In the UK it is 75 kHz for Radio and 50 kHz for Television sound for 100% modulation. In order to improve signal-to-noise ratio, the frequency modulation transmission and reception standard incorporates 50 μs pre-emphasis (75 μs in the USA), i.e. the output of the transmitter increases with frequency and a complementary response is incorporated into the receiver. When this standard was introduced it was no doubt designed to take account of the fact that, in normal circumstances, the average distribution of audio power favours the lower-middle end of the spectrum, the high frequency sounds and those comprising the harmonics of the basic sounds being relatively low in volume.

Unfortunately these assumptions no longer hold true with some types of modern sound-balancing technique. The use of multi-microphone setups, with very close balance and variable-frequency amplifiers, can result in unnatural emphasis being accorded to very high-pitched sounds, e.g. piccolo, finger cymbals, percussive instruments, etc., especially in respect of their harmonics. The use of compressors, which tend to increase the average level of all sounds, increases this effect which is particularly noticeable in sibilants.

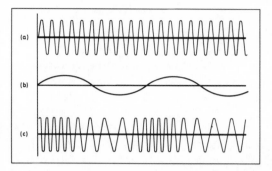

Fig. 23.5
Frequency modulation leaves the carrier amplitude constant but changes its instantaneous frequency in accordance with the audio signal amplitude

When an instrument is played very close to the microphone, the sound tends to have a crisp 'attack' due to the preponderence of high harmonics. This may be a very desirable feature as far as the originated sound is concerned. As heard on the studio monitoring loudspeaker it may sound excellent but this may not be true at the receiving end, since over-deviation of the transmitter can result in serious harmonic distortion.

If the transmitter is protected from over-deviation by a limiter which responds in accordance with the 50 μs pre-emphasis, a remarkable effect can result in which small high-frequency components in the sound appear to take control of apparently much louder, lower frequency, sounds to reduce the volume dramatically and for no obvious reason.

The effect is most noticeable if the transmitter limiter has a long recovery time. It can be mitigated by the use of variable de-emphasis limiters which, on receipt of a signal with an abnormally high-level high-frequency content, cause a momentary reduction in pre-emphasis, thereby effecting a temporary reduction in high-frequency response at the receiver without reducing the gain at lower frequencies.

Obviously the safest way to guard against these undesirable effects is to be cautious in the use of shaping filters and compressors in close-microphone balances.

Programme meters

Having set the technical and artistic limits for programme control, it is necessary to provide the means to assess and adjust volume levels in order that these limits can be achieved.

First of all it is important to establish that programme control is exercised only at the point of origin. Any subsequent adjustment should be concerned only with ensuring that the level remains the same throughout the broadcast chain. What is of particular significance in broadcasting is the type of programme meter employed, as it has a dual rôle to perform: (a) to enable the sound controller to assess his levels and work within the prescribed parameters, (b) to enable engineers at various subsequent points in the chain to judge the levels and carry out checks between them while the programme is in progress.

There are two types of programme meter in general use, the Volume Unit Meter and the Peak Programme Meter (Fig. 23.6), and a basic description appears in Chapter Five.

1. The Volume Unit Meter met in broadcasting has two scales, arranged one above the other. One is calibrated in figures 1–100 usually printed in black and occupying about two thirds of the scale. The calibration is arbitrary and the figures are intended to represent 'percentage utilization of the channel'. The other scale is calibrated in decibels (volume units) with the figure 0 corresponding to the 100% figure on the other scale. The figures below this have negative notation and those above (usually marked in red) positive.

The decibel calibration is meaningful only on steady tone, when the dynamic characteristics of the meter can be ignored.

The main problem in the use of VU meters is that the meter readings vary in relation to the electrical signal strength according to the type of pro- gramme material being measured. Short staccato sounds can tend to make the meter overshoot and thereby read high relative to long sustained signals of equal magnitude. Because of the rapid movement of the needle, it is not easy to agree levels between stations by means of meter checks on pro- gramme. As a large proportion of the scale is taken up with a range of only 3 dB approaching 100% modulation, the needle tends to fluctuate wildly with peaky material.

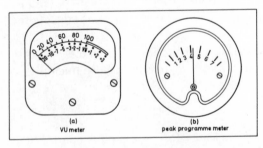

Fig. 23.6
Comparing the basic scale markings on (a) VU meter, (b) peak programme meter

2. The Peak Programme Meter measures the peak or crest values of the programme signal. It has a very rapid rise time (approximately 4 ms) and a slow recovery time (approximately 3 s). The rapid rise time gives a good indication of the maximum crest values of the signal, even in the case of sudden transients and peaks, which is the main purpose of a meter used for programme control to keep the signal within the broadcast parameters. The slow recovery time makes the meter easy to read, even with peaky material, and the fact that the peaks tend to be clearly defined and can be read off separately makes it possible to compare meter readings at different points in the transmission chain with a reasonable degree of accuracy.

The BBC PPM meter is calibrated 0 to 7. The use of a quasi-logarithmic law enables the divisions between each indication to be reasonably equally-spaced, being 4 dB between each pair over the major part of the scale (figures 2–7) and 6 dB between 0 and 1 and 1 and 2. It is normal to line up equipment at 8 dB below peak level (4 on the PPM scale), full modulation being represented by 6.

Peak Programme Meters are normally calibrated in white on a black background to reduce eye strain. Other versions include the Optical PPM (a form of mirror galvanometer in which the indication is given by a light projected on to a ground-glass screen, intended to accompany television monitors) and meters in which the mechanism is replaced by a row of lamps (usually light-emitting diodes). These may be arranged in the form of an arc or in vertical rows (with changing colours) which forms a convenient arrangement if a number of channels have to be watched simultaneously. Stereo equipment is usually fitted with dual PPM movements, with red and white needles superimposed so that both channels can be measured and compared simultaneously.

The need for rules

Unfortunately no type of meter so far devised is capable of giving more than a rough indication of loudness, which is largely subjective. In addition to the strength of the signal, apparent loudness is influenced by such factors as the harmonic structure of the sound, the spectral distribution of energy and even by the listener's appreciation of the programme material. As mentioned earlier, unwanted sound can sound much louder than wanted sound of the same power. It is necessary, therefore, for people engaged in sound control to judge volume mainly by listening to high-quality loud-speakers using the PPM as a means of calibrating the ear. With practice it becomes possible to judge sound levels accurately with only occasional reference to the meter.

There is no suggestion that all programmes or their individual ingredients should sound equally loud in a broadcast medium, but it is necessary to lay down a set of rules relating to programme meter readings for specific types of programme material. This is in order that the output resulting from the efforts of different operators will sound consistent and also to enable engineers monitoring at subsequent points in the chain to assess whether the levels are within normal limits for the type of programme, or if action is necessary. In the case of low levels, the question of time is important. There are likely to be moments of low level, or even silence, in most types of programme. What is important is to know for how long it should continue before a fault is indicated. To this end a set of rules exists, based on many years of study of listeners' preferences. In general they stipulate average peak levels of approximately +2 dB to +8 dB ($4\frac{1}{2}$–6 on the PPM) for most forms of speech, a range of about 22 dB to full modulation for serious music, with the allowance to let the readings fall below figure 2 for up to half a minute before warning continuity. Light music is allowed a range of about 16 dB (3–6) with only short excursions below 2, while 'pop' music and the related speech would be mainly compressed into the top 4–6 dB range. Drama productions are allowed a range of about 16 dB for dialogue with narration about 8 dB below full modulation. It must be remembered that some items (particularly instruments such as harpsichords) sound much louder than their meter readings suggest.

With average stereo material the A+B signal will register about 3 dB higher than A or B and this sum signal is normally used for control.

The importance of listening levels

When considering any type of programme material for broadcasting purposes, it is important to bear in mind the sort of volume levels at which it is likely to be heard. In general this is likely to be much quieter than in reality so that, unless the volume range is suitably compressed, the balance immaculate and the reproduction clear, many of the finer points will be lost upon the listener. For this reason it is important to resist the temptation to monitor continuously at very loud levels.

People engaged in the balance and control of sound tend to monitor at a loud level because it aids concentration and assists in the detection of distortion, noise and minor deficiencies of balance. Another reason is the natural tendency of operators to want to 'wind up the gain' when they are enthusiastic and enjoying the programme.

Unfortunately there are inherent dangers in this practice. Apart from the risk to the operator's hearing incurred by long exposure to high volume sound, there is the fact that high volume can make the sound unrealistically impressive and tends to give the impression that points of balance are less important than they are. It is possible to listen through loud sounds (especially in stereo) to quieter ones which may not be audible at lower volume. It is important to remember the listener in mono who is able to exercise much less discrimination. Generally the best answer is to monitor at reasonably high level, but to have provision for dimming the loudspeaker volume from time to time so as to acquire a realistic impression of how the balance will sound to the average listener.

Live broadcasting technique

As stated at the beginning of this chapter, most of the sound balance techniques for broadcasting are very similar to those used for recording. Where differences exist they are likely to be due to the stringent requirements for programme control and the need to work 'live' or with unrehearsed or unrepeatable material, or where the layout and microphone arrangements are dictated by factors outside the sound balancer's control.

A typical feature of 'live' music broadcasts, even where a good rehearsal is possible, is a tendency for the instrumentalists, and particularly the vocalists, to save their efforts for the performance. As a result, the volume output of the performers tends to increase by a factor of several dB, especially in the case of the brass. This factor is usually much smaller for recording on a rehearse-record basis and, even if it does result in upsetting a fine balance, it is usually possible to record it again having made the necessary adjustments. With a live performance, it will be necessary to make adjustments during the performance and that means allowing sufficient leeway, adopting a technique that keeps sufficient adjustment in the balance in hand to cater for all likely contingencies.

This can be achieved in a variety of ways; one is to use a rather closer, possibly more numerous, microphone technique than may be called for under controlled conditions, and then 'opening out' the sound with a subtle addition of more distant 'atmosphere' microphones and artificial reverberation. Another useful arrangement is to employ in the balance some microphones with variable directivity patterns that can be adjusted remotely at the control position. These can be especially useful when employed as a stereo pair used for 'atmosphere', or as a main microphone in the stereo balance.

An important factor in live music broadcasts is the provision of a good score or lead sheet because, with a continuous performance, it is not possible to rely on memorizing the orchestration. Music scores should preferably be full-score unless they are likely to be too unwieldy, in which case piano or miniature scores (suitably marked up) should suffice. In the case of lead (control) sheets for light music orchestrations, there is much to be said for two-line writing. The upper stave should indicate the solo or lead parts and the lower the accompaniment. Where no lead sheets are provided, the author has developed a simple form of 'shorthand' which can be written in while the rehearsal is in progress. It consists of a single line divided into segments to fit the construction of the music: e.g. a typical popular song might be 4 bars (intro) 8 (chorus) 8 (chorus) 8 (middle eight) and 8 (chorus reprise) with possibly a 4 bar coda. The lead, vocal, or solo part is written above the line with the important features of the accompaniment, such as solo figures and brass mutes, below.

Audience reaction

Another feature of the 'live' performance that calls for special attention is the handling of audience reaction. Usually the requirement is to make the audience sound at least as numerous as it is and, particularly in the case of comedy, to retain an effect of intimacy: i.e. as though a large number of people are reacting at close range to the listener. These are likely to be rather conflicting requirements. It usually means employing a large number of reaction microphones, each placed near to a group of audience, and strategically arranged to minimize pick-up from the PA loudspeakers if used. The microphone outputs should be controlled by a group fader for ease of control, especially if it is required to 'milk' the audience, i.e. to 'swell' the reaction by bringing up the level just after the natural start of each laugh; but they should each have an individual fader also so that distinctive or irritating reaction or focusing effects can be eliminated.

CHAPTER TWENTY-FOUR

Television

Glyn Alkin

Quite a large proportion of the sound elements in television, and the techniques required to produce it, are very similar to those for recording and radio broadcasting. In fact recordings made for domestic use form quite a substantial part of the output. There are, however, some types of programme material and many production circumstances that create the requirement for a particular character of sound and the application of a specialized technique.

The required quality of sound
The requirements for sound as far as technical quality is concerned are very similar to those for recording and broadcasting, and just as stringent. Certainly the fact that there is a picture does not provide any sort of excuse for poor sound production or a lowering of standards (though it may sometimes provide the reason for it). In some respects the picture makes a demand for extra clarity from the sound because, since the camera direction is invariably motivated by the script or score, what the picture is doing most of the time is drawing the viewer's attention to what he should be hearing.

If an important source of sound cannot be heard clearly, the fact that one is presented with a picture of it, apparently at very close range, only tends to increase the frustration. This point is easily confused by the fact that speech can be made clearer by the ability to see the speaker's lips, in fact some people are able to lip-read without any sound, but this ability varies considerably between individuals and certainly cannot be relied upon as far as the transmission is concerned. It would be a clever person indeed who could hear the notes of a musical instrument by merely watching the fingering.

Regarding technical quality, it is easy to assume that, because television sets tend not to be renowned for their sound reproduction, this suggests a lack of interest on the part of the audience. It may be true that the sound element is a feature not uppermost in the minds of the public when choosing a television set, because their attention is usually diverted by the more obvious appeal of the picture and the cabinet. If, subsequently, the sound is found to be lacking, this tends to be blamed on the transmission.

In fact the shortcomings of the receivers, coupled with the fact that a great many viewers tend to set their volume controls to a low level because they leave their sets switched on for long periods, imposes on the sound the need for a high degree of clarity.

There are, however, encouraging signs of improvement in the standard of sound reproduction of many of the newer sets, especially the colour ones, and some have provision for connection to hi-fi equipment. There is also a large, and growing, number of people buying special tuners to enable them to hear television sound under high quality conditions. So it is true to say that the quality parameters are very similar to those for radio (taking programme type for type) with possibly a little less latitude in overall volume range and a particular emphasis on clarity.

The required character of sound
One of the major functions of television sound is to underline the realism of the pictures, and it is all too easy for it to do the opposite and *undermine* them. One has only to watch a film in which the picture and sound have become misaligned to realize how a speaker can be made to look ridiculous, and somehow unreal, by even a small error in lip-synchronism. This may be an obvious example but there are other, more subtle, ways in which the two media can conflict. These may be subjective but they can give the viewer a deep, though possibly inexplicable, sense that something is wrong. This is particularly true of visual and aural perspective.

Anyone who listens to radio drama must be aware of the ability of sound to conjure up mental images without the aid of a picture. Sound can evoke a sense of movement, environment, distance and atmosphere. Obviously television sound will do the same, whether the viewer realises it or not, so that it is vital that the sound image and the picture are in agreement.

The television viewer tends to credit the camera with the faculty of hearing and accepts it as normal that he will hear what he can see. Unfortunately, in practice it is all too easy for an artist moving towards the camera to move away from the microphone. His voice will therefore appear to recede as his picture approaches, so that the perspective will be reversed. In a situation like this, where the sound and picture are contradictory, the picture will normally take control, because people tend to believe their eyes, but the viewer will be left with a sense of frustration that could undermine his enjoyment of the programme and the credibility of the performance.

Microphone technique
The requirements for sound pick-up in television can be roughly divided into

two categories, (a) occasions where it is permissible to see microphones in shot, and (b) where it is not.

Nowadays it is generally accepted that microphones, provided that they are neat ones, may be seen in the picture in most circumstances except those in which their appearance would destroy the apparent realism of the setting. This was not always the case and throughout the early days of television sound standards, especially in the case of music, were bedevilled by the insistence on the part of producers that microphones should be kept out of the picture. This created innumerable problems of acoustic effect and lack of separation. Acceptance of the fact that microphones are as much a part of the light music scene as the musical instruments has been the greatest step forward in the production of live television sound.

Microphones in shot

An important feature of microphones for use in shot is a neat and unobtrusive appearance. This requirement varies to some extent according to the situation in which the microphones are being used. Generally speaking, large micro- phones can be acceptable when used for sectional balance within orchestras, but not for vocal work, where they are more likely to mask the artist from the camera.

Hand-held microphones

A possible exception exists in the case of hand-held microphones for vocalists. Here there is little purpose in minimizing the size of the microphone beyond the point where it could become difficult to handle. In any case, microphone mannerisms usually become a feature of the artist's routine. So, far from trying to make the microphone unobtrusive, they are sometimes fitted with coloured close-talking shields as a decoration. Artists can usually be relied upon not to mask their faces from the camera when carrying their own microphone, as they tend to be more concerned with their appearance than their sound (until they hear the recording). The choice of directional characteristics for a hand-held microphone depends upon the circumstances and upon the mobility and expertise of the artist or interviewer.

If loudspeaker reinforcement (PA) is involved, or it is necessary to dis- criminate against a loud accompaniment or noise, unidirectional charac- teristics would be an advantage provided that the artist can be relied upon to keep the microphone pointed towards himself and away from the unwanted source. Unfortunately this is by no means always the case, and artists who continually wave the microphone about, altering the angle with respect to their mouth, can cause considerable problems for the sound engineer which can be only partially mitigated by the use of a compressor in the microphone circuit. It is often better, in these circumstances, to use an omnidirectional microphone and rely upon the relative proximity to the wanted sound source to provide the necessary discrimination.

Another reason for choosing an omnidirectional microphone could be to reduce the risk of wind-blasting, with artists who tend to whisk the microphone around rapidly. In general, omnidirectional microphones tend to be less prone to pressure-change effects due to rapid movement, 'popping' and the proximity effect (bass boost) due to close working.

Stand microphones
When microphones that are to be seen in shot are required to be fixed in position, it is usual to mount them on stands (rather than suspend them on slings). In general, microphones look better when supported from below than suspended from above because, unless the point of suspension can be seen, this tends to leave an uncomfortable query in the mind. Fixed microphones present a very real risk of masking camera shots, and this does not seem to be nearly so acceptable when the artist is not holding the microphone. Therefore a slim and neat appearance is essential.

Normally a microphone with a cardioid or hypercardioid characteristic would be chosen to give maximum separation from the accompaniment, PA or noise. It would probably have to be positioned rather lower than the optimum to prevent visual masking. In general, microphones that have their live face in line with their principal axis (end-fire) are better for this purpose than side-sensitive types because, when used under the shot, they tend to look better being angled towards the artist.

Stand/hand-held microphones
There is often a requirement for a microphone that can be used on a stand and then taken off easily for hand-holding. For this purpose the most useful device is a plastic clip which attaches to the top of the stand and grips the microphone around its middle, but encompasses only a little more than half its circumference. The microphone can then be pulled out of the clip and returned to it with ease, and without having to thread the cable.

Extension tube microphones
Where there is no need to handle the microphone, an obvious choice for an unobtrusive stand microphone is the electrostatic type in which a length of thin co-axial tube can be fitted between the capsule and the head amplifier (e.g. the AKG C451 series). These microphones, normally cardioid in response, are usually supplied with alternative lengths of extension tubes.

The longer extension, with the head amplifier mounted on a short stand, makes a very neat arrangement when it can be seen in long shot, the top section being particularly unobtrusive in close-up when only the thin tube and capsule are visible. Hinged capsule adaptors are also available which, while they slightly add to the obtrusiveness, enable the capsule to be angled as required relative to the tube. The short extension tube can be very useful for low instruments, and can make a very convenient form of gallows arm for such purposes as hovering over a piano with the amplifier mounted on a microphone stand. An example of the use of a long and short extension occurs when a singer accompanies himself on a guitar. Special adaptors have been made to accommodate the two microphone amplifiers on a single base for this purpose. Another important use for microphone extension tubes is to sling microphones in circumstances where they are required to be as unobtrusive as possible, e.g. over large orchestras at public concerts and above the stage in opera theatres etc. When such microphones are hung upside down, they can be almost invisible if they dip into a long shot, provided that they do not produce reflection from the lights into the camera lens. For this purpose it is advisable to give the microphones a matt black finish or to cover them with a 'stocking' made of black open-weave material.

Personal microphones

One method of picking up sound from an artist, while allowing him to move about, is to attach a microphone to his clothing. Special miniature micro-phones are available for this purpose, equipped with lanyards by which they can be slung around the neck, or tie clips to enable them to be clipped on to the clothing. 'Lavalier' microphones, to give them their proper name, usually contain moving coil or electrostatic elements, although some have been produced with piezo-electric elements. The microphones can be con-nected to the control equipment either by wire or a radio link, involving a miniature transmitter which is also carried on the person. It is essential that the cable from the microphone is very slender and pliable, to prevent the transmission of noise due to its rubbing against the clothing.

When a wire connection is used, it is usual to make a plug and socket con-nection at a distance of about 1·5 metres from the microphone so that a more robust cable can be used to connect to the wall point. This has the advantage of preventing the part of the cable that comes into contact with the artist from becoming dirty, and also makes it easier to thread into the clothing. The most usual method (at least in the case of male artists) is to thread the cable through a trouser leg and attach it to the waist and ankle by means of tape.

It is possible to hide personal microphones completely under the clothing, provided that the material is thin and of a reasonably open weave, but this always brings an attendant risk of loss of high frequency response and excessive rustling, to which some microphones are more prone than others. Whatever type of personal microphone is used, and even if no attempt is made to conceal it, there exists the problem inherent in the 'lavalier' position, which is a very unnatural one from which to pick up the voice. As it is low down, the microphone often becomes shielded from the mouth by the chin, which can produce an 'off-mike' quality and loss of intelligibility. Some types of lavalier microphone have a non-linear frequency response which peaks in the 'presence' region (between about 4 and 6 kHz) to restore clarity of diction. One example has a moveable clip, to which the lanyard is attached, which can be slid over the end of the microphone. The resultant lip forms a cavity with a resonant frequency of around 5 kHz, thereby giving the microphone a peak in response in this region.

Electrostatic personal microphones

Some miniature personal microphones work on the electrostatic (capacitor) principle. They require a head-amplifier, which must be in close proximity to the microphone capsule. This usually takes the form of a cylinder which is fed from a supply unit by means of a multi-core cable or a 'phantom power' connection along the microphone leads. For microphones which use conventional electrostatic elements, the supply unit has to include a polarizing potential of about 50 V to energize the capsule. In some more recent examples, this requirement has been eliminated by the use of an electret diaphragm.

As was mentioned in Chapter Three, this consists of a material (typically a high-polymer plastic film) which has been given a permanent electrostatic charge, rather in the manner that ferrous metal can be magnetized. As a result, the assembly can be made extremely compact and the head amplifier (usually an FET) can be supplied by a small battery cell contained within it.

Radio microphones

Electrostatic microphones are particularly suitable for use with miniature transmitters which can be carried by the artist, either in a pocket or a special pouch on a belt around the waist or sewn into the clothing. There is also a type in which the microphone and transmitter are combined into a cylindrical 'baton' which can be held in the hand. This type is especially suitable for vocalists or interview situations.

Frequency-modulated transmission is used, the choice of carrier frequency depending upon the circumstances, the frequencies for which the user is licensed, and the clear channel space available in the particular area.

Typical frequencies are in the 100/200 MHz or 400/500 MHz range. A radio frequency power of the order of 50 mW is quite sufficient, as the receiving aerial can usually be mounted quite close to the action. However, where several artists are equipped with radio microphones operating on different frequencies, it is important that their respective receiving aerials are not too close, otherwise there can be a risk of a transmitter working on an adjacent frequency 'pulling' a receiver off tune.

Sometimes problems occur due to reflections from metal structures causing null points as the artists move about. These can usually be mitigated by employing more than one aerial per channel to give a simple form of 'diversity' reception.

Super-directional microphones

Television cameras are usually equipped with a turret containing a number of interchangeable lenses of different focal length, or with Zoom lenses. In either case, it is possible to change the angle of view and alter the apparent distance of the subject, either by moving the camera or by changing the angle of the lens. In fact close-up pictures can be taken from a considerable distance.

Obviously, in order to pick up the corresponding sound, what is needed is a 'zoom microphone', i.e. a microphone capable of adjusting its acceptance angle to match that of the camera, and thereby pick up sound with clarity and separation from the background at an equal distance.

Unfortunately, due to the fundamental difference between the two media, this is extraordinarily difficult to achieve. Sound wavelengths are very much longer than light wavelengths and are able to curve around objects that are smaller than the wavelength. Thus, in order to focus sound as one is able to do in vision, it would be necessary to have an acoustic lens or focusing reflector with a diameter comparable in size with the longest wavelength it is required to receive, i.e. about five metres. In practice, the bass response for a small reflector tends to be better than might be expected from a simple consideration of wavelength, due to the 'pressure doubling' effect that occurs when a microphone is placed in proximity to a reflective surface.

Without doubt, a microphone placed at the focus of a parabolic reflector is the most efficient method of picking up sound from a considerable distance (see Fig. 24.1). Assuming that the wavefront of a sound source on the axis is practically plane, which is likely to be the case when it arrives from a distance, the path lengths of the reflections from the parabolic surface are equal at the point of focus, so that they all arrive at the face of the microphone in phase. The sound reaching the microphone directly is likely to be out of phase with the reflected sound and will cause some cancellation. Thus uni-direc-

Fig. 24.1
A parabolic reflector gives improved directivity and is useful, for example, in birdsong recording (photo courtesy Eric Hosking)

tional microphones should be used, positioned at the focus with the dead side towards the wanted sound.

A microphone should be selected which has an acceptance angle just wide enough to encompass the whole area of the dish. Parabolic reflectors of about one metre in diameter are about the largest that can conveniently be used in most circumstances. With these, the response tails off rapidly below about 300 Hz, which tends to limit their use to such applications as recording birdsong and picking up sound effects at cricket matches, race meetings, etc.

Line (gun) microphones

A less efficient, but much less cumbersome, method of picking up sound at not too great a distance is the line microphone, often called the 'gun' or 'rifle' microphone. Unlike the parabolic reflector, the gun microphone relies for its directionality not on a focused collection of sound but on rejecting sounds from unwanted directions.

The 'gun' microphone consists essentially of a sensitive transducer, in later models normally an electrostatic cardioid, coupled to a tube which has a series of apertures or a slot with transverse baffles along its length. In some cases the tube, including the capsule, is an accessory which can be substituted for the normal capsule of an electrostatic microphone. The microphone achieves its directionality by virtue of the fact that sound arriving on axis passes straight down the tube to the diaphragm, whereas sounds from other directions enter via the slot, travel differing distances down the tube and therefore tend to cancel when they reach the diaphragm in random phase.

It will be evident that the above principle holds completely only for plane waves. The system becomes less effective if the source is radiating spherical waves, e.g. a person speaking close to the tube, or if the sound arrives from all directions in random phase as can occur in reverberant conditions. For this reason, gun microphones tend to have better discrimination when used out of doors than in reverberant rooms.

Electrostatic models which can be mains or battery powered, with tubes of about 0·5 metre, have a considerable application in television and film operations. They can be fitted with a pistol grip for hand-holding, used with a special suspension mounting on a boom, or attached to a camera. Large plastic windshields are available to enable them to be used out of doors. Hand-held, they form an excellent basis for sound pick-up for small location sequences. In the studio they can be very useful for covering awkward areas in drama sequences, or for picking up distant speech in audience participation programmes.

Microphone booms (Fig. 24.2)

The most useful and versatile tool for picking up sound, at least as far as TV studio work is concerned, is the microphone boom (see Fig. 24.2). The boom consists of a telescopic arm on which a microphone can be mounted, with a counterweight at the other end. The arm is balanced on a pivot attached to a mobile three-wheeled 'pram', which also supports a platform on which the operator stands. The operator can extend or retract the boom arm by turning a handle with his right hand. This action also causes the counterweight to execute a smaller, complementary, movement so that the arm remains in balance. Simultaneously, using his left hand, the operator can adjust the microphone for position (by rotating the arm), height (by tilting the arm about its pivot), direction (by turning a lever) and tilt (by squeezing the two components of the same lever together). The whole boom, with the operator standing on it, can be tracked (steered by the back wheel) or, in the case of the larger booms, 'crabbed', i.e. moved in any direction with all three wheels steering together.

Booms are available in various sizes from small portable ones, with a reach of about 2·3 to 3·3 metres, to large ones with arms extending between 2·4 and 5·1 metres. The larger booms are fitted with seats intended only for slow sequences or resting periods. Some have been made with seats designed for continuous use, which the operator can orientate by means of foot pedals, but these have not proved very successful for television work where rapid boom swings to follow artists in quick-moving sequences demand that the operator stands with his legs braced to overcome the inertia of the boom arm.

The big advantage of the boom is its continuous manoeuvrability. Anyone with experience of microphones will know that, for any given situation, there is one optimum position for the microphone. If the action is fluid, with the artists moving and continually facing in different directions, it follows that the microphone should be mobile.

The art of boom operating is to follow the action, keeping the microphone in the correct relationship to the artists to maintain a proper sound balance between them (and possibly the accompaniment), with due relation to the camera shots, in terms of perspective and directionality, while keeping the equipment and its shadow out of the picture.

To some extent, the business of keeping the microphone out of the picture and matching visual and aural perspective are synonymous, as it is necessary to raise or retract the boom to clear a long shot and close it in for close-ups.

In practice, of course, the dictates of practicability do not necessarily produce the ideal result, and the operator is required to exercise a fine degree of judgement as to the optimum position for the microphone at each point in time. The boom operator is not able to hear the results of his efforts with a high degree of clarity, so he must rely upon direction via head-phones from the sound mixer, who is listening in controlled conditions while watching a vision monitor with which he can judge the visual and acoustic match.

The boom operator is not able to read a script while operating, for even a brief glance away could mean getting the microphone in shot or even causing injury to the artists. He is therefore provided with a brief 'shot list', giving him basic positions to work from and he relies on the sound mixer to give him action cues. Conversely, the boom operator is often in a much better position to see the action than the sound mixer and can often provide him with useful information. For instance, a large set with dialogue between widely-spaced or rapidly moving artists, or changing camera angles, may require two or even three booms. The operators are often in the best position to inform the sound mixer of the right moment to fade from one to the other. For this purpose, the operator is provided with a microphone and a reverse talkback key.

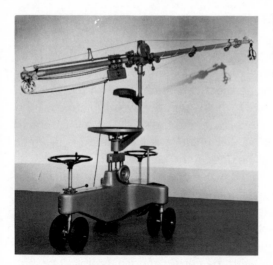

Fig. 24.2
Typical microphone boom and pram, giving flexible control of position, height and tilt (photo courtesy Berkey Colortran UK)

The whole essence of the television operation relies upon co-operation between the various sectional interests concerned. Practically all the production decisions made regarding the picture will reflect upon the sound operation and vice versa. A successful sound mixer and boom operator will therefore understand the rudiments of optics and lighting, and a good lighting or camera man will have a basic knowledge of the requirements of sound.

Music

As stated at the beginning of this chapter, there is little difference between the techniques involved in balancing music for compatible monophonic recording and television. Most successful records are destined to be played on television sooner or later, and recordings made specifically for television (usually as introductory or theme music) are often made into commercial gramophone records. After all music is music, and a good balance, in which all the elements of the composition are reproduced with the proper quality and volume relationship to each other, is a good balance in any medium. Nevertheless there are two important aspects of the televising of music which have a particular bearing on the sound technique.

1. The subjective effect of close-up shots of the instruments, which can effect the desired quality of the sound.

2. The problem of achieving good musical balance in 'live' television, which is often broadcast under unsuitable acoustic conditions with orchestral layouts designed to suit visual, rather than sound balance, considerations.

The first point principally concerns the televising of orchestral concerts where it is usual to maintain visual interest by causing the camera viewpoint to roam around the orchestra, taking close-ups of the various instruments or sections, as their part becomes musically predominant and, it is hoped, suitably prominent in the balance. Most orchestral records or broadcasts present an aural image equivalent to an overall wide-angle shot of the orchestra, in which the geographical and perspective relationships are fixed throughout. It would not be satisfactory to hold such an overall picture of the orchestra for the entire performance as, due to the small size of the screen, the viewer is not able to vary his viewpoint to concentrate on different areas as they take his interest, as he does in the concert hall.

The sound mixer can thus be faced with a dilemma. A distant overall perspective of sound can appear most incongruous with close-up pictures of the instruments, and yet any attempt to adjust the balance from instant to instant to match the picture would be musically disastrous. The answer lies in producing an immaculate sound balance, in which all the instruments are not only reproduced clearly and with the correct musical prominence, but have a degree of 'presence'. With this character of sound, which is also characteristic of many of the best recent gramophone records, it is possible to take any close-ups which make musical sense without creating conflict between eye and ear.

Live light music balance
The main problems in televising light music live are:

1. If the orchestra appears in shot, the layout is likely to be arranged more for visual than for sound balance considerations.

2. There are likely to be problems of separation between the various sections, and in particular in between the orchestra and soloist.

For visual reasons, sections such as saxophones which in the recording studio could be grouped in a tight semicircle are usually spread out in a straight line. Only small, and rather ineffective acoustic screens can be used to contain the drums or separate the sections without obscuring them from the camera and, of course, the vocalist can hardly be accommodated in an acoustic booth!

In the early days of television, when every effort was made to keep microphones out of shot, the problem of separation was acute, due to excessive microphone distances when using booms. Even when the vocals were clearly audible above the accompaniment, this was often at the expense of the orchestral balance which was ruined by pick-up on the vocal microphone. Eventually, good sense and the persuasive powers of the pioneer sound mixers prevailed, resulting in the most significant advance in the technique, the acceptance of microphones in shot for vocalists, or even allowing them to carry their microphones.

Separate orchestral studios

Where it is required to use booms for vocalists, and the orchestra is not to be seen in shot, there is much to be said for accommodating the orchestra in a separate studio, or an acoustically screened-off section of the same studio, and playing the accompaniment to the artist via a loudspeaker.

This procedure is frequently used in the production of opera, where a very large orchestra is involved. The use of mobile loudspeakers which track with the booms keeps the accompaniment playback close to the action, prevents the risk of time-lag which can occur when large areas are involved, and enables good separation to be obtained even with quite large microphone distances. A closed-circuit television system can be used to relay a picture of the conductor to monitor screens ranged around the sets. The singers then have a better chance of seeing the beat, without falsifying their eye-line, than would probably be the case with the conductor in the same studio. Sometimes an auxiliary conductor will relay the beat while watching the monitor.

Mime

Undoubtedly the easiest way to achieve good vocal/orchestral balance under television conditions is to resort to miming to the playback. This has been the standard method used in the film industry since the early days of the talkies. Unfortunately in television production, unlike in films, there is not usually time to synchronize by forming mime sections into loops for dubbing and then continually repeating them until lip-sync is perfect, so the artifice is often exposed. Another feature that can give away the fact that mime is used is the difference in comportment of an artist who is not actually singing. Singers should be encouraged to use their full singing voice, even though no sound is being picked up from the set. Playback loudspeakers should be loud enough to encourage them to do so.

The addition of music and effects

Improvements in recording and editing of videotape have encouraged producers to adopt, much more than previously, a discontinuous-take technique, particularly for drama productions. Synonymous with this is the need to add incidental music and sound effects to the final edited version.

Cut editing

Prior to the development of electronic editing, or where only one videotape machine was available, editing (with quadraplex machines) was accomplished by cutting the tape. This is a difficult and time-consuming operation which is complicated by the problem that the vision recording is displaced from the sound track (on the same tape) by approximately 23 cm, so that the sound leads the picture by about 0·6 sec. In order to make a physical cut in the tape, it is therefore necessary either to allow a sufficient period of silence at the point of joining or to 'lift off' the sound on to a separate recording, usually on a 6·25 mm ($\frac{1}{4}$-inch) machine, and subsequently re-record it on to the videotape after the join has been made.

A limited amount of adjustment can be made to the sound track during this process, but only short sequences can be attempted due to the difficulty of maintaining synchronism between the sound and vision recorders.

Electronic editing

Electronic editing is a method of dubbing from one machine to another, or sometimes two machines to one, to achieve editing. It must be remembered that videotape editing is much more complicated than audio tape editing because picture synchronism must be maintained, the cuts can only be made at specific points in the waveform (during frame blanking) and joined in a particular sequence which, in the case of colour, occurs only every four fields (two picture frames).

The process employs a device that automatically, on receipt of a cue pulse recorded on the cue track of the videotape, changes the mode of one of the machines instantly from replay to record. It also enables the two machines, one containing the end cue (which will be the record machine) and one with the material to be added, to be run up synchronously. The transition is effected by pressing a button which records a cue pulse on the tape. The position of the edit can be checked by running the tapes over the transition point in the rehearsal mode, when only the monitoring changes from machine to machine on receipt of the cue, both machines remaining in repro mode. The position of the cue can then be moved, if necessary, to achieve the right effect before the process is repeated in the record mode. This time the record machine changes to record on receipt of the cue and the edit is completed.

Time-code editing

As an extension of this principle, it is possible to record a time code in digital form on the cue track of the videotape. This can be displayed in numerical form as hours, minutes, seconds and frames superimposed on the picture on a monitor. It can also be used to control the functions of the tape recorders, in computer fashion.

In order to save wear on the transmission tape, it is possible to make a copy on to a cheaper (domestic quality) videotape machine, and use this to select and rehearse the edit points which can be located by means of the time code, also recorded on the tape. Finally, cue pulses recorded on the domestic (helical-scan) tape can be used to programme the original (quadraplex) recorder to perform the editing function.

Multitrack dubbing

When complex sound editing is required, e.g. the addition of music, dubbed dialogue or effects, a copy of the vision-edited videotape, complete with time-code, can be made on a domestic quality machine. Simultaneously, a copy of the videotape sound track and the time-code is recorded on two tracks of a multitrack audio recorder.

The multitrack recorder can then be run in synchronism with the domestic video recorder so that the picture can be seen on a monitor while music, effects or dialogue are added to the other tracks of the audio tape. When the required tracks have been built up, they can be mixed down to a single track (still using the domestic videotape as the vision monitoring source) the whole remaining in synchronism. Finally the reduction track can be dubbed back to the original quadraplex recording, synchronized by comparing the time codes recorded on each, to replace the original sound track.

CHAPTER TWENTY-FIVE

Film

Edgar Vetter

'Recording Sound for Motion Pictures' (as the ASMPTE Textbook called the art in 1936) used to be an entirely separate technique, unrelated to the making of gramophone records. However, all media now share the use of magnetic tape in the early stages of production, though this similarity is misleading and, even at the first stage, three essential requirements separate film from other forms of recording:

1. The tape machine must start, stop, and remain accurately synchronized with a picture camera, which may or may not itself hold accurate speed.

2. In nearly all cases the microphone (and its shadow) must remain invisible.

3. Though not now so critical as it once was, the sound recording must give satisfactory reproduction in large auditoria.

The choice of the photo-optical, as against the magnetic track, for the final medium of reproduction is not so important as it was once thought to be. The optical method, if carried out with the care and respect it deserves, is a technique with many advantages. Like the gramophone record, it was said to be doomed by the advent of magnetic recording but has stood up well to competition on grounds of both quality and economy.

In recent years, the motion-picture producer has responded to the growth of television competition by moving away from studios to the great outdoors for this background material (see Fig. 25.1) and equipment and technique have had to be adapted accordingly. The advantages of compactness, mobility, and quality are to be found in the small, high-priced recorders which can all be powered, if need be in the middle of the desert, by small, torch-type cells, but still produce studio-quality sound.

In the earlier days, when the photo-optical method was used in all stages of recording for picture production, the result of a day's work could not be confirmed as satisfactory until the sound film had been sent to the laboratory for developing, a print made and the report as to quality sent back to the

Fig. 25.1
Typical busy scene during filming on location (courtesy Fox Photos)

location or studio. This could sometimes take two or three days, though the normal timing for home-based units was a twelve-hour lab service with a 'rushes' report available first thing on the following morning. Instant playback has done away with most of these delays.

The greatest difference in technique arises from the need to keep the microphone invisible. When one thinks of a pop studio or television broadcast with microphones close to the performers and even attached to some musical instruments, the gulf seems enormous. In the earliest talking-picture days, the Jenkins and Adair condenser microphones, for example, weighed about 3 kilograms (6·5 lb) and were coupled by a cable up to 20 mm thick. Mobility was very limited but, as microphones got smaller and more directional, and overhead boom mounts lighter and more controllable, it became possible to follow artists around between furniture and even up and down stairs (lighting camera men permitting). The art of boom operating became very skilled and a good boom operator was much sought after, partly for his skill but almost equally for his personality, as he represented the sound department in the centre of the action. Regrettably the camera personnel have always slightly resented the arrival of sound and the fact that they, and their equipment, must now operate silently.

Types of camera

Cameras have improved optically and operationally but, sad to say, the modern camera is noisier than its counterpart of twenty years ago. At the same time, although film actors have always tended to be chosen for their appearance rather than their vocal powers, the style of acting has changed. The stage production voice has been abandoned in favour of such styles as 'The Method', which are often almost inaudible to the director and crew but somehow supposed to be satisfactorily recorded—even with a noisy camera only a metre or so away. Frequently, in a close-up scene, the microphone has to be closer to the camera than to the artist, to avoid being in the picture.

The types of camera used for 35 mm feature productions have been reduced by successive closures of equipment manufacturers to two, one German and the other American. The German type is small, reliable, and comparatively inexpensive. It is still based on a design worked out for war reporting and which had to be considered expendable. It was noisy, but this did not matter much in a war situation unless it made so much noise that it attracted the attention of the enemy (the British Vinten Normandy was even noisier). Its basic design has not changed materially, so that a satisfactory 'blimp' (soundproof cover) has to be larger and thicker than usual and, when extended to include a zoom lens, requires two men to lift it. The exterior controls have to be flexibly coupled to the mechanism in order not to transmit noise. Not unnaturally, the camera crew prefer to work 'un-blimped' and tend to groan when the director requires sync sound. They will ask for scenes to be made 'post sync' whenever possible.

The American standard camera is highly sophisticated and beautifully machined. It comes from a long tradition of precision tool making and is 'self-blimped'. That is to say the movement is finely balanced to reduce noise at every stage, and then the walls are double skinned and insulated from the moving part. However, in order to end up with a device which is reasonably compact and light, the noise leakage is still only just tolerable. In fact it is customary at a major studio to submit every camera to expensive

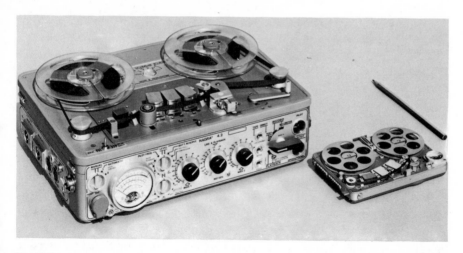

Fig. 25.2
A miniature tape recorder, the Nagra SN (right), shown alongside the Standard Nagra 4.2 model to illustrate the relative size

modifications by the camera department before putting it into service. If the sound mixer objects to the noise of a particular camera, he is liable to be reminded by the camera department that the manufacturer's specification states that microphones must be kept at least 2 metres from the camera. This can lead to conflict unless considerable restraint is exercised by all parties.

All this has led to the use of highly directional 'gun' or 'rifle' microphones which have to be aimed very accurately at each character a split second *before* he speaks. Once again the skill of the boom operator comes in, though he may in modern technique use a pistol grip or hand stick, as the current method of production in real locations often precludes the use of the more cumbersome overhead boom.

The use of a zoom lens in the picture camera brings added complications. Because of its large size, the need to make it accessible to its focus operator and its large radiating surface, there is increased chance of leakage of camera motor pull-down mechanism noise. Also, whereas an experienced boom operator would previously enquire what angle lens was being used and calculate his safe distance for the microphone accordingly, the zoom can turn everything upside down. A car might be seen in medium shot driving round a corner and pulling up on the opposite side of a square: then, instead of the car going away from the camera into long shot, the zoom may come into operation and the shot may end in a close-up of the passenger getting out and saying something to the driver—which the director wants to hear.

Two devices have been developed to meet this situation, the radio micro-phone and the vest-pocket recorder. The radio microphone suffers, in this country and some others, in that the frequencies on which it would work most reliably are not permitted since they have already been allocated to essential services. (TV networks are allowed to use their own station fre-quencies, when these are not in use for public service.) The modern radio microphone is greatly improved but is still unpredictable in city conditions, and some freak effects can always be expected. Artists can be 'wired for sound' and everything go well on rehearsal but, when the camera runs on the take, its motor ruins the recording by radiating static. Some camera motors even blot out the assistant director's 'walkie-talkie'. Another odd situation arose in a cowboy picture when Don Murray, specializing in expertise with a Winchester instead of a six-gun, rode in waving the rifle as he spoke. The signal came and went with every movement and it turned out that the Winchester barrel was the exact tuning length of the aerial.

More reliable, but expensive, is the vest-pocket tape recorder (Fig. 25.2). This can be crystal controlled for sync, set running and concealed on the artist before the shot starts. One machine can be given to each actor in a scene and the results transferred to sprocketed magnetic film, edited to include the relevant lines from each character and so make up the scene as finally heard. This is expensive in time and material—and, of course, the hire of the machines—but it gets results which are not obtainable by other means. The cost of the recorder tends to be proportional to the degree of miniaturi-zation.

The American soundman is perhaps helped to some extent by the more penetrating tone of American speech. However, in spite of the British habit of quiet speech, the average British sound mixer prides himself on recording the highest proportion of usable live sound, especially in documentary subjects; and a documentary technique has largely taken over in feature film production at present. On the Continent, perhaps due to the limited use of any one language, they tend to think that we are mad even to try to record sound on location, and they post sync most of their films (often quite carelessly). They have become so innured to seeing, for instance, an Italian actress dubbed into French with Dutch sub-titles, that it does not seem to worry them too much.

Synchronization

The problem of synchronization between picture and sound was satis-factorily solved at a very early date, though in a rather clumsy manner. The earliest technique used a 420 mm (16-inch) diameter gramophone record running at $33\frac{1}{3}$ rpm to provide 15 minutes of synchronized sound, running from a standing start with the pickup on a marked spot on the spiral groove at the *centre* of the disc—the amount of nearly silent groove corresponding to the length of numbered leader on the picture strip. The 15-minute running time of the reel of film was due to the fact that the film then ran at 350 mm (1 ft) per second for the 300 metres (1,000 ft) reel. In general this was fairly satisfactory, unless some mishap took place in the cinema projection room, but the loss of sync occurred often enough to provide much hilarious material for the rather jealous theatre comedians.

The movie producers reacted promptly, to protect both their dignity and their investment, and encouraged the less technically perfect, but operationally secure, method of 'Sound on Film', the optical method still largely used today. To obtain satisfactory results from this method, the film speed had to be increased by half, from 16 to 24 frames, or 450 mm ($1\frac{1}{2}$ ft) per second.

The extra costs of material and the extra light used for exposure in the studio were resented at first but the improved steadiness and smoothness of the picture image was soon appreciated by the public. To provide room for the sound track, the camera men had to give up some of the image bearing surface of the now standard 35 mm film and, after some preliminary arguments, the 'Academy Aperture' was adopted as an industry standard, with the picture area reduced to retain the familiar aspect ratio of five units of width to four of height. The grain structure of the film could only just accommodate this smaller image but, as emulsions improved, the industry indulged in further reductions of image bearing surface to provide 'Wide Screen' and other aspect ratio experiments, leading to the use of anamorphic lenses of the Cinemascope type and ultimately to the use of 70 mm film for specialized presentations. On the sound side, the earliest 'sound on film' results were not so good as with the disc method, but the cinema projectionists and their investors could relax.

With the large investment, and even larger earnings, of a very success-conscious industry, adequate funds were available for research and the introduction of various improvements. It would be safe to say that the major advances in the technique of recording for all purposes were a by-product of the dedication and keen competition between the heads of the movie producing centres during the next thirty years. At first, almost equal investment was made (by the same basic small group of financiers) in each of the rival optical systems, i.e. Variable Density and Variable Area. Each system had its own advantages in use: it was only the general adoption of colour printing for big musicals, where density systems were at a disadvantage, that finally decided the issue, and this system was reluctantly dropped by the studios who had championed it.

During the production stages, the industry continued with the use of three-phase synchronous motor drives to both picture and sound cameras. The film path scanning speed was metered by sprocket holes which were punched in the film edges and engaged on toothed rollers driven by accurately machined gear trains. Synchronization was exact, provided both drive motors were connected to the same electrical supply.

Where mains electricity was not available, use was made of heavy and relatively inefficient rotary converters run from large storage accumulators. This equipment was so big and heavy that it was found most practicable to have it permanently mounted in the sound truck. Studios vied with each other in providing large and beautiful teak panelled trucks, complete with a built-in dark room for loading and unloading film magazines and conducting daily dip tests of short lengths of sound negative, and equipment for accurate measurement of track location and density. When at home, the truck was kept in a garage built into a corner of the sound stage, but was ready to rush off like a fire engine to any location sessions.

By custom, the sound truck always provided the power to run the picture cameras and the crew usually had to service the motors when not in use. Unfortunately most of the power was used in turning the alternator and only a fraction went to the motors, so the system was not very efficient but was sufficiently massive to provide adequate power. To reduce weight on location, especially for newsreel work, the multi-duty motor was developed. This was basically a DC motor with a small built-in three-phase alternator. The camera took its running power from a local and independent battery and the alternators were linked (or 'netted') by a cable providing a locking voltage between cameras.

Tape synchronization

After the end of the 1939–45 war, and with the wide adoption of 6·25 mm ($\frac{1}{4}$-inch) magnetic tape as a system of recording, Norman Leevers developed the idea of 'magnetic sprocket holes' in order to make tape usable in film production. This British development used make-and-break contact, mounted on the picture camera, to provided pulses of the signal from a small oscillator and recorded these on the lower track of the tape. When displayed on one beam of an oscilloscope, and compared with the trace from a reference source derived from the mains on which the optical recorder was run, this allowed the sound on tape to be accurately transferred to the optical medium at base, in a manner that gave synchronization with the picture camera from which the pulses had been derived. The tape reproducer had to have a motor capable of small changes of speed, and was manually controlled to keep both traces in step.

This was a considerable breakthrough in technique and was recognized as such by leading sound technicians all over the world. Swiss and German designers soon developed the idea into a Piloton standard, using the technique of placing the pulse track in opposite phase on each outside edge of the tape, so that almost a full-track recording could be used for the speech as against the half-track of the Leevers system. If all goes well, the pulse tracks cancel out when the full-track is scanned. In practice, this system was subject to damage of the edges of the tape or inaccuracy of tape scanning. Kudelski in Switzerland came up with the now standard 'Neo Piloton' system, in which the two out-of-phase tracks are disposed down the centre of the tape, and this is much more reliable. He further developed the system so that the tape reproducer would follow its own pulse as referred to the mains. This is a neater system than that in which the sprocketed recorder ran from an amplified signal derived from the recorded pulse itself. The Neo Piloton is the system generally accepted today for all location shooting when 6·25 mm ($\frac{1}{4}$-inch) tape is used.

In transcription to the sprocketed material used at the editing and subsequent stages of production, the Neo Piloton pulse signal is referred to a lightweight transistorized discriminator which compares the signal from the tape being copied with a comparable voltage derived from the mains used to drive the sprocketed recorder. The product of the comparison is fed back to the tape reproducer drive motor in such a way as to adjust the free running speed to correspond to the picture camera speed, together with any stretch or shrinkage factor developed in the tape since the time of recording. Where large changes of temperature or humidity are involved, this is a most important factor.

The Nagra, or other similar recorder, is set up to receive a sync signal of 1 V at 50 or 60 Hz. This voltage is derived from a small alternator rigidly mounted on the camera body or, if the camera is being driven by a sync motor, by a transformer reading one phase of the camera mains supply. More recently, both camera and sound recorder may be used with independently crystal controlled units, so that no connecting cable is required between them, a very great advantage on news coverage or where filming is taking place in public places or crowds. A word of warning may be given here. It is not satisfactory to run one unit on crystal and one on mains. The mains supply will vary in frequency slightly, while the crystal is dead accurate. There are no tolerances in film synchronization and the resultant loss of sync will be noticed.

So far we have been talking about synchronization when running. It is just as important to match the start of the section (or shot) accurately. Many systems have been tried for semi-automation of the starting signal with information which will identify the shot; none has so far proved entirely satisfactory. The favourite is still the crude, but reassuring, 'clapper board', sometimes referred to as the 'slate' (because the information can be written in chalk and later wiped off). Slating a shot means photographing the Title, Scene, and Take No. simultaneously with the recording of a voice giving the same information, and a clap made by closing the hinged flap at the top of the board, before the director calls for action to begin. Sometimes, for the sake of a nervous or sensitive artist, children, or animals, the clap is reserved to the end of the take. This is called an end slate and is announced as such to help the editor.

The crew

By custom, by Union agreement and by the requirements of smooth operation of the job, the sound crew for feature film production consists of four grades. Sound mixer, boom operator, camera operator, and maintenance. In specially large or complicated productions, other supplementary grades are included such as playback operator, boom assistant, assistant maintenance, etc. Advertising productions for both TV and the cinema are regarded as features, and crewed as such. Documentary and news rate smaller crews, and here there is some call for rationalization, but in every case the smooth running of the job must be the overriding factor as running costs are inevitably high.

The sound mixer is the leader of his crew. He used to be salaried and permanently employed by the studio—one of a stable of half-a-dozen or so carried by the studio, assigned and charged out to productions as they were booked. He was responsible to the sound supervisor, worked with the crew assigned to him, and used equipment owned and sometimes developed by the studio sound department.

This has nearly all changed. More and more, the sound mixer tends to be a sub-contractor, owning the tools of his trade and employing or at least choosing the members of his supporting crew. The risks are greater; if he buys the wrong gear or chooses the wrong assistants, his own earnings may have to pay for the correct model, the latest microphone or the replacement crew member. But if he gives good service, has a likeable personality and maintains a cheerful crew, the rewards can be greater too. However, he will have to look after the administrative chores, maintain the cash flow between crew payments and the production payments to him, and generally provide an advisory service and trouble-shooting bureau.

But, when all is going well, the sound mixer should be free to liaise with the Director on creative matters and plan the general strategy of the sound department in advance of the daily shooting schedule. A thorough working knowledge of all the equipment is essential, though perhaps his chief assets are a good ear, a sense of 'theatre', and an ability to keep in his head an image of what the completed scene should be like. Then a dialogue sequence shot over a period of days will match for quality, level, and presence from long shot to close-up, reverse angle, establishing shot, etc, and it can be put together in the cutting room as one continuous performance. It is no good getting superb quality close-up material that will not cut into yesterday's establishing shot, or have camera noise jumping in level with the change of angle.

The boom operator is more accurately called the 'Mic Man' in America. Booms are still widely used in television studios but location film working has largely done away with them. Personality and an ability to learn dialogue at least as fast as the artists themselves remain his most important qualifications.

The maintenance man on location with good equipment must use intelligent anticipation by having the most useful spares in reserve. On foreign locations his job becomes more onerous. He will be expected to travel with the equipment and have some knowledge of local customs regulations and what must be carried to give continuous service. Transportation of equipment is expensive, but a hold-up in production would be more so.

The sound camera operator, as the title suggests, is a crew position which is a hangover from the past and only rarely applicable today. It relates to the days when all film production sound was recorded optically. The earliest magnetic recorders used for film work were converted optical cameras, making the best use of an excellent, sprocketed, film-pulling mechanism but with the enclosing doors removed or left open and a magnetic head mounted (sometimes in addition to the optical gate). When tape recorders came into use, the BFPA/ACTT union agreement was already so firmly established that the designation has remained, in spite of the anachronism. On small productions his presence is difficult to justify, but on a full feature in continuous operation for a number of weeks, his job is to identify all tapes accurately, make out the log sheets, and liaise closely with continuity department and the camera crew to ensure that all information to the cutting rooms and laboratories will tally. He has also to despatch recorded tapes and completed log sheets to the centre where the wanted material will be copied (or transferred) to sprocketed tape so that it can be matched and seen, or rather heard, with the picture rushes and subsequently edited. In between, he assists with the movement of equipment, liaises with the production department, and generally acts as the junior member of the sound crew.

There are a few, probably not more than a dozen in this country, who still operate a sound camera, and the industry could not exist without their services. They tend to be scattered around in sound centres, closely linked to a laboratory service. The operation is more and more divorced from the hurly-burly of production and has become a backroom 'transfer operation'; much like the cutting operation in the disc industry. Almost the whole of the cinema output has to pass through their hands, and their scrupulous attention to detail is essential to the survival of the industry.

Presentation

Finally there is the matter of theatre reproduction. Much work, notably by Douglas Shearer in America and Britons from P. G. A. Voigt onward, has been expended on behalf of better reproduction and better acoustics in large auditoria.

The 4,000-seat 'Super Cinema', once the legitimate pride of the industry, has given way with very few exceptions to the neighbourhood 'Two in One' or 'Four in One' cinema group with auditoria not much larger than a lecture room. Even here the acoustic situation is far from that of a domestic living-room. In consequence, the sound has to be reproduced larger than life, partly to rise above the noises created by the audience, air conditioning, etc., but more to match the larger than life close-up images of the players on the screen. The economics of building construction rarely allow enough rigidity or weight in large wall surfaces, and low frequency reverberation or overhang can be a disturbing feature and reduce intelligibility. To avoid this, a certain amount of bass cut has to be introduced in the recording chain (though music is usually left comparatively flat) whether the reproduction is from magnetic or optical track.

Due to the requirements of early equipment and techniques, reduction of high-frequency response was also introduced on the recommendation of a Committee of the Academy of Motion Picture Arts and Sciences. This became known as 'the Academy roll-off'. Intended originally to counteract harshnesses from the high-frequency horns used in the loudspeaker arrays, which highlighted peak clipping on tracks and amplifiers, this well intentioned standard came to be regarded as a serious limitation by sound mixers and dubbing theatre crews. Intent on getting better sound for their producers, successive generations introduced presence filters, mid-lift speech equalizers, etc. This technique of pre-emphasis and de-emphasis did reduce system noise, valve hiss, exciter lamp hiss, and photocell flicker noise.

To keep the high frequency response relatively free from distortion became the chief aim of sound camera operator and laboratory together. Thus each new batch of sound recording negative material had to have an exposure factor fixed by a series of cross-modulation tests to secure optimum cancellation effect in the printing or positive cycle. Remembering that the positive emulsion and development would always be chosen for best picture quality, the maintenance of sound standards had to be fought for at every stage. Nevertheless, the best products were very good indeed. We hardly realized how good at the time; subsequent reproduction for television, without the doubtful benefit of the Academy roll-off, has surprised many.

As with gramophone record companies, although all studios paid lip service to the AMPTE curves and standards, each dubbing theatre, through which the studio output had to pass, had its own private recipe for success, arrived at more or less by empirical methods but backed up by a lot of expensive research. However, a large measure of success was achieved in the last few optical-only productions in which the print that the public heard was only one, or at the most two, generations away from the original sound negative shot on the floor of the studio. The late John Cox, head of the sound department at Shepperton Studios and many times an Oscar winner, was firm in his belief that the last optical-only sound productions were of considerably better quality than later magnetic productions or mixed magnetic/optical tracks.

This view has since been confirmed by experiments and practical work carried out at the EMI studios at Elstree by Tony Lumkin and a member of the Dolby organization, Ioan Allen. In a paper presented to the British Kinematograph Sound and Television Society in 1974 Mr. Allen introduced himself as a newcomer to film sound who had decided to start from scratch and test out the optical method for himself, free from any preconceived ideas. He declared his opinion that optical sound, if carried out with the care it deserved, was a very satisfactory recording medium. Its capabilities were being limited by practices, ritually observed and inherited from the early days of the industry, mainly stemming from the observance of the Academy roll-off at the reproducing end of the chain. He reported that he had found as much as 15% distortion being fed into the optical system negative arising from the use of presence equalization at each stage.

He therefore advised the removal of the reproduction roll-off and a restriction of presence equalization to one stage, preferably in the dubbing theatre where its effect could be accurately assessed.

Following this, hundreds of cinemas have already been re-equalized, either permanently or on a switchable basis, and a number of recent film sound tracks have been Dolby encoded at the optical stage. Mr. Lumkin explained that a Dolby encoded track reproduced in a non-Dolby cinema was found acceptable with the Academy roll-off, as the Dolby treatment produced a raising of high-frequency level similar in some respects to mild presence lift but with a more controlled characteristic, so that a high degree of compatibility existed even in cinemas without Dolby playback facilities.

Improvements in the grain structure of sound-recording negative and print positive emulsions, coupled with replacement of the old high impedance photocell used in reproduction by a much more practical transducer which produces up to 1 V of signal into the first stage of amplification at the comfortable impedance of a few hundred ohms, contribute to an overall reduction in background noise, and therefore allow a greater dynamic range. The much improved reproduction of old films on television is a by-product of all this work, and confirms that the old product was capable of good reproduction, even though it was equalized to suit theatre horn systems rather than domestic loudspeakers.

The industry has flirted with a number of stereo and multitrack sound systems. Disney produced *Fantasia* with six-track stereo 'Fantasound' as long ago as 1938; the Wide Screen 'Cinemascope' had four-track magnetic stereo, Todd AO and other 70 mm Systems can have six tracks, the Russian Kino Panorama has nine, and so on.

However, a good mono optical track, when properly reproduced, still seems to satisfy most audiences. Such prints are much easier to distribute than the magnetic multitrack presentations which tend to be used only in first-run cinemas in the major cities.

Much of what has become standard practice in sound recording for other media owes its beginnings to the film industry and the time and money which it could afford for research and development during its best period. One has only to look through the reference works of the Academy of Motion Picture Arts and Sciences and other learned societies connected with the film industry to realize that most of what we now take for granted was developed there.

Films were using multitrack and complicated mixdown techniques a generation ago: playback and overdub techniques were all in use soon after the start of the talking picture. It also seems certain that optical sound will continue to make a solid contribution to the survival of the film business.

APPENDICES

Appendix I—Units

The SI system of units (Système International d'Unités) is an extension and refinement of the traditional metric system (MKS=metre, kilogramme, second) and is moving towards world-wide acceptance. The main features of SI can be summarized as follows:

1 There are six basic units:

quantity	unit	symbol
length	metre	m
mass	kilogramme	kg
time	second	s
electric current	ampere	A
thermodynamic temperature	kelvin	K
luminous intensity	candela	cd

N.B. symbols for units do not take the plural form.

2 Fractions and multiples of units are normally restricted to steps of a thousand. However the full list of possible fractions and multiples would include the following:

fraction	prefix	symbol	multiple	prefix	symbol
10^{-1}	deci	d	10	deka	da
10^{-2}	centi	c	10^2	hecto	h
10^{-3}	milli	m	10^3	kilo	k
10^{-6}	micro	μ	10^6	mega	M
10^{-9}	nano	n	10^9	giga	G
10^{-12}	pico	p	10^{12}	tera	T

3 Various derived SI units have special names, including the following:

quantity	unit	symbol	definition
energy	joule	J	$kg\ m^2/s^2$
force	newton	N	$kg\ m/s^2$
power	watt	W	$kg\ m^2/s^2$
frequency	hertz	Hz	$1/s$
electric charge	coulomb	C	$A\ s$
electric potential	volt	V	W/A
electric resistance	ohm	Ω	V/A

4 Other derived units include the following:

quantity	SI unit	symbol
area	square metre	m²
volume	cubic metre	m³
	(also litre = 1 cubic decimetre)	(l or dm³)
density	kilogramme per cubic metre	kg/m³
velocity	metre per second	m/s
pressure	newton per square metre	N/m²
	(or pascal)	(Pa = N/m²)

TABLE OF CONVERSIONS

Length

1 thou = 25·4 μm	1 μm = 0·04 thou
1 inch = 25·4 mm	1 mm = 0·039 inch
1 foot = 304·8 mm	1 cm = 0·39 inch
1 yard = 0·9144 m	1 m = 39·37 inches
1 mile = 1·609 km	1 km = 0·62 miles

Area

1 sq. in. = 645·2 mm²	1 mm² = 0·00155 sq. in.
1 sq. ft. = 0·093 m²	1 m² = 10·764 sq. ft.
1 sq. yd. = 0·836 m²	= 1·196 sq. yd.

Volume

1 cu. in. = 16·387 cm³	1 cm³ = 0·061 cu. in.
1 cu. ft. = 28·317 litres	1 litre = 61·023 cu. in.
1 pint = 0·568 litres	= 0·0353 cu. ft.
1 gallon = 4·546 litres	1 m³ = 35·315 cu. ft.

Weight

1 oz = 28·35 g	1 g = 0·0353 oz
1 lb = 453·59 g	1 kg = 35·274 oz
= 0·4536 kg	= 2·2046 lb

Appendix II—Standards

The following lists show only a selection of the more relevant standards published at the time of writing. Readers are recommended to check on the existence of further standards, or more up-to-date re-issues, with the issuing authority.

(a) *British Standards* (British Standards Institution, 2 Park Street, London, W1)

BS 204: 1960   Glossary of terms used in telecommunication (including radio) and electronics
BS 661: 1969   Glossary of acoustical terms
BS 1568: Part 1: 1970   Specification for magnetic tape recording equipment. Part 1. Magnetic tape recording and reproducing systems, dimensions and characteristics
BS 1568: Part 2: 1973   Part 2. Cassette for commercial tape records and domestic use, dimensions and characteristics
BS 1928: 1965   Specification for processed disk records and reproducing equipment
BS 2498: 1954   Recommendations for ascertaining and expressing the performance of loudspeakers by objective measurements
BS 2750: 1956   Recommendations for measurement of airborne and impact sound transmission in buildings
BS 3383: 1961   Normal equal loudness contours for pure tones and normal threshold of hearing under free-field listening conditions
BS 3638: 1963   Method for the measurement of sound absorption coefficients (ISO) in a reverberation room
BS 3860: 1965   Methods for measuring and expressing the performance of audio-frequency amplifiers
BS 4197: 1967   Specification for a precision sound level meter
BS 4297: 1968   Specification for the characteristics and performance of a peak programme meter
BS 4847: 1972   Method for measurement of speed fluctuations in sound recording and reproducing equipment
BS 4852: Part 1: 1972   Methods of defining and measuring the characteristics of disk record playing equipment. Part 1. Disk record players

(b) *German Standards* (Beuth Vertrieb GmBH, 1 Berlin 30, Burggrafenstrasse 4–7)

45510   Magnetic sound recording: terminology (1971)
45511/1   Tape recorder for recording on magnetic tape 6·3 mm (0·25 in.) wide: mechanical and electrical specifications (1971)
45511/2   Tape recorder for 3- or 4-track recording on magnetic tape 12·7 mm (0·5 in.) wide: mechanical and electrical specifications (1971)

455.11/3   Tape recorder for 4-track recording on tape 25·4 mm (1 in.) wide: mechanical and electrical specifications (1971)

45512   Magnetic tapes for sound recording
      Sheet 1: Dimensions and mechanical properties to be stated (1968)
      Sheet 2: Electroacoustic characteristics (1969)

45513   Sheet 1: DIN test tape for magnetic tapes for 76·2 cm/s tape speed (1968)
      Sheet 2: Ditto 38·1 cm/s tape speed (1967)
      Sheet 3: Ditto 19·05 cm/s tape speed (1966)
      Sheet 4: Ditto 9·5 cm/s tape speed (1968)
      Sheet 5: Ditto 4·75 cm/s tape speed (1972)
      Sheet 6: Ditto 3·81 mm (0·15 in.) wide and 4·75 cm/s tape speed (1972)

45514   Sound recording and reproduction, magnetic tape apparatus: Spools (1961)
45520   Magnetic tape recorders: measurement of the absolute level of the magnetic flux and its frequency response on magnetic tapes (1973)
45521   Measurement of crosstalk in multitrack tape recorders (1963)
45523   Remote control by signals from magnetic tape recorders (1968)
45524   Evaluation of the tape speed of magnetic tape recorders (1968)
45536   Monophonic disc records M.45 (1962)
45537   Monophonic disc records M.33 (1962)
45538   Definitions for disc reproducing equipment (1969)
45539   Record reproducing equipment: directives for measurement, markings and audio-frequency connections, dimensions of interchangeable pickups, requirements of playback amplifiers (1971)
45541   Frequency test record St.33 and M.33 (1971)
45542   Distortion test record St.33 and St.45 (1969)
45543   Crosstalk record St.33 (1969)
45544   Rumble measurement test record St.33 (1971)
45545   Wow and flutter test records 33 and 45 rpm (1966)
45546   Stereophonic disc records St.45 (1962)
45547   Stereophonic disc records St.33 (1962)

(c) *American (NAB) Standards* (National Association of Broadcasters, 1771 N. Street, N.W., Washington, D.C. 20036)

Disc recordings and reproductions (1964)
Cartridge tape recording and reproducing (1964)
Magnetic tape (reel-to-reel) recordings and reproductions (1965)
Audio cassette recording and reproducing (1973)

(d) *International Electrotechnical Commission (IEC) Recommendations* (1 Rue de Varembe, Geneva, Switzerland)

IEC Publication 50   International electrotechnical vocabulary
IEC Publication 94   Magnetic tape recording and reproducing
IEC Publication 98: 1964 Processed disk records and reproducing equipment
IEC Publication 200 Recommended methods of measurement for loudspeakers

(e) *International Organization for Standardization (ISO) Recommendations* (1 Rue de Varembe, Geneva, Switzerland)

R131 Expression of the physical and subjective magnitudes of sound or noise
R357 Expression of the power and intensity levels of sound or noise
R532 Procedure for calculating loudness level

Appendix III—Bibliography

General

G. von Bekesy, *Experiments in Hearing* (New York, 1960)
H. Fletcher, *Speech and Hearing in Communication* (New York, 1953)
R. Gelatt, *The Fabulous Phonograph* (London, 1956)
E. Haydn Jones, *Audio Frequency Engineering* (London, 1961)
F. Langford-Smith, *Radio Designer's Handbook* (London, 4th Ed. 1954)
H. F. Olson, *Music, Physics and Engineering* (New York, 2nd Ed. 1967)
Lord Rayleigh, *Theory of Sound* Vols. I and II (London, 1896, republished 1960)
O. Read and W. Welch, *From Tin-Foil to Stereo* (New York, 1959)
C. E. Seashore, *Psychology of Music* (New York, 1938, republished 1967)
H. M. Tremaine (Ed.), *The Audio Cyclopedia* (New York, 2nd Ed. 1969)
A. Wood, *The Physics of Music* (London, 1947)
F. Winckel, *Music, Sound and Sensation* (New York, 1967)

The Studio

L. L. Beranek, *Acoustics* (New York, 1954)
L. L. Beranek, *Music, Acoustics and Architecture* (New York, 1962)
C. Gilford, *Acoustics for Radio and Television Studios* (London, 1972)
V. O. Knudsen, *Architectural Acoustics* (New York, 1952)
G. W. Mackenzie, *Acoustics* (London, 1964)
V. S. Mankowsky, *Acoustics of Studios and Auditoria* (London, 1971)

The Equipment

BBC Monographs (various titles)
J. L. Bernstein, *Audio Systems* (New York, 1966)
J. G. Frayne and H. Wolfe, *Elements of Sound Recording* (New York, 1949)
M. L. Gayford, *Acoustical Techniques and Transducers* (London, 1962)
J. W. Godfrey (Ed.), *Studio Engineering for Sound Broadcasting* (London, 1955)
E. J. Jordan, *Loudspeakers* (London, 1963)
A. McWilliams, *Tape Recording and Reproduction* (London, 1964)
A. E. Robertson, *Microphones* (London, 2nd Ed. 1963)
H. G. M. Spratt, *Magnetic Tape Recording* (London, 2nd Ed. 1963)
W. Earl Stewart, *Magnetic Recording Techniques* (New York, 1958)
K. R. Sturley, *Sound and Television Broadcasting* (London, 1961)

Techniques

J. Bernhart, *Traité de Prise de Son* (Paris, 1949)
A. D. Blumlein, British Patent No. 394325 (1933)

L. Burroughs, *Microphones: Design and Application* (New York, 1974)
J. Culshaw, *Ring Resounding* (London, 1967)
A. Douglas, *Electronic Music Production* (London, 1973)
N. V. Franssen, *Stereophony* (Eindhoven, 1962)
H. Burrell Hadden, *High Quality Sound Production and Reproduction* (London, 1962)
H. S. Howe, *Electronic Music Synthesis* (New York, 1975)
D. Kirk, *Audio and Video Recording* (London, 1975)
A. Nisbett, *The Technique of the Sound Studio* (London, 3rd Ed. 1974)
A. Nisbett, *The Use of Microphones* (London, 1974)
R. Oringel, *Audio Control Handbook* (New York, 4th Ed. 1972)

Manufacturing Processes

P. J. Guy, *Disc Recording and Reproduction* (London, 1964)

Allied Media

G. Alkin, *Sound with Vision* (London, 1972)
G. Alkin, *TV Sound Operations* (London, 1975)
R. L. Hilliard, *Radio Broadcasting* (New York, 2nd Ed. 1974)
J. S. Johnson and K. K. Jones, *Modern Radio Station Practices* (Belmont, California, 1972)
G. Millerson, *The Technique of Television Production* (London, 9th Ed. 1972)
M. Z. Wysotsky, *Wide-Screen Cinema and Stereophonic Sound* (London, 1971)

Appendix IV—APRS Information Sheets

No. 1 Procedure to be taken when tapes are submitted for transfer to master lacquers or direct play-back disc (January 1974)

A   *The tape box must indicate:*

1   Client/Artist/Title.
2   The speed. Minimum speed 19 cm/s (7 ½ ips).
3   Full-track mono, half-track mono or two-track stereo etc.
4   The duration of each item; the total playing time including spacers.
5   The recording characteristics: IEC, NAB etc.
6   Speed and size of disc to be cut.
7   Disc matrix reference number (if applicable).
8   Any other information, i.e. if stereo XY or MS or quad etc.; state if Dolby system used.

B   *Leaders, spacers, and trailers*

1   *Beginning* 2 metres (6 feet) of leader tape white or green must be joined to the beginning of the tape to within 12 mm ($\frac{1}{2}$ inch) of the programme.
2   *End* 2 metres of red trailer must be joined after the reverberation ends.
3   *Spacing* Where scrolls are required on the disc a minimum of four seconds (unless otherwise specified) of white spacer must be inserted at the desired position in the tape.
4   Tapes must be wound trailer end out.
5   Spacers must be matt side to head to reduce static.

C   *Recommendations*

1   Spool and tape box should be identified with each other.
2   For half-track recording, use new tape and ensure *all* the width is fully erased before recording.
3   If Dolby system used, add 30 seconds of Dolby tone at start of tape.
4   At the start of a tape a 30 second band of 10 kHz tone should be inserted

at a level of at least 10 dB below peak programme level for head alignment, followed by a 30 second band of 1 kHz tone at peak programme level.

5   Standard play tape of 0·052 mm (1½ mil) base thickness is normal, though tape of 0·035 mm (1 mil) may be acceptable.
Double or triple play tape is not acceptable.

6   Recording levels should be in accordance with accepted commercial standards and relative to a standard test tape.

7   A cue sheet containing content and duration should be supplied with each tape.

No. 2   Recommended conditions for custom pressing

A   *Minimum requirements for lacquer masters submitted for processing*

1   Only discs manufactured specially for processing should be used.

2   Studios are recommended to make themselves familiar with the requirements of BS 1928: 1965 and AMD 856.

3   Cutting styli made to comply with the requirements of BS 1928: 1965 and AMD 856 must be used.

4   It is recommended that should the first attempt fail, a fresh blank be used. Do not turn blank over.

5   For 30 cm (12 inch) pressings a 35 cm (14 inch) recording blank should be used. For 18 cm (7 inch) and 25 cm (10 inch) pressings reference should be made to the processing factory before cutting blanks to confirm which size of blank best suits the factory's equipment.

6   Discs for processing must be without drive holes or labels.

7   Titles or numbers should be lightly scribed on the edge of discs.

8   Master lacquers must not be played.

9   Recorded levels should agree with normal commercial practice.

B   *Handling and packing of lacquer masters*

The container—preferably metal—for transporting the masters should be free from dust. Discs should be space packed, i.e. with a bolt through the centre hole and at least one spacer between each disc, each spacer to be not less than 1·6 mm thick. Where several discs are packed the bottom one should be face up and all others face down. The whole stack to be bolted firmly. The lid should be sealed with adhesive tape to prevent entry of dust.

C   *Processing and Pressing instructions*

Full information must be given in an envelope securely attached to the outside of the container. The instructions should include:

1   Details of contents of container; matrix numbers and size.
2   Name of cutting studio.
3   Name of client studio.
4   Any observations by the cutting engineer which will assist the manu-
    facturer's quality control.

Where the cutting studio is itself the client studio, the following additional
information should be included.

5   Whether full or half process is required.
6   Order number for pressings.
7   Source of labels.

D   *Limits of responsibility*

1   Whilst every care is taken with discs received for processing, the factories
    do not normally accept any responsibility for damage that may occur
    during the various operations or processing. If a faulty master lacquer is
    submitted to the pressing factory, re-processing is chargeable; if pro-
    cessing is faulty, normally re-processing is free of charge, but the client
    must provide a new master lacquer.
2   Stampers made by the factories from lacquer masters remain their
    property and will not in any event be deliverable to the customer.
    (Note: The lacquer masters are not returnable.) 'Masters' and 'Mothers'
    (positives) remain the property of the customer, and are stored at the
    customer's risk. As processing charges are usually contributory, an extra
    charge is made if 'Master' or 'Mother' plates are handed over to clients.
    It is recommended that they be kept for two years after the date of the
    last order, after which factories reserve the right to dispose of them.

E   The above are subject to the manufacturer's own terms of business.

No. 3   Copyright and sound recording (January 1968)

The Copyright Act, 1956 and the *Dramatic and Musical Performers Protection
Acts*, 1958 and 1963, give monopoly rights to certain classes of copyright
holders enabling them to restrict the use of their works.

1   *Authors and composers* (and publishers, arrangers etc.) can refuse per-
    mission for their works to be published, performed in public or recorded.
2   *Musicians and actors* (and even speakers, if they are using a script or
    text as opposed to speaking impromptu) can refuse permission for their
    performances to be recorded.

3 *Gramophone recording companies* (and private recording studios) can refuse permission for their recordings to be copied.*

4 *Broadcasting organizations* (sound and television) can refuse permission for their programmes to be recorded (except by a person for his own private and domestic use—when the permission of any copyright holders and performers is still required).

These separate restrictions add up to a formidable maze of copyright difficulties. Unauthorized recording 'off the air' of a broadcast of a musical gramophone record, for example, would mean the infringement of several copyrights at once.

Briefly, recording studios should take action on the rights of these four categories of copyright holders as follows:

1 Authors and composers

Most British copyright holders have appointed the Mechanical Copyright Protection Society Ltd., Elgar House, 380 Streatham High Road, London, S.W.16 to act as their agents. MCPS can therefore issue a licence granting permission for recording, subject to certain conditions:**

(a) The studio must compile a monthly list of copyright music recordings, giving enough information for the copyright owner to be identified, i.e., title of work, publisher, composer etc. Forms on which these returns can be made are available from MCPS.

(b) The studio (or client) must pay a royalty of $6\frac{1}{4}$% of the retail selling price (less tax) of each record with an agreed minimum payment per copyright work. (This assumes that the recording is made in this country and not from an imported master, and that the musical works have previously been issued on a commercial gramophone record in the UK.)

(c) The studio (or client) must affix a royalty stamp to all copyright recordings. These stamps are supplied free of charge by MCPS as required.

(d) The studio (or client) must ensure that the label bears the words—in bold type—'REPRODUCTION, RESALE, BROADCASTING OR PUBLIC PERFORMANCE PROHIBITED WITHOUT LICENCE'.

2 Musicians and actors

An artist has no copyright in his performance (whether live, broadcast or

---

*The owner of the mechanical copyright in a recording is the studio or person who made the recording. However, where a person commissions the making of a recording and pays for it, that person is entitled to hold the copyright—in the absence of any agreement to the contrary.

**Members and Associates who participate in the APRS Copyright Scheme can, by paying a single annual fee, avoid the need to make separate applications, returns and royalty payments to MCPS—where up to 25 copies are concerned.

recorded) but he is protected against having it re-recorded, broadcast or filmed.

The studio (or client) must ensure that he has the written consent of every artist, amateur or professional, whom he wishes to record.

3 Gramophone recording companies

Re-recording of gramophone records is expressly forbidden without the permission of the recording company or studio concerned. This permission is rarely granted and if it is, the full royalty is still payable to MCPS.

4 Broadcasting organizations

Except where recordings are made 'for private purposes', off-the-air recording is only possible when prior permission has been granted. The studio (or client) must obtain this permission and in addition that of any artists or copyright holders concerned.

5 Public Performance

Recording studios are sometimes involved in outside events where sound recordings are reproduced over loudspeakers. This constitutes a public performance, which is forbidden without a licence, by the warning notice printed on all record labels.

Where records are used for this purpose, the performance involves both the musical work and the copyright recording. Therefore two licences are usually required, the first from The Performing Right Society Ltd., 29–33 Berners Street, London, W.1, in respect of the musical works, and the second from Phonographic Performance Ltd., 62 Oxford Street, London, W.1, who act on behalf of most British record companies for that purpose.

Appendix V—High Sound Levels and the Impairment of Hearing

The purpose of this paper is to draw attention to recent findings concerning the effect of high sound levels on the human hearing mechanism and to consider what these findings may mean to those of us engaged in the sound recording industry.

That prolonged exposure to loud noise can produce deafness has of course been acknowledged for a long time, indeed the term 'boiler-maker's deafness' has been known to medicine for over a century. Although research into the subject started in the 1930s it is only in the last few years that the results of detailed studies have become available. Similarly it is only in the last few years that developments in power amplifiers and loudspeakers have raised monitoring and playback levels into a range comparable with those to be found on the factory floor or the airport runway, thus making these medical findings extremely important to the recording engineer, whose hearing is the most valuable asset he possesses.

Briefly stated, these findings are that EXPOSURE TO HIGH-LEVEL SOUNDS CAN GIVE RISE TO PERMANENT HEARING LOSS AFTER MUCH SHORTER PERIODS OF EXPOSURE THAN HAD BEEN EXPECTED. That said, let us examine the subject in more detail.

Measurement of Sound Levels

There is an internationally agreed standard for the minimum audible sound threshold for the average normal human hearing mechanism, which varies with frequency. 1,000 Hz is taken as the reference frequency and the threshold figure is 2×10^{-5} newtons/metre² (2×10^{-4} dynes/cm²). For ease and convenience the more usual sound field intensities are described in decibels of sound pressure above this figure.

Typical figures for average normal hearing are:

	Sound pressure level
Whispered speech	30 dB
Normal speech	65 dB

Loud speech	80 dB
Discomfort level—short term	120 dB
Maximum safe upper limit—short term	134 dB
Dangerously high level	140 dB
Eardrum rupture level	144 dB upwards

It is usual to measure actual environmental sound pressure levels with a portable sound level meter which is weighted in its frequency response to take account of the fact that the human hearing mechanism is not a linear device. Greater pressures are required at frequencies both below 1,000 Hz and at the higher audio frequencies to produce the threshold condition. This is the so-called 'A' weighting. However, at high sound levels (i.e. 120 dB and above) the variation with frequency is relatively negligible and then a 'C' weighting may be used.

The weighting used is shown as a suffix to the dB measurement, e.g. dBA, dBC. A, B and C weightings are shown in Table A.1. Weighted sound pressure levels are nowadays used in preference to perceived loudness levels measured in phons (derived by Fletcher and Munson from their set of equal loudness curves) as they can be read off directly from a sound level meter, whereas mathematical calculation is needed to arrive at the loudness level in phons.

Table A.1: relative responses for sound level meters

Frequency (Hz)	Curve A (dB)	Curve B (dB)	Curve C (dB)
63	− 26·2	− 9·3	− 0·8
125	− 16·1	− 4·2	− 0·2
250	− 8·6	− 1·3	0
500	− 3·2	− 0·3	0
1,000	0	0	0
2,000	1·2	− 0·1	− 0·2
4,000	1·0	− 0·7	− 0·8
8,000	− 1·1	− 2·9	− 3·0
16,000	− 6·6	− 8·4	− 8·5

Curve B is not much used. There is also a D curve for measurement of aircraft noise.

However, since these weightings effect only the extreme ends of the spectrum, and since we shall be considering the effects of frequencies lying mainly in the range 1,000–6,000 Hz, we can for our present purposes take dB, dBA, dBC and phon measurements as being approximately equal.

Other typical sound pressure levels are:

| VC10 over runway | 130 dB |
| Thunder (close) | 120 dB |

Riveter	110 dB
Full orchestral fortissimo (at rostrum)	105 dB
Weaving shed	100 dB
Heavy lorry (kerbside)	90 dB

Ten years ago the accepted maximum listening level in control rooms was about 90 dB. Today levels can exceed 120 dB.

Physiological Effects

The human hearing mechanism is a very sophisticated piece of apparatus which has remarkable capabilities of adaptation. When subject to rather loud sounds it switches in an attenuator so that a mild degree of deafness results. When the sound source is removed there is a quick recovery of hearing acuity. If the loud sounds are experienced for a long period, or if the sound level is increased for shorter periods, the duration of the temporary impairment is lengthened so that it may take several hours before complete recovery. Repeated subjection to lengthy periods of high intensity sounds can lead to the recovery taking as long as two days. This condition is known as 'temporary threshold shift'. Further continued exposure to high level sound can result in 'persistent threshold shift' for which a period of weeks in quiet conditions may be necessary to effect recovery.

The next stage, 'permanent threshold shift', comes if the exposure to high level sounds is prolonged and without long periods of rest. This condition is caused by physical damage to the hair cells in the cochlea, that part of the inner ear which transmits information to the auditory nerve and thence to the brain. This damage is irreversible.

Symptoms

The loss first occurs in a relatively narrow band of frequencies around 4,000 Hz, causing a dip in hearing acuity in this region. Continuing the process of exposure to high sound levels causes this dip to increase in both depth and width until it becomes a slot. At this stage the subject will notice this loss in ordinary environments as a syllabic loss in listening to normal speech. The danger is that the subject may not become aware of the threshold shift until it has reached the persistent or permanent stage.

It is a natural process that with advancing years, from age 24 approximately, there is a gradual lifting of the threshold level—most noticeable in the upper frequencies. Anyone who by virtue of exposure to high-level sound over very prolonged periods has developed a slot will be at an even greater disadvantage with increasing age. Whereas a normal person at age

40 can expect his hearing at 6,000 Hz to be some 12 dB down relative to 500 Hz, for a person with permanent threshold shift this figure may be as high as 50 dB. This brings the subject into the range where he has frequent difficulty in understanding normal speech.

Intensity and Duration of Exposure

It is impossible to arrive at a precise quantitative relationship between hearing impairment and exposure to sound. For one thing the effects of exposure vary considerably from person to person. For another, scientifically valid results could be obtained only by tracing the aural experiences of a group of people from birth and then testing their hearing to destruction.

The wide scatter of results obtained from group tests in identical circumstances is remarkable. For example, in one experiment to determine threshold shift the median value of shift for the whole group was 20 dB, but 10 per cent of the group showed a shift of 60 dB. This scatter can partly be accounted for by physiological differences between individuals, but some of it must be due to previous exposures experienced by the subjects. (This paper is concerned with the effects of exposure to high sound levels, but it is worth digressing to note that the 'noise climate' in which a person lives has a direct effect on his hearing and helps to determine the rate at which his hearing will deteriorate under severe exposure. There is evidence that the hearing of rural dwellers tends to be better than that of urban dwellers, while a series of tests conducted in a remote African tribe living in a 40 dB SPL environment showed quite extraordinary acuity even in the 70–80 age group.)

The practical difficulty of determining the point of onset of permanent threshold shift has been overcome by the indirect method of measuring the temporary shift produced by short exposures and then applying corrections to deduce the permanent shift that would have resulted if these exposures had been prolonged. The results show that, while the relationship between threshold shift and duration of exposure is roughly linear, that between threshold shift and intensity of exposure is not. At levels above 90 dB the rate of shift begins to increase rapidly, and above 100 dB it increases very rapidly indeed. The practical recommendations which emerge from these findings are summarized in Table A.2 (Burns).

It will be noted that these levels lie within the range to be found in some control rooms, and refer only to single exposures in one 24-hour period. A simplified form of this table, with calculations of daily exposures, is given in the Department of Employment pamphlet *Noise and the Worker* (3rd edition, 1971) published by HMSO.

Table A.2: values of sound pressure level in specific frequency bands which indicate a hazard to hearing at stated daily durations for one exposure

Octave band specified as centre frequency (Hz)	Sound pressure levels at specified durations (dB)					
	4 hrs	2 hrs	1 hr	30 mins	15 mins	7 mins
63	100	103	106	110	116	122
125	94	97	100	104	110	116
250	90	93	96	100	106	112
500	87	90	93	97	103	109
1,000	85	88	91	95	101	107
2,000	83	86	89	93	99	105
4,000	82	85	88	92	98	104
8,000	81	84	87	91	97	103

The Pop Scene

With millions of people exposed to industrial and transport noise as part of their daily lives, it is only to be expected that research into hearing impairment should have been directed to these sources, and it will have been noticed that most of the evidence so far quoted relates to industrial noise.

As regards music, the same basic principles apply and although the nature of the source may be different it is the intensity and duration of exposure which affect hearing. Traditional bands and orchestras present a relatively minor problem. A symphony orchestra can produce about 105 dB but only for a few seconds and at close quarters. The Big Band probably produces a similar level for longer periods, indeed it is said that the late Ted Heath had his hearing impaired by continued exposure to his own brass section.

However, the intensities and durations of traditional music become insignificant when compared to those of the synthesized and amplified sound of the pop group which relies for effect as much on its sheer volume as on its texture. To quote a member of a leading American group, 'our single aim in life is to get louder'. Dr David Lipscomb of the University of Tennessee, who is investigating the physiological effects of loud music on guinea pigs, uses a sound level of 122 dB for his experiments. He uses this level because he found it typical of the discotheques in the locality.

The same university, in common with many others, tests the hearing of all students on entry. In one intake of 1,500 students it was found that 61% suffered from some form of hearing impairment, and that one in seven had the hearing acuity that might be expected in a person of 55 or 60. Dr Lipscomb attributes this to exposure to high-level pop music. Reference to Table A.2 suggests that Dr Lipscomb is probably right.

The danger of this situation to the studio engineer is twofold. First, the levels mentioned are in themselves quite high enough to damage his hearing. Secondly, as his clients (the groups and their producers) become progressively deafer so they will demand higher and higher listening levels.

Hearing Impairment as an Industrial Injury

In the case of Berry v Stone Manganese Marine Ltd. in December 1971 the High Court for the first time awarded damages for hearing impairment sustained as a result of working in high sound levels. The plaintiff, Frank Richard Berry, aged 50, was employed by the defendants in making marine propellers, a process which involves chipping away surplus metal using pneumatic hammers. He began his employment in 1957 at which time his hearing was normal. In 1960 he became aware of some loss of hearing and attributed this to the high noise levels encountered at work. He took no action at the time but in 1964 he saw a doctor and in 1968 consulted his trade union.

Giving judgement, Mr Justice Ashworth said that the plaintiff had been working in noise levels of 115 to 120 dB, as compared with a tolerable level of 90 dB. The defendants were aware of the high noise levels and made available two types of earplug. The selection and fitting of earplugs should not have been left to the individual, but required expert supervision, e.g. by a nurse at the first-aid post. The defendants were in breach of duty in not seeing that this was done.

Each case must depend on its own facts. In some cases the danger would be obvious and protection simple, and the mere provision of protection would suffice so long as the workmen were made aware that it was available. In other cases the danger might be far from obvious and resulting injury both serious and also insidious, so that much more was required than mere provision of a safeguard. The defendants were not negligent in failing to arrange for testing the man's hearing by audiometry. The employers' duty did not involve taking steps to find out whether a workman's hearing was being affected.

Although hearing was measured by reference to decibels, his Lordship knew of no tariff for measuring compensation by reference to a loss in decibels. Mr Berry stated that when he was with companions at his club he had difficulty in taking part in conversation and felt out of it: similarly in regard to radio and television he was handicapped. But his deafness did not affect his work. Damages were assessed at £2,500 but because part of the claim was 'statute barred' (i.e. made too late) the sum awarded was £1,250. Stay of execution for six weeks was granted pending a possible appeal.

Among the number of interesting points raised by this judgement, three in particular stand out:

1   The court considered a 'tolerable' noise level to be 90 dB. This accords with the figures given in Table A.2.

2   Damages were assessed at £2,500 although the plaintiff's deafness did not affect his work. What might the damages have been if it had?

3   The court found that the defendants were not negligent in failing to give the plaintiff audiometric tests. This is at variance with expert medical opinion that audiometric tests must be made before employment and at intervals during employment if a hazard to hearing is thought to exist.

Conclusions

Our hearing mechanism is subject to wear just as much as is our recording equipment. The more roughly it is treated the greater will be the wear.

Exposure to sound levels greater than 90 dB presents a hazard to hearing and should be avoided. When it cannot be avoided it must be followed by a period of rest to enable the ear to recuperate.

Repeated and prolonged exposure to high sound levels results in permanent hearing impairment which is not only detrimental to an engineer's professional ability but will in later life prove to be a social handicap as well.

Recommendations

The Executive Committee *most urgently recommends* that *in your own interest and that of your staff* you make sure that everyone in your studio reads this paper and is made aware of its conclusions.

Further, the Committee recommends that in studios where listening levels above 85–90 dB are to be found, facilities should be made available to staff members being subjected to these levels for regular audiometric tests carried out by a qualified audiologist.

Acknowledgements

The Committee wishes to express its thanks to Dr T. G. Hammerton, Ph.D., M.Inst.P., C.Eng., for his invaluable help in preparing this paper and for reading the final manuscript, and to Mr R. G. Macbeth, MA., DM., FRCS., for also reading the final manuscript.

References

W. Burns, *Noise and Man* (John Murray, 1968)

W. Burns and D. W. Robinson (for Department of Health), *Hearing and Noise in Industry* (HMSO, 1970)

P. H. Beales, *Noise, Hearing and Deafness* (Michael Joseph, 1965)

Department of Employment, *Noise and the Worker* (HMSO, 3rd Ed. 1971)

Documentary Film, *The Noise Invasion* (BBC, 1971)

The Times Law Reports, 7th December 1971

GLOSSARY

Glossary

Absorption	1. Damping of a sound wave on passing through a medium or striking a surface.
	2. The property possessed by materials, objects or media of absorbing sound energy.
Absorption coefficient	The fraction of the incident sound energy absorbed by a surface or material at a given frequency and under specified conditions. The complement of the sound energy reflection coefficient under those conditions, i.e. it is equal to 1 minus the sound energy reflection coefficient of the surface or material.
AC	Abbreviation for alternating current, which periodically reverses its direction, as opposed to DC (direct current).
Academy roll-off	Control of the upper frequencies in terms of total response heard by the audience in a cinema, to minimize the effect of unwanted random noise in the system.
Acetate	Alternative term for Lacquer disc.
Acoustics	1. The science of sound.
	2. Of a room or auditorium. Those factors that determine its character with respect to the quality of the received sound.
ADT (Automatic Double Tracking)	Duplication of a voice or instrument track with a delay of a few milliseconds to increase the impact or simulate the effect of more performers (see Double tracking).
Advance	Sound is printed on film, and scanned, at a point in advance of the picture aperture by an amount equal to 20 picture frames for 35 mm optical track, 26 frames for 16 mm optical and 30 frames for 16 mm magnetic. N.B. 35 mm striped films such as Cinemascope and 70 mm prints are scanned for sound after picture.
Aerial	(American: Antenna.) Wire or system of wires supported at a height above the ground for the purpose of radiating or of collecting electromagnetic waves.

Alignment	The process of positioning tape heads and amplifier presets for optimum tape performance.
Ambience	The combination of reverberation and background noise which characterizes the sound in a given hall or studio.
Ampere (Amp.)	Practical unit of electric current.
Amplifier	A device in which an input signal controls a local source of power in such a way as to produce an output which bears some desired relationship to, and is generally greater than, the input signal.
Amplitude	Of a simple sinusoidal quantity. The peak value.
Amplitude distortion	That part of non-linearity distortion which is an undesired variation of gain or sensitivity with change of signal level.
Amplitude modulation (AM)	Modulation in which the amplitude of the carrier is the characteristic varied.
Analogue (Analog)	Electronic signal whose waveform resembles that of the original sound (c.f. Digital).
Anechoic	Without echo. An anechoic chamber is a chamber or room where walls are lined with a material which completely absorbs sound.
Antenna	(See Aerial.)
Aspect ratio	Proportion of height to width.
Atmosphere microphone	Microphone placed at some distance from the performers to pick up the general ambience.
Attack time	Time taken for a limiter or compressor to produce the necessary gain change.
Attenuation	Reduction in current, voltage, or power along the transmission path of a signal.
Attenuation distortion (or amplitude/frequency distortion)	An undesired variation of gain or sensitivity with frequency.
Audio frequency (AF)	(Low Frequency, deprecated): Rate of oscillation corresponding to that of sound audible to the human ear (i.e. within the range from about 20 to 20,000 Hz).
Auto-locate	Tape machine facility giving fast location of chosen points on the tape.
Azimuth	The angle between the gap in a tape head and the longitudinal axis of the tape (should be 90°).

Backing	Accompaniment, as when a group of vocalists record a 'backing track' to which the soloist listens on headphones when recording.
Back-tracking	The production of a composite recording by combining live sound with a previously recorded backing track.
Baffle	General expression for wall, board or enclosure carrying a loud-speaker. The purpose of the baffle is primarily to separate the front and back radiations from the cone or diaphragm which would otherwise cancel each other.
Balance	Placing of artists, speakers or other sources of sound in relation to a microphone or microphones, or vice versa (hence, 'balance' test).
Balanced line	Programme cable in which the twin signal wires are both isolated from earth.
Band	Portion of the recorded surface on a disc separated by a marker space or scroll.
Bandwidth	The interval between the cut-off frequencies or -3 dB points in a response curve, expressed in octaves or as a frequency difference in Hertz.
Beats	The periodic variations of amplitude resulting from the addition of two periodic quantities of the same kind but of slightly different frequency.
Bel	A scale unit used in the comparison of the magnitudes of powers. The number of bels, expressing the relative magnitudes of two powers, is the logarithm to the base 10 of the ratio of the powers. One bel equals 10 decibels.
Biasing	The superposition of a magnetic field on the signal magnetic field during magnetic recording. This additional field may be alternating at a frequency well above the signal frequency range (HF bias). Alternatively, the additional field may be steady (DC bias).
Bias trap	Low-pass filter in tape replay circuit designed to attenuate any high frequency bias present.
Bi-directional	Type of microphone having a figure-of-eight directivity pattern.
Binaural hearing	1. Normal perception of sounds and/or of their directions of arrival with both ears.
	2. By extension, the perception of sound when the two ears are connected to separate electroacoustic transmission channels.
Blimp	Soundproof cover device for a camera. Later models of studio camera are 'self blimped', that is they have a double skin suitably insulated.

	N.B. The term 'silent camera' is a misnomer as it refers to a camera which can be used only for making silent films and is usually very noisy.
Boom	A mobile carrier for a microphone which includes a moveable arm from which the microphone is suspended.
Break jack	A jack arranged to break the normal circuit when a plug is inserted.
Buchmann and Meyer pattern	The pattern formed by the spread of reflections from a modulated groove when a parallel beam of light is caused to fall normal to the surface of one or the other wall, and when the groove is viewed from the direction of the light source. It is used as a measure of the maximum modulation of either wall of the groove in the calibration of the performance of recorders, and for the measurement of levels on test records.
Bulk eraser	Electromagnet designed to erase a reel of tape in a few seconds.
Bump	Colloquial term for making an interim reduction of, say, 4 tracks to 2 to make room for more material on a multitrack tape (also called 'Jump').
Burnishing facet	The portion of the cutting stylus directly behind the cutting edge which smooths the groove.
Burwen	Proprietary noise reduction system.
Bus Bar	Common earth or other contact wire.
Butterfly head	Type of multitrack head with a flared guard band to give improved crosstalk performance.
Cans	Colloquial for headphones.
Capacitance	The magnitude of the capability of an element, or a circuit, to store electric charge. Measured in microfarads (μF).
Capacitor microphone (sometimes called Condenser or Electrostatic)	Type of microphone in which the signal is generated by the variation in capacitance between the diaphragm(s) and a fixed plate.
Capstan (American: Puck)	Drive spindle of tape machine.
Cardioid microphone	Class of microphone having a heart-shaped directivity pattern.
Carrier	The wave which is intended to be modulated.
Cartridge	1. Easy-loading magazine of magnetic tape; generally refers to the 8-Track Stereo format.
	2. Disc reproducing head.

Cassette	Easy-loading magazine of magnetic tape; generally refers to the Philips Compact Cassette format.
CCIR	Comité Consultatif International des Radiocommunications: International standards organization.
Chip	American term for swarf (q.v.).
Chromium dioxide (Cr O$_2$)	Magnetic tape coating permitting higher levels at high frequencies than the conventional ferric oxide.
Clapperboard (or slate)	Primitive but efficient system for simultaneously giving an identification to the picture camera and an audible and visual synchronizing point at the start or finish of a filmed section or 'take'.
Clean feed	Version of a programme signal which omits one source (e.g. voice, to allow overdubbing in another language etc.).
Clipping	Form of distortion due to severe overloading.
Cocktail party effect	The faculty of selecting one stream of information out of a number of voices speaking at the same time.
Coincident	Refers to microphone arrangements in stereophony. Two microphones are said to be coincident if they are placed immediately adjacent to each other so that any differences in the times of arrival of the sound are negligible.
Colouration	Change in frequency response caused by resonance peaks.
Compandor	A combination of a compressor at one point in a communication path for reducing the volume range of signals, followed by an expander at another point for restoring the original volume range. Usually its purpose is to improve the ratio of the signal to the interference entering in the path between the compressor and expander.
Compression moulding	The process of forming a disc by compressing a quantity of suitable plastic in a cavity.
Compressor	Means for reducing the variations in signal amplitude in a transmission system according to a specified law.
Concentric (Finishing groove)	The closed circular groove which succeeds the lead-out groove.
Concert pitch	System of music tuning based on a frequency of A = 440 Hz.
Continuity studio	A small studio from which an announcer, supervising the running of a sequence of programmes, makes opening and closing announcements, and interpolates interlude material when required.

Copy master

Reserve or replacement metal negative produced from the positive for use as a master.

Crossfade

To fade in one channel while fading out another in order to substitute gradually the output of one for that of the other (e.g. to create the impression of a change of scene). Hence 'crossfade' (noun).

Crossover frequency

As applied to a dividing network. That frequency at which equal power is supplied to each of two adjacent frequency channels.

Crosstalk

Form of interference caused by break-through of signals from one circuit or tape track to another.

Cutterhead

A recording head with cutting stylus for electromechanical or mechanical recording.

Cycle

Of a periodic quantity. The sequence of changes which takes place during the period of a recurring variable quantity.

Cycle per second (c/s)

Unit of frequency, now generally superseded by Hertz.

Damping

That property of a circuit which tends to cause decay in amplitude of oscillations or reduce resonant peaks.

DBX

Proprietary noise reduction system.

DC

Abbreviation for direct current, which flows in one direction only, as opposed to AC (alternating current).

Dead studio

Studio having very little reverberation.

Decibel (dB)

A unit of transmission giving the ratio of two powers. One-tenth of a bel.

De-emphasis

A change in the frequency response of a reproducing system, complementary to pre-emphasis.

Diffraction

Form of interference by means of which longer wavelength sounds effectively bend round obstacles.

Digital

Refers to signals which have been converted from the normal 'analogue' form to a series of coded pulses.

DIN

Deutscher Industrie Normenausschus: German standards organization.

Direct disc

Lacquer recording blank which is intended for reproduction without further processing.

Direct injection

Process of recording a guitar or other electronic instrument by feeding the electronic signal direct to tape instead of via a microphone.

Directivity pattern	Graph showing the response of a piece of equipment such as a microphone at all angles in a given plane—sometimes called a polar diagram.
Distortion	The unwanted change in waveform which can occur between two points in a transmission equipment or system.
Dolby	Noise reduction system named after its inventor, Dr Ray Dolby. Dolby 'A' is used in professional tape mastering; Dolby 'B' is a simpler system used for example in domestic cassette recorders.
Doppler effect	The change in the observed frequency of a wave caused by time rate of change in the length of the path between the source and the observer.
Double tracking	Overdubbing a voice or instrument 'playing along' with a previous track of the same musical line (see also ADT).
Drop-in	Process of inserting a recorded sound by playing up to a chosen point and switching one or more tracks to the record mode.
Dropout	Momentary loss of signal caused by a fault in tape coating, or dust etc.
Dubbing	1. The combining of two or more recordings into a composite recording. 2. The recording so obtained. Misnomer sometimes used to describe 're-voicing' (in the original or a foreign language) the dialogue spoken by an actor appearing on the screen.
Ducking	Process of automatic compression, e.g. when the announcer's voice signal causes the level of music to be attenuated.
Dummy head stereo	(German: Kunstkopf Stereo.) System of recording using microphones placed in the ears of a model head (or of a wearer).
Dynamic range	Of a programme. The range within which its volume fluctuates. (The term is applied to the original sounds and to the electric currents produced by them.)
Echo	Sound which has been reflected and arrives with such a magnitude and time interval after the direct sound as to be distinguishable as a repetition of it.
Echo chamber	A reverberant room, containing only a microphone and a loudspeaker, through which an output from a studio or hall is passed in order to allow a variable degree of reverberation to be added to the direct output from the same source. The microphone output is combined with the output of the programme source and controlled in volume to give a desired degree of reverberation.

Editing	Process of cutting, rearrangement and selection of recorded material.
Efficiency	Of mechanical or electrical plant, the ratio (expressed as a percentage) of the output energy in the required form to the total input energy.
Eigentones	(German.) Resonances set up in a room or enclosure at frequencies determined by the physical dimensions.
Electret	Non-conductor which has been given a permanent electrical charge: used in microphones and other transducers.
Electromagnet	Coil of wire, possibly having a core of soft iron, which behaves as a magnet only while a current is passing through it.
Electron	Smallest charge of negative electricity which may exist by itself or as part of an atom. (From the Greek 'elektron' = amber.)
Electronic crossover	Frequency dividing circuit using split amplifiers rather than passive circuits.
Envelope	Graphical representation of the changing amplitude of a complex wave.
Equalization (EQ)	The process of modifying the amplitude/frequency response in a recording and reproducing system to produce flat overall characteristics, minimize noise or give an artistic effect.
Erase head	The component in a magnetic recording system that obliterates previous recordings so that the recording medium may be used afresh.
Expander	Means for increasing the variations in signal amplitude in a transmission system according to a specified law.
Farad	Unit of capacitance, which for convenience is sub-divided into one million microfarads (μF).
Feedback	The return of a fraction of the output of a circuit to the input. *Note.* Feedback may be either positive or negative, i.e. tending to increase or decrease the output.
Figure-of-eight	Polar response shape of a bi-directional microphone.
Film speed	1. Scale of sensitivity of photographic emulsion.
	2. Rate of film travel, related to 24 frames per second.
	N.B. For Television, in order to avoid stroboscopic effects, the nearest multiple of mains frequency is used. In Europe this is 25 frames per second, which raises the pitch of reproduced sound by a noticeable amount. For films commissioned for television, the speed of 25 frames/sec is adopted.

Filter | Electrical network composed of inductors, capacitors or resistors, or a combination of these, designed to discriminate between currents of different frequencies.

Flanging | Coarse phasing effect like that obtained by placing a finger on the supply spool of a tape machine (c.f. Phasing).

Fletcher and Munson curves | Set of equal-loudness graphs showing frequency dependent behaviour of human hearing.

Flutter and wow | Undesired forms of frequency modulation introduced by the recording/reproducing process; for example, by irregular motion of the recording medium.
Note. 'Wow' usually refers to the range of fluctuation frequencies between about 0·1 Hz and 10 Hz and is perceived as pitch fluctuations.
'Flutter' usually refers to fluctuation frequencies above about 10 Hz.

Flutter echo | A rapid multiple echo of even rate.

Flux density | Measure of the concentration of an electric field or magnetic field. (Magnetic flux density is measured in lines per square centimetre, or gauss, or Webers per metre of tape width.)

Foldback | Process of feeding microphone or tape signals to headphones or loudspeakers as a cue to artists during recording.

Formant | A band of frequencies in the spectrum of a complex sound which may be associated with a resonance in the mechanism of the production of the sound.

Note 1. Vowel sounds may possess more than one formant in different parts of the spectrum.

Note 2. The term may also be used in relation to musical instruments.

Frequency | Of a periodic quantity. The rate of repetition of the cycles. The reciprocal of the period. The unit is the Hertz (Hz).

Frequency correction | (See Equalization.)

Frequency modulation (FM) | Modulation of a sinewave carrier in which the instantaneous frequency of the modulated wave differs from the carrier frequency by an amount proportional to the instantaneous value of the modulating wave.

Fringe effect | Misleading increase in low frequency output when a full-track test tape is used on a multitrack machine.

Fundamental frequency | The highest common factor of a series of harmonically related frequencies in a complex oscillation.

Fuse	Wire or strip of metal connected in an electric circuit so as to act as a protective device by melting, and thus interrupting the circuit, if the current exceeds the maximum safe value.
Fuzz	Deliberate use of distortion for special effect with electronic guitars etc.
Gain	1. The ratio of the output load power to the input power.
	2. The ratio of the output and input voltages, or currents, under specified conditions of impedance termination.
	Note. In this case the terms should properly be 'Voltage gain' and 'Current gain' respectively.
Gap alignment	The adjustment of the magnetic gap in relation to the magnetic medium.
	a. Azimuth alignment. The adjustment of the orientation of the magnetic gap in relation to the direction of motion of the magnetic medium.
	b. Lateral alignment. The adjustment of the magnetic gap parallel to the plane of the magnetic medium and normal to its direction of motion.
	c. Pole face alignment. The rotation of the contact surface in a plane at right angles to the direction of motion of the magnetic medium in order to effect satisfactory contact over the full length of the gap.
Gate	Special amplifier circuit which has zero output unless the input level exceeds a chosen threshold level.
Gramophone record	A processed copy of a disc recording from which sounds may be reproduced by a mechanical or an electromechanical system.
Graphic equalizer	Frequency correction device giving selective control in narrow bands and having slider controls which indicate the approximate response curve chosen.
Groove	In a mechanical or electromechanical recording. The track inscribed in the recording medium by the cutting or embossing stylus.
Groove shape	The geometric form of the cross-section of a groove. It is defined in terms of the radius of the bottom of the groove (bottom radius) and the included angle between the walls of the groove (groove angle).
Guardband	Spacing between tracks on a multitrack tape.
Gun microphone	(American: Rifle microphone.) Type of microphone employing a long tube and being narrowly directional along the axis.

Haas effect	An effect concerned with the apparent location of the source when the same sound is heard from two or more sources (as in a public address system). Within certain limits of the relative intensities of the separate sounds, and of the time intervals between their arrivals, the sound appears to come from a single source, namely that from which the sounds first arrive, even though the later sounds are more intense.
Harmonic	A sinusoidal oscillation having a frequency which is an integral multiple of a fundamental frequency. A harmonic having double the fundamental frequency is called the second harmonic and so on.
Harmonic distortion	A constituent of non-linearity distortion, consisting of the production in the response to a sinusoidal excitation of sinusoidal components whose frequencies are integral multiples of the frequency of the excitation.
Headroom	Amount of increase above the working level which can be tolerated by an amplifier or tape etc. before the onset of overload distortion.
Helmholtz resonator	A resonator consisting of a cavity in a rigid structure communicating by a narrow neck or slit to the outside air. *Note.* The frequency of resonance is determined by the mass of air in the neck resonating in conjunction with the compliance of the air in the cavity.
Hertz	Unit of frequency (= 1 cycle per second).
Hill and dale recording	A mechanical or electromechanical recording in which the modulation is perpendicular to the surface of the recording medium.
Howlround (Howlback)	Instability in a sound reinforcement or other system when feedback is allowed to build up between the output and input.
Hum	Low frequency noise at the AC mains frequency and its harmonics.
Hunting	Fault condition, where the transport mechanism or motor is alternately reaching synchronous speed and falling back again in rhythmic fashion.
Hybrid transformer	Type of transformer having two secondary windings with minimum crosstalk between them; used to split signal to 'echo send' for example.
Hyper-cardioid	Class of microphone having a directivity pattern intermediate between cardioid and figure-of-eight.
IEC	International Electrotechnical Commission: International standards organization.

Impedance	That property of an element, or a circuit, which restricts the flow of an alternating current. Measured in ohms.
Inductance	The magnitude of the capability of an element, or a circuit, to store magnetic energy when carrying a current. Measured in Henrys.
Injection moulding	The process of forming a disc by injecting a liquified plastic material into a die cavity.
Insulator	Substance or body that offers a very high resistance to the flow of an electric current and may therefore be used to separate two conductors from each other.
Intensity	Of a sound, the objective strength of the sound expressed in terms of the rms pressure in dynes per square centimetre (or bars)—more recently in Newtons per square metre or Pascals—or in terms of the power in Watts per square metre (c.f. Loudness).
Intermodulation distortion	A constituent of non-linearity distortion consisting of the occurrence, in the response to co-existent sinusoidal excitations, of sinusoidal components (intermodulation products) whose frequencies are sums or differences of the excitation frequencies or of integral multiples of these frequencies.
Internal balance	Placing adopted by the performers in a musical combination in order to secure a satisfactory relationship between the sounds produced by each of them, as heard in the studio or other place of performance.
ISO	International Organization for Standardization.
Jack	A device used generally for terminating the permanent wiring of a circuit, access to which is obtained by the insertion of a plug.
Jump	(See Bump.)
Kilo (k)	Prefix signifying one thousand.
Kunstkopf stereo	(See Dummy head stereo.)
Lacquer disc	A disc for mechanical or electromechanical recording usually made of metal, glass or fibre and coated with lacquer compound. It may be coated on one side (single-sided) or both (double-sided).
Land	The uncut surface between adjacent grooves.
Lateral recording	A mechanical or electromechanical recording in which the

groove modulation is perpendicular to the motion of the recording medium and parallel to its surface.

Leader	Uncoated tape, usually white, spliced to the beginning of a recording tape.

Lead-in groove — The length of plain groove that starts at the periphery of the record and the pitch of which is greater than normal recording pitch.

Lead-out groove — The length of plain groove which succeeds the recorded surface and the pitch of which is greater than the normal recording pitch.

Level — Intensity of a continuous tone used for test purposes (measured in decibels by comparison with the standard reference level, or zero level, of 0·775 volt rms, which is equivalent to a power of 1 milliwatt in a resistance of 600 ohms); colloquially, intensity of programme output or of noise. Hence 'level test'.

Limiter — Device for automatically limiting the volume during programme peaks so as to prevent accidental overmodulation of a transmitter or overloading of other equipment. (As the volume applied to the input of the limiter increases, the volume at the output increases linearly up to a certain critical point, after which a further increase in input volume produces a much smaller increase in output volume. When the applied volume exceeds the critical value, the device necessarily introduces amplitude distortion, but ought not to introduce excessive non-linear distortion.)

Lissajous figure — Locus of displacement resulting from two signals applied at right angles. The form of ellipse obtained indicates relative phase.

Live —
1. Programme broadcast or recorded at the time of its performance to an audience (as distinct from a studio recording).

2. Studio having a comparatively long reverberation time, and therefore tending to give a brilliant acoustic effect (c.f. Dead studio).

3. Connected to electrically sensitive part of a circuit.

Logarithmic scale — Scale of measurement in which an increase of one unit represents a tenfold increase in the quantity measured.

Loudness — An observer's auditory impression of the strength of a sound.

Loudspeaker — An electroacoustic transducer operating from an electrical system to an acoustical system and designed to radiate sound.

Magnetic field — Field of force in the vicinity of a permanent magnet or an electric circuit carrying current.

Magnetic tape	Recording medium in the form of a plastic tape (e.g. cellulose acetate, polyvinyl chloride, polyester), coated or impregnated with magnetizable powders.
Masking	1. The process by which the threshold of hearing of one sound is raised due to the presence of another.
	2. The increase, expressed in decibels, of the threshold of hearing of the masked sound due to the presence of the masking sound.
Master	A recording, in edited or approved form from which copies can be made.
Matching transformer	A transformer designed for insertion between two circuits having different impedances to reduce the reflection at the junction and increase the power transferred.
Matrix	1. Generic term applied to all processing electroforms.
	2. Circuit designed to mix or separate electrical signals.
Matrix number	Serial number engraved or embossed on the lacquer or subsequently on the metal parts.
Matt backed tape	Type of recording tape with a dulled finish to facilitate proper winding, even on open hubs.
Mega (M)	Prefix signifying one million.
Micro (μ)	Prefix signifying one millionth part.
Microgroove	A groove of which the unmodulated width at the top is less than 0·076 mm and which is intended to be played with a stylus having a tip radius less than 0·025 mm.
Micron (μm)	One millionth of a metre.
Microphone	An electro-acoustical transducer operating from an acoustical system to an electrical system.
Milli (m)	Prefix signifying one thousandth part.
Mixer	An apparatus by means of which the outputs of several channels can be faded up and down independently, selected individually, or combined at any desired relative volumes.
Modulation	The process by which the essential characteristics of a signal wave (the modulating wave) are impressed upon another wave (the carrier wave).
Modulation noise	In a recording and reproducing system. That part of the total noise which varies with signal amplitude.
Monaural hearing	The perception of sound by stimulation of a single ear.

Monitor	1. (Verb.) To check the technical quality of a transmission.
	2. (Noun.) An apparatus for comparing the technical quality of a programme at one point in the transmission chain with that of the same programme at another point and for giving an alarm if there is any significant difference between the two.
Monophonic (mono)	A transmission system in which, at some point, only a single signal exists.
Mother	Electroform produced from the Master.
Moving coil	Of a microphone, loudspeaker etc. depending for its action on the movement of a coil in a magnetic field.
Mumetal	An iron alloy used in tape heads and for magnetic screening.
NAB or NARTB	National Association of Radio and Television Broadcasters: American standards organization.
NAB operating level	Equivalent to 0 VU.
Neopilot head	Improvement on the original Piloton system of sync pulse in which two thin tracks are positioned at the centre of the tape (where they are more reliable) recorded in opposite phase (push-pull) and so do not reproduce in a full-track scan.
Newton (N)	Unit of force.
Noise	Sound which is undesired by the recipient. Undesired electrical disturbances in a transmission channel or device may also be termed 'noise', in which case the qualification 'electrical' should be included unless it is self-evident.
Noise gate	(See Gate.)
Noise rating curves	An agreed set of empirical curves relating octave band sound pressure level to the centre frequency of the octave bands, each of which is characterized by a 'noise rating' (NR), which is numerically equal to the sound pressure level at the intersection with the ordinate at 1,000 Hz. The 'noise rating' of a given noise is found by plotting the octave band spectrum on the same diagram and selecting the highest noise rating curve to which the spectrum is tangent.
Noise reduction	Process using gain control devices to improve the signal-to-noise ratio. (See Burwen, DBX and Dolby.)
Non-linear distortion	That part of the distortion arising in a non-linear system (i.e. a system whose transmission properties are dependent on the instantaneous magnitude of the excitation) which is due to the non-linearity of the system.

Normalled jacks	Sockets on a jackfield having permanently wired interconnections.
Notch filter	Bandpass filter tuned to a very narrow frequency band.
Octave	1. A pitch interval of 2:1.
	2. The tone whose frequency is twice that of the given tone.
Ohm (Ω)	Practical unit of resistance or impedance.
Ohm's Law	Fundamental generalization describing the flow of direct current in an electrical circuit, by stating that the magnitude of the current is proportional to the potential difference, provided the resistance is constant. (The practical unit of potential difference, the volt, has been so chosen that 1 volt is produced across a resistance of 1 ohm when 1 ampere is flowing through it, so that:

$$\text{Current (amperes)} = \frac{\text{p.d. (volts)}}{\text{resistance (ohms)}}.$$

Omni-directional (or Non-directional)	Equally sensitive in all directions.
Open circuit	Circuit which is not electrically continuous and through which current cannot therefore flow.
Optical sound track	A narrow band, usually on cinematograph film, which carries a photographic record of sound.
Oscillator	Apparatus for producing sustained oscillations, usually by means of positive feedback between the output and the input of an amplifying valve or transistor.
Overtone	A component of a complex wave which may or may not be an integral multiple of the fundamental.
Pad	A network of resistors designed to introduce a fixed loss, or for impedance-matching purposes.
Pan	To shift a sound image as desired between the positions occupied by the loudspeakers in stereo or quadraphonic reproduction.
Pan-pot	(Panoramic potentiometer.) Ganged volume control used in panning.
Parabolic reflector	A light, rigid structure which reflects sounds to a focus at which a microphone is placed.
Parametric equalizer	Frequency correction device which allows both the frequency and the bandwidth of the boost or cut to be selected.
Pascal (Pa)	Unit of pressure = 1 Newton per square metre.

Patch	To connect reserve equipment by means of flexible cords and plugs, so that the connections to the normal equipment are automatically broken by break-jacks.
Peak Programme Meter (PPM)	An instrument designed to measure the volume of programme in a sound channel in terms of the peaks averaged over a specified period.
Peak value	Of a varying quantity in a specific time interval. The maximum numerical value attained whether positive or negative.
Phantom power	Method of sending DC supply to a capacitor microphone by connecting the positive side to both signal wires of a balanced line and the negative to the screen.
Phase distortion	Form of distortion in which wave-trains of different audio frequencies travel with different group velocities, owing to the characteristics of the medium (e.g. a landline).
Phasing	Trick effect obtained by splitting a signal to two tape machines or networks and introducing a time delay in one of them (c.f. Flanging).
Pilot tone	A signal wave, usually a single frequency, transmitted over the system to indicate or control its characteristics.
Pink noise	Random noise signal having the same amount of energy in each octave (c.f. White noise).
Pitch	1. That attribute of auditory sensation in terms of which sound may be ordered on a scale related primarily to frequency. 2. Number of grooves per inch.
Plane wave	A wave in which successive wavefronts are parallel planes.
Polar response	A plot of the variation in radiated energy with angle relative to the axis of the radiator. Similarly used for receivers and microphones.
Post sync	Recording of music, effects or dialogue to synchronize with a previously filmed picture.
Potentiometer (colloquial: pot)	Potential divider or variable attenuator used, for example, to control the volume of a programme.
Pre-echo	The undesired transfer of a recorded signal from one groove to another. N.B. Post-echo can also occur.
Pre-emphasis	A deliberate change in the frequency response of a recording system for the purpose of improvement in signal-to-noise ratio, or the reduction of distortion (see also De-emphasis).

Prefade listening (PFL)	Listening to a programme before it is faded up for transmission or recording; technical facilities provided for this purpose.
Presence	Degree of forwardness in a voice or instrument achieved by boosting in the frequency region 2–8 kHz.
Pressing	Moulding of thermoplastic material produced from the stamper by the application of heat and pressure and subsequent cooling.
Pressure gradient operation	Method of responding to sound signals in which the sound wave has access to both sides of a microphone diaphragm.
Pressure operation	Method of responding to sound signals in which the sound wave has access to only one side of a microphone diaphragm.
Print-through	The undesired transfer of recorded signal from one layer to another of the recording medium when these layers are stored on spools.
Production Master	Copy of a master tape recording to be used for production of copies in quantity.
Proximity effect	Increase in low frequency response which occurs at distances less than about 1 metre from pressure gradient operated microphones.
Public Address (PA)	Arrangements of microphones, amplifiers and loudspeakers used to reinforce speech or music over a large audience area.
Pulse code modulation (PCM)	Modulation in accordance with a pulse code.
Q-factor	A measure of the sharpness of resonance.
Quadraphony	System of recording and reproduction using four channels and four loudspeakers in an attempt to recreate a 360° sound field around the listener.
Quantization	A process in which the range of values of a wave is divided into a finite number of smaller sub-ranges, each of which is represented by an assigned or 'quantized' value within the sub-range.
Radio microphone	Type of microphone incorporating a small radio transmitter to give reception at short distances without the need for cables.
Recording head	A transducer whereby the state or configuration of the recording medium is changed in conformity with the signal.
Recovery time	Time taken for a limiter or compressor to return to its quiescent state on removal of the high level signal.

Rectifier	Device for transforming an alternating current into a direct one.
Reduction	The mixing from a multitrack recording to produce a mono, stereo, or quadraphonic recording as a production master.
Reflection	A return of energy due to the wave striking some discontinuity in its supporting medium.
Relay	A device, operated by an electric current, and causing by its operation abrupt changes in an electrical circuit (making or breaking the circuit, changing of the circuit connections, or variation in the circuit characteristics).
Release time	(See Recovery time.)
Reproducing head	A transducer whereby the signal is re-created from a recording.
Resistance	That property of a substance which restricts the flow of electricity through it, associated with conversion of electrical energy into heat. Measured in ohms.
Resonance	A condition resulting from the combination of the reactances of a system, in which a response to a sinusoidal stimulus of constant magnitude reaches a maximum at a particular frequency.
Reverberation	In an enclosure. The persistence of sound due to repeated reflections at the boundaries.
Reverberation time	Of an enclosure, for sound of a given frequency. The period of time required for the sound pressure in the enclosure, initially in a steady state, to decrease, after the source is stopped, to one-millionth of its initial value, i.e. by 60 dB.
Re-voicing	Post-synchronization in the same language as the original but with a different artist.
Ribbon microphone	Type of microphone in which currents are generated by the movements of a metal ribbon suspended in a magnetic field.
Ring modulator	Device which may be used to produce sum and difference frequencies of two signals applied to the input.
Rise time	The interval between the instants at which the instantaneous value of a pulse or of its envelope first reaches specified lower and upper limits, namely 10% and 90% of the peak value unless otherwise stated.
Root mean square (rms)	Of a varying quantity. The square root of the mean value of the squares of the instantaneous values of the quantity. In the case of a periodic variation, the mean is taken over one period.
Rumble	Low-frequency vibration mechanically transmitted to the

	recording or reproducing turntable and superimposed on the reproduction.
Rushes	First prints (usually made overnight or at speed) from any new material for a film. Usually screened in a pre-view theatre.
Safety Master	Copy of a master recording made for protection purposes.
Scale distortion	Loss of fidelity when the sounds from a large concert hall, for example, are reproduced in a small listening room.
Scroll	Portion of the recorded surface where the groove pitch has been increased to mark the separation of two successive bands of recording.
Sel-sync	The adding of live sound to a spare track to synchronize with recordings on a multitrack tape or film by the temporary use of other tracks of the record head for replay.
Sensitivity	Of an electroacoustic transducer. The ratio of the response to the stimulus under specified conditions. *Note.* This is usually expressed in decibels relative to a reference sensitivity.
Separation	Degree to which individual microphones reject unwanted voices or instruments and give effective control of the desired source.
Signal-to-noise ratio	The ratio of the magnitude of the signal to that of the noise, usually expressed in decibels. *Note.* This ratio is expressed in many different ways, for example, in terms of peak values in the case of impulsive noise and in terms of root-mean-square values in the case of random noise, the signal being assumed sinusoidal (see also Weighted noise).
Sinewave	Waveform of an alternating quantity which varies according to a simple harmonic law, so that the amplitude at any instant is proportional to the sine of the quantity: $2\pi \times$ frequency $\times$ time (the time being reckoned from the instant when the quantity is zero and becoming positive in sign).
Slate	Term used for recording spoken 'take' numbers or cues on tape by analogy with the chalked cues on a film clapperboard.
Slope	Steepness of the sloping part of a response curve, usually stated in dB/octave.
Solenoid	Form of electromagnet permitting remote operation of switches etc.
Sound pressure level (SPL)	The sound pressure level of a sound, in decibels, is equal to 20 times the logarithm to the base 10 of the ratio of the rms sound pressure to the reference sound pressure. In case of doubt, the reference sound pressure should be stated.

In the absence of any statement to the contrary, the reference sound pressure in air is taken to be 2×10^{-5} N/m² $(= 20 \mu Pa)$.

Sound reinforcement	(See Public Address.)
Splicing tape	Special dry adhesive tape used in butt editing of tape recordings.
Spot effects (Hand effects)	Sound effects created in a studio where the scene of which they form part is taking place.
Stamper	Metal negative, produced by electroforming from the positive or mother and used for the production of pressings.
Standing waves	An interference pattern characterized by stationary nodes and antinodes.
Stereophony	A process designed to produce the illusion of a spatial distribution of sound sources, by the use of two or more channels of information.
Stripe	A narrow band of magnetic material applied as a coating on cinematograph film and which carries the sound record. (Further similar bands are frequently applied to the film for control and other purposes.)
Stylus	The needle, generally diamond or sapphire tipped, in a cutterhead or pickup cartridge.
Subjective	As judged by the senses: opposite of objective, i.e. measured.
Swarf	(American: chip.) The material removed from the recording blank by the cutting stylus.
Swinger	Record in which the hole is not at the exact centre of the groove spiral.
Sync facility	Feature on some tape machines permitting individual tracks of the record head to be switched to act as replay heads, for example to provide synchronous foldback to artists during overdubbing.
Synthesizer	Device used in electronic music giving flexible control of the pitch, timing, and tonal quality of signals.
Take	Recording of whole or part of a musical item. Thus a long work or one which is difficult to perform might consist of many 'takes' to be edited together.
Talkback	A circuit enabling spoken directions to be given from a studio control cubicle or television control room, or from a production panel to a studio, or other programme source, for the purpose of directing a performance or rehearsal.

Timbre	That subjective quality of a sound which enables a listener to judge that two sounds having the same loudness and pitch are dissimilar.
Time constant	Shorthand method of specifying the values of resistor and capacitor to be used in a frequency correction network by reference to the time taken for the voltage across the capacitor to fall to 37% (approx.) of its original value through the resistor. Equals the product of R and C: stated in microseconds (μs).
Tracing distortion	Non-linear distortion due to the different shapes of the cutting and reproducing styli.
Tracking error	The difference between the curved path followed by a pivoted pickup and the straight radial path of the cutter.
Tracks	Regions of the tape of specified width scanned by the tape heads.
Transducer	A device designed to receive oscillatory energy from one system and to supply related oscillatory energy to another.
Transferring	Copying by re-recording on a different medium.
Transformer	Component having two coils of wire, the primary and secondary, whose lengths (number of turns) are in a fixed ratio to permit voltages to be stepped up or down and circuit impedances to be matched for maximum power transfer.
Transient	A phenomenon which occurs during the change of a system from one steady state to another.
Transmitter	Equipment for converting the audio-frequency electric currents corresponding to a programme into a modulated carrier wave which can be radiated by an aerial.
Uni-directional	(See Cardioid microphone.)
Variable-area	System of optical recording in which the modulation varies the area through which light is transmitted.
Variable-density	System of optical recording where the width is constant but the transmission factor is varied. This system has largely fallen into disuse with the increased popularity of colour film.
Vari-groove	The technique of varying the groove spacing in relation to displacement amplitude of the cutting stylus.
Velocity	Distance travelled in unit time (e.g. velocity of sound in air at 20°C = 344 metres per second; velocity of electromagnetic waves (light and radio) = 300,000,000 m/s).

Velour effect	Difference in performance of a magnetic tape when it is run in the opposite direction; caused by asymmetrical distribution of the magnetic particles in the coating.
Volt	Practical unit of electrical pressure or of electro-motive force, of such a magnitude that if a pressure of one volt is applied across a resistance of one ohm, a current of one ampere will flow (see Ohm's Law).
Volume	Intensity of programme, or of noise, expressed in decibels relative to a standard reference volume or zero volume, according to the readings of a programme meter, the characteristics of which must be specified in order to define the volume accurately (see also Level and VU).
VU (Volume unit)	A unit for expressing the magnitude of a complex electric wave such as that corresponding to speech or music. The volume in volume units is equal to the number of decibels by which the wave differs from a reference volume.
VU meter	A volume indicator the specification of which is given in American Standard 'Volume Measurements of · Electrical Speech and Program waves', C16.5-1942.
Watt	Practical unit of electrical power equal to one joule per second. (In a DC circuit the number of watts is equal to the product of the volts and amperes; in an AC circuit it is equal to the product of the volts and amperes multiplied by the power factor.)
Waveform	The shape of the graph representing the successive values of a varying quantity.
Wavelength	Of a sinusoidal plane progressive wave. The perpendicular distance between two wavefronts in which the phases differ by one complete period. Symbol λ. *Note*. The wavelength is equal to the wave velocity divided by the frequency.
Weber	Unit of magnetic flux.
Weighted noise	The noise measured within the audio frequency band using an instrument which has a frequency selective characteristic.
White noise	Random noise signal having the same energy level at all frequencies (c.f. Pink Noise).
Wow	(See Flutter.)
Zero level	Standard of reference used when expressing levels. (The zero level generally chosen is one milliwatt, which corresponds to a voltage of 0·775 volt rms across a resistance of 600 ohms.)

Index